Doing Grief in Real Life

A Soulful Guide to Navigate
Loss, Death & Change

Shea Darian

A Doing Grief Publication from Gilead Press

Doing Grief in Real Life

By Shea Darian

© 2022 by Charlene DeShea Bagbey Darian

All rights reserved. Reproduction, distribution, or transmission of this book in whole or in part in any form is strictly prohibited. Brief quotations for review and other non-commercial uses as permitted by copyright law are appreciated. Permission requests: contact info@gileadpress.net. Printed and bound in the United States of America.

Library of Congress Cataloging-in-Publication data
Names: Darian, Shea, author.
Title: Doing grief in real life: a soulful guide to navigate loss, death & change / Shea Darian
Description: first trade paperback edition | Sun City: Gilead Press, 2022 | Includes bibliographical references and index.
Identifiers: LCCN: 2021920398 | ISBN: 978-0-9675713-4-8 (paperback) | ISBN: 978-0-9675713-3-1 (e-book PDF edition)
Subjects: LCSH: Grief | Loss (Psychology) | Adaptation (Psychology) | Family Relationships | BISAC: PSYCHOLOGY / Grief & Loss
Classification: LCC BF575.G7 2022 (print) | LCC BF575.G7 (e-book/PDF) | DDC 155.9/3–dc23

ISBN: 978-0-9675713-4-8 (paperback – Feb 28, 2022)
ISBN: 978-0-9675713-3-1 (e-book PDF edition – Oct 30, 2021)

Disclaimer: This book is designed to provide information and motivation to our readers. It is made available with the understanding that the author and publisher are not engaged to render any type of professional advice or healthcare. It is not meant to be used to diagnose or treat any medical condition or mental disorder. Consult your healthcare providers for medical needs and conditions. The author and publisher are not responsible for any damages or negative consequences from any action or application by any person reading or following the information in this book. All references and listings are provided for convenience and do not constitute an endorsement of any websites, products, services, or opinions. Seek out the resources that are right for you. Our views and rights are the same: You are responsible for your own choices, actions, and results.

The names and identifying details of some individuals whose stories are related in this book have been changed to protect their privacy.

A Note from the Author: I greatly appreciate you taking the time to read my work. Please spread the word about *Doing Grief in Real Life* with your family, friends, and colleagues. These days, we humans have a lot of healing to do.

Cover artwork by Benjavisa Ruangvaree

1 2 3 4 5 6 7 8 9 10

♥

Dedicated to

Maggie Jezreel who was brave enough
to walk beside me in the dark

&

Morgan Darian who is the light that saw
me through to the other side

♥

May it be a light to you in dark places
when all other lights go out.
        J.R.R. Tolkien

Table of Contents

- ◈ An Invitation: *Doing Grief in Real Life*   1
- ◈ Why This Book? What This Guidebook Asks of You   5

Part I ◈ The Underbelly of All Good Things: Exploring the Paradoxes of Grief, Grieving & Healing   11

Chapter 1 ◈ Letting it Out: Grief Doesn't Belong in a Box   13
- ◈ Outrageous Fortune: Seeing Grief From a Different Perspective   14
- ◈ The Unabridged Version: Grief as a Life Force   15
- ◈ Taking It Personally: A Grief Story   17
- ◈ No Such Thing: Normal Grief is an Oxymoron   19
- ◈ On the Other Side of Normal: Defining Grief on *Your* Terms   21
- ◈ Intimate Exposure: Guided Contemplations to Inspire Self-Reflection   22

Chapter 2 ◈ Don't Fix What Isn't Broken: Grieving as Self-Expression   31
- ◈ Viva la Différence! The Relationship Between Grief and Grieving   32
- ◈ Refracted Darkness: Grieving in All Directions   34
- ◈ No End in Sight: When Grief Keeps on Giving   35
- ◈ Authentic Grieving: Breaking the Bonds of Convention   38
- ◈ What's a Griever to Do?: Re-envisioning the Human Grieving Process   40
- ◈ Caught Between a Rock and a Hard Place: The Model of Adaptive Grieving Dynamics Explained   42
- ◈ Intimate Exposure: Guided Contemplations to Inspire Self-Reflection   44

Chapter 3 ◈ In Good Company: Grieving Alone Together in Four Dimensions   51
- ◈ Walking in Your Own Shoes: Gaining Compassionate Perspective   52
- ◈ In the Center of the Storm: Finding Your Bearings in Four Dimensions   54
- ◈ Painful Possibilities: Lamenting Alone Together   55
- ◈ Playing the Renegade with Grief: Heartening Alone Together   60
- ◈ Reinventing Life With Loss: Integrating Alone Together   64
- ◈ You Deserve a Break Today: Tempering Alone Together   68
- ◈ Among the Band of the Wounded: Grieving & Healing Alone Together   73
- ◈ Intimate Exposure: Guided Contemplations to Inspire Self-Reflection   76

Part I Wrap-Up ◈ Know Thyself: Grieving as a Path to Self-Awareness   91

Part II ◈ Enough Grief for a Lifetime: Healing From Birth to Old Age   93

Chapter 4 ◈ From the Mouths of Babes: Grieving & Healing in Infancy   97
- ◈ Born Grievers, Born Healers: An Infant's Natural Genius for Grieving & Healing   98
- ◈ For Crying Out Loud: Lamenting in Infancy   99
- ◈ Playing With Grief: Heartening in Infancy   101
- ◈ A Matter of Survival: Tempering in Infancy   104
- ◈ You and Me, Baby: Integrating in Infancy   106

- ◈ The Great Imitator: Companionship Needs of the Grieving Infant   108
- ◈ Do-It-Yourself: Self-Guided Contemplations for the Infant Within You   110
- ◈ An Infant's Healing Chest: Approaches to Grieving & Healing in Infancy   112

Chapter 5 ◈ Coming to Our Senses: Grieving & Healing in Childhood   113
- ◈ Childhood Smarts: A Child's Natural Genius for Grieving & Healing   114
- ◈ Mother (or Father) May I?: Lamenting in Childhood   119
- ◈ Gathering Wildflowers: Heartening in Childhood   124
- ◈ As If By Magic: Tempering in Childhood   127
- ◈ Everyday Grieving, Everyday Healing: Integrating in Childhood   131
- ◈ Build It & They Will Come: Companionship Needs of the Grieving Child   134
- ◈ Do-It-Yourself: Self-Guided Contemplations for the Child Within You   142
- ◈ A Child's Healing Chest: Approaches to Grieving & Healing in Childhood   144

Chapter 6 ◈ Stressing Love & Intimacy: Grieving & Healing in Youthhood   145
- ◈ Bridging the Gap Between Me, Myself & I:
  A Youth's Natural Genius for Grieving & Healing   146
- ◈ Love, Love Me Do: Lamenting in Youthhood   150
- ◈ The Power to Change for Good: Heartening in Youthhood   157
- ◈ Give Me a Break: Tempering in Youthhood   161
- ◈ If a Youth Were a Feeling, What Feeling Would It Be: Integrating in Youthhood   166
- ◈ Feeling Your Way to Healing: Companionship Needs of the Grieving Youth   173
- ◈ Do-It-Yourself: Self-Guided Contemplations for the Youth Within You   186
- ◈ A Youth's Healing Chest: Approaches to Grieving & Healing in Youthhood   188

Chapter 7 ◈ Mi dolor es su dolor: Grieving & Healing in Adulthood   189
- ◈ Serving the Greater Good: An Adult's Natural Genius for Grieving & Healing   190
- ◈ Bringing the Lessons of Dying to Life: The Practice of Breaking Down Your Grief   196
- ◈ Bridging the Great Divide: The Practice of Healing Relatedness Pain   200
- ◈ Beyond Shame & Blame: The Practice of Healing Forgiveness Pain   208
- ◈ Hope Against Hope: The Practice of Healing Hopelessness Pain   223
- ◈ Grasping the Meaning of Meaning: The Practice of Healing Meaning Pain   233
- ◈ If Not You, Who?: Companionship Needs of the Grieving Adult   246
- ◈ Do-It-Yourself: Self-Guided Contemplations for the Adult Within You   249
- ◈ An Adult's Healing Chest: Approaches to Grieving & Healing in Adulthood   252

Chapter 8 ◈ Harvesting Curative Wisdom: Grieving & Healing in Elderhood   253
- ◈ Making Good Use of Old Age: An Elder's Natural Genius for Grieving & Healing   254
- ◈ Making Good of a Bad Thing: Lamenting in Elderhood   261
- ◈ The Silver Lining: Heartening in Elderhood   283
- ◈ Escaping Pain for Good: Tempering in Elderhood   289
- ◈ In the Crucible of Life & Death: Integrating in Elderhood   296
- ◈ Responding Healer to Healer: Companionship Needs of the Grieving Elder   305
    Polaris: Serving as a North Star for Grieving Adults of all Ages   307
- ◈ Do-It-Yourself: Self-Guided Contemplations for the Elder Within You   312
- ◈ An Elder's Healing Chest: Approaches to Grieving & Healing in Elderhood   315

Part III ◆ The Healing Chest: Gathering Your Own Best Medicine   317

Endless Possibilities for Doing Grief in Real Life:
Wisdom from Everyday Grievers, Professional Healers, Artists & Care Providers   318

◆ Healing Through Nonfiction & (Mostly True) Stories   318

Abuse Awareness & Prevention ◦ Addiction Prevention & Recovery ◦ Apologies ◦ Art & Creativity ◦ Bibliotherapy ◦ Breathing & Relaxation ◦ Caregiving ◦ Ceremonies & Celebrations ◦ Cinematherapy ◦ Cognitive Healing ◦ Community-Building ◦ Conscious Eldering ◦ Crying ◦ Dance ◦ Death Care ◦ Dreaming & Visitations ◦ Dying a Good Death ◦ Emotional Healing & Expressing Feelings ◦ Exercise, Body Awareness & Physical Release ◦ Forgiveness ◦ Funeral Planning & Memorial Services ◦ Grieving & Healing Perspectives ◦ Habit-Building ◦ Helping Others ◦ Hope ◦ Illness Tending ◦ Integrative Care & Complementary Therapies ◦ Laughter & Humor ◦ Listening ◦ Massage, Reiki & Comforting Touch ◦ Meaning-Making ◦ Memoir & Autobiography ◦ Memorials & Remembrance ◦ Metaphors, Objects & Symbols ◦ Mindfulness & Meditation ◦ Movement, Yoga & Posture ◦ Music & Sound Therapy ◦ Natural Remedies for Pain Relief ◦ Nature ◦ Parenting Mindfully ◦ Pets & Animals ◦ Pilgrimages, Labyrinths & Hiking Treks ◦ Play, Fun & Games ◦ Poetry ◦ Prayer ◦ Repairing Broken Relationships ◦ Sanctuary & Sacred Space ◦ Self-Injury Recovery ◦ Sexual Healing & Intimacy ◦ Sleeping ◦ Stories & Storytelling ◦ Suicide Prevention & Survivor Support ◦ Talking Cures ◦ Theater & Speech ◦ Trauma Recovery ◦ Wonder ◦ Writing

◆ Healing Through Novels & Picture Books   341

◆ Healing Through Movies & Documentaries   347

◆ Healing Through Community Connections   350

◦ Healing Through Sports & Exercise
◦ Healing Through the Arts
◦ Healing Through Nature
◦ Healing Through Education & Support Groups
◦ Healing Through Therapeutic Counseling & Spiritual Direction

Index   351

Works Cited: Giving Credit Where Credit is Due   353

Gratitude   357

◆ Those Who Helped & Inspired   358
◆ Those Who Led the Way ◆ In Memoriam   359

An Invitation
Doing Grief in Real Life

> There are only two or three human stories, and they go on repeating themselves as fiercely as if they had never happened before.
>
> Willa Cather

Some books tell you how to grieve. Some books tell you how to "get over" a broken relationship, how to forgive, how to "deal with" all kinds of unimaginable loss. Some books even tell you how to die or watch someone you love die. This is not one of those books.

Doing Grief in Real Life asked to be written at a time when brokenness and grief threatened to consume me. It was at a time I lost hold of my belief in the goodness of the world and humanity. So, it's a book that doesn't have much patience for formulas that prescribe a particular path to mental, emotional, or spiritual healing. That's why I may as well tell you upfront: *Doing Grief in Real Life* fails to pay homage to well-known grief theories that offer a one-size-fits-all grieving process. Theories can't heal us. They may bring momentary comfort or insight, but they can also give us a false sense that we can manage what is not manageable.

Generalizing about grief is like generalizing about love. It throws a profoundly subjective personal experience into an abyss of anonymity. It denies the very aspects of grief that are a grieving person's saving grace: *motivation for self-reflection and the prospect of discovering for oneself what the sources of one's true healing will ultimately be.*

Doing Grief in Real Life is a book of reflection and practice. It's a book that will invite you to enter with courage into the dark inner sanctum of your grief and the grief of your loved ones. In that place, you may well encounter mystery thick as mud up to your mouth. It's a book that asks how *you* choose to grieve, how *you* choose to live, how *you* choose to die. It's a book that asks how *you* choose to mourn the deaths of loved ones or any life change that speaks to you of grief.

In our 21st century Western culture, many of us spend a good portion of our lives holding grief at arm's length. We hire others to care for our dead and tell us how to mourn. We depend upon our legal system to negotiate for us our broken relationships. We enlist clergy to enact rituals and ceremonies that oftentimes only vaguely hint at the intimate sorrows and excruciating changes they represent.

Doing Grief in Real Life asks you to carry your own sorrows, observe them, listen to them, and discover what they are calling forth in you. It asks you to encourage your family members and friends of all ages to do the same. Although you may find comfort in these pages, if you come seeking it, you may be disappointed – as C. S. Lewis wrote in his book, *Mere Christianity:*

> " . . . comfort is the one thing you cannot get by looking for it. If you look for truth, you may find comfort in the end: if you look for comfort you will not get either comfort or truth – only soft soap and wishful thinking to begin with and, in the end, despair."

May these pages prompt you to look truthfully, gaze fearlessly into your grief, and discover how your grief might be a catalyst for healing.

Each grief experience is as unique as the person who embodies it, each death as unrepeatable as any birth. If only we can learn to attend death as witnesses and participants of *life*. Then, we may come to know grief as a teacher. Then, we are capable of seeing that the darkness of our grief can become the most exquisite canvas. Upon that canvas, the light of mourning is utterly distinguishable. In measure, it reveals the wondrous and varied landscapes of the human soul.

This is one of the many paradoxes of grief. Silently, mournfully, it hollows a space to make room for something new. What that something is, is up to you.

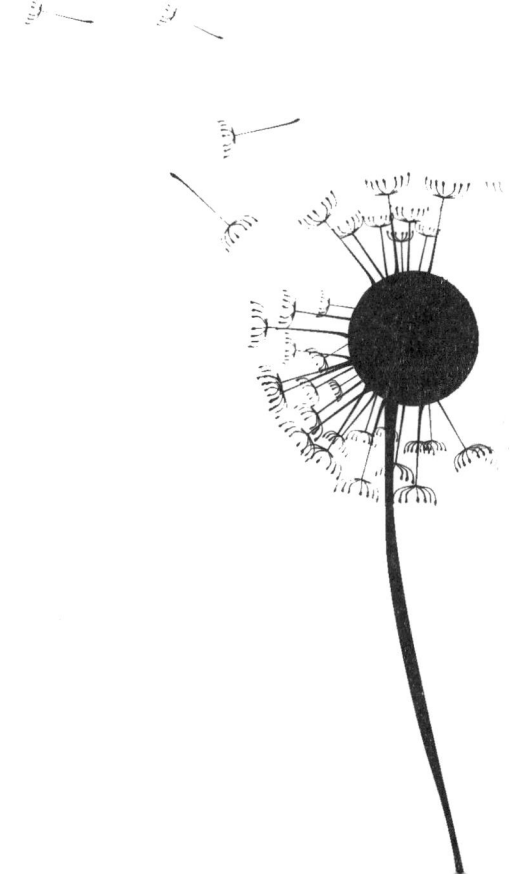

Why This Book?

What This Guidebook Asks of You

There are times in everyone's life when something constructive is born out of adversity . . . when things seem so bad that you've got to grab your fate by the shoulders and shake it.

author unknown

Walk the Walk

You may be reading this book because you or a loved one already came face to face with excruciating grief. If not, my kudos for your bravery. Most people don't dwell on grief unless they must. What's more, when grief descends upon your world, you can choose to run from it as if life depends on it. Sometimes life does. Depend on it. Sometimes denial is the safest way our psyches come through grief with a semblance of sanity. But if you opened this book, you know denial isn't a place most people can bear to live forever – at least, not if a person is bent on finding cherished meaning or true happiness, or living a mostly authentic life.

Doing Grief in Real Life doesn't contain a magic formula or sure-fire approach to ease your suffering. It's likely to be as beneficial to you as you make it. If you're in the throes of grief, this book can provide solace, inspiration, activities, and approaches to grieving and healing that are immediately useful. If you're seeking a new perspective on grief to increase self-awareness, enhance family intimacy, or enrich your work as a professional healer, this book offers sustenance for a lifelong journey.

This guidebook is a soulful invitation for you to gather the scattered shards of your grief and melt them down in the crucible of change. Transformed grief can be shaped into one of life's most useful possessions – the strength and courage to heal your deepest wounds.

A Step at a Time

Ultimately, this guidebook is about *your* journey with grief. In the end, it is a story about you carrying your grief-related burdens into the heart of healing to see what grief can make of you and what you can make of your grief. There may be times during your journey with grief that you seem to skip along past the pain to make a beeline for healing and other times when the way of grief is tediously and painfully confusing or slow-going. Sometimes your grief may ask you to stay put or retrace your steps to get your bearings. Your journey may be winding or suddenly change course. Wherever and however you find yourself on this path, remember to walk the walk with grief as you are – from wherever you find yourself in the present moment. Take your journey a step at a time, knowing that many small steps will get you there. Set your own pace. Adjust your path. Trust your inner compass to guide you.

Acknowledge Life and Death Changes

For many, grief is synonymous with bereavement of physical death – your own or that of a loved one. No doubt, physical death can open a person up to profound grief, but death is only one of many losses we humans face in the course of a lifetime.

Doing Grief in Real Life broadens the scope on passages of loss, death, and change. Broken relationships through divorce, betrayal or conflict, illness or injury, sudden loss of belongings, beliefs, or cherished daily rhythms and routines, experiencing violence, injustice, disappointment, loneliness, shame, or failure may be for some grievers a death worse than death. The illusionary great divide between living and dying is filled with all sorts of life-altering changes that breed grief.

Grief is mixed in, too, with life changes that are thought to be happy occasions: marriage, graduation, giving birth or adopting a child, developmental passages that bid innocence or youth farewell, or retirement, to name some. Looking into the kaleidoscope of human experience, it may surprise you to see that grief weaves itself through good times, too. To live fully, we are obliged to befriend grief and tune into its healing potential in times of sorrow and celebration.

Explore Your Unique Ways of Doing Grief With My Model of Adaptive Grieving Dynamics

Unfortunately, for those living in the United States, our greatest expertise regarding grief may be our collective knowledge of infinite possibilities for numbing the pain of it. One recovering addict says pointedly: "Addiction is a direct result of unresolved grief." Drugs and alcohol, sex, entertainment, work, electronic media, shopping, eating – all of these diversions can become addictive when we use them to shove grief underground.

Even those who willingly face our grief may be terribly challenged by grief's complexities. Most of us have only a vague understanding of what grief is and how it affects us. Today's foremost grief experts argue among themselves about how to define grief and grieving. A massive dilemma in seeking common answers to grief-related questions is that each person's grieving process is unique and so are approaches to healing. If we accept this knowledge at face value, we might be inclined to leave each griever to fend for healing alone, waiting until grieving becomes problematic to give a griever the curative support that's needed. But grieving is as much a social endeavor as it is a personal one. That's why building a common language to communicate highly personal experiences of grief and grieving can be useful. When we learn to speak, observe, and listen in a common language of mourning, compassionate understanding among grievers becomes more possible.

Part I of this book, "The Underbelly of All Good Things: Exploring the Paradoxes of Grief, Grieving, and Healing," provides soulful guidance for you to

- Experience grief as a catalyst for personal growth and needed social change,
- Explore the curative relationship between grief, grieving, and healing, and
- Utilize your unique grieving responses to ease and heal your suffering.

You'll be introduced to my Model of Adaptive Grieving Dynamics (MAGD) that highlights four types of grieving responses – lamenting, heartening, tempering, and integrating (see pages 40-42). These four dynamics are universal among grievers but experienced and expressed differently by you and anyone who suffers grief.

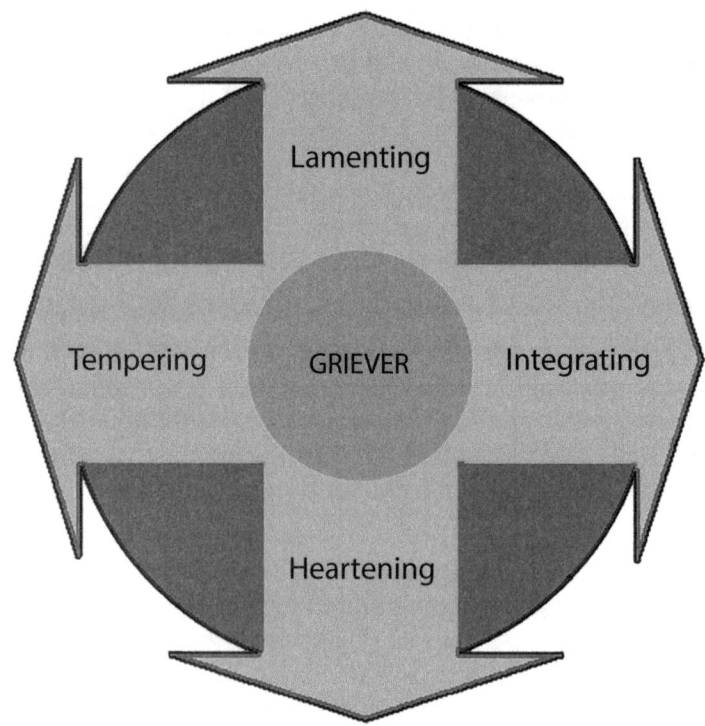

Model of Adaptive Grieving Dynamics © 2014 by Charlene DeShea Bagbey Darian

Doing Grief in Real Life invites you to use the MAGD as a compass to help guide you as you grieve and heal. Each chapter in Part I concludes with a section called "Intimate Exposure: Guided Contemplations to Inspire Self-Reflection" that will help you to explore your unique experiences of grief and your responses to it. *As you read and reflect, engage in the contemplations that are most helpful and relevant to you.*

Heal Yourself, Heal Your Family
(However Family is Defined for You)

Doing Grief in Real Life sheds light on personal and social healing from an intergenerational perspective. An ongoing challenge with grieving alongside your loved ones is knowing when, where, and how to tend to your own suffering and when, where, and how to tend to the suffering of another. An oft-used metaphor for self-care is the airline directive that reminds a passenger to "put your own oxygen mask in place before helping those around you." However, the reality is that most of us grieve and heal *while* we are caring for children, aging parents, or those who are injured, ill, or dying. At the very least, we often grieve in tandem with those we love, requiring attention to be shared between one's self-healing and encouraging another's healing alongside.

Most of us don't have the luxury to disappear into the grieving cave for long without damaging our connections with loved ones who may be in as much pain as we are. Rest assured, there are facets of grief you can only face alone. No doubt you will be of greater assistance to others when you learn how to heal your solitary suffering. There may even be times you retreat temporarily to attend to your personal healing. But woe to the one who fails to mourn and heal with those they love. *Authentic and deep healing is a lifelong proposition, so while we learn to meet grief on our own terms, at once, we must learn to meet grief in our loved ones – on their terms.*

In Part II, "Enough Grief for a Lifetime: Grieving and Healing from Birth to Old Age," you'll be invited to consider developmental changes and characteristics that influence a person's grieving responses throughout the stages of the human life cycle: infancy, childhood, youthhood, adulthood, and elderhood. Adaptive strengths for grieving and healing that we humans generally acquire during each of these developmental cycles can snowball into phenomenal capacities to heal grief more fully as we mature. Thus, healers of all ages from the newly born to the eldest of the elders can make valuable contributions to a family's healing journey – however "family" is defined for you.

May this book help you to become more familiar with the dance between self-healing and healing with others of all ages. For those who learn this dance, healing becomes more (oh, so much more) than the victory of one. This is how healing expands exponentially. This is how healing changes the world – one person, one relationship, one family at a time.

Heal the Whole Griever – Body, Heart, Mind & Spirit

Until recently, most therapeutic approaches to grief focused on *emotional* pain. However, grief permeates the whole person – physically, emotionally, mentally, and spiritually. It can reside in one dimension of a griever's being more greatly than another, given a person's age, personality or temperament, family and community conditioning, body chemistry, grieving tendencies, loss experiences, and the like. If a griever or their caregiver focuses overly much on emotional distress, grief residing elsewhere in a person's being may go undetected. Perpetually unacknowledged grief can deepen its hold on the body, psyche, or spirit to play havoc with physical health, the vibrancy of one's inner life, and intimate relationships. *Doing Grief in Real Life* guides you to heal all aspects of your being – body, heart, mind, and spirit.

Gather Your Healing Medicine

Part III, "The Healing Chest: Gathering Your Own Best Medicine," offers a plethora of resources on personal and family healing. This section will guide you to the curative wisdom of some of the most innovative healers of our time – counselors, therapeutic caregivers, art advocates, naturalists, athletes, scientists, spiritual guides, death and dying practitioners, and more. From among the bounty, you'll be prompted to create healing chests that include the "medicine" that works best for you, your family, and anyone who walks beside you as a grieving companion.

Forge a Trail

Doing Grief in Real Life is my attempt to offer a caring presence as you forge a trail to the deep river of healing that grief can open up in you. I hope this guidebook will be a trusted companion as you walk the walk – whether you take it a step at a time or blaze the trail like there's no tomorrow. Either way, healing is the journey of a lifetime, because healing can change everything – grief, love, even death. But now I'm getting ahead of myself. First, healing requires you to become familiar with the nuances of your grief. Indeed, your grief is the sickle with which to clear the trail to the river.

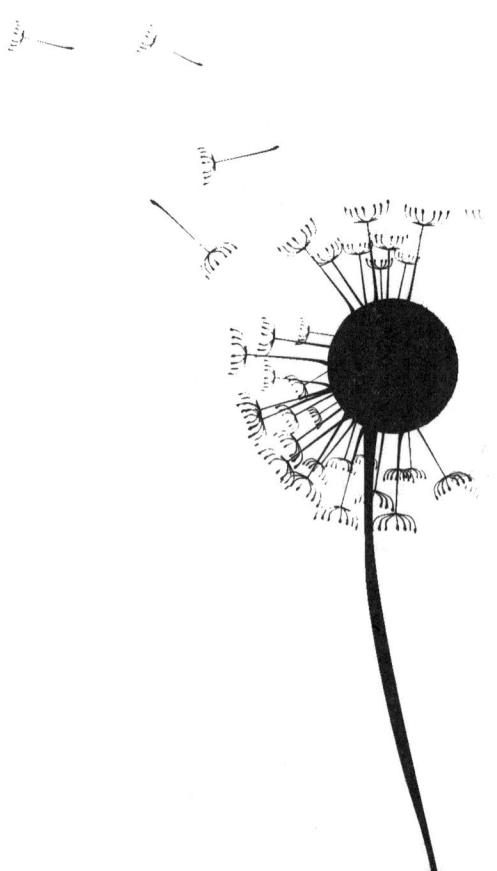

❧ Part I ❧
The Underbelly of All Good Things

Exploring the Paradoxes of Grief, Grieving & Healing

> Smooth seas do not make
> skillful sailors.
> Proverb

Braving the Monsters of Grief

In ancient times, there was born a legend of two sea-faring dangers: Scylla and Charybdis. The two monsters dwelt on opposite shores of the Strait of Messina. They were poised to destroy anyone courageous or ignorant enough to pass between them. It was told that Scylla and Charybdis had once been strong, beautiful sea nymphs transformed into monsters by their adversaries.

Scylla's enchanting form was morphed into that of a raging six-headed beast. Charybdis was transmuted into a more deceptive foe who spent most of her time sulking beneath a fig tree. Charybdis stirred only to guzzle all the water in the strait and many a seafarer, besides. Scylla and Charybdis made it nigh impossible to navigate through the Strait of Messina. Of those who attempted the passage, only a roughened few survived.

The passage of grief can seem equally daunting. On either shore of the passage, the beauties of life can rise up as hellish fiends. What we love and cherish may suddenly appear repulsive or frightening. What we usually depend upon for sustenance and direction may throw itself as a horrific obstacle into our path.

Grief is busting full of clashing contradictions that do battle within a solitary grief-stricken soul. So, when we hear that the legendary protagonist, Odysseus, and a few of his crew survived the passage between Scylla and Charybdis, we may feel torn. The success of Odysseus (at piloting through those troubled waters) calls to us like a death-defying challenge to live.

Paradox is the meat of human existence. Raging Scylla and sulking Charybdis each stake a claim at the center of human suffering. How you respond to these claims depends upon your unique relationship with grief.

Part I of *Doing Grief in Real Life* provides navigational tools to help you become more familiar with the watery terrain of your own personal Strait of Messina. Some of these tools will be more helpful to you than others. Use them as they're useful to you and remember: whatever tools you use to guide you, you're the only one who can steer your ship through these roiling waters. You're the only one who can ensure safe passage.

Be forewarned: Once you pass safely through your Strait of Messina, having faced your Scylla and Charybdis within, such passage doesn't necessarily obliterate your grief. Your grief may always be with you. But braving the fiercest part of the passage can ease your suffering and make you strong. As Josephine Hart put it: "Damaged people are dangerous. They know they can survive."

So, take your courage with you, and let the journey begin.

Guidepost 1

If you want to heal your pain, you can't be afraid of your own shadow.

1 ❧ Letting It Out

Grief Doesn't Belong in a Box

> Grief.
> The pain now is part of the happiness then.
> That's the deal.
> C. S. Lewis

Outrageous Fortune
Seeing Grief from a Different Perspective

Proverbial wisdom says that all good things must come to an end. In the same breath, it declares that all good things come to those who wait. Such are the contradictions of grief. Grief is a private waiting room where you sit brooding for such attendants as love, joy, hope, and meaning to return. So, the suffering of grief is every bit as much about the goodness of life as it is about heartbreak. Sorrow is the sister of delight, and grief is their mother.

Why, then, does grief get such a bad rap in our culture? Most of us think of grief in the same way we imagine the Grim Reaper – as a reality we hope to hide from as long and often as we possibly can. But how would your life be different if you learned to regard grief as no less a gift than happiness? How would our children and grandchildren be different if families learned to embody the lessons grief teaches?

Perhaps it's a ridiculous proposition. Grief hurts. Grief threatens to break our hearts and minds into a million shard-like pieces. Grief comes when loved ones die or disappear or when they leave, lie to, or betray us. Grief comes with violence, storm, flood, or a system of injustice. It comes with loneliness, injury, illness, or isolation. Grief comes when life changes are too much for a heart, body, psyche, or soul to bear.

Yet, grief may also come when one gives birth or adopts a child, commits to a life-long partnership, gets a new job, or moves to a new home. Grief comes when one grows to a new age or stage of development and recognizes that illusions we once depended upon (the irreversibility of death or the heroic invincibility of a guardian) no longer serve us. It comes in subtle, elusive ways when our favorite season or time of day passes and we must wait another year or another day to recapture the joy and meaning we find in it. Grief is the courier of change.

We humans often confuse grief with the sadness we feel over something we lose, but grief is something more and different. To experience grief, what we lose must be something dear to us. Grief keeps us abreast of that which we love, that in which we find our greatest happiness.

Shakespeare, in the tragedy of Hamlet, deems grief as a fortune – an "outrageous fortune," to be sure, but a fortune, all the same. Here's the rub with the outrageous fortune of grief: You can squander it. You can use it to wield power over others. You can even hold onto it tight as a starving miser. But you can also learn to use grief as a resource to make your life, family, and world a more loving and hopeful place to reside. Your suffering is an able torchbearer. It can lead you to the center of meaning, hope, joy, love, forgiveness, and yes, to the very center of healing – where you can see for yourself that grief is *not* the Grim Reaper.

Guidepost 2

Grief turns everything on its head. Even itself.

The Unabridged Version
Grief as a Life Force

Physical death is often regarded as the ultimate grief-striking loss – the common denominator of our species. But death is hardly the most common loss we humans endure. Some of us make it all the way to middle age without experiencing the death of an intimate or seriously contemplating the inevitability of our own physical decay. Grief is not so elusive and can come in many forms.

For over a decade, my family was hit with a series of profound losses involving the deaths of family members – two who were murdered, a slew of broken family relationships, and scathing injustice encountered within the Broward County, Florida probate court system. For the first six years, the layers of grief descending upon our little corner of the world threatened to suffocate any hope that deep-seated joy would return to our home and family. My spouse, Andrew, and I each faced numerous grief-striking losses in our younger years. In many ways, we each exemplified resilience and certainty that the pains of life could not, would not defeat our joy or gratitude. But some losses are akin to a shrieking nightmare that finds its way to daylight.

It was in facing this series of losses that I fully digested the wisdom that physical death is not necessarily the worst loss that my loved ones or I can suffer. These losses that shook my family to the core forced me to take numerous treks across the wastelands of my inner being. It was upon such a trek that I learned to place physical death in perspective alongside all the other losses known to humanity.

As overwhelming as the fear of physical death can be, grievers worldwide experience other types of loss as "a death worse than death" – betrayal, shame, failure, injustice, lost love, abuse, violence, war, desolation, the loss of home or homeland, poverty, hunger, debilitating illness or injury, impotence, and the list goes on. If we desire to gain a fuller understanding of grief, we must explore the more nebulous psychological, emotional, physical, and spiritual deaths that threaten to consume our joy, meaning, hope, faith, and love.

Grief and death are inherent in all life. We humans dare to dream and we are devastated by our dreams. We awaken to innocence and we are disillusioned. We sacrifice autonomy for relationship and relationship for autonomy. We celebrate the birth or adoption of a child and we are terrified of parenthood. We love and we refuse to love, and we love again. Every change we encounter requires us to lose *something*, no matter how precious the gain. We're forced to die into relationship just as we die into aloneness. Grief is everywhere because change is everywhere.

What grief-striking losses have you encountered that you met easily and without delay? What losses were more difficult to face? Have you ever suffered a loss that for you was a death worse than death? Perhaps you endured an abusive relationship, debilitating injury, painful illness or addiction. Perhaps you were betrayed by (or betrayed) your beloved or were the victim of a violent attack or grave injustice. Perhaps the loss that sends you over the edge of hope or joy or meaning is watching a loved one suffer from increasing dementia, or experiencing failure, impotence, poverty, loneliness, rejection, or an unrelenting foreboding for the future of our planet.

Discover what is more painful to you than the reality of death and you will discover what you value more than life itself. What you value more than life is the secret to understanding the grief you carry. Grief is more sweeping and comprehensive than the bereavement of physical death; it is likely to arise in you whenever you attempt to reconcile the excruciating paradox of pain and pleasure in the human experience.

In Ernest Becker's Pulitzer Prize-winning book, *The Denial of Death*, he writes of the difficulties we encounter when we attempt to reconcile the grief of physical death. Becker deems the "denial of death" a human necessity. He tells us that hiding from ourselves the knowledge of our certain physical annihilation is a must if we desire to retain the will and interest to live. When we become overly focused on our mortality, says Becker, we risk mental illness and even insanity.

There is a fine line between denial and acceptance that allows us to hang in the balance between life and death. But, according to Becker, even those who can balance on that fine line, live, by design, in a constant state of grief. We are mostly unaware of it. But grief is there, just beneath the surface of our lives, and not only grief surrounding physical death but grief related to all kinds of unspoken, unheeded losses.

The folktale character Uncle Remus once said, "You can't run away from trouble. There ain't no place that far." The same is true for grief. Grief is as sure as life and death. Grief cannot be eradicated. Humans have been living with it for ages. Some of us reconcile our grief more easily and completely than others. But for all of us, grief is a given – as much an aspect of a human being as blood and bones.

So, the first step in accepting the reality of grief is to accept that grief resides in the contours of our human consciousness – however latent or active it may be. No human is exempt from grief – ever. A central human task, then, is to engage with grief not as if it's the Grim Reaper, but as the Life Force it can be – a Life Force that guides us back to hope, cherished meaning, joy, forgiveness, and relationship. Grief only becomes problematic when we are unable or unwilling to move it through our being, reconcile it, transform the sometimes-paralyzing pain of it.

I wrote the following poem as I resurfaced from the darkness of my six-year hiatus in which debilitating grief was my constant companion:

> Let us never
> Grow too comfortable
> With the surface of things,
> Be it pleasant or painful.
>
> Let us forever reach
> Beneath our grief and gratitude
> To find a deeper pain,
> A greater pleasure.
>
> It is not only ours to reconcile
> Our Sorrow and Joy together.
> It is ours to breathe from them
> All the Life that is theirs to give.

Guidepost 3

Grief is a Life Force to be reckoned with.

Taking It Personally
A Grief Story

When I was a senior in high school, my best friend Sheri died in an accident. She was on a date with a young man whose car went out of control and hit a tree. Eric, the driver of the car, was severely injured in the crash. All I could think to do at the time was to be strong in the only way I knew how at seventeen: I consoled friends, sang at Sheri's funeral, helped to create a "get well" video for Eric. I performed in a play a few nights after Sheri's death and wrote her obituary for the school newspaper. Purposeful action was the only thing that kept my world from completely caving in on me.

It was over three months after the accident when I began to face the devastating void. I was without my most intimate confidante and kindred spirit. When I finally began to cry over the loss, my mom – who in my estimation had braved a lifetime of grief and was doing her best to provide the support I needed – thought my delayed crying was abnormal. To avoid seeing a therapist, I quickly dried my tears.

About the same time, a school guidance counselor chastised me when I confided to him that the victorious celebration thrown for Eric after he was discharged from the hospital, left me feeling alone in my grief. Others seemed only thrilled to welcome our champion home, though he came back to us with brain damage, a reconstructed face we did not recognize, and the weight of another's death on his shoulders. After that, I decided it was less painful to go it alone than to trust others with my suffering.

The horrific sorrow I experienced after Sheri's death came as naturally to me as breathing. There was simply no other way for me to feel. The person who best personified life and joy for me had been eradicated from the face of the earth. Every time I turned around, I expected to see her, yearned to spill out to her the depths of my pain. Instead, I learned to *cope*, as they say. I learned to *deal with* my grief in ways that were acceptable, comfortable, even admirable to those around me.

During grad school, I sought out therapists to help facilitate my healing. Each one insisted that I was emotionally stuck because I never allowed myself to feel anger. At the time, in the mid 1980s, Elizabeth Kübler-Ross's five stages of death and dying (which included anger as the second stage after denial) were being routinely misapplied to grievers everywhere. "Where is your anger?" the therapists questioned. "Where is your anger at Sheri for leaving you behind? Your rage to indict the boyfriend? Your blame to hold God accountable for allowing the tragedy to occur?"

Psychology professors in college and grad school taught me that such responses to grief were considered normal, even justifiable. But no matter how completely I scoured my inner being, I couldn't detect more than a shred of anger – and none of it was pointed in Sheri's, Eric's, or God's direction. Sheri had confided premonitions of her early death. She didn't seem to fear the possibility, but I knew her absence was not intended to hurt me. I was told that the car accident was the result of a mechanical malfunction that occurred when Eric decided to show off his car at too high a speed. That alleged mistake cost him dearly. Witnessing Eric's pain after the accident, I could easily forgive him. Forgiveness, in fact, seemed irrelevant. As for God, I've never imagined a God who moves people through life like a puppet master. Accidents happen. To me, it's a miracle that the universe is created in such a way that we earthlings don't go spinning off into oblivion in droves every day.

No, my grief wasn't about anger. It was about missing the physical presence of a person who continues to be utterly irreplaceable. It was about my earthly joy being so shattered that sorrow would forever seep through the cracks of it. It was about facing the harrowing reality that to trust one's heart completely in the hands of another is to throw oneself wildly into the path of unfathomable heartache.

Ironically, my deepest healing after Sheri's death came when I found another human soul who was as trustworthy with my heart as Sheri had been. Andrew and I had been dating a few months when we took a trip to the ocean. Being near that massive body of water connected me with life and death, meaning and mystery. The first night we were there, I curled up in Andrew's arms and let go of the torrent of tears I'd been holding back for seven years. For me, that was a turning point, the moment I knew I could trust life, love, and joy again – not only in appearance but truly from the deepest cavern of my wounded soul. Thankfully, Andrew didn't push me to explain my need for that cathartic expression of suffering. Brave and loving being that he is, he simply held my pain as I let go a mother lode of it.

Sheri's death wasn't the first devastating loss I experienced and it isn't the last. What makes this loss unique is that it provided an opportunity for me to recognize that no grief "expert" can assess better than I what is true or useful to me in my grieving process. I waited seven years to release a stockpile of pain related to Sheri's death because I needed the presence of someone strong enough to accept and help me hold it without judgment or advice. I realized then that authentic grief gives little heed to what others deem "normal." It cares little for cultural conventions, even when we choose to abide by them outwardly – for our own sake or the sake of another.

Any professional healer – therapist, grief counselor, spiritual director, nurse, doctor, life coach, minister, priest, imam, or rabbi – whose guidance is worth their weight in gold, knows that each griever is their own best grief expert. Moreover, true healers make this knowledge the cornerstone of their work. Excepting young children or those whose mental or emotional capacities are severely impaired, there is no substitute for a griever's self-awareness. We healers cannot conjure such a substitute, no matter how wise or learned we may be.

Guidepost 4
Grief cannot, will not, be coerced.

No Such Thing
Normal Grief is an Oxymoron

Since Sigmund Freud explored the human grieving process in his paper, "Mourning and Melancholia" in 1917, grief and bereavement experts have tried to give us a handle on grief. Trouble is, grief doesn't have a handle. Our confusion in attempting to give it one is clearly reflected in a broad sweep of the scientific and medical literature on the subject. Is grief a crisis, an illness or disease, a survival instinct, a search for meaning? Is it a natural response to loss and change? Can "normal grief" be reduced to a series of emotional, behavioral, physical, or mental responses, or be given a time limit? Many theoretical models of the grieving process have been proposed by researchers and practitioners – to name a few, Erich Lindemann, John Bowlby, Colin Parkes, Therese Rando, William Worden, Margaret Stroebe and Henk Schut, and (best known among laypeople) Elizabeth Kübler-Ross. Kübler-Ross's model of grief was presented in her book, *On Death and Dying* in 1969. The model includes five stages of grief: (1) denial, (2) anger, (3) bargaining, (4) depression, and (5) acceptance. Unlike the others, Kübler-Ross's model caught the widespread attention of the medical establishment and the interest of the general public.

Over the past three decades, grief researchers have compiled a growing body of scientific evidence indicating that grief has no clear universal course, but Kübler-Ross's model remains a mainstay of contemporary grief mythology. The model took its form out of the five stages of grief Kübler-Ross observed in terminally ill patients who received the "catastrophic news" of their impending deaths. Soon, the model was misapplied by practitioners as a prescriptive tool for those grieving the deaths of loved ones and, eventually, to anyone suffering grief. Although Kübler-Ross also applied her model to a more general experience of grief in her final book, *On Grief and Grieving* (2005), even *she* qualifies the broad misapplication of the model in her opening paragraph:

> "The stages have evolved since their introduction, and they have been very misunderstood over the past three decades. They were never meant to tuck messy emotions into neat packages. They are responses to loss that many people have, but there is not a typical response to loss. There is no typical loss. Our grief is as individual as our lives."

Despite being misunderstood and misapplied, Kübler-Ross's work was influential in bringing a new sense of compassion to the process of death and dying for those of all ages. She suffered for it, too. In 1994, Kübler-Ross's house was burned down, allegedly by those who opposed her work. Moving beyond our cultural denial of death takes courage. We owe much to such pioneers and change agents. But the problem with most prevailing models of the grieving process, including Kübler-Ross's five-stage theory, is that many of these theories fail to sufficiently account for human diversity. Grief standards that depict a "normal" grieving process deny a wide range of possibilities and cast a shadow on many perfectly useful and sincere grieving responses that become suspect of being abnormal, immature, self-absorbed, or even pathological.

A heart-rending and brilliant account of grief is Ann Hood's book *Comfort*. The book takes us down the trail of grief upon which Hood was forced to embark after the death of her five-year-old daughter, Grace, in 2002. After receiving a litany of encouragement to seek the advice of other grievers, including those whose children died, Hood's prose drives into the core of her grief when she writes: "But none of them lost Grace. They do not know what it is to lose Grace."

To face grief is to face the knowledge that your grief is yours and yours alone. No one experienced your grief before you, and no one – not even you – will experience your grief the same way again. We humans are multi-dimensional creatures. As we grieve, we process countless nuanced emotions, mental states, physical sensations, behaviors, and spiritual perceptions. By default, *you* are the foremost expert on your grief. But, due to the complexities of your being, there will be times even you have no idea what your grief is asking of you or how to satisfy its needs. As a grief-stricken Ralph Waldo Emerson once wrote, "Sorrow makes us all children again – destroys all differences of intellect. The wisest know nothing."

If we humans are to untangle the great psychological mess we've gotten ourselves into by pretending that grief is a predictable and categorically simple process, we must first admit our ignorance. We must clear the table of all the answers and look instead to the questions that rise up in us as we stand smack dab in the middle of our unique grief experiences. Moreover, we each have to be willing to accept grief as an aspect of our being. Your grief doesn't have a life of its own; it can't reside apart from you. If you regard grief as an enemy to be eradicated, you do battle with your own soul.

Do this. Pretend you're observing, sensing, feeling, thinking, being in your grief as if for the first time. Lay down the burdens of expectation you carry, forget the knowledge you've acquired, suspend your beliefs and judgments about your grief. Now, close your eyes, take a few deep breaths, and simply be with this grief that is you – because it *is* you or, at least, a part of you.

Guidepost 5

Grief is a stranger you know by heart.

On the Other Side of Normal
Defining Grief on *Your* Terms

Put simply, *grief is the spontaneous suffering you experience when you are subject to a real or imagined loss of someone or something you greatly value or cherish*. But, what makes grief so difficult to define in explicit terms is that it comes in all shapes and sizes. Not only can grief's pain and suffering be experienced differently from griever to griever; it can be changeable within each of us – depending on the time of day, the season, the setting, or the situation. Grief can ease with the passage of time. It can intensify as one significant loss is piled on another. It can wax and wane as one's psyche blocks grief from view or allows grief to come more fully into daily or momentary consciousness.

If you desire to know the ins and outs of grief, you have to be willing to observe your own. Grief can be a feeling, an emotion. It can be a physical sensation or a way of thinking. It can be a certain energy that surrounds your being or a fidgety frustration that takes over when you stop to dwell on your loss. It can present itself as an illness or spiritual crisis – a nebulous gnawing at your psyche that alludes to an absence of meaning or hope or joy. It can be a raw burning in your chest, or a lifting of a veil that once protected some aspect of your innocence or naiveté. Grief can come as a sense of aloneness. It can even come as a bittersweet love of what used to be.

Think about it. Right now. What is grief to you? You're the only one who can answer the question. You're the only one who can feel what you feel, think what you think, and be in your grief the way you are. So, ask the question often, every day if need be: *What is grief to me?* Think about it. Contemplate it. Write about it. Draw it or dance it, if you choose. Talk it out with a loved one. The effort will be worth it, because if you get to know your grief, you can discover your path to healing.

Guidepost 6

Your grief contains its own antidote.

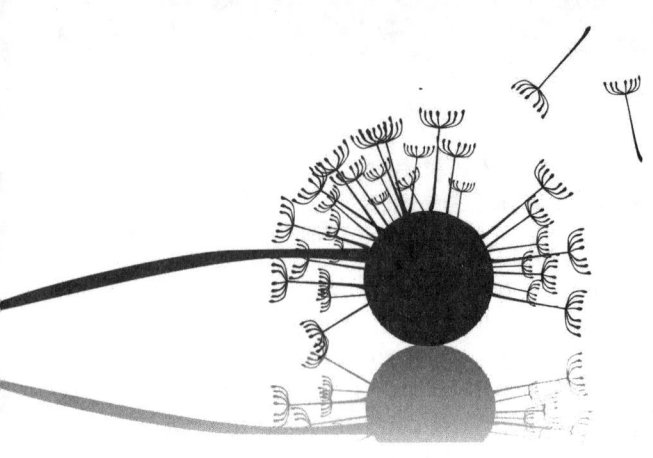

Intimate Exposure

Guided Contemplations to Inspire Self-Reflection

Self-awareness. As adults, there's no getting around it. You can try, of course, and many of us die trying. So it may be tempting to skip over the Guided Contemplations that focus on self-reflection and move on to the next chapter without pausing to consider the ins and outs of your intimate relationship with grief. There's no crime in that if it works for you. Sometimes self-awareness is a matter of timing. Sometimes a grief-striking loss is so raw and present to you, there is little need to become more aware of your responses to it than you already are. But don't let too much time get away without taking a closer look at your relationship with grief. Too often, we hold our grief at arm's length until the eleventh hour – perhaps that's why grief has become so synonymous with death.

Death and dying educator Richard Groves, who is co-author of *The American Book of Living and Dying*, focuses his life's work on helping the dying and their families resolve grief with one another before a death takes place. Groves calls it "transforming spiritual pain." He asserts that no matter how prepared you may be to face the reality of your death or that of a loved one, no one is immune from death-related spiritual pain in one form or another.

At one of Groves' training sessions for care providers that I attended through The Sacred Art of Living Center, I was struck with a notion that completely changed my relationship with grief. As Groves shared one death story with us after another, it became apparent to me that the types of spiritual pain encountered in each death were rooted in the types of spiritual pain each person encountered long before death came to call. It suddenly dawned on me: *If the grief of death is the grief of life, then we'd best get on with learning to resolve grief in our lives continually!* The effort seems especially significant since some of us will never see death coming. Why save up the challenge of healing all of our grief for the last big hurrah?

The following contemplations are intended to help you explore the nuances of your personal grief. Choose any or all that are relevant for you. Use each one as it's useful to you. Adapt it as you see fit. No one can contemplate your way to healing better than you.

Guidepost 7

The grief you heal now is part of the peace you find then. That's the deal.

Contemplation 1
A Mother, the Buddha & Some Mustard Seed
A Traditional Buddhist Grief Story Retold

Audio version available at DoingGrief.com

Focus: *To contemplate a Buddhist folktale regarding heartbreak and apply its wisdom to your personal experiences of unbearable loss.*

Once upon a time, yet not so long ago, there lived a loving and wise young woman named Kisa Gotami. Kisa Gotami was an orphan and grew up in poverty, but she always found a way to bring goodness and prosperity to everything she touched.

When Kisa Gotami reached a certain age, she met and married the son of a wealthy merchant. Soon, the happy couple gave birth to a beloved son. But their son was not very old when suddenly, without warning, the little boy died. In her crushing grief, Kisa Gotami carried her dead little boy from house to house, asking each of her neighbors to give her medicine to heal her son. The neighbors could not speak at the sight of Kisa Gotami's grief. They merely shook their heads and closed their doors to her pain. Behind their closed doors, they spouted to one another, "Kisa Gotami has lost her senses! It is clear that the boy is dead!"

But there was one old man who took pity on the young mother and lovingly replied, "Dear woman, I cannot give you medicine to heal your son, but I know someone who can."

"Please sir," Kisa Gotami cried, "tell me where I can find this Physician?" So, the old man sent her to visit none other than the Buddha.

To the Buddha, Kisa Gotami pleaded for medicine to heal her child. The Buddha replied, "To cure your son I will need a handful of mustard seed." Upon hearing this, the young mother was overjoyed! "I will go to get it at once!" she exclaimed. But the Buddha stopped her and said, "Before you go, I must tell you: this mustard seed must come from a home where no one has lost a child, parent, spouse or friend."

Kisa Gotami thanked the Buddha and went off determined to find such a home where she could procure the blessed mustard seed. At each house, her neighbors were glad to hear of her request, anything to save the poor woman from her pain. "Here, is the mustard seed!" they exclaimed, "Take it!"

But when Kisa Gotami asked if the mustard seed came from a home where no one had lost a child, parent, spouse, or friend, the people looked at Kisa Gotami in disbelief: "The living are few, the dead are many. Do not remind us of our grief." And they sent her away.

After searching far and wide long into the evening, Kisa Gotami finally understood. There was no home where death was a stranger. With this understanding, Kisa Gotami became weary and hopeless. She stooped to sit by the wayside, watching the lights of the city until they were extinguished. Darkness reigned everywhere.

In the morning, Kisa Gotami buried the body of her dead son in the forest. Then, returning to the Buddha, she took refuge there, seeking medicine to soothe and heal the pain of her broken heart.

⋏ ⋏ ⋏

Consider Kisa Gotami's grief experience in light of your own:

- ◈ Have you ever experienced a loss that caused you such unbearable grief that it was difficult for you to comprehend the reality of it?
- ◈ How did you avoid accepting the reality of your loss?
- ◈ What took place before you could begin to accept your unbearable grief?
- ◈ How did you seek the needed "medicine" to soothe and heal your suffering?

You may want to journal about your discoveries or share them with a trusted counselor or loved one. What was good medicine for you in the past may be of use as you find your bearings to face present and future losses.

⦀⦀⦀

⁞ Contemplation 2 ⁞
Plenty to Lose
Taking a Personal Inventory

Focus: *To reflect on common types of loss and identify which of your firsthand losses are easily tended or difficult for you to heal.*

⦀⦀⦀

We humans are utterly resilient. It may not appear to be so when we take stock of the current statistics on depression, addiction, suicide, and mental illness. However, as a species, we're able to assimilate monumental grief-striking losses daily:

- One's own imminent death or the death of a loved one
- Loss of home, homeland, or property
- Loss of health, body function, or body image
- Loss of future ideals, plans, or dreams
- Loss of independence, freedom, mobility, or control
- Loss of safety or protection
- Loss of mental or physical abilities
- Loss of core beliefs or values

We rise and rise again from the ashes of devastating grief experiences that are born of compounded losses. Consider the layers of grief that pound us from widespread disease such as COVID-19 or natural disasters – hurricanes, tornados, earthquakes, wildfires, tsunamis. Such tragedies may encompass the deaths of friends, family members, and pets; losses of income, home, property, or prized possessions; loss of access to food, water, employment opportunities, community assistance, freedom to travel, aid and protection, etc. Such compounded losses present entire communities and nations with an entangled web of grief to process.

What's more, our grief experiences may be layered with losses that are ambiguous, painful to acknowledge, or culturally taboo, such as:

Losses experienced within the family or private sector:
- Divorce, separation, or interpersonal conflict
- Physical or psychological abuse or abandonment
- Drug or alcohol abuse or addiction
- Economic hardship
- Demands of caregiving
- Experiencing intense shame, guilt, or failure
- Losing a valued object
- Placing a child for adoption

Non-death losses related to powerlessness:
- Unemployment, hunger, or homelessness
- Spiritual or existential crises
- Being a victim of acts of violence (vandalism, physical attack, bullying, etc.)
- Political or social oppression
- Rejection by intimates, peers, co-workers, etc.
- Psychological or social liabilities
- Being subject to an ineffective or corrupt legal system

Losses related to sexuality:
- Sexual dysfunction
- Infidelity
- Unrequited love
- Unplanned or unwanted pregnancy
- Planned or spontaneous abortion
- Infertility
- Hormonal imbalances
- Becoming sexually active
- Feeling sexually unattractive
- Sex-related addictions
- Being a victim of rape, sexual abuse, or incest
- Rejection or self-loathing due to sexual orientation, gender identity, or sexual behavior

Losses related to developmental passages:
- Disillusionment from the magical thinking of childhood
- The onset of puberty
- Menopause
- Aging

Life cycle passages commonly celebrated within the family, community, or culture that include loss related to independence, identity, security, youth, etc.:
- Birth or adoption of a child
- Graduation
- Retirement
- Marriage

Whether real or imagined, any life event, circumstance, or experience that a griever perceives as an undesirable loss can conjure grief.

Wherever love and happiness are treasured priorities, there is unending potential for grief-striking loss. As you consider the breadth of possibilities, you may be surprised to discover how many grief-striking losses you endured without giving them much thought. Sometimes, we humans simply do what's required of us and move on with life. But when grief-striking losses leave you wounded and hurting, simply moving on with life isn't a viable option, because unacknowledged grief gets played out in unconscious ways that may cause further harm to you and those around you.

A crucial question for grievers who are seeking healing is: *How do I tend to my grief without getting bogged down in the mire of my suffering?* Figuring out which losses require your thoughtful healing intention and which losses are easily addressed in the course of everyday life is an art. As you ponder this for yourself, it may be helpful to ask:

- Which of the losses in the lists (on pages 24-26) have I experienced firsthand?
- Are any of my grief-striking losses missing from these lists?
- Which losses cause me intense pain and suffering or are heaviest for me to carry?
- Which losses are devoid of intense distress or are easily tended?

Don't judge yourself for experiencing excessive grief that may appear to be out of line with the type of loss you suffer. Grief takes root within the complexities of your beliefs, values, expectations, loves, and desires. Mark Twain once wrote: "Nothing that grieves us can be called little: by the eternal laws of proportion a child's loss of a doll and a king's loss of a crown are events of the same size."

Contemplation 3
The Power of a Name
Giving Your Grief an Identity

Focus: *To acknowledge personal grief that is not attached to an obvious loss event and explore your grief through free-form writing.*

You may suffer grief but can't identify its source. Unidentified grief can play havoc with your health and well-being. So, it's fortunate that grief is painful because that's how it lets you know when something within you is amiss – even if you don't have a name for it yet. Grief will jump up and down on your heart and head (and any other part of you it finds especially vulnerable) until it gets your attention – your *undivided* attention.

Sometimes the source of grief is easy to identify: the death of a loved one, divorce, foreclosure on the family home, job loss, injury, illness. But grief may slip in through the back porch of your psyche like a wanderer seeking shelter from an unrelenting storm. You may not even know it's there until you stumble over it in the dark.

If you can't identify the source of your grief, ask your grief the same questions you might ask a stranger from out of town:

- What's your name?
- Where do you come from?
- What's the reason for your visit?

As you get to know your grief better and acquaintance turns into companionship, you can ask your grief more pointed questions:

- What would you like to communicate to me?
- What are you asking of me?
- What do we need to accomplish together?

Free-form Writing: Asking Your Grief a Question

Free-form writing may help you to discover new insights about your grief. Find a quiet place to sit and contemplate. Have paper and pen/cil handy. Ask your grief a question – any question you choose. Meditate on the question for a few quiet moments. Hold it in your mind and repeat it silently to yourself. When you're ready, begin writing. Write uninterrupted for 10-15 minutes. Don't think about the words. Allow your grief to answer your question in whatever way it chooses to do so. If you get stuck, just write your question over and over again, until the answer re-emerges in your writing. Some free-form writers switch to writing with their non-dominant hand to inspire a more spontaneous process.

As you contemplate what you've written, you may be surprised and heartened by the answers you receive. The real beauty of naming your grief is that acknowledged grief often begins to heal of its own accord. Like most of us, grief often responds favorably to a little loving attention.

⋮ Contemplation 4 ⋮
Location, Location, Location
Discovering Where Grief Resides in You

Audio version available at DoingGrief.com

Focus: *To engage in a guided contemplation that helps identify your experience of grief in all aspects of your being – body, heart, mind, and spirit.*

There is more than one road to track down your grief and discover how it affects you, because your grief can live in every aspect of your being. Grief may cause intense *emotional* suffering for you. It may play havoc with your *mental* capacities and thinking patterns. You may experience grief in your *physical* body or within your *spiritual* life and relationships. Your body chemistry, personality or temperament, age, emotional maturity, mental habits, type of loss, spiritual relationships, and hormonal levels can amplify grief in one dimension of your being more than another.

Taking stock of where grief resides within you can help you to attend more directly to your suffering. If you experience grief intensely in your physical body, physical care may become an immediate priority. If grief causes obsessive, unrelenting thinking patterns, finding ways to calm and balance your mental state may be crucial.

If grief is especially present and raw for you, it may be helpful to ask a capable and trusted counselor, spiritual director, friend, or family member to guide you through this process. Or you can listen to the audio version of this contemplation on my website at DoingGrief.com. As you contemplate, be patient with yourself. It may take time and practice to learn to trust your grief as an enlightening aspect of your being.

Self-Assessment: Discovering the Location of Your Grief

- ◈ **Preparation:** Before you begin, create a quiet relaxing space to explore your grief and have paper and pen/cil handy to jot down any insights that come to you during or after your contemplation.

- ◈ **Your Loss:** Revisit the story of "A Mother, the Buddha, and Some Mustard Seed" on page 23. Imagine yourself in the place of Kisa Gotami suffering a loss you know firsthand that threatened to crush your spirit. What loss have you carried in your arms, searching everywhere for a cure, longing to reverse it, if only there was a way?

  Whatever the loss is, don't judge it. Don't justify it, minimize it, or push it away. Simply hold it in the arms of your being. Accept it, observe it, be with it as you are. Feel what you feel. Think what you think. Breathe deeply and acknowledge your grief – however it may present itself.

- ◈ **Your Physical Body:** Once you acknowledge your grief quietly within, notice where and how your grief lives in your body. You may feel your grief more intensely in your chest or gut. You may feel it in your brain, heart, neck, back, genitals, jaw, or the site of a recent injury or organ affected by disease. Check in with each part of your body. Notice if the pain of your grief resides strongly in a particular place. Does your grief cause your body to feel immobile or weary, fidgety or in need of constant activity?

Reflect on each physical sensation related to your grief. As you identify each one, don't judge it. Don't justify it, minimize it, or push it away. Simply hold it, accept it, observe it, be with it – however it may present itself. Write notes of any insights that come to you.

- **Your Thinking:** Once you self-assess your body, consider where and how your grief lives in your thinking. What thinking habits or patterns have changed since your grief-striking loss occurred? Perhaps your grief prompts denial, doubt, hopelessness, a lack of meaning or safety, numbness or disorientation, a sense of doom or disbelief. Grief can also spur a person toward belief, hope, cherished meaning, protection, understanding, forgiveness, clarity, a sense of purpose or acceptance. Perhaps your grief presents itself as an obsessive compulsion to stay awake thinking of every nit-picking detail of your loss experience. Or perhaps your grief numbs your mind, making it easy to sleep 24/7.

As you uncover each mental habit or thinking pattern that dominates you in your grief, don't judge it. Don't justify it, minimize it, or push it away. Simply hold it, accept it, observe it, be with it – however it may present itself. Take as much time as you need. Write notes of any insights that come to you.

- **Your Emotions:** Once you self-assess your thinking habits and patterns, consider where and how grief lives in your emotional life. Make a list of all your grief-related emotions. Perhaps your grief elicits sorrow, anger, depression, frustration, yearning, bitterness, hatred, or apathy. Your grief may just as easily elicit love, joy, humor, relief, peace, calm, compassion, or affection. The nuances of emotion related to grief can be multi-layered, complex, and sometimes in opposition to one another. Write a list of the grief-related emotions you experience.

Identify and reflect on each grief-related emotion. As you detect each one, don't judge it. Don't justify it, minimize it, or push it away. Simply hold it, accept it, observe it, be with it – however it may present itself. Write notes of any insights that come to you.

- **Your Spirituality:** Once you self-assess your emotional life, consider where and how grief lives in your spiritual relationships. *Spirituality is broader than religious faith.* Spiritual intuitions, imaginations, and inspirations can be experienced through any realm that brings cherished meaning to our lives. Beyond religious faith, spirituality can be nurtured through philosophy, science, sociology, psychology, or any discipline in which a person discovers valued meaning concerning our human existence in an ever-expanding universe. Spirituality can be nurtured through intimate relationships, visual and performing arts, silent meditation, literature, poetry, nature, athletic endeavors, and the spoken word.

Before your loss: Consider sources of spiritual meaning and sustenance in your life. Recall how you experienced spiritual meaning *before* grief-striking loss changed your life as you know it.

After your loss: When you're ready, consider how your spiritual relationships and understanding changed in light of your loss. Perhaps your spiritual relationships were damaged or your previously held convictions seem too weak to hold you in your pain. Perhaps your grief gave you access to new spiritual experiences or drew you intimately into the solace of your faith community or the peace and beauty of nature. Perhaps your grief motivated you to delve into whatever art form, philosophical perspective, or scientific discipline you find most useful or inspirational to discover valued meaning. Take time to reflect on where and how your grief lives in your spiritual life.

With each change you discover in your spirituality, don't judge it. Don't justify it, minimize it, or push it away. Simply hold it, accept it, observe it, be with it – however it may present itself. Write notes of any insights that come to you.

- **Your Discoveries:** What did you discover about your experience of grief? In which aspect/s of your being is your grief:
  - Most present and observable?
  - Most problematic for you?
  - Most easily processed or helpful?
  - Least noticeable?

You may want to share your insights with a trusted counselor, spiritual director, friend, or family member who is an especially supportive listener. Since your relationship with grief is fluid, revisit this contemplation to take stock of how you experience your grief differently over time.

Reflecting on your body-heart-mind-spirit relationship with grief can help you to figure out the most effective ways to care for yourself when you're suffering. But griever beware: genuine self-awareness requires both persistent practice and knowing when enough self-awareness is enough – for now. As you discover the healing balance, be patient and gentle with yourself in the process.

Guidepost 8

Grief is like an old friend:
you can always take up where you left off.

2 ❧ Don't Fix What Isn't Broken

Grieving as Self-Expression

One who does not grieve, hardly exists.
Antonio Porchia

Vive la Différence!
The Relationship Between Grief and Grieving

Grief. Grieving. What's the difference? Grief is to grieving as the eye is to seeing, as the ear is to hearing. Think of grief as an invisible organ of perception. Think of the difference between grief and grieving as the difference between what a person is and what a person does. Grief is a part of you. Grieving is responding – consciously and unconsciously – to the part of you that is grief.

In 21st-century Western culture, we tend to speak of grief and grieving as one and the same – an emotion of sorts that happens to us. Whether it erupts like spontaneous combustion or simmers beneath the surface of the daily round, grieving is often regarded as personal pain over which a griever has little control.

It's true, as the modern proverb says, "shit happens" – to us, our loved ones, and to those on the other side of the world who we will likely never know by name. Every day our human collective suffers common, extraordinary, unthinkable grief-striking losses we would never choose for one another or ourselves. So, most of us, if only we had the magic power, might elect to eradicate grief-striking losses from the face of the planet – forever. But we don't and we can't. Instead, most of humanity learns to coexist with grief. I beg you to do more.

It may sound delusional, but your grief deserves your respect and affection. Grief is like the irritatingly wise and learned teacher who prods you to consider the incomprehensible – the mentor you go back to thank years later for imparting the lessons you were so resistant to learn.

Grief is laced with healing wisdom but sometimes that message gets lost in translation: A griever (or their caregiver) may respond to grief in ways that intensify or prolong suffering. What's more, the human psyche can ignore grief so completely that grief and grieving reside as perfect strangers on opposite sides of a massive chasm within a person's being. Why the rift? How can grief and grieving become utterly unfamiliar with one another?

Perhaps it's like this: A healthy eye can see, but cannot observe. A healthy ear can hear, but cannot listen. It takes a whole person – a breathing, thinking, feeling person – to fully observe what the eye sees and fully listen to what the ear hears. Likewise, it takes a whole person to grieve. Your grief needs you – all of you – to make itself useful.

You write your grieving biography in the ways you choose to grieve. When you engage fully in the grieving process, it becomes clear that grieving isn't merely something that happens to you. Whether your grieving choices are made consciously or unconsciously, spontaneously or methodically, they will determine whether your grief-related suffering diminishes or enhances your life and relationships. For good or ill, how you grieve impacts those you hold close, including yourself.

Consider this story from India that serves as an allegory for the intense challenge a griever faces in responding to grief:

Little Bird

A youth wanted to befuddle the elder of the village. The old one was said to be exceedingly wise. But the young challenger imagined that youthful wit could outdo the wisdom of the rickety old sage. So, the youth caught a little bird, carried it to the elder, and hiding it between young hands not yet worn or weary, the youth announced:

"I have a riddle for you, old one. Here in my hands is a bird. Tell me – is the bird alive, or is it dead?"

The youth delighted in the game. There was no way for the elder to win. If the old one ventured to guess "dead," an open hand would release the little creature and the bird would fly free. If the elder guessed "alive," the youth would set a fist and crush the bird at once.

But the old one looked into the eyes of the young seeker and replied with care, "The answer, my child, is in your hands."

Such is the puzzle of grieving. Grieving is a life-and-death challenge to which your spirit inquires, however silently or soulfully: "How will I hold my grief?" Will it be with a fist or an open hand?

Guidepost 9

Grief is a noun.
Grieving is a verb – it's something you do.

Refracted Darkness
Grieving in All Directions

Grief scatters darkness as a prism scatters light. So, when we respond to grief, we're forced to take a soulful journey in all directions. No doubt, it would be easier if grieving were more orderly. If only there were three, or five, or even ten grieving assignments we could line up and knock off one by one. But grieving isn't as simple as all that. Like grief, grieving is multi-dimensional.

Imagine a person facing a divorce who simultaneously experiences love, bitterness, relief, regret, depression, and anticipation about ending a marriage. Add to that, possible custody battles, property disputes, and the necessity of redefining relationships with family members and friends, including in-laws and (sometimes) stepfamily. A person experiencing divorce often acquires layer upon layer of interrelated losses to process, evoking emotions, mental states, physiological changes, behaviors, spiritual perceptions, and social dynamics that may conflict with one another.

Take a moment to reflect on a personal grief-striking loss experience – past or present. You might call to mind a death, divorce or betrayal, a loss of job, home, health, safety, or a grave disappointment or failure. Consider how your grieving responses to your loss impact/ed your relationships with yourself, others, your living space, and patterns of daily life. Some relationships may be improved and others damaged, including

- Your relationships with loved ones, co-workers, acquaintances, God or other spiritual companions;
- Your self-image or your relationship to your body, work, play, sexuality, beliefs, values, spirituality, or religious faith;
- Your relationship to your home or workplace, food, sleep, money, alcohol, drugs, or daily routines and rhythms; and
- Your priorities, goals, or aspirations.

You can't separate grieving from the rest of your life or confine your grieving responses to a singular relationship. Grief permeates everything, whether you're aware of it or not. That's why grieving can be so all-consuming and overwhelming at times. A holistic approach to grieving requires you to know yourself through and through. No, not just know yourself, but also be willing to stake your healing on it. In her book, *The Neurotic Personality of Our Time*, Karen Horney wrote that the most comprehensive formula for healing is wholeheartedness, that is "to be without pretense, to be emotionally sincere, to be able to put the whole of oneself into one's feelings, one's work, one's beliefs." So, try it – for an hour, a day, a lifetime. Wholeheartedly commit yourself to grieving as a path to healing.

Guidepost 10

Authentic grieving is like looking into a broken mirror and seeing your whole reflection as if for the first time.

No End in Sight
When Grief Keeps on Giving

Many grief-striking loss experiences are not realized in a singular instance, but may occur as a series of losses over days, weeks, months, or years. Consider the "perfect storm" of loss that began to descend on my family in the fall of 2004:

A Family Story of Unrelenting Loss

It all began when my father announced that he was living and dying with cancer. When we found out, Andrew and I with our two children (who were teenagers then) moved from McFarland, Wisconsin to Phoenix, Arizona to be closer to my Dad as he negotiated the passage of death. We moved into our Phoenix home in 112-degree August heat. Arizona heat may be a "dry heat," as they say, but sweat was pouring from every pore. Even then, we had no idea how metaphorically scorching that first Phoenix summer would become for us.

Three weeks after our move, on a leisurely Sunday evening, we received a phone call that shook our world: Andrew's father, Jim, and Martha (Jim's wife of five years) had been murdered by Martha's son from a previous marriage. There is no sufficient way to describe the horrific shift of perspective that took place for us when that senseless act ripped Jim and Martha from the earth.

Amazingly, to our devastated hearts, things only got worse. Ironically, it wasn't the violence of the murderous act that became the most difficult aspect of our grief to navigate. There were more insidious violent acts that we experienced at the hands of the Broward County, Florida probate judge assigned to the case.

The murders took place at a vacation home Jim owned in North Carolina on September 3, 2004. Jim and Martha drove to the home to escape a hurricane threatening the coast of Ft. Lauderdale, Florida, where they lived for most of the year. When they entered the North Carolina home, Martha's son, Tom, was hiding like a sniper in military attire. He shot them both before fleeing the scene.

There was no criminal trial. Tom was quickly and easily apprehended in Florida, allegedly making his way toward the home of his father. Tom pleaded guilty, was indicted, and received two life sentences without parole by the North Carolina criminal court. That fact brought some sense of closure to the tragedy, but our shock and devastation were ignited repeatedly as Andrew discovered he was named as executor and trustee of his father's multimillion-dollar estate with no knowledge or preparation of it before his Dad's death. Suddenly, we were grieving our monstrous loss, taking on what the top probate lawyers in Ft. Lauderdale considered to be one of the most convoluted probate cases they had encountered, and navigating through the inefficient and highly questionable Broward County probate court process.

While hurricanes continued to threaten the Florida coast, we were forced to evacuate twice as we planned a double funeral with Martha's daughter and son-in-law. Soon, compassionate overtures morphed into adversarial attacks as Martha's daughter (who was the sole heir of her mother's sizable estate) filed a claim to win the lion's share of Jim's estate on behalf of her dead mother.

Since Jim and Martha died at approximately the same time, simultaneous death laws applied in the case, so the assets of each estate were to be distributed as if each spouse had predeceased the other. Neither Jim nor Martha had named the other's children or grandchildren as beneficiaries of their separate wills or trusts. Given these facts, at first, the daughter's claim seemed to us like a shot in the dark, perhaps an emotional reaction to grief that would be quickly dismissed by the probate court.

However, as we began to wade through the muddy legal mess in the aftermath of the murders, stories about the ineffectiveness of the Broward County probate court system began to pour in. All too soon, we were among its casualties, entangled in a seemingly never-ending stream of contentious court hearings and demanding "mediations" that mostly served to diminish Jim's estate assets, batter the already wounded souls of his children and grandchildren, and cause family relationships among beneficiaries and in-laws to become increasingly problematic.

For the first nine years, the judge who was assigned to the probate case never spoke a word of consolation to the families. As the case bumbled along, his egoistical courthouse demeanor vacillated between nonchalant arrogance and abrasive tirades. He dragged hearing proceedings out for years with promises of expediency and no explanation for the delays. What's more, relevant laws were completely ignored in the probate judge's "final judgment" regarding Jim's estate assets. Irrelevant and misinterpreted common law cases were used as his justification. The bizarre outcome, which took over five years to acquire, was this: *After Jim's life was taken by Martha's son, the majority of Jim's assets was granted to Martha's daughter.* It was like rubbing salt in an open wound. We were so emotionally exhausted by then, it would have been easy to give up the fight, but fighting was the only option we had to honor Jim's final wishes, life's work, and the provisions he bequeathed to his family members, co-workers, and friends.

Our estate lawyers immediately filed for an appeal. However, we were told that the lower court's decision might well be "rubber-stamped" at the district level. We weren't holding our breath for a positive outcome. By then, we knew: no matter who wins the court battle, no one really wins. There was plenty of loss to go around for a good long while. So, imagine our astonishment when after two more years of waiting, we received the news that the appeals court had overturned the probate judge's earlier decision, citing the same simultaneous death law that should have protected Jim's estate from the beginning.

The probate case was finally closed almost 13 years after Jim's death. By that time, we were well aware that the damages suffered could never be repaired in a court of law. Even if the court awarded damages in the amount of the total financial loss, there is no way for the court to compensate a family for years of suffering caused by the negligence and error of its representatives. Judges are protected by law from being held accountable for harmful consequences of their erroneous judgments. So, in the end, my family's saving grace is our resilience and willingness to heal our grief, despite a slew of broken relationships, squandered assets, and disillusionments we encountered as we battled our way through the Broward County probate court. Thank heavens that our healing is something we don't have to depend on a judge to acquire.

After Jim's death, my family members and I learned to gather every gift we could uncover from the wreckage of Jim's murder and probate case. Fortunately, amid the damage, we found opportunities to honor and celebrate Jim's life and legacy; re-think goals, priorities, values, and beliefs; clarify and deepen intimate relationships; re-establish connections with estranged loved ones; and transform disillusionments into meaningful life lessons. We learned that the more grievous our loss, the more we stand to gain by healing our pain and suffering.

The Lawful Truth of It

Since my family's "up close and personal" awakening to the potential deficiencies of the U.S. court system, we are keenly aware that we're some of the fortunate ones. Some grievers fighting legal battles in probate, divorce, family, civil, or criminal court who are up against an inefficient, uninformed, or corrupt system, don't always have the resources, opportunities, or appeals outcome we do. What's more, some victims stand to lose a great deal more than time, money, or faith in the legal system.

Consider Mario Rocha, the subject of the documentary *Mario's Story*, who went to jail at the age of sixteen and spent twelve years fighting a conviction for a murder he didn't commit. During his ten-year incarceration, Mario suffered severe injuries twice when fellow inmates knifed him. Fortunately, due to the persistence of a creative writing teacher Mario met in juvenile hall (when he was awaiting his first trial) and the unrelenting efforts of the pro bono lawyers she acquired for him, Mario was finally released temporarily from prison after an appeals court ruled that he was not adequately represented in his original trial. After waiting another two years for the Los Angeles County prosecutors to decide that Mario's case would not be retried, Mario's lengthy legal nightmare finally came to an end.

No doubt, Mario Rocha and his family members know that he's one of the lucky ones, too. Once a person is convicted of a crime in Los Angeles County, an appeals case is rarely heard. Only a minuscule number of convictions are overturned without retrial. What's more, not everyone has the emotional, psychological, or physical stamina of a Mario Rocha. Unlike the resilient Mario, whose creative writing and indomitable spirit sustained him through his imprisonment, there are others unjustly incarcerated who are psychologically and spiritually damaged beyond recognition.

How can we hope to define "normal" grieving behavior when life after loss gets that messy? When tragedy strikes, the blow can resound with ongoing tremors that create pain and havoc for years on end. So, when we assess "normal" grieving responses for ourselves or others, let's put "normal" in its proper place alongside all that is abnormal. Grieving can be complicated. Feel free to color outside the lines.

Guidepost 11

Grieving becomes simpler only when you accept its complexities.

Authentic Grieving
Breaking the Bonds of Convention

In 21st-century Western culture, those suffering grief are expected to express intense sadness, anger, fear, yearning, even depression in the weeks and months following a loss and then to quickly "get on with life." Turn it on. Shut it off. Advice on how to do so is often conflicting. Some imagine tears as the ultimate answer to ease the pain of grief, while others say laughter or impassive resolve is the remedy. Some promote talking cures, while others say that silence is instructive. There is advice to "get busy" and advice to "stop and be still." Some counsel that it's good to be alone with your grief, others that relationships are a refuge. But just as each of these grieving responses can cure, they may also add fuel to your suffering or obstruct genuine healing. What is "good medicine" for one griever may not alleviate another's pain, or may be a help in one instance and a hindrance in another. Given the varying outcomes of such curatives, how does a griever or caregiver figure out the most effective approach to acknowledge, ease, tolerate, and heal the pain of grief?

Sometimes, friends, family members, and caregivers are at a loss to know which healing path to suggest to a griever, so they fumble or fall silent. Some imagine they will only make the pain worse. Others hope to pray the grief away. After my friend Sheri's death in high school, my teachers, parents, coaches, and mentors, even my minister, had no idea how to respond to my pain or show me the way to heal it. Their floundering in the face of grief was as frightening to me as the fact that my dear friend could disappear from the earth in a flash. Just like that, she was gone, and none of us knew what to do about it. No one could show me the way home to myself.

How I wish I knew then what I know now. How I wish this wisdom for all my dear ones: Grieving is more than emoting over the pain of grief. It is more than talking about your distress. Grieving is not so different from living. We cry. We laugh. We carry our sorrows, we set them aside. We forget. We remember. We resist. We embrace. Grieving is responding to the all of grief: the pain and the relief from pain, the joy and the sorrow, the love and the bitterness, the aloneness and togetherness, the unthinkable agony and the unexpected miracle that arises out of the paradox of losing what you cherish.

If life were only pain, who among us would resist death? If life were only pleasure, who among us would resist being lulled into a blasé stupor in which joy, love, hope, and faith are no longer relevant? It is life's rationing of pain and pleasure, the juxtaposition of sorrow and joy, that gives life its meaning. We must embrace all of it or die a life of discontent.

Above all else, grief asks you to remember what it is to be human. Grief may ask for tears or laughter. It may ask for your story or silence, your action or stillness. Grief may require your resolute strength, or inspire a purging of the wildly foreign sounds of despair that lodge themselves in your gut. It may throw you into the heart of love, joy, or hope, or it may ever so gradually unveil the meaning of life beyond misery. Grief may ask you to perform Herculean tasks that come as easily to you as taking a breath or that sap every last ounce of your love, self-compassion, or interest in keeping on. At times, grief may even ask you to ignore it, deny it, put it down.

Know this: authentic grieving is breaking through what others do or do not do, to discover what grief asks of *you*. It may require various responses – not just a specific series of emotions, a particular way of thinking, or a line of grieving tasks you can knock off one by one. Grief requires you to live with it – eat, breathe, and sleep with it. It requires you to despair and hope with it, to nurture and (even) neglect it.

Unfortunately, we humans don't have a common understanding of what grieving entails. Even the grief experts disagree on how to define essential aspects of the grieving process. In the void, grief counselors may witness such emotions as sadness or anger as obvious responses to grief, and say, "Come, this is the way!" Scientists may stack up statistics and define "normal" by way of the majority. If you don't fit the profile, you may be labeled as being emotionally or psychologically impaired. What's more, in an age of the "isms" and political correctness – in which we strive to give voice to those of all genders, ages, and ethnicities – we may fail to see the unique responses of each griever because we're striving so diligently to understand people in groups of likeness. Statistical norms are easily translated into expectations.

According to speculation about human tendencies, if you're a woman experiencing grief, you'll talk about your grief with someone. If you're a man, you'll respond to your grief by throwing yourself into mental or physical tasks. According to tendencies: Black/Afro-Americans defeat the pain of grief; Asian-Americans lean into it; Euro-Americans numb it; Hispanic Americans purge it; those of indigenous cultures in North America learn from it. But anyone with an eye for observing human behavior knows that these tendencies – which may or may not be documented through scientific study – are typecast pictures of us.

I repeat: no two grievers are exactly alike in the ways we perceive and respond to grief. No matter a person's age, race, personality or temperament, family expectations, community influences, or gender, each griever's loss experience involves a unique combination of grieving responses. So, identifying commonalities among subsets of grievers is not the same as knowing a loss experience as another person perceives it and grieves it.

Honoring diverse responses among grievers requires a common understanding of the human grieving process that accommodates everyone, especially those who don't fit into statistical or cultural norms. Grieving is complicated enough without a griever feeling pressured by medically sanctioned prescriptions, social expectations, or faulty personal beliefs. So, in your grieving, seek out the people, places, and corners of your soul that allow you to express and explore your honest-to-goodness grieving responses, and encourage others to do the same. Anything less will only keep you from yourself and those you love.

Guidepost 12

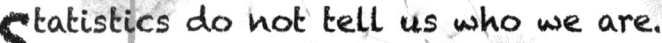

Statistics do not tell us who we are.

What's a Griever to Do?
Re-envisioning the Human Grieving Process

Grieving is what you make of it. There is no universal cure for the grief that ails you. Even so, grief remains one of life's most complex and problematic certainties, and a lifeline for grievers is surely in demand – one that is useful for *everyone* and does not divide us into camps of the supermajority and everyone else.

Through three decades, as I studied the grieving process and observed grievers of all ages and walks of life in my work as a family educator, minister, and spiritual director, a niggling question distilled itself (oh-so-gradually) within me: *What navigational tool might be of practical use to grievers in charting a course to healing?* Searching for answers wasn't a conscious process. In truth, I doubted that any bona fide answers existed. But the grief-related suffering I witnessed in my work and personal life prompted years of exploration and pondering.

After years of contemplation, it suddenly came to me – my Model of Adaptive Grieving Dynamics (MAGD, page 41). The MAGD is a picture of the grieving process that integrates four types of grieving responses that are universal to all grievers, but experienced and expressed uniquely by you and anyone who suffers grief. My MAGD is not a paint-by-numbers grieving model or a prescriptive cure for grief. It won't tell you what to do with your grief-related pain, but it does provide a sense of relational direction, wherever you find yourself in the grieving process.

The Model of Adaptive Grieving Dynamics – explained in greater detail in the following section and chapter – is a new way to think about grieving. It's a sketch that provides broad strokes of the grieving process so you can fill in the details. It's a compass to help you and your loved ones navigate your landscapes, heartscapes, and mindscapes of grieving – no matter how far you venture from "normal."

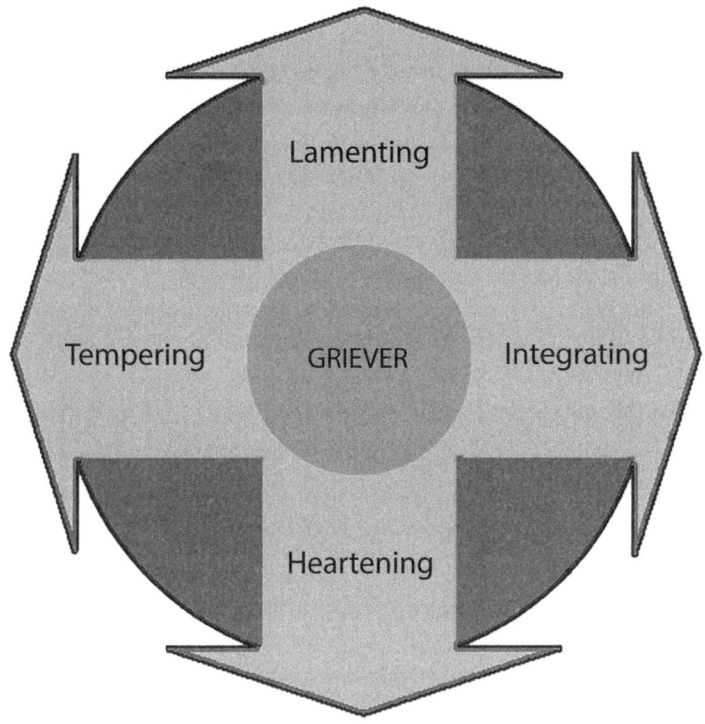

Model of Adaptive Grieving Dynamics © 2014 by Charlene DeShea Bagbey Darian

For those interested in a detailed description of the MAGD and its scientific justification and theoretical underpinnings, see my journal article, "A New Mourning: Synthesizing an Interactive Model of Adaptive Grieving Dynamics" in *Illness, Crisis & Loss*, volume 22:3, 2014.

Guidepost 13

A new way of seeing is a new way of being.

Caught Between a Rock and a Hard Place
The Model of Adaptive Grieving Dynamics (MAGD) Explained

The MAGD illustrates four types of responses to grief that naturally occur in the grieving process. Engaging in all four of these grieving dynamics in ways that are meaningful and effective for you is the essence of adaptive grieving. Together these responses provide needed release, relief, and reprieve from your suffering and help you to recreate your life and relationships as you adjust to personal, social, and environmental changes brought about by a grief-striking loss. Specific grieving responses (emotions, thinking patterns, behaviors, physiological changes, spiritual perceptions, etc.) fall into one or more of the following categories:

- **Lamenting:** Experiencing and expressing grief-related pain, distress, or disheartenment.
- **Heartening**: Experiencing and expressing what is comforting, uplifting, or (even, surprisingly) pleasurable within the grieving process.
- **Integrating:** Attending to the life-shifting changes brought on by a grief-striking loss and incorporating these changes into everyday life.
- **Tempering**: Taking a break from grief – that is, suppressing grief-related suffering, or avoiding grief-related changes and realities that distress or overwhelm a griever physically, emotionally, mentally, and/or spiritually.

A compelling example of a griever navigating among these four dynamics of adaptive grieving is the film *127 Hours* that recounts an excerpt from the life of wilderness adventurer and mountain climber, Aron Ralston. In a mere 97 minutes, the film takes us through the 127 hours of misadventure that changed Ralston's life forever – after his arm became trapped beneath a boulder on a solo hike in Blue John Canyon near Moab, Utah. For hours, Ralston waited for help that never came. He ultimately took his fate into his own hands by breaking his arm and cutting it off with a dull-bladed knife he'd thrown into his pack before setting off on what was supposed to be an eight-hour excursion.

Through the lens of the film, Ralston clearly experiences and expresses all four dynamics of grieving. Amid his death-defying composure, we listen to him *lament* his fate with angry outbursts and tearful regrets for not connecting with his loved ones before setting out into the middle of nowhere by himself. We see him *temper* his grief with fantasies and dreams of a previous girlfriend and by succumbing to much-needed sleep. We witness his willingness to *integrate* his life-threatening predicament as he strategizes to care for his physical needs and as he faces the possibility of his death by saying good-bye to family and friends on his video camera. We cheer him on in fleeting moments as he finds humor to *hearten* himself and as he balances his pain and devastation with hope, cherished meaning, inspiration to persevere, and courage to take the ultimate risk.

It's all there – the suffering, the laughter, the numbing of the pain, the ability to risk life to resolve the grief of injury and death. No doubt, Ralston is a brave soul, and his death-defying story is a crystal-clear reflection of the human spirit fully engaged in the grieving process.

Grief-striking losses provide the opportunity to unearth potentials that lie dormant within you. If you face the challenge, your grieving responses can help you to excavate the gifts of your humanity. Of course, at times, you may lose your bearings and find yourself adrift on an uncharted sea. In such times, let the four dynamics of adaptive grieving serve together as a compass in your pocket. And remember: the usefulness of any compass is relative to where you find yourself at present and which way is home.

Guidepost 14

There is no moving away from grief.
There is only moving with it in a new direction.

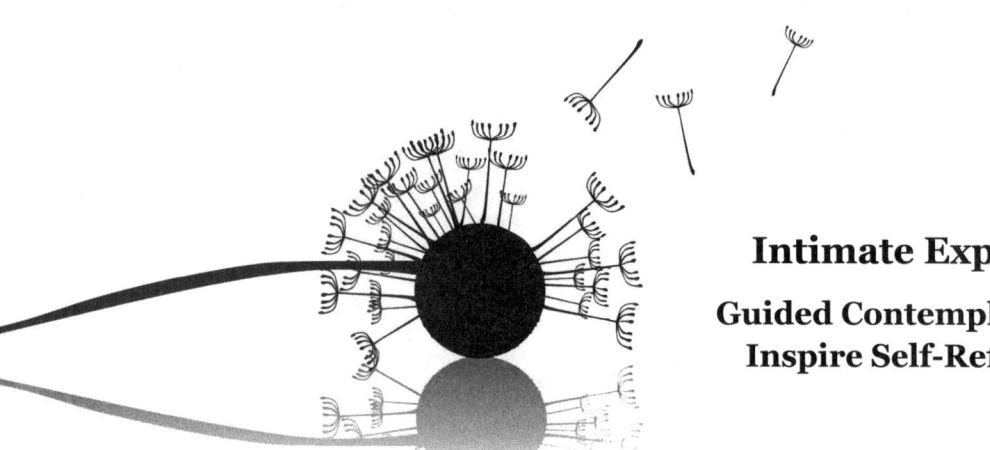

Intimate Exposure
Guided Contemplations to Inspire Self-Reflection

It may be that loss and grief accompanied you into the world – wailing as you left the warmth and safety of your mother's womb. Grief-striking losses, little and large, pepper every age and stage of your human journey and shape your perceptions of yourself, others, and the world in which you live. Ask yourself:

- What influential losses have I experienced from infancy to the present that define my identity, worldview, and relationships with myself and others?
- What anticipated losses of the future tend to stir up grief for me in the here and now?

The following contemplations help you to identify grief-striking losses that have shaped you and your relationships – for good or ill (or both at once). Engage in whichever contemplations are relevant for you. Use each one as it's useful to you. Adapt it as you see fit. No one can contemplate your way to healing better than you.

|||||||||||||||||||||||||||||||||||||||||||||||||||||||||||||||||||||||||||||||||||

Contemplation 5
Your Grieving Map
Picturing a Lifetime of Loss

Focus: *To create a map of your significant grief-striking losses – those you already encountered and those you anticipate in the future.*

|||||||||||||||||||||||||||||||||||||||||||||||||||||||||||||||||||||||||||||||||||

This contemplation guides you to create your grieving biography in the form of a map that can speak for you in ways that defy words. There are no hard and fast rules here. Your map can be as simple or elaborate as you choose. Follow your muse.

- ◈ **Materials:** Depending on your preferred artistic medium, you might create your grieving map with (1) drawing utensils of your choice; (2) photographs and/or magazines, glue sticks, and scissors to create it collage style; (3) digital art/design tools; (4) watercolor paints; or (5) another art form of your choice.

- ◆ **Your Life's Path:** Create the background for your map to represent the various phases of your life — perhaps, the stages of the life cycle (infancy, childhood, youthhood, adulthood, and elderhood) or past, present, and future. No need to include your losses on your map just yet. Take as much time as you choose to design your map. Create it as a flowing river, nature trail, conventional road map, interlacing circles or spirals, a mountain range, or whatever reflects your life journey as you see it.

- ◆ **Which Direction to Take?** You may want to add losses to your map chronologically as they happened or begin where you are now and add losses as you remember them from the past or realize anticipated losses of the future. Whichever direction you take, include on your map (in words or images):

  - **Past Losses:** Any life experiences or events involving a grief-striking loss from your long-ago or not-so-distant past.

  - **Present Losses:** Any recent losses that are presently causing or intensifying your experience of grief.

  - **Future Losses**: Losses you imagine in the future can be every bit as grief-striking as the present-life variety. Look into your future and identify losses you often anticipate happening to you or your loved ones in the days, months, or years to come that elicit a sense of foreboding, disheartenment, or pain. In words or images, add these losses to the "future" sections of your map.

- ◆ **Pacing Yourself:** You may want to create your entire grieving map all at once or let it evolve over several days. As you read through Part II: "Enough Grief for a Lifetime: Healing from Birth to Old Age," your reading may prompt you to recall overlooked or long-forgotten losses from earlier stages of your life. If so, add these to your map as you remember them. Check in with yourself from time to time to determine how much reflection on grief-striking losses is enough for one day. Be gentle with yourself and, if needed, ask for support from a trusted friend, family member, or counselor as you chronicle your grieving experiences.

- ◆ **Ongoing Reflection:** Once your grieving map is complete (for now), you may want to display it or store it in a special place, so you can add to it, reflect on what your grief experiences continue to teach you, and discover new opportunities for growth and healing.

Contemplation 6
Coming to Attention
Your Grieving Hotspots

Focus: *To identify grief-striking losses that are especially difficult for you to acknowledge or tend – that may be calling for your loving attention.*

Please note: *This contemplation is not intended to "fix" your grieving hotspots or make them go away, but to help you acknowledge intense grief related to a loss that is difficult for you to express or explore openly with yourself or others.*

When grief-related suffering is especially tender to the touch, your grief may be difficult to face at the same time it demands your undivided attention. Such contrasting responses to grief denote a "hotspot" – any grief-striking loss (past, present, or future) that causes intense distress that you may not want to think or talk about, but is impossible to ignore. As you reflect on your hotspots, allow your creativity and self-compassion to guide you. . .

◈ **Map or List Your Losses:** To identify the grief-striking losses that are your personal "hotspots" at present, use your grieving map from Contemplation 5 *or, if you didn't create one,* make a quick list of your losses, choosing a word or phrase to represent each loss – past, present, and those you anticipate in the future.

◈ **Symbols of Suffering & Healing:** Create three distinct symbols to place beside each of your losses included on your map or list by (1) sketching, (2) printing copies of your symbols to cut out and glue, or (3) digitally copying and pasting (if you're working on a computer):

- *Grief Symbol* to represent each loss that stirs up grief for you now – for example, a teardrop, broken heart, dark cloud, upside-down flag, etc.

- *Healing Symbol* to represent each loss that carries with it an expansive sense of healing, resolution, growth, or gratitude for you – for example, a rainbow, Asclepius wand (snake coiled around a staff), peace symbol, lotus flower, cross, Kokopelli, phoenix rising, bursting seed/sprout, etc.

- *Hotspot Symbol* to represent each loss that is difficult to acknowledge, stirs up intense suffering in you when you call it to mind, or causes debilitating or chronic problems for you, personally or socially – for example, a warning sign (exclamation point inside an equilateral triangle), S.O.S., thermometer showing a high-grade fever, warning flare, alarm sounding, skull and crossbones, etc. or by circling each hotspot in red or orange.

- ⬧ **Choose One Hotspot Only:** If you were able to identify more than one hotspot, choose only one to contemplate daily for a few moments, at a time of day that is convenient for you. You don't have to fix it, resolve it, heal it, or make it go away. Simply observe how your loss continues to affect you. In these brief interludes, you might name your loss, write a few words or sentences in a journal about this particular source of suffering, or create a song, art piece, or poem to express your intense grief. If your grief-striking loss is one you hadn't recognized before, strive to see it as an opportunity to know yourself better. If you need support, seek out the help of a trusted family member, friend, or counselor.

- ⬧ **Nurture Yourself:** Do something kind for yourself each day as you become more familiar with your hotspot of grief. You may want to go for a hike or prayer walk, engage in a hobby, build something, plant a garden, talk about your reflections with a great listener, journal, knit, express yourself artistically, commune with nature, rock in a swing or rocker, take a soothing bath, get a massage, or whatever might ease your burden as you reflect on your grief-related suffering.

- ⬧ **Locate Your Hotspot:** When you're ready, willing, and able, it may be helpful to take a personal inventory of how you experience and perceive your hotspot in your body, heart, mind, and spirit by returning to Contemplation 4, "Location, Location, Location," on page 28.

- ⬧ **Seek Healing Wisdom:** As you read *Doing Grief in Real Life*, take note of any approaches to healing that you imagine might be useful to release, relieve, and transform the pain related to your hotspot. Choose one simple way to tend to your hotspot of suffering each day – even if it is only for a few brief moments that, eventually, stretch into a few minutes…a few hours…an afternoon.

⋮ Contemplation 7 ⋮
The Language of Grieving
A Cinematic Exploration

Printable spreadsheet available at DoingGrief.com

Focus: *To become better acquainted with the MAGD's four types of grieving responses (page 42) by watching a film to reflect on the movie characters' or documentary subjects' grieving responses to a loss.*

Alone or in a group setting, choose a movie that focuses on a grief-striking loss experience. Make sure the film is one that offers a sense of resolution and a balanced outlook of the joys and challenges of the human experience. If laughter is needed, choose a comedy or dramedy that allows for a humorous reprieve. If information or guidance is of the essence, you may want to choose a documentary that provides insight and direction. For adults and teenagers becoming familiar with the four dynamics of adaptive grieving, the movie *127 Hours* (mentioned on page 42) might be a good place to start. This movie is based on a true story and has only one main character who vividly demonstrates all four types of grieving responses. (For other movie suggestions, see "Healing Through Movies & Documentaries" on page 347.)

A note on age appropriateness: If you view a film in an intergenerational setting, make sure the film is age appropriate for the youngest in the group. This contemplation is intended for ages fourteen and up after all participants have been introduced to the four dynamics of adaptive grieving, but an astute older child (eight or nine and up) may find it interesting to explore which movie character or documentary subject is most like the child and how the child responds (or imagines responding) to a grief-striking loss in ways that are similar or different from that character or subject. With a young child, you may want to explore such similarities and differences of response by choosing a relevant grief-related book to read together. For book suggestions, see "Bibliotherapy" (page 320) and "Healing Through Novels & Picture Books" (page 341).

❖ **Review the Four Dynamics of Grieving**: Revisit the definitions of lamenting, heartening, tempering, and integrating on page 42.

❖ **Questions to Ask Before Watching the Film:** Choose any or all of the following questions to contemplate as you view the film:

- How does a particular person in the film lament, hearten, integrate, or temper their grief? (Give specific examples.)

- Does this person engage in all four grieving dynamics or usually stick with one or two?

- How do a person's grieving responses affect their relationships with themselves or others – positively or negatively?
- Is there a person in the film with whom you empathize or identify, or who prompts negative judgments or reactions in you?
- Does anyone in the film grieve a loss in ways that are similar to you?
- Does anyone in the film grieve a loss in ways that are similar to one of your intimates? (In a group setting, be sure to share insights and observations about one another with the utmost care and respect for one another's unique grieving responses.)
- What idea, insight, or line of dialogue from the film is especially helpful, heartwarming, or thought-provoking for you?

◈ **Optional Supplies:** If it's helpful, have paper and pen/cil available for jotting down notes and insights as you watch the film.

◈ **Optional Spreadsheet:** Jotting notes on a spreadsheet with names of your film's characters/subjects and columns for the four dynamics of grieving may make it easier to remember ideas, insights, and inspirations as you view the film. *Print a spreadsheet at DoingGrief.com or create one by following the instructions below:*

- Create columns: In landscape view, fold a piece of paper accordion style into five sections, so five columns are visible (legal size paper works well but letter size will do).
- Title columns: At the top of the far left column, write "Character's Name" or "Subject's Name." At the tops of columns two through five, write the names of each of the four dynamics of grieving – lamenting, heartening, integrating, and tempering – one for each column.
- Add names: Before or during the film, the names of the film's main characters or subjects can be listed in the left-side column. Leave space between names for jotting notes on each character or subject.

◈ **Reflecting as You Go:** You may want to stop the film occasionally to reflect together on what you've seen and heard. In a group setting, there may be different preferences – to watch uninterrupted or pause together to process thoughts and feelings that arise, so come up with a plan that works for everyone.

◈ **Insights & Inspiration:** After the film, reflect again on the questions you asked before viewing it. In a group setting, you may want to prepare food to enjoy as you share insights, questions, thoughts, and feelings about the film. As you converse, invite everyone to contribute, but don't push a reluctant participant to engage in the conversation. For some participants, listening to others and then writing or talking more in depth about the experience at a later time may be more beneficial.

❦ ❦ ❦

In traumatic situations, you'll be drawn to the type of grieving response that offers you the greatest and most immediate relief from distress. But over the long haul, authentic healing is found in the interplay of all four types of grieving responses – lamenting, heartening, integrating, and tempering. So, count it as good fortune when those closest to you are well-versed in tried-and-true grieving responses that complement your own.

That harrowing Sunday evening when Andrew received the call letting us know of the murder of his dad and stepmom, a flurry of instantaneous grieving responses was set in motion. In the days, weeks, and months following the tragedy, each family member displayed certain "superpowers" for grieving and healing that helped us (individually and as a family) to find greater balance as we lamented, heartened, integrated, and tempered our grief.

My reaction was to discover myriad ways to integrate this horrific loss and tap into each family member's needs to experience and express both painful and uplifting aspects of the grieving process. Morgan (who was sixteen at the time of her beloved grandfather's death) displayed an intense ability to temper grief. Her capacity for tempering helped me to balance integrating so that other family members and I wouldn't be overwhelmed by my tendency to relentlessly face our grief until we each find resolution. My spouse Andrew often brings heartening responses to our family life. He is skilled in knowing just the right moment to bring a sense of levity, joy, and humor to an otherwise unbearable situation. His ability to do so helps other family members learn to reciprocate for him when hopelessness or devastation takes over his usually optimistic demeanor. Willa, the youngest (she was fourteen when her grandparents were killed) was able to lament, hearten, temper, and integrate her grief as the moment required. Now, as an adult, Willa continues to deepen her connections with each of these four dimensions of grieving, as we all do.

The grief you seek to heal is bound to the grief of others so delicately, at times, so ferociously that along with your own unique superpowers for grieving, you can make good use of the superpowers of your loved ones, too. Mutual compassion shared among grievers can help you to grow mighty capacities for healing that you might not discover on your own. So, be patient with others in the grieving process, and be patient with yourself. Self-compassion is a primer for developing compassionate relationships that can serve as a healing balm for everyone.

Guidepost 15

Grieving together requires a willingness to dance to everyone's favorite song.

3 ❧ In Good Company

Grieving Alone Together in Four Dimensions

> Solitude is where one discovers
> one is not alone.
>
> Marty Rubin

Walking in Your Own Shoes
Gaining Compassionate Perspective

As a culture, we're bent on swapping grief stories with one another – through confessions and confidences, tittle-tattle and hearsay, movies and memoirs, and a daily diet of grief stories reported in bloody detail by our local, national, and global news teams. Swapping grief stories reminds us that we're not the only one. It reminds us that our personal grief-striking losses are, after all, not as bad as it can get.

As the fable goes, a hundred grievers walk into a room. Each is asked to remove their shoes and place them in a pile. The shoes bear the weight of each owner's grief. So, as the grievers remove their shoes, there is visible relief – sighs, wiggling toes, tears of solace, giggles of pleasure. Then, the grievers are told to try on other shoes and choose a pair before they go. No pair may be left behind. For a good long while, the grievers take turns trying on one another's shoes. Some shoes are so heavy for their guest that walking is impossible. Some shoes are too pinching or too massive. Gradually, one-by-one, each griever chooses to leave the room wearing the same pair of shoes they wore when they walked in.

This wisdom story oozes with perspective: If you get to know the grief-striking losses of others, you're bound to see more clearly the slew of blessings (or the single miracle) that makes your grief possible. That's perspective. If you're willing to look into the face of another's loneliness, you're more likely to appreciate the circle of loved ones (or even the one soul) willing to stay the journey with you. That's perspective. But, if you find yourself lonely and broken, that's perspective, too. Healing your personal grief requires you to heal the grief that's woven into the fibers of your kinship and connection with others. When you're lonely and broken, tending to the grief that spans the distance between loneliness and kinship can be your saving grace.

As a griever, you don't choose to carry the weight of your grief-striking losses because they're the lightest or easiest. You carry them because they're relative to the joys and pleasures of your life and relationships. You carry them because you need their wisdom to show you the way out of your suffering. So, if you're ever tempted to swap shoes with another griever, you have to ask yourself: Who, better than I, knows how to honor what is lost from the bounty of my life?

Wisdom fables aside, of course, you have no choice. You alone must bear the weight of your suffering. You're the only one who can fully perceive the nuances of your grief or understand what your grieving requires of you. But, on the flip side of grief, your aloneness is neither terminal nor complete. As humans, we come into this world wired with remarkable empathic abilities to share in one another's suffering. We're set up from the get-go with an existential paradox that's as challenging as any to reconcile: *We earthlings are destined to grieve alone together.*

By ourselves, one-on-one, in families and communities (near and far) – as friends, kin, lovers, co-workers, acquaintances, and strangers – we each grieve our losses within the solitary confines of our personhood and as social beings who are hopelessly (and hopefully) entangled in one another's lives. So, even though we may all choose to leave the room in the same grief-laden shoes in which we arrived, there's something about taking the time and making an effort to walk in another's shoes that makes the weight of our personal grief more bearable.

That room where you swap shoes with other grievers – it's the place where your compassion labors into being: compassion for others and compassion for yourself, compassion for life and God, and the human condition. It's the place where you recognize that the grief that is yours alone to heal not only lives within your being; it also lives in the spaces between you and everyone else whose life touches your own.

Guidepost 16

Lonesomeness is a mighty illusion.
Even a hermit grieves alongside the rest of humanity.

In the Center of the Storm
Finding Your Bearings in Four Dimensions

Grief often comes bearing with it a question: "How do you stop the freakin' pain?!" Or as John Green asks in his novel, *Looking for Alaska*, "How do you get out of the labyrinth of suffering?" Whether consciously or unconsciously, you ask and answer these pain-stopping questions within your private hovel of existence – even as you stand elbow-to-elbow with other grievers who are asking and answering these questions for themselves. As we search for answers, sometimes we move together – in sync and agreeable. Sometimes, I go this way and you go that but, somehow, we both end up in the heart of healing. At other times, our pain-stopping answers cause us to crash into one another or leave a loved one out in the icy cold and (whether we intend to or not) we deepen our wounds and hurt even those we love.

Think of grief as a storm – whether it builds suddenly or gradually – a cyclone that gathers the pieces of your life and the lives of your loved ones, and scatters them to the winds. Amid the whirring chaos, you reach for the quiet center of the storm and, if you're given half a chance, you hold on to your loved ones for dear life and do your best to take them with you. In the eye of the cyclone, the deadly winds are weakest and you can gather your life-sustaining forces.

The four dynamics of grieving: lamenting, heartening, integrating, and tempering (illuminated in the following sections) create a life-giving space like "the eye of the storm." From that center space, you can find your bearings and listen more attentively for answers to the question, "How do you stop the freakin' pain?!" At times, the answers will come quickly and easily, flowing from your natural reactions and intuitions. At other times, you may be numb or confused, and need to be reminded of the multiple possibilities for moving beyond the pain of grief. Moving beyond the pain is what four-dimensional grieving is all about.

At a given moment, engaging in only one type of grieving response may suffice to stop your grief-related suffering and help you find balance amid the storm. But the opposite is equally true. Each type of grieving response – lamenting, heartening, integrating, and tempering – come with unique curative properties *and* problematic limitations. So, setting up camp in only one type of response can backfire. It can throw you off-balance and fling you or your loved ones back into the worst part of the storm or, in more subtle ways, can make healing more difficult.

There are no one-answer cures to the pain-stopping question. In a life punctuated by grief, your ultimate task as a griever is reckoning the healing interplay of the four types of grieving responses for yourself and your loved ones, so you can regain your balance and find your way into the life-giving center of the storm.

Guidepost 17

Moving beyond suffering is learning to live with and without the pain in more ways than one.

Painful Possibilities
Lamenting Alone Together

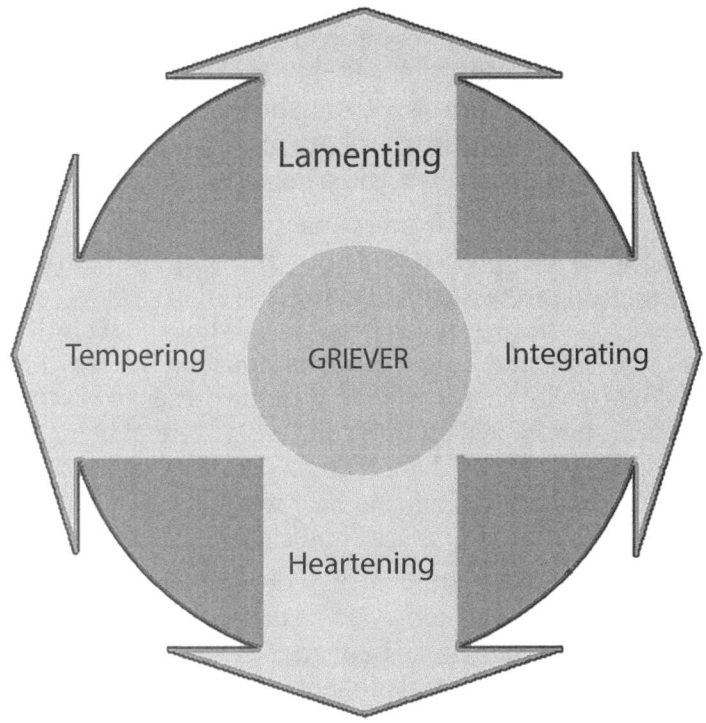

Model of Adaptive Grieving Dynamics © 2014 by Charlene DeShea Bagbey Darian

Grieving begins with pain. Before anything else, suffering. So, lamenting – that is, *experiencing and expressing grief-related pain, distress, and disheartenment* – isn't a choice for a griever, it's a given. The million-dollar question is, how capable are you when it comes to acknowledging and communicating your grief-related suffering?

Gifted lamenters are expert at acknowledging and expressing grief. In 21st century Western culture – especially in the United States, where we pride ourselves on being invincible and resilient – capable lamenters may be regarded as weak, deficient, ill, or broken. Grievers are expected to express grief intensely in the first weeks and months following a loss and then to quickly put sorrow away, keep it in private lock-down so everyone can get on with life as usual. That plan doesn't work for all of us, nor should it be thrust upon anyone, least of all, those who show us how to lament fully and powerfully without allowing sorrow to swallow us whole.

The novelist Ann Hood is a prime example of a gifted lamenter. Through her memoir *Comfort*, that chronicles Hood's relationship with grief after the sudden death of her five-year-old daughter Grace, the author clears a wide trail for others to join in her suffering. The anguished mother grants her readers permission to crawl inside her utterly wretched despair, described by Publisher's Weekly as "a tightly controlled scream."

After Grace's death, Hood cannot move a muscle without experiencing agony. In her writing, she captures the essence of grief so strikingly that one is compelled to turn page after sorrow-filled page without a sliver of hope that Hood will lace her memoir with anything but pain. There are no take-backs in birthing or burying a child. In the end, Hood's promise of "comfort" resides for the reader not so much in her willingness to re-imagine family life with her husband and son, or even in the adoption of their new daughter and sister, Annabelle. But an odd sort of comfort resides in bearing through Hood's searing story of pain and accepting with the author that her thunderous grief is every bit as enduring as her fervent love for Grace.

It takes effort to hide your pain from yourself and others. If you're in pain, your natural human instinct is to express it. So, not expressing the pain of grief may intensify your distress. Lamenting a grief-striking loss allows you to communicate the depths of your pain and suffering. It can bring your whole being into greater balance as toxic emotions, debilitating thinking patterns, spiritual distress, or physical pain is acknowledged and released. When you lament in the presence of others, those listening and observing can gain insight into your inner state of being – to know better how to encourage and support you. Lamenting a common loss with others can build a sense of intimacy, caring relationship, and community as the pain, distress, and disheartenment of grief is mutually shared and consoled.

Lamenting is so central to the grieving experience that some grief counselors regard lamenting as the be-all and end-all of healing grief. Rest assured, it isn't. Excessive lamenting can sharpen the pain of grief as well as diminish it – potentially causing long-term depression, physical ailments, mental disturbances, and social conflicts. Lamenting without reprieve can be consuming and exhausting – emotionally, physically, mentally, and spiritually. Crying non-stop can dehydrate the body. Releasing anger through violent actions (even if not intended to harm) can foster more anger and violence. What's more, those who lament freely with little regard for the opposing needs of others may find themselves being avoided or isolated socially. Given the benefits and limitations of lamenting, the gulf between not enough and too much is filled with a boatload of questions: When and where and with whom is lamenting most helpful? For how long? How intensely? How often?

The Challenges of Lamenting for Ourselves & Others

Think of lamenting as a wonder-drug with no side effects – if the correct prescription and dosage are given and taken properly. That's a big "IF" with several hitches involved:

Hitch #1: We humans don't always have control over how much lamenting we do. Much of our lamenting involves spontaneous, involuntary reactions.

Hitch #2: We each have a unique threshold of tolerance for pain and particular types of loss. So, even when grievers experience a comparable loss, some may need to lament more or less intensely than others and for varying stretches of time.

Hitch #3: Each griever has a unique threshold of tolerance for engaging in lamenting responses. Whatever is too much lamenting for a particular griever can cause suffering to worsen.

Hitch #4: We humans are naturals at tuning into and absorbing the pain and distress of others. So, empathic grief may become a source of borrowed pain and the need to lament others' grief, a complex necessity.

The pain and possibility of empathic grief are explored in the 1999 film, *The Green Mile*, which is based on a science fiction novel by Stephen King. The protagonist, John Coffey (played flawlessly by the late Michael Clarke Duncan) is a paradox of a man – a towering, soft-spoken giant on death row who is afraid of the dark. As Coffey awaits the date of his execution, the corrections officer in charge discovers that the convict has a mystical ability to intuit the pain of others and physically heal them. The healing act involves Coffey taking the other person's suffering into himself. After the gentle giant heals a person, he attempts to purge himself of their pain by regurgitating specks of darkly iridescent energy that evaporate into thin air. However, with each healing gesture, the pain Coffey assimilates saps him of his life forces. It appears that large-hearted grief kills the healer in the end.

The empathic abilities of John Coffey are the stuff of which myths and legends are made. Still, we each have intuitive capacities to tune into the grief-related pain of others. Among loved ones, such empathic grieving is common. All compassionate souls are susceptible to it. But, unlike the fictional John Coffey, the pain we absorb from another seldom heals the sufferer; oftentimes, it only multiplies grief. So, it's critical to identify and acknowledge when you're carrying the grief of another. Because, even if a grief-striking loss doesn't have your name on it, once you take it into your being, it's yours to lament and yours to heal.

Consider empathic grief you absorb in your intimate relationships. For me, this borrowed pain includes intergenerational trauma due to the suffering of my grandmother and mother who, as children and youths, were both victims of incestuous sexual abuse in an extended family that can trace the illness back for generations. I have no memory of being sexually abused by any of my maternal relatives, but for over three decades I detected the pain of this multi-generational grief within me and experienced visceral reactions connected to it. Finally, as a young adult I realized that, whether I was a firsthand victim or not, I carry this wound in my psyche as part of my family legacy. So, it's up to me (not to heal the whole of it, but yes) to heal whatever part of this family wound lives in my body, heart, mind, and spirit.

In addition to intergenerational trauma, if you're in a helping profession that services grievers – if you're a nurse, doctor, counselor, clergyperson, firefighter, EMT, spiritual director, social worker, physical therapist, teacher, or the like – the grief of others may weigh heavy on your body, psyche, and soul in ways that result in compassion fatigue. What's more, in an age of electronic media, empathic connections extend far beyond your interpersonal relationships. Today, most of us have instant access to grief-striking losses worldwide that put us into contact with grievers from all over the planet every day. So, in global dimensions, you may subliminally absorb and stockpile the grief-related suffering of others. Unchecked, this empathic grief can morph into a vague sense of doom or impotence related to your inability to cure the grief-related suffering of others. That's why healing your grief requires you not only to lament your personal losses; it also requires you to acknowledge and lament the grief-striking losses you experience by way of compassion and connection with the rest of humanity, near and far.

Self-Prescribing the Proper Dosage of Lamenting

Given the breadth and depth of our experiences with personal and empathic grief, and varying thresholds of tolerance for grief-related pain, how are we to figure the just-enough-but-not-too-much dosage of lamenting for ourselves? How can we know how much lamenting will set the wheels of healing in motion without letting the cart run away with the horse?

What's more, there are hundreds of ways to lament a grief-striking loss. So, in addition to discovering how much lamenting is enough, there is the question of which lamenting responses will be most effective for you to relieve and release grief's painful hold. This question is ever-expansive as you lament solo, one-on-one, in small groups, and collectively with others, because how you lament by yourself may be markedly different from the ways you lament in the presence of other grievers.

When you think about your lamenting responses to grief, what comes to mind? Do you. . .

- Experience emotional distress – anger, sadness, fear, guilt, loneliness, etc.?
- Lash out at those responsible for your loss or blame yourself?
- Go for a drive, run, hike, or swim, or withdraw into a quiet place or activity to contemplate your grief-striking loss in solitude?
- Seek out others with whom to lament your loss, or seek spiritual companionship in prayer or meditation?
- Shed light on the difficulties of experiencing a loss you know firsthand – through public speaking, advocacy, education, writing, political action, etc.?
- Find ways to honor the gravity of your loss through commemorative celebration, artistic creation, philanthropic contributions, or a ritual of mourning?
- Go over and over every detail of your loss, or stay up till all hours trying to solve a grief-related problem or shake a bad memory?
- Cry, wail, rage, or sulk with your pain?
- Express your grief physically – sighing, trembling, picking physical fights or taking violent action against yourself or others, engaging in contact sports, consciously or unconsciously re-enacting the circumstances of a loss, etc.?
- Become ill, lethargic, irritable, depressed, or feed a death wish?
- Tell and retell your story of sorrow to anyone willing to listen?
- Sit still or get busy with your pain?

Perhaps none of the above typifies your lamenting responses to grief, or perhaps you're familiar with every one of these and more. From time-to-time, consider the lamenting responses that are true for you. Take stock in how – for good or ill – your lamenting responses impact you, your intimates, and your circles of community. Ask yourself: Is a particular lamenting response beneficial or harmful? When, where, and with whom is it most helpful? For how long? How intensely? How often? Answer these questions for yourself alone and together with those lamenting alongside you.

Sitting too long in the seat of sorrow can be deadly. Lamenting your grief is essential, but it can't be sustained non-stop without doing damage to your body, heart, mind, or spirit. So, whenever enough is enough for now, then it's time to take a different path into the heart of healing. For example, for months and years after her daughter Grace's death, Ann Hood found that knitting was one of her only effective answers to the pain-stopping question, because focusing on knitting patterns created a mental distraction from her suffering.

What do you imagine might keep you from overdosing on your grief-related pain? Only you can unravel the mystery of what will provide you with the just-enough-but-not-too-much dosage of lamenting that is right for you. Lamenting is a double-edged sword. Let it heal you, not kill you.

Guidepost 18

Though your grief may be large,
your inner wisdom to heal it is larger still.

Playing the Renegade With Grief
Heartening Alone Together

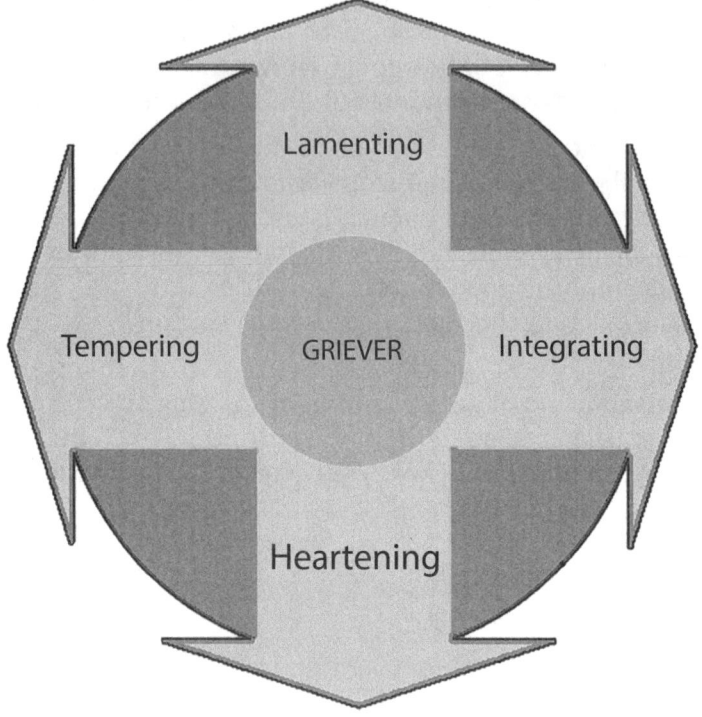

Model of Adaptive Grieving Dynamics © 2014 by Charlene DeShea Bagbey Darian

After the fateful car crash that killed my friend Sheri, I can vividly remember the moment I first laughed. It shocked me that I was capable of laughing amid such indescribable pain. But, oh, how that laughter rippled through my being – like a fountain pouring into every parched fiber of my soul. And why not? Laughter had been a mainstay of my relationship with Sheri. Why wouldn't it be part of missing her, searching for her, loving her, wanting her back in the aftermath of her sudden death?

Heartening – *experiencing and expressing what is comforting, uplifting, or pleasurable as you grieve a loss* – may seem contrary to the grieving process. But researchers tell us that heartening is common for grievers and may be a source of resilience in the face of loss. Heartening may include embracing the oddities, comic pleasure, and funny incongruences that are woven throughout a loss experience. However, humor is only one door to heartening; there are multitudes:

- Reframing a situation to see it in a more positive light
- Solving a problem or strategizing a plan to impact positive changes
- Practicing self-care to renew your body, heart, mind, or spirit
- Experiencing hope, joy, inspiration, laughter, pleasure, etc. in a circumstance, relationship, or activity related to your loss

- Finding solace in religious, spiritual, or philosophical beliefs and practices
- Experiencing relief with an ending that clears the way for a new beginning
- Fostering mutually caring relationships as you grief and heal with others

Heartening responses to grief answer the question, "What is there to celebrate, despite my loss?" Heartening brings a sense of levity. It can provide balance, comfort, and safety. Even in the direst circumstances, many pleasures – including laughter and engaging in loving, supportive relationships – produce endorphins (the body's natural pain relievers) that help to ease physical, emotional, mental, and spiritual pain. What's more, even some lamenting responses to grief – crying, telling the story of your loss to an attentive listener, celebrating mourning rituals, etc. – can help you to find relief and comfort. So, lamenting and heartening are not simply opposites, but complementary grieving responses that can be experienced simultaneously.

Some grievers habitually use heartening responses to temper the pain, distress, and disheartenment of grief; others have a natural tendency to optimistically see the cloud of grief-striking loss with a silver lining. However, when a griever is experiencing intense distress, it may be necessary to intentionally seek out and cultivate emotions, perceptions, behaviors, beliefs, relationships, etc. that re-engage heartening capacities. In his book, *Return from Tomorrow*, George Ritchie relates a poignant example of a griever making the most of heartening responses to loss:

Heartening to Heal: A Prisoner's Love Story

As a U.S. soldier, George Ritchie helped to liberate a concentration camp near Wuppertal, Germany after World War II. There, he met a Polish man who'd been a prisoner in the camp for six years – eating the same starvation diet and sleeping in the same dank and diseased barracks as the rest of the prisoners. Though the other liberated captives seemed beaten down and emaciated with hunger, this man stood tall with shining eyes and a face full of compassion.

The U.S. soldiers called this man "Wild Bill Cody" because he had a handlebar mustache like the legendary Buffalo Bill Cody of the Old West and because his real name was a string of polish syllables that the U.S. soldiers couldn't pronounce. Wild Bill was unlike any prisoner Ritchie met during the liberation of the camp. The man was fluent in five languages. Day after day, he tirelessly led and assisted the exhausted soldiers as they relocated survivors – some whose entire families or hometowns had been annihilated during the war. In a camp in which many prisoners of various nations hated one another only slightly less than they hated the Germans, every group in the camp considered Wild Bill to be a friend.

At other liberated camps, many prisoners sought vengeance by shooting the first German who crossed their path. Wild Bill was quick to reason with the different vengeance-seeking groups at Wuppertal and counseled them to forgive the German people. One day, when Ritchie commented to Wild Bill that it was difficult for many former prisoners to forgive the Germans after all they endured, Wild Bill responded by telling Ritchie the story of his capture and imprisonment. Ritchie relates:

> "Wild Bill leaned back in the upright chair and sipped at his drink. 'We lived in the Jewish section of Warsaw,' he began slowly, the first words I had heard him speak about himself, 'my wife, our two daughters, and our three little boys. When the Germans reached our street they lined everyone against a wall and opened up with machine guns. I begged to be allowed to die with my family, but because I spoke German they put me in a workgroup.'
>
> "He paused, perhaps seeing again his wife and five children. 'I had to decide right then,' he continued, 'whether to let myself hate the soldiers who had done this. It was an easy decision, really. I was a lawyer. In my practice I had seen too often what hate could do to people's minds and bodies. Hate had just killed the six people who mattered most to me in the world. I decided then that I would spend the rest of my life – whether it was a few days or many years – loving every person I came in contact with.'
>
> "Loving every person . . . this was the power that had kept a man well in the face of every privation."

Loving every person was also how Wild Bill chose to grieve his losses. "Really? Loving as a form of grieving?" you might ask. It's true. Grieving through tears, depression, withdrawal, or angry tirades are not the only possible expressions of grief. Grief can also be channeled into benevolent or purposeful action.

Wild Bill's absence of tears and rage didn't indicate a deficiency to lament his monumental losses. He wasn't in everlasting "denial" or avoiding the effort it takes to heal his grief. Wild Bill was grieving and healing all the while by refusing to forever identify himself as the worst thing that had ever happened to him or his loved ones. He couldn't bring his loved ones back to life or free himself from the Nazis' cruel imprisonment, but there was something he could do. Even as a victim of outrageous injustice that could never be set right, Wild Bill imagined living with his pain in more ways than one.

A Heart for Heartening: My Father's Legacy

When you're able and willing to see beyond your suffering, there's no telling what acts of compassion, great or small, may be sifted from the ashes. Of course, there's no need to make your heartening responses to grief into the stuff of which heroes are made. Heartening in the face of suffering is heroic enough – because heartening can leave you open to love, and love can heal the world one person at a time.

I experienced such a legacy of love through my father's approach to his impending death from cancer. Despite the encroaching physical pain that plundered his strength and will to live, Dad was determined to excavate everyday blessings from the circumstances of his departure. He enlightened his children and grandchildren again and again of all we had to be grateful for – even in the circumstances of his death that, in his words, was "not a tragedy." At times, he continued to be the ornery, scheming man he could be and, in private, he occasionally shared an annoyance or regret. But mostly Dad infused his final months on earth with love – generously inviting us into the wonder of his life and the mystery of his death.

When Dad finally became bed-ridden in his final days before death, a hospital bed was set up for him in the living room of his home. At night, Dad's spouse, children, and grandchildren scattered to various beds and blow-up mattresses on the floor in adjoining rooms. But my brothers insisted on being by Dad's side through those last few nights – Roger sitting in the lounge chair, Jim lying on the couch.

One night, when my dad's catheter was accidentally pulled loose, Jim and Roger struggled to wrap Dad in a father-sized diaper to keep him dry until the hospice nurse's morning visit. The picture was riveting: two strong, caring sons, awkwardly doing their best to tenderly roll Dad this way or that to secure the diaper, hoping to avoid causing any more pain. Suddenly, out of his sleepy, drugged stupor, Dad's feeble voice piped up, "Well, if I ever had more fun than this, I can't remember when." Even dying, Dad could joke. Roger and Jim doubled over in laughter. After that, they could relax enough to finish the task without too much pain of their own.

Dad asked us to throw a party after he was gone. He helped us to plan an old-fashioned wake and memorial service that left his family and friends feeling grateful, even buoyant. After his memorial, a long-time friend told me over the phone long-distance, "You sure don't sound like a person who's just been to a funeral!" I didn't. It was unlike any death experience I had ever witnessed. Before my dad showed me the way, I had no idea that death could be that beautiful.

Heartening can ease pain and suffering, relieve stress, build a sense of intimacy and community, and broaden your perspective of what grief and grieving entail. But, like all four dynamics of grieving, heartening also has a downside. In excess, heartening can be a means of chronically tempering the pain of grief, obstructing authentic healing. Misplaced heartening responses can also alienate other grievers who are consumed with lamenting and may feel their pain is being discounted. So, finding a healing balance between lamenting and heartening often requires give-and-take between your own momentary grieving needs and the needs of those who are lamenting and heartening alongside you.

Whatever dosage is needed at any given moment, be sure to make room for heartening and all heartening represents – joy, gratitude, comfort, relief, faith, hope, and love. In Robert Harling's script, *Steel Magnolias*, the beauty salon owner, Truvy (played by Dolly Parton in the movie version) reveals, "Laughter through tears is my favorite emotion." With these few words, Harling lights upon the truth of it: tears and laughter together are so much more than the sum of their parts.

Guidepost 19

A radical cure is realized when suffering becomes celebrating.

Reinventing Life With Loss
Integrating Alone Together

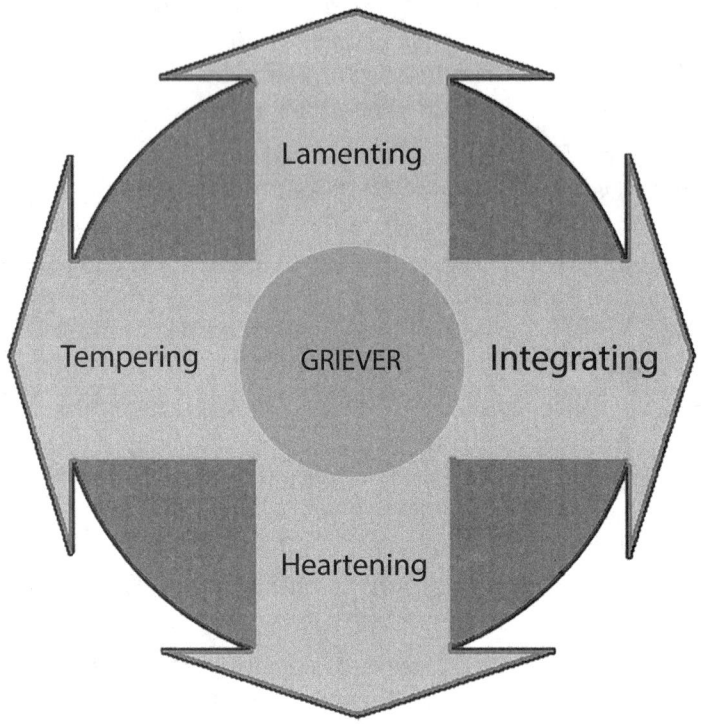

Model of Adaptive Grieving Dynamics © 2014 by Charlene DeShea Bagbey Darian

Grief-striking losses wreak change. Whatever the loss, life as you know it is over and you're forced to reinvent the wheel without all its parts. So, integrating – *giving attention to the life-giving changes brought on by a grief-striking loss and incorporating these changes into everyday life* – can be a tall order.

The stressful impact of grief-related change is a matter of perception. Some grief-related changes are so subtle that they may evade immediate detection. Only later, you notice that you're limping along and sense that something important is missing, or see that some unexpected little gain has sprouted up in the middle of your suffering. Other grief-related changes are more obvious or earth-shattering and impossible to ignore. But the stressful impact of change for a griever isn't relative only to the griever's relationship with who or what is lost or gained, it's also relative to the griever's relationship with change.

Those who find comfort and safety in the sameness of life's daily rhythms and relationships may experience even small or beneficial changes as catastrophic. Since change is inherent in all of life, people opposed to change may be in a perpetual state of grief. For example, animal science professor and autism activist, Temple Grandin (who is the subject of the movie that bears her name), asserts that change can be particularly difficult for those with autism. She likens her firsthand knowledge of autism (that includes hypersensitivity to sound, movement, touch, light, and shadow) as being "tied to the rail and the train's coming." Perhaps unwittingly, Grandin describes this autistic experience as a type of chronic anticipatory grief – an impending loss of comfort and safety that causes ongoing fear and distress. Her story demonstrates how integrating responses can transform and heal the pain of grief:

The Great Integrator: A Woman's Will to Embrace Change

As a child and youth, Temple Grandin experienced chronic anxiety and fear of her surroundings. Physical touch was abrasive. In middle school and high school, she suffered ridicule for being different in the ways she processed information and related socially. She repeated words over and over again. She didn't understand social cues and was unable to interpret emotions – her own or those of others. But with the help of her mother and other cherished mentors, Grandin ultimately discovered that her differences of perception, thinking, and behavior were not only personal and social liabilities, they were also a gold mine of creativity and invention.

Grandin describes her autistic way of thinking as "sensory-based picture thinking." To process information, she translates sensory perceptions and words into movie-like projections in her mind. Because she's developed this picture-processing ability, Grandin is sometimes able to resolve her fears of change by translating them into symbolic images. For example, as a teenager and young adult, Grandin translated each significant life change or social challenge that terrified her (moving to college, going to grad school, approaching a potential business contact, etc.) into an image of a door that was meant for her to open and walk through – a practice she willed herself to do again and again. Now, as a seasoned adult, Grandin continually uses her remarkable autistic thinking capacities to help others who are facing grief-striking losses and fears.

As an autism rights activist, Grandin labors to communicate the nuances of her autistic experiences, so that she and others with autism may be better understood and assisted by their teachers, care providers, and loved ones. As an animal rights activist, Grandin capitalizes on her abilities to sense and picture the world from the perspective of a cow or a dog to suggest improvements in animal care practices. In her work to implement more humane standards for slaughterhouses and livestock farms, Grandin sometimes designs entire equipment systems in her imagination.

Understandably, the scholar, inventor, and activist no longer regards her autism as a misfortune. Now, Grandin's so-called, "disability" is to her (and those for whom she advocates and teaches) more gain than loss. But it took a boatload of integrating to get there for Grandin and her loved ones, particularly her mother who never lost faith that her daughter could rise to the challenges of developing the gifts of her autistic mind.

Although Grandin's autism isn't as severe now as when she was a child or youth, her "different" way of thinking continues to be both a curse and a blessing. Grandin still struggles at times to be comfortable in social settings and in processing the overload of sensory stimuli so prevalent in contemporary Western culture. But the activist and educator knows how to re-invent the wheel of her life with a smooth and sturdy roundness. Her courage to do so defies the sharp edges of grief she encounters as she strives to make a place for herself in a world in which she feels like an alien – or, in her own words, an "anthropologist from Mars."

Integrating the Whole Loss Experience

Temple Grandin epitomizes what integrating grief is all about: making your peace with what is, rearranging the pieces of your life to accommodate past, present, and future losses, acknowledging the pain, distress, and disheartenment of grief without allowing it to render you joyless or powerless. When you discover useful and graceful ways to integrate loss-related changes into daily life, a sense of health and wholeness can flourish, despite your continued suffering.

Look around you and identify those you know personally who are skilled integrators. Perhaps someone you know continues to honor the love shared with a spouse who died, even as the person engages in a meaningful relationship with a new partner. You may know divorced spouses who, despite their marital brokenness, create a harmonious shared parenting plan. Perhaps you know of a birth parent who creates a ceremony of blessing on the date of a child's birth previously placed for adoption, or an athlete who chooses to re-engage in a favorite sport after the amputation of a limb, or a friend who makes the most of breast implants after a full mastectomy. Integrating gestures such as these speak of reinventing life when loss is mixed into the big middle of everything.

Given its benefits, integrating may seem like a perfect place to cast anchor when it comes to healing grief, but alone it will not suffice. Perpetual integrating can exhaust the body, heart, mind, and spirit of a person. Thus, even able integrators like Temple Grandin need a break now and then from the effort it takes to digest and adjust to grief-striking changes. That's why, as a teenager, Grandin invented an ingenious device to take her away from suffering.

While spending the summer at her Aunt's cattle ranch, Grandin noticed that many cows calmed down when they were in the "squeeze chute" – a device that holds cows when they're receiving inoculations. She tried the squeeze machine herself and found that Deep Pressure Stimulation (DPS) offered her a sense of calm and relaxation. So, Grandin invented a human-sized version of the squeeze box. Whenever she used it, she no longer sensed a "train coming" to run her over. In the comfort of her self-made hug, anxieties and fears fell away, and she was blanketed with peace. Although Grandin claims she now prefers hugs from people, her hug-in-a-box is widely used as a therapeutic tool by children and adults with autism and other hypersensitivity disorders.

Grieving and healing with loved ones who have special needs (related to physical, mental, emotional, or social functioning) frequently involves facing grief-striking losses daily. Those who learn to do so have much to teach us about integrating grief-related change. Years ago, after a friend gave birth to a son with Down syndrome, she sent me a beautifully written essay by a parent whose child suffered the same congenital disorder. In the essay, the author likened giving birth to a child with Down syndrome to taking a trip to a beloved country where you know the language and customs, but instead you're rerouted and flown to a country in which you're forced to learn a new language and a different way of being. The unexpected destination isn't a bad place. Eventually, you may regard the deviation in plans as a blessing, but a mixed blessing, all the same.

Integrating grief requires stouthearted honesty, an ability to view a loss for what it is. Of course, the real test in integrating grief is learning to live amicably with both the pains and pleasures of what is. That's what Temple Grandin does every day. Despite her ongoing distress from living in a noisy, busy world of people who are mostly alien to her, Grandin is inclined to build herself an imaginary door, put one foot in front of the other, and walk through that threshold. She is ever curious to know what blessed possibilities await on the other side of her fear.

Guidepost 20

Courage is forged by fear that refuses to give up hope.

You Deserve a Break Today
Tempering Alone Together

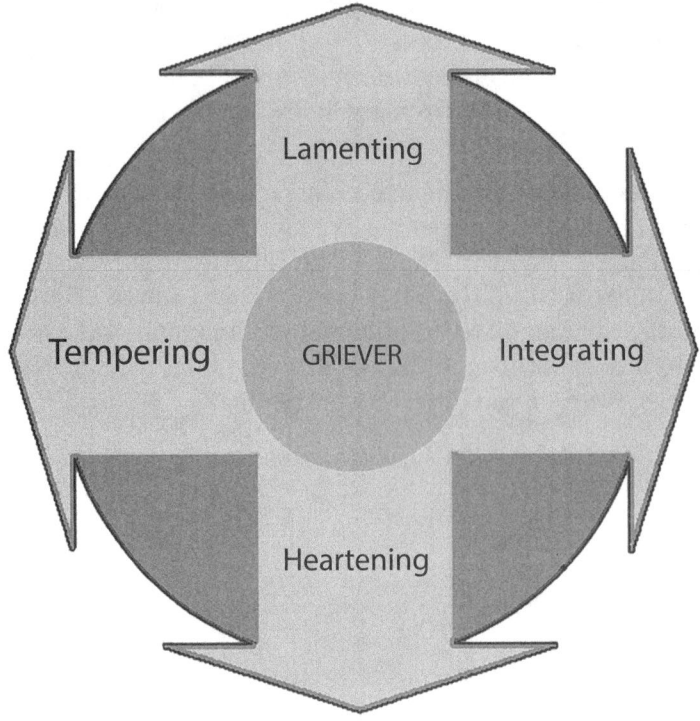

Model of Adaptive Grieving Dynamics © 2014 by Charlene DeShea Bagbey Darian

In some healing circles, denying your grief is to be avoided at all costs. Ever since Freud postulated the concept of "denial," grief-related denial has gotten a bad rap. It's reckoned by some to be an immature, unhelpful, and sometimes dangerous response to harsh realities that a griever isn't able or willing to accept. And, well, it can't be denied – chronic repression, avoidance, or comfort-seeking are at the root of many physical, psychological, and social maladies.

Despite denial's dicey reputation, today we're given the high sign from grief researchers who tell us that denying the reality of a loss in brief interludes (through avoidance, suppression, comfort-seeking, etc.) can be like taking a "mini-vacation" from grief. What's more, in life-threatening situations or when you have no power to change ongoing loss-related circumstances, tempering grief – *denying or avoiding grief-related changes and realities* – may be far more beneficial to your health and well-being than integrating a loss. For example, those experiencing warfare may ignore losses of life, safety, and home to seek refuge from a storm of grief-related pain and minimize future losses. A child who is repeatedly abused may find relief by imagining the details of an abusive situation differently or creating a fantasy of another world where the child is safe and secure from harm – at least until help comes. Because grieving requires so much of a person in body, heart, mind, and spirit, there's a definite boon in being able to suppress, ignore, or be downright apathetic about integrating the changes caused by a grief-striking loss. Such tempering responses to grief can provide an oasis for a griever to rest and rejuvenate.

When my father died after his bout with cancer, my sister Rebecca and I had the privilege of engaging in the ancient custom of washing our father's body and blessing it in preparation for the old-fashioned wake that was planned. My father's five-year-old great-granddaughter, Kaylynn, was the only person present who chose to join us in this intimate rite of passage. Because this ancient custom is generally unfamiliar today, it can be awkward or frightening for those who grow up in a culture in which dead bodies are quickly whisked out of sight. Kaylynn hovered around us unafraid. She observed for a few minutes at a time and occasionally questioned us about "Pappaw's" dead body; the next instant, she happily ran off to play. A few minutes later, she was back to take in more of the ceremonial washing with a regained sense of solemn curiosity.

Some of the ablest tempering practitioners are among the very young. A young child's magical thinking can make it easier for a child to hold onto grim realities more loosely than adults. What's more, a child's attention span is briefer, so a child tends to change focus more readily. These developmental differences enhance a child's ability to slip in and out of facing and avoiding the changes impacted by a grief-striking loss with remarkable skill.

Kaylynn's intermittent desire to run off and play as she integrated the death of her great-grandpa is an example of an instinctual tempering response. Grievers of all ages temper grief through a variety of conscious and unconscious, spontaneous and intentional means: Temple Grandin used her homemade "squeeze box" as a tempering device to ease her ongoing fear and anxiety of what was coming at her in the immediate future. Ann Hood used knitting patterns to divert her attention from the relentless pain of lamenting her daughter's death. Wild Bill threw himself into his self-elected work as a peacemaker and used heartening responses – notably, his exceptional capacities for compassion and caring – to temper the agony of his imprisonment after his family's execution. Most likely, you and your loved ones use a variety of methods to temper your grief, perhaps some or all of the following:

- Throwing yourself into work or play
- Escaping into an imaginative fantasy
- Seeking comfort in food, sex, or some other captivating sensual experience
- Suspending consciousness through meditation, prayer, or visualization
- Caring for children or animals, or helping others in need
- Submerging yourself in some form of electronic or written media (reading an engrossing novel, watching a captivating film, playing a video game, etc.)
- Using prescription or recreational drugs or drinking alcohol
- Sleeping for extended periods or frequent napping
- Going shopping or taking a trip

- Focusing on an engrossing project
- Avoiding people, places, activities, thoughts, objects, news programs, TV shows, movies, etc. that remind you of your loss or intensify your grief
- Engaging in a demanding physical activity (competitive or recreational sports, playing an instrument, woodworking, knitting, etc.)

From these examples, it's easy to see how some tempering behaviors may lead to over-indulgence and addiction. No doubt, prolonged or chronic tempering can drive grief underground, forcing it to resurface as a physical ailment, emotional or mental disturbance, social conflict, or spiritual crisis. So, it's critical to pay attention to the ways tempering behaviors may intensify or prolong grief, or cause additional harm. However, excluding addictive substances and behaviors, if an age-appropriate tempering response is used in moderation, it may provide respite from the 24/7 challenges that a grief-striking loss presents.

Tempering responses allow you to focus on day-to-day needs and responsibilities, practice self-care, and renew your inner resources for lamenting, heartening, and integrating grief. While grievers sometimes temper a loss experience entirely, tempering can also be useful *selectively*. The following story related by Eddie Ogan demonstrates how the Ogan family tempered a particular grief-related change to integrate a loss more effectively:

The Gifts of Tempering: One Family's Story of Abundant Loss

The year was 1946 and Eddie Ogan was 14. Eddie and her family were familiar with hardship. Eddie's father died in 1941. Her mom faced the difficulties of raising seven children without a penny to her name. Some seasons were thinner than others, but the Ogans stuck together and learned to make the most of their difficulties. By the spring of '46, four of the older children were grown, so Eddie lived with her mother and two sisters.

A month before Easter, the pastor of Eddie's hometown church announced that a special offering would be collected on Easter Sunday to help a family in need. He encouraged everyone to "give sacrificially." When Eddie's family got home, they imagined together how they could make a difference for a family in need and immediately got to work. The Ogans saved on their electric bill by keeping their lights and radio turned off. They bought fifty pounds of potatoes to save twenty dollars on their grocery bill. Eddie and her sisters cleaned homes, did yard work, babysat, and made potholders to sell.

Eddie remembers that month as "one of the best" months of her family's life. In the evenings, they sat in the dark and imagined how excited the chosen family would be to receive the money from the church. Eddie writes,

> "Every day, we counted the money to see how much we had saved . . . We had about 80 people in the church, so figured whatever amount of money we had to give, the offering would surely be 20 times that much."

At last, Easter was only a day away and the girls took all the change they saved to the grocery store to exchange it for three brand new 20 dollar bills and a ten. That evening, their anticipation mounted. Without a care that they couldn't afford new Easter clothes or their own Easter banquet, they were thrilled to help make someone else's Easter lavish and memorable. Eddie recalls, "We couldn't wait to get to church!"

A torrential rain drenched the Ogan family as they walked the mile trek to church. One of the sisters had holes in her shoes and the cardboard she'd stuffed in them came apart. Sitting in the second pew from the front, Eddie and her sisters were a stark contrast to the other girls in the church who were donning their Easter best and whispering about Eddie and her sisters with their old, tattered clothes. Even so, the Ogan girls felt proud and rich.

When it was time for the offering, Eddie's mother placed a ten-dollar bill in the offering plate and each of the girls added a twenty. Afterward, they walked home singing. "At lunch," Eddie writes, "mom had a surprise for us . . . a dozen eggs . . . we had boiled Easter eggs with our fried potatoes." The joy and excitement they felt that day was one of the happiest memories they ever shared. But their delight stopped short late that afternoon. Eddie recalls:

> ". . . the minister drove up in his car. Mom went to the door, talked with him for a moment, and then came back with an envelope in her hand . . . she didn't say a word . . . (just) opened the envelope and out fell a bunch of money . . . three crisp $20 bills, a $10 bill, and seventeen $1 bills – for a total of eighty-seven dollars."

The girls were shocked and saddened to find out that they had been chosen as the "poor family" in their town who needed help. Eddie remembers, "We sat in silence for a long time. Then, it got dark and we went to bed." All that week, they puzzled over what to do with the money: "What did poor people do with money?" Eddie writes, "We didn't know. We'd never known we were poor."

Eddie, with her sisters and mother, had so tempered their awareness of their financial burden that when their church community selected them as the "poor" family in town, the label didn't jive with the Ogan family's identity of themselves. For them, facing the realities of their poverty on that Easter Sunday was less about their lack of money and more about their lack of friends who knew them as they were – perhaps, in many ways, the richest family in the county whose joy of giving was stripped from them.

But, of course, that's not the end of the story. True to their resilient form, Eddie and her family followed through with their intention to make good use of their sacrifice. They returned to church and the community who did not yet know them. One Sunday, Eddie's family gave their offering to a missionary who was visiting the church. The money would pay for the roof of a new church being built in Africa.

For Eddie and her family, the bridge between integrating and tempering their financial poverty was paved with a refusal to regard their poverty as a devastating burden. That refusal helped them to develop vast inner resources for hard work, simple living, and frugality that became deep-rooted assets in their lives. So much so, that Eddie and her sisters never even knew they were poor until someone told them. Thank heavens Eddie's family enjoyed a different sort of wealth that was built on something the church folks didn't understand – an ability to temper their grief through unity of purpose, the will to persevere, imagination for creative problem-solving, and joy in the simple pleasures of life together.

Tempering serves to lift you from the clutches of suffering. Whether you temper your grief completely now and then or temper a specific problematic change over time (as Eddie and her family did with their financial poverty), tempering can liberate you from your pain. It can inspire your belief in the goodness of the present moment. As you strive for balance in your grieving process, the healing properties of tempering cannot be denied.

Guidepost 21

Sometimes healing grief is making sure you don't fall into the hole where life is missing.

Among the Band of the Wounded
Grieving & Healing Alone Together

Never doubt the reaches of grief's pain and possibility. The stories of those whose grief experiences grace this chapter bear witness. Grief can sink you to the bottom of an ocean of despair. It can destroy everything that makes life worth living. Grief can invade every cell of your body with anxiety and fear, and it can threaten to suck the goodness of life right out of you. But the usefulness of grief is equally formidable. Courage is built on it. The reach of kindness is extended by it. Grief can hollow a gorge for your happiness and it can set you up for a miracle. So, four-dimensional grieving makes room for it all: the pain, the avoidance of pain, the unexpected joys, the getting on with life in spite of everything. No, not just in spite of everything, but because of it.

To some, panning for gold in the riverbed forged by suffering may seem a colossal waste of time and energy, but it's nothing compared to a life of misery. So, if you learn anything in this lifetime, let it be that grief's pain is a sign of promise and that grief-striking loss can be an opening for opportunity. Let your life be a continual seeking of those sweet spots in the riverbed where gold comes in swaths – that place where your grieving gives way to healing.

Of course, the sweet spots of healing are fluid and changeable, so you may get to know the riverbed of suffering differently each time you wade into that river. What's more, if your heart is home to anyone, that elusive place of abundance will be sought and shared by a company of the wounded. Love makes it impossible to excavate the riverbed of suffering by yourself, even when you think you're alone.

As I read *Comfort* (introduced on pages 55-56) in which Ann Hood bravely invited me into her agonizing rail against the death of her daughter, I was riveted by a story she tells involving her son that made me wish I could read his version of *Comfort*. After three years of leaving her daughter Grace's belongings as they were in her bedroom on the day she died, Hood finally musters the courage to dismantle the hauntingly beloved memorial of her daughter's childhood possessions. As the grieving mother begins the dreaded task, her son comes to the doorway and asks if she wants him to help. Hood tells her son it's something she has to do alone. At that moment, I so wanted to ask the boy a flurry of questions – if only I could and if only he knew: Was asking your mom to help an effort to make it easier on her, to let her know you understood how difficult the task? Were you relieved, mad, sad when she turned you away? Did you (as much as she) need to experience firsthand this monumental act of mourning your sister's death? Did you (as much as she) require a ritual to reorganize how Grace's memory lived on in your family, in you, and in the spaces between you and your mom?

I doubt Hood's inclusion of this detail of her story was unintentional. I imagine as a battle-scarred griever that Hood gets it – how intense suffering can cause us to neglect what is of great value, even when it stands before us in all its radiance. In grieving and healing alone together, what is one griever's solitude may be another's loneliness.

When you're pelted by a storm of grief, the adjoining path between your honest-to-goodness grieving responses and those of a loved one can elude you. Even if the path to join your loved one is well-marked, you may choose to turn back and steal away with a bundle of sharp-edged questions jabbing at you: How do I share with you what only I can know? How painful will it be (for me or you) if I turn my tormented soul inside out while you're watching? How do I know that you grieve as lavishly as I do for what has been (or will be) lost? How do I straddle the divide between your grieving and healing needs and mine without tearing myself apart? How do I make room for you in a heart swollen with pain?

In grieving alone together, a griever isn't allowed to crawl into a private cocoon of suffering and stay there, although some of us may try and try again. Hood felt compelled to go through her daughter's belongings in private, but the way she tells the story, she was at least peripherally aware of her son's need (whatever it was) and may have understood that he was every bit as deserving as she to honor and mend his brokenness. Just as grief can send us flying into one another's arms, it can also erect between us monuments of pain. It took years for Hood, along with her son and spouse to integrate the changes born of Grace's death and reimagine a home and family without her shining presence. With their common love at the center of their pain, the only choice Grace's family ever had was to make that transformation alone together. If you're part of a family (however "family" is defined for you), you're likely to find yourself forever balancing your personal needs and preferences for grieving and healing privately while you're holding the hand or foot or head of each of your loved ones who are attempting to do the same.

The art of grieving and healing alone together is a labor of love that transcends the "golden rule." You know the one; it shows up at the center of almost every good-hearted religion known to humanity. It tells you to treat others as you want to be treated. Such well-meaning advice may be a good place to start, but grieving and healing alongside others requires a good bit more than reciprocity of your own desires. Even in the most ideal grieving situations – my father's home death among them – a grief-striking loss can send family members to opposite curves and corners of the grieving process. Misunderstandings between family members may arise.

When my father's body gave way to death and we children placed him in the homemade coffin we'd built for his wake and the transport to the crematory, his wife responded immediately with a desire to clean the whole house. While other family members still needed time to integrate the details of the death, my stepmom was moving into high gear, shouting out orders to children and grandchildren as if her life depended on it. The purpose of her fevered cleansing frenzy appeared to be two-fold: to temper her painful feelings by throwing herself into housework and to remove all signs of illness and death from the common living space. It was a spontaneous and understandable response: After months of accompanying her spouse to the doors of death, she was heaving a volcanic sigh of relief. But when a few of the grandchildren burst into tears because of her abrupt demands and the feeling that the house was being "wiped clean" of their grandpa's essence, my stepmom was able to calm herself and apologize for the outburst. Then, together, as a family, we renegotiated how we could meet our contrasting needs, balancing activities in which some grievers continued to process the death experience and others cleaned and prepared for the three-day wake that was planned.

At that place where your singular path of woe meets another's, there is a bighearted trail to the river of healing that's wide enough to walk it hand-in-hand with others at your side – those who may or may not be lamenting, heartening, integrating, or tempering grief when, where, and however you do. Whenever you and your loved ones meet at that merging trailhead, may you accept every challenge grief throws down to you as an opportunity to live and love more fully. May you trust in the healing possibilities of the present moment even when it has pain written all over it.

Guidepost 22

The golden rule of grieving and healing alone together: Do unto others as you want them to do to you – only from the other's perspective.

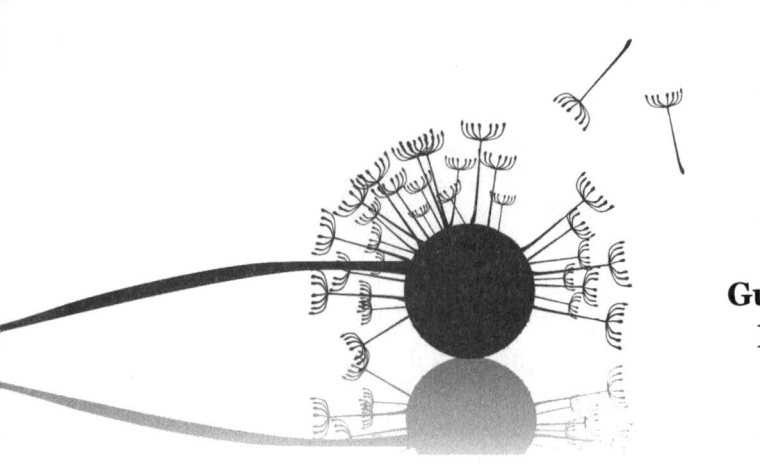

Intimate Exposure

Guided Contemplations to Inspire Self-Reflection

When we humans create intimate bonds of affection with one another, we discover it is only possible to heal our grief abundantly if each of our loved ones is doing the same. When even one griever among intimates is unable or unwilling to heal grief-related pain and distress, everyone who is anyone to the person suffers. That's the way love is. So, if you can't find the motivation to seek healing for your own good, do it for your loved ones and their loved ones and their loved ones' loved ones.

Think about it: how would your life and relationships be different if you made grieving and healing a daily priority? What if families, friends, co-workers, and acquaintances explored the unique grieving responses that serve to dishearten or encourage, alienate or unify, wound or revive us within our expanding circles of community? What if each of us learned to grieve exquisitely in ways that uplift, harmonize, and heal?

Whether other grievers join you in your quest for healing or not, your personal healing is likely to radiate outward toward those around you. So, if you want to make the world a better place, nourish the seeds of healing that lie dormant in the seedbed of your soul – the singular place where you have the most power and influence to change the world for good.

The following contemplations are intended to help you foster faith and confidence in your natural abilities to heal your grief-related wounds – both privately and in the company of others. Choose the contemplations that are relevant for you. Contemplate alone or together with others. Use each contemplation as it's useful to you. Adapt it as you see fit. No one can contemplate your way to healing better than you.

⋮ Contemplation 8 ⋮
Grieving in Style
Doing It Your Way

Printable checklist available at DoingGrief.com

Focus: *From a checklist of grieving responses, (a) identify your grieving tendencies, preferences, and needs for lamenting, heartening, integrating, and tempering, and (b) contemplate your strengths and growing edges as a griever and healer.*

Pause to reflect on each of the four dynamics of grieving – lamenting, heartening, integrating, and tempering. Which type of response do you regard as the healthiest or most likely to lead you or a loved one to healing?

⋏ ⋏ ⋏

You may have strong feelings or opinions about which type of grieving response is best, depending on your past experiences with grief. But, generally speaking, none of the four types of response is superior or more likely to lead to healing than any other. Each grieving dynamic can inspire health and wholeness just as easily as it can obstruct a person from resolving the pain of grief. Although healing can take place within a singular dimension of grieving, holistic healing is more possible by becoming proficient in all four. By developing your capacities for each type of grieving response whenever grief comes to call, you build for yourself a storehouse of tools to use when grief comes to call again – as grief inevitably will.

As you become more aware of the various ways you respond to grief within the rhythms of everyday life (even when no great loss is in clear view), you may be surprised how frequently your grieving responses show up in a day. Pay attention. You're the only one with a bird's eye view of your grieving process. Take your self-knowledge to heart and let it teach you ever more about who you are as a griever and a healer.

Asleep or awake, consciously or unconsciously, you respond to the cacophony of grief impulses that surge through you. As you move among the four dynamics of grieving, in which direction/s are you apt to move?

Lamenting Grief – *Your* Way

As you contemplate your lamenting responses to grief, ask yourself: *How do I usually experience and express grief-related pain, distress, and disheartenment?*

My usual modes of lamenting grief include:

- ☐ Experiencing painful, distressful, or disheartening emotional reactions (sadness, depression, despair, anger, fear, irritation, impatience, guilt, shame, loneliness, etc.), specifically: _____
- ☐ Experiencing physical symptoms (tightness or burning in the chest, dizziness, nausea, trembling, heart palpitations, headaches, exhaustion, insomnia, loss of appetite, etc.), specifically: _____
- ☐ Frequent sighing, moaning, or other spontaneous vocalizations
- ☐ Withdrawing from social situations or feeling unwelcome by others
- ☐ Seeking out others who are grieving so we can lament together
- ☐ Engaging in solitary activities (exercise, household chores, gardening, artistic creation, meditation, etc.) that allow me to be alone with my grief-related thoughts, feelings, and perceptions, specifically: _____

- ☐ Crying, wailing, sobbing, or sulking
- ☐ Lashing out at others; spewing rageful words or actions
- ☐ Experiencing physical or verbal outbursts privately or socially
- ☐ Blaming myself or others
- ☐ Going over and over the details of my loss mentally or verbally
- ☐ Experiencing disturbing memories or flashbacks related to a loss
- ☐ Experiencing fitful sleep, bad dreams, or nightmares
- ☐ Talking to someone about my grief (a person or spiritual entity), specifically: _____

- ☐ Educating others about a particular type of loss experience that I know firsthand
- ☐ Telling or writing my grief story
- ☐ Feeling sorry for myself
- ☐ Feeling sorry for my loved ones
- ☐ Becoming ill, lethargic, depressed, or suicidal
- ☐ Becoming irritated, intolerant, or engaging in erratic or risky behavior

- ☐ Participating in a celebration, memorial, ceremony, or simple ritual to honor what or who is lost, specific examples include: _____
_____

- ☐ Reliving or reenacting distressful aspects of a loss experience (mentally or physically), for example: _____

Other lamenting responses I experience (not listed above):
_____
_____

I usually don't experience lamenting responses to grief, because:

- ☐ I am unaware of experiencing or expressing grief-related pain, distress, or disheartenment.
- ☐ I choose not to lament as I grieve. Why? _____
_____

Heartening Grief – *Your* Way

As you contemplate your heartening responses to grief, ask yourself: *How do I usually experience or express what is comforting, uplifting, or pleasurable in my grieving experience?*

My usual modes of heartening grief include:

- ☐ Permitting myself to be happy despite my pain
- ☐ Embracing the oddities, comic pleasure, and funny incongruences that are woven throughout my loss experience
- ☐ Problem-solving and strategizing to meet or transform grief-related challenges
- ☐ Carrying through with plans and strategies to impact a grief-striking loss experience in a beneficial manner, for example: _____
_____

- ☐ Retaining hope that something good will come from my grief
- ☐ Seeing a loss as an opportunity for personal growth
- ☐ Reframing my grief in a positive light – for example, finding cherished meaning, purpose, a sense of destiny, etc. in it
- ☐ Creating humor and joy for others who are grieving
- ☐ Imagining how much worse things could be
- ☐ Engaging in self-care, pleasurable activities and/or relationships that are uplifting, comforting, or inspirational while grieving a loss, specifically:
_____

- ☐ Making light of my grief; "this loss is nothing in the grander scheme of things"
- ☐ Making light of others' grief; attempting to cajole others out of their pain
- ☐ Finding solace in my chosen religious, philosophical or spiritual perspective
- ☐ Using heartening responses to ease, suppress, or avoid grief, for example:

  _____

- ☐ Enjoying the intimacy or mutual sense of care that is built up among those grieving with me
- ☐ Making the most of others' gestures of support or sympathy
- ☐ Recognizing the unexpected benefits of a loss experience, for example:

  _____

Other heartening responses I experience (not listed above):

_____

_____

I usually don't experience heartening responses to grief, because:

- ☐ I am unaware of experiencing or expressing what is comforting, uplifting, or pleasurable in my grief experience.
- ☐ I choose not to hearten as I grieve. Why? _____

  _____

Integrating Grief – *Your* Way

As you contemplate your personal integrating responses to grief, ask yourself: *How do I usually perceive life-shifting changes brought on by a grief-striking loss and incorporate these changes into everyday life?*

My usual modes of integrating grief include:

- ☐ Accepting how a loss experience impacts my life and relationships – I'm a realist and easily resolve myself to "what is"
- ☐ Identifying which grief-related changes are most pressing to attend at the present moment and taking action to do so
- ☐ Identifying which grief-related changes I can impact beneficially and taking action to do so
- ☐ Finding ways to incorporate my loss into daily activities (creating simple acts of remembrance or grief-related artistic creations, talking or writing about my loss/grief, taking new approaches to life, work, relationships, etc.), specifically:

  _____

  _____

- ☐ Allowing a loss experience to guide my choice of work or volunteer projects (perhaps in ways I can help others who are suffering a similar loss)
- ☐ Discovering new ways to relate to a deceased or estranged loved one (prayer, meditation, letter-writing, ongoing memorials or birthday celebrations, identifying metaphors and signs of a loved one's continued presence, etc.)
- ☐ Fostering an understanding that such human experiences as love and joy give rise to grief as much as loss and sorrow
- ☐ Acknowledging both lamenting and heartening responses in my grieving and healing process – for example, experiencing and expressing a wide range of emotions or psychological states related to grief (joy, sorrow, comfort, regret, acceptance, rage, love, despair, hope, guilt, shame, faith, fear, etc.)
- ☐ Rearranging pieces of my life to accommodate past, present, or future loss-related changes, for example: _____

_____

- ☐ Identifying who or what is to blame for the circumstances of a loss and making adjustments so that similar losses don't happen again
- ☐ Identifying who, if anyone, is to blame for the circumstances of a loss and seeking ways to resolve my anger, bitterness, etc. or offer forgiveness to myself or others
- ☐ Tempering (avoiding, relieving, denying, etc.) particular aspects of a grief-striking loss so that other aspects of a loss can be integrated more effectively
- ☐ Accepting grief as an integral part of life and envisioning grieving (and healing) as an ongoing process that I experience throughout my lifetime

Other integrating responses I experience (not listed above):

_____
_____

I usually don't experience integrating responses to grief, because:

- ☐ I am unaware of ways I make sense of life-shifting changes brought on by a grief-striking loss or how I incorporate these changes into my everyday life.
- ☐ I choose not to integrate as I grieve. Why? _____

_____

Tempering Grief – *Your* Way

As you contemplate your tempering responses to grief, ask yourself: *How do I usually avoid grief-related changes that stress and overwhelm me? How do I subdue, take a break from, or deny my grief through repression, avoidance, numbing, suppression, or seeking solace in what is comfortable, familiar, or pleasurable?*

My usual modes of tempering grief include:

- ☐ Throwing myself into work or volunteer efforts
- ☐ Refusing to take notice of my pain
- ☐ Hiding my grief from others
- ☐ Distracting myself with an engaging activity (sport, art, project, etc.)
- ☐ Watching an entertaining movie, reading an engrossing novel, or losing myself in some other form of electronic or written media, specifically:

  _____

- ☐ Self-medicating with alcohol
- ☐ Finding comfort in food
- ☐ Engaging in pleasurable fantasies about the past, present or future
- ☐ Self-pleasure or sex with a partner
- ☐ Numbing myself with prescription or recreational drugs
- ☐ Enjoying hobbies or taking care of others (people or pets)
- ☐ Enjoying pleasurable sensory experiences, such as _____

  _____

- ☐ Forcing myself not to think about my loss
- ☐ Not watching news programs, TV shows, or movies that intensify or spark my grief
- ☐ Avoiding people, situations, activities, places, or objects that remind me of my loss

Other tempering responses I experience (not listed above):

_____
_____

I usually don't experience tempering responses to grief, because:

- ☐ I am unaware of ways I avoid grief-related changes that stress and overwhelm me.
- ☐ I choose not to temper as I grieve. Why? _____

  _____

Putting It All Together

Once you take stock of your tendencies and preferences for lamenting, heartening, integrating, and tempering grief, it may be helpful to ask yourself:

❖ Which of the four grieving dynamics do I tend to engage in spontaneously without hesitation or forethought?
☐ Lamenting ☐ Heartening ☐ Integrating ☐ Tempering

❖ Which do I avoid or find especially difficult to experience?
☐ Lamenting ☐ Heartening ☐ Integrating ☐ Tempering

❖ In which of the four am I most comfortable and confident engaging?
☐ Lamenting ☐ Heartening ☐ Integrating ☐ Tempering

❖ Do I lament grief in a variety of ways or stay with one preferred mode of lamenting? (Ask this question regarding each of the other grieving dynamics – heartening, integrating, and tempering.)

❖ As I consider specific ways that I lament, hearten, integrate, and/or temper grief, which particular responses from the checklist tend to provide the greatest source of healing for me? In what ways?

❖ Are any of my grieving responses debilitating, or do they cause harm to others or me?

❖ Which dynamic of grieving might I engage in more often to foster a greater sense of healing balance – within me and in my relationships with others?

❖ What are my healing strengths as a griever? My growing edges?

※ ※ ※

When you lose a cherished part of yourself or your world as you know it, it can be more difficult than ever to face who and what you are in light of your grief-striking loss. Give yourself a bounty of grace as you contemplate your strengths and needs for healing. Once you take note of your grieving preferences, tendencies, strengths, and growing edges, you may want to journal about your discoveries or share them with a trusted listener. You might also invite other family members or friends to engage in this contemplation and share your insights and discoveries.

⋮ Contemplation 9 ⋮
All Shall Be Well
Guided Visualizations of Hope & Healing

🎧

Audio version available at DoingGrief.com

Focus: *To recall the goodness of your life and relationships that made your grief-striking loss possible and the blessings of hope and healing that may yet arise despite your suffering.*

Grief-related disheartenment, worry, and distress can produce chemical reactions in your body that make it more difficult to resolve and heal your grief over time. As you experience personal and empathic grief, heartening yourself now and then with gratifying memories and visualizing positive outcomes in the future can give you a break from your grief-related suffering and provide inlets in your psyche and soul for hope and healing.

The following visualization is a means of heartening yourself with a sense of trust in the unfolding future. It invites you to revisit your grief story, visualize it, and tell it to yourself from three different perspectives – (1) the story that made your grief-striking loss possible, (2) the story of your loss experience, and (3) the story of healing possibilities that are already arising or may yet arise from the realities surrounding your loss. *If you prefer, listen to the audio version of this contemplation at DoingGrief.com.*

- ◈ **Supplies:** Prepare a space to sit and contemplate. Gather paper and pen/cil, and optional sketching pencils or crayons. For a touch of beauty and comfort, you may want to add a symbolic object such as a candle, plant, or vase of flowers.

- ◈ **Meditative Focus:** Choose a simple blessing to begin and end your contemplation, one that stirs hope and comfort in you, for example, this verse from Julian of Norwich:

    > "All shall be well. All shall be well.
    > And all manner of things shall be well."

- ◈ **Visualization:** To begin your visualization, close your eyes or observe a candle flame (or other object) and breathe naturally and easily, releasing all tension from your body with each exhalation. When you're ready, read through the following instructions (one bullet point at a time). After reading each bullet point, close your eyes or observe your chosen object and visualize each scenario one at a time – past, present, and future.

- **Celebrating the Past:** Call to mind a time when you were enjoying your life and relationships before a loss. Past joys and pleasures are the very things that made your loss possible (the presence of a loved one who has since died, enjoying health and well-being before an injury or illness, relational intimacy before a conflict, etc.). Take a "mental snapshot" of an image that represents these good times.

    When you have your mental snapshot clearly in mind, write a few sentences or paragraphs describing what it represents, or draw a simple sketch of the image that is symbolic, realistic, or abstract.

- **Clarifying the Present:** Call to mind your present loss experience and the cause/s of your disheartenment, worries, or distress. What are your specific concerns and how do you imagine the situation might become worse? Take a mental snapshot of the image that comes to you.

    When you have your mental snapshot clearly in mind, write a few sentences or paragraphs describing it, or draw a simple sketch of the image that is symbolic, realistic, or abstract.

- **Letting Go For Now:** Do something for yourself that helps you to ease your disheartenment, worries, or distress – at least momentarily.

    You may want to try this simple breathing exercise:
    - Inhale slowly and deeply.
    - Hold your breath for a moment.
    - Exhale fully and, as you do, imagine your disheartenment, worries and distress spilling out of your body, heart, and mind.
    - Pause momentarily; inhale slowly and deeply, and imagine a peaceful, comforting energy breathing into every atom of your being.
    - Pause momentarily; then, repeat the breathing cycle three or more times as it's useful to you, so that your disheartenment, worry, and distress is softened or released; as you breathe, imagine a deep sense of peace and comfort surrounding you and filling your body, mind, heart, and spirit with each breath.

    If this breathing exercise isn't effective for you, try taking a walk, preparing a healthy snack or beverage to enjoy, or engaging in a soothing physical activity - for example, coloring or sketching, singing, or playing a musical instrument for a few minutes to take your mind off your worries and distress.

- **Imagining Good Things to Come:** Once you experience a sense of release from present sorrows and concerns, call to mind a place that provides you with a sense of safety and comfort in the future. See yourself (and/or your loved one/s) clearly in that place – whether days or weeks from now or a few years down the road. Imagine enjoying and celebrating all the good things that have transpired. Take a mental snapshot of the image that comes to you.

    When you have your mental snapshot clearly in mind, write a few sentences or paragraphs describing it, or draw a simple sketch of the image that is symbolic, realistic, or abstract.

- **Observing Good Things in the Here and Now:** Consider your life and relationships at present. Is there any evidence (even a hint) of your future visions of hope and healing beginning to emerge or take form?
  - Write a list of how these visions are already materializing and express gratitude for each good thing.
  - If you can't think of any, ask yourself: "What actions might I take to help create my future visions of hope and healing in the here and now?"
- **Telling the Whole Story:** To conclude your contemplation, you may want to write a letter of hope and comfort to the downhearted part of yourself, sharing any insights you gained through your contemplation. In the days to come, whenever a new insight comes to you, add it as a "P.S." to your letter. When your letter feels complete, you might want to put it in a self-addressed, stamped envelope and ask a friend to mail it to you at a random date a few months in the future.
- **Blessing Yourself With Hope:** To conclude your contemplation, repeat the simple blessing you chose for yourself to begin. Use your blessing whenever you are feeling downhearted and need to revisit hope and healing.

Contemplations for the Whole Family
Getting to Know Your Loved Ones as Grievers & Healers

The people we know and love best may be the ones we spend the least time getting to know better – as if knowing a person is a once-and-for-all proposition. Our perceptions of one another may become frozen and so we see one another as we were once upon a time (whether last week, or some thirty or forty years ago), engaging in the same old beliefs, feelings, thoughts, and behaviors. The reality is that, from birth to death, we humans are changing – some more or less swiftly or willingly than others, but changing all the same. If we stop paying attention to one another's process of becoming, these myriad changes make us strangers to one another.

How would your interactions with your loved ones be different if each day – in your gestures and interest – you silently asked a question that is a shining mantra of intimacy: "How have you changed today?" Not "have you changed," but "how?" It may seem to be a presumptuous question, but we ask it all the time concerning an infant's or toddler's becoming. We expect them to change: to learn a new word, take a first step, grasp a new game, see something in the world for the first time. Hm. So, when do we stop expecting one another to learn the world anew each day? And when do we stop expecting it of ourselves?

If you desire to keep knowing those you know best, learn to bear witness to the striking and subtle changes that occur in your loved ones every day – especially when grief strikes. Change is at the core of grief and no matter how well-versed you are in the art of grieving, you don't have an inside track on someone else's grieving process. Even when you think you know someone through and through, you may not have a clue about what they are going through or how they are changing in light of a loss.

Blind spots between grievers proliferate: Cultural decorum prompts some grievers to hide their pain away. Children may not be able to articulate the nuances of their grief in ways their elders understand, nor elders their young ones. Gender expectations may cause men to hide tears and women to camouflage rage. Some grievers have no idea how grief is affecting them, so cannot confide to others what they do not know. Introverts or those suffering depression may have no motivation to bridge the chasm between aloneness and togetherness in grief. Some grievers refrain from sharing grief with family members or friends for fear that revealing their pain will hurt those they love.

Among family or friends, a loved one may harbor debilitating distress over an aspect of a loss that you integrate easily or you may find yourself brooding over what others consider to be an inconvenience. Some may resolve grief over a particular loss in a matter of days or weeks, while others carry the weight of a loss around in their front pocket for the rest of their lives. Thus, grieving may rattle on as a mystery that lurks in the shadows between you and those you love.

Don't take it personally when another griever's path diverges from your own. Honor and accept your similarities and differences in ways that foster self-compassion and build empathy. The following contemplations may be a good place to start.

Contemplation 10
What Do You See?
Creating the Big Picture of Your Family Grieving Dynamics

Focus: *For family members age 8 or 9 and up to explore and reflect on family grieving dynamics by creating a mural or collage.*

- **Materials:** Create a large canvas of the Model of Adaptive Grieving Dynamics (MAGD) as shown on page 41 – perhaps using Kraft paper or poster board, or a cardboard box (taped shut on the bottom and open on top; cut the corners that join the sides so you can lay the box flat in one piece). Be creative and let your canvas reflect your artistic flare.

- **Creating Your Big Picture:**
  - Write one or more losses in the center square of your canvas – for example, "after Fido died," "after Grandpa's cancer became terminal," "after the divorce," "after the car accident," "after mom lost her job," etc.
  - Label each section of the MAGD with the corresponding grieving dynamic or initial and a few words or phrases to describe each. In age-appropriate ways for the youngest family members, collaboratively describe each of the dynamics and give examples.
  - Ask everyone to (a) draw pictures (for a mural) or (b) cut out words and images from magazines (for a collage) to glue on your canvas – that represent the various ways you see yourselves and one another responding to a loss both privately and together as a family.
  - Match each of your images to the grieving dynamic it represents (some may be drawn or placed in between two or more dynamics). If need be, help younger participants match their chosen words and images to the corresponding grieving dynamic/s.
  - After your mural or collage is complete, stand back and take a good long look. What do you see?
  - Invite each person to describe the meaning of the images they contributed (if they choose to do so) and reflect together on what your cocreated mural or collage reveals to you about your personal and family grieving dynamics.

⋮ Contemplation 11 ⋮
Now You See Me, Now You Don't
Grieving Alone & In the Company of Others

Focus: *For family members age 8 or 9 and up to explore (and draw or collage) how you grieve differently when you are alone or together with one another.*

- **Materials:** A paper plate or paper bag for each person (grocery bags or lunch bags work well); your choice of art tools: (a) drawing utensils or (b) magazines, scissors, and glue for cutting and collaging images.

- **Grieving Remembrances:** Take time to reflect on and talk about a grief-striking loss (or series of losses) that you experienced as a family. Give examples of ways you grieved your loss/es together in the past, for example planning or attending a memorial celebration, crying, talking, hugging, sharing remembrances, providing care for someone who was hospitalized, ill or injured, etc.

- **Grieving Together:** Before you draw or cut out images, ask yourselves, "When we are together as a family, what are some ways that I usually grieve?" Draw pictures or choose magazine images for the *upside of your plate or the outside of your bag* that represent the ways you tend to grieve in the company of others. As you draw or collage your images, it may help to ask the following questions:

  - *Lamenting*: How do I show or tell others when I am sad, angry, or hurting?
  - *Heartening*: How do I show or tell what brings me joy, hope, or pleasure?
  - *Tempering*: How do I show or tell that I don't want to remember, think, talk, or hear about our loss/es – at least for now?
  - *Integrating*: How do I show or tell others that I am okay with remembering, talking, or hearing about our loss/es during daily interactions?

- **Grieving Alone:** Contemplate how you respond to a loss in private when you are by yourself. Draw pictures on blank paper or cut out words and images from magazines *for the backside of your plate or to drop inside your bag* that represent the ways you tend to grieve when you are alone.

- **Sharing Your Creations:** When your plates or bags are complete:
  - Share images on the front side of your plate or outside of your bag.
  - Invite those who are willing to share images (or insights they gained) from the backside of their plate or the inside of their bag.
  - Ask yourselves: How are my "alone" and "together" grieving images similar or different from one another?

- **Circle of Gratitude:** You may want to conclude by sharing one new thing you learned about yourselves or another family member, or offer thanks for specific gestures of love and grieving support you receive from one another.

☙ Part I Wrap-Up ☙

Know Thyself

Grieving as a Path to Self-Awareness

> Know Thyself?
> If I knew myself I would run away.
> Goethe

The human quest for self-awareness is seldom easy. Some say it's futile – that getting to know yourself can be as complex as unraveling the cosmic mysteries of the universe. It can be scary, too. But make no mistake: self-awareness can be a mighty ally when cherished things go missing from your personal universe. Knowing and trusting yourself as a griever (and allowing your intimates to know and trust you, too) can vanquish fear and doubt. If you look your grief in the eye with confidence, you're likely to see your strength and integrity as a healer in its reflection.

Your self-knowledge as a griever will evolve to your journey's end, so too your need for healing. Always and forever, life involves change in which loss begets gain as gain begets loss, and so it goes. If you make room for one, the other is never far behind. What's more, gain and loss will come to your door tethered knee bone to knee bone, talking out of both sides of their mouths. Even so, you're obliged to let them in.

As for me, whenever I am tempted to send grief from my door without welcome, I check myself by imagining my being in spirit before I was conceived in my mother's womb, hovering just beyond the veil of this human existence. I see myself signing up for this life, agreeing to come because I had people to see and things to do that only a human being on earth can accomplish. I like to think that I was told of the suffering I might encounter and chose it anyway because I knew in my heart of hearts that there was something awe-inspiring to learn from it and a great measure of healing to be had by it. To you, my vision may be nothing more than a flimsy hope; but, for me, it's one of the sweet spots of healing.

Where are your "sweet spots" of gold on that gritty riverbed of grief – the times and places, imaginations, situations, and relationships in which you unearth healing riches? If you're awake and aware, you'll discover the gold that's mixed in with the grit of your pain. So, come to the riverbed of suffering as a hopemonger and a light seeker. Be on the lookout for the sweet spots where loneliness gives way to solitude, and togetherness lends itself to unity. Be on the lookout for the places where fear opens the dam for joy, and where lack polishes the luster of abundance. Look for the sweet spots where sobs of laughter are no less welcome than chortles of tears, and where the voices of laughter and weeping fall into silent repose.

The sweet spots of healing can be found in any old beginning and every new end. So, alone and together in the company of your wounded loved ones, dally long and often in the healing that the riverbed of suffering provides.

Guidepost 23

When all is lost,
    there is nothing left but new beginnings.

❧ Part II ❧
Enough Grief for a Lifetime

Healing From Birth to Old Age

As long as you keep getting born,
it's alright to die sometimes.

Orson Scott Card

The Healer Within

Everyday we face change. As Arthur Schopenhauer wrote, "Each day is a little life: every waking and rising a little birth, every fresh morning a little youth, every going to rest and sleep a little death." For some grievers, morning breaks with dirges of death, and sleep serves as a portal to rebirth. Regardless of your slant on the day's shadow and light, the daily round pushes you up against the inevitability of change.

Fortunately, just as change is a breeding ground for grief, it's also the seedbed of healing. We can survive grief and transform it because we're adaptable. From birth to death, the lessons of healing resound with a common theme: *If you want to heal your grief, you have to be willing to change your relationship to the source of your suffering.* Resilience is the name of the mothership that carries many a traveler through grief. This old parable serves as an object lesson:

The Farmer & His Donkey

Once there was a farmer whose donkey fell into a well. The animal cried so pitifully that it nearly broke the farmer's heart. But, try as the farmer might, he could figure no way to retrieve the trapped donkey. Finally, when the farmer could stand the animal's cry no longer, he decided to put the poor creature out of its misery. After all, the farmer told himself, the donkey was old, and the well was dried up and needed to be covered. So, the farmer invited his neighbors to come and help him with the task. They each grabbed a shovel and began to throw dirt into the well to bury the donkey.

The animal's pathetic cry rose to a fevered pitch as the cold, biting weight of the dirt piled upon the donkey's back. The gravediggers worked quickly to put the animal out of its pain. Finally, when the donkey's cry was no longer heard, the farmer looked into the well. To his astonishment, the donkey was still alive! With each shovel of earth that fell, the animal shook the dirt off and used it to take a step up toward the light at the well's opening. Soon, to everyone's surprise, the creature stepped up over the edge of the well and trotted off to safety and freedom.

The moral of the parable: When life's burdens pile heavy on your back, shake them off and use them to create something life-giving.

※ ※ ※

Change your relationship to the source of your suffering. It's a lesson that you're likely to spend a lifetime learning, so you may assume that older humans are the most proficient when it comes to making the changes that healing requires. But this is a troublesome misunderstanding. Every stage of life lends itself to healing genius. So, it's wise to get to know yourself as a healer from the beginning.

A number of mental health professionals in recent decades encouraged us to regard the hurt aspects of our psyches and souls as "helpless infants" or "wounded children." Some therapists suggest that (as adults) we need to revisit and re-parent our younger, more vulnerable selves, and rightfully so. Certainly, a healthy adult psyche can assist you in healing aspects of your self-identity that you regard as "helpless" or "wounded." But if you imagine your infant-self as always helpless and your child-self as forever wounded, you're apt to ignore the healing instincts and intuitions that came naturally to you in your younger years. Being helpless and wounded isn't the whole story.

How you perceive yourself as a griever is everything. In adulthood, when you adopt a view of yourself as a helpless infant or wounded child who has others to blame for your grief-related pain, there's at least a part of you that surrenders to suffering and allows it to have its way with you indefinitely. Learning to see yourself as a healer who wisely tends to your grief-related wounds throughout all the ages and stages of your life drastically changes your relationship with grief. It inspires you to discover healing anywhere and everywhere – even at the core of your most agonizing loss experience.

As a self-aware human, your identity is an instantaneous sum of who you know yourself to be at present, who you remember yourself to be in times past, and who you imagine becoming in the future. So, your potential for self-healing multiplies exponentially when you call forth the healing wisdom of the infant, child, and youth within you. Add to this cast of characters the elder within – that is, the sage healer you imagine becoming as you continue to mature – and, no matter what your age, you can be as ripe with healing wisdom as you choose to be.

Think of yourself as a time traveler who can visit and revisit the infant, child, youth, adult, and elder healers within you. Seek audience with each one and ask "What healing wisdom can you offer to help me heal my pain and suffering?" Carry this question along with you as you grieve and heal with loved ones of all ages and as you read and reflect on the following chapters that highlight the healing expertise commonly shared among grievers in each stage of life.

Take heed in your reading and your living: there are no absolutes when it comes to stage-related grieving and healing. Although certain tendencies among age-group peers can be identified, the nuances of response among grievers is forever variable. What's more, a person can straddle more than one stage of life at a time. Divisions of developmental change aren't usually neat and tidy. As you encounter up close and personal losses, you or a loved one may reel into the thick of perceptions or behaviors that dominated an earlier stage of development. Or, grief may propel you toward healing knowledge and skill sets beyond your years. Depending on your grieving needs and challenges in the here-and-now, either direction of "time travel" may be a burden or a gift – and sometimes, both at once.

Let healing be a central theme of your grief story as you tell it and live it. As you do, trust the infant, child, youth, adult, and elder within you to be your guides. Shake off the weight of your suffering. Step up toward the light. The freedom of healing awaits you.

> Before you delve into the bulk of Part II, choose your chapters wisely. There is no need to read these chapters chronologically from infancy to elderhood. Feel free to skip around to whichever stage of life is most relevant to your personal journey with grief or to your work as a parent, caregiver, or professional healer.

Guidepost 24

There are no fancy devices to transform the substance of your grief. There is only you and your willingness to change how you see yourself.

4 ❧ From the Mouths of Babes
Grieving & Healing in Infancy

> Don't forget that compared to a
> grownup person every baby is a genius.
> Think of the capacity to learn!
> May Sarton

Born Grievers, Born Healers
An Infant's Natural Genius for Grieving & Healing

In his poem, "Infant Sorrow," William Blake wrote, "My mother groaned, my father wept./Into the dangerous world I leapt . . ." Birth is as close an experience to death as we humans encounter. Because we are born physically helpless, at birth we are utterly dependent upon the generosity of love and care provided by others.

It's been said that infants commune with angels, that babies and toddlers are protected by spiritual powers from beyond. This seems only right when one considers the vulnerability of the newborn. We are miracles made out of nothing more than a father's wetness and a mother's roundness. At birth, we lay mostly powerless in the cradle of our infancy.

Angel theories aside, as an infant, your fate predominantly rests in the arms of your intimate caregivers. So, it's no wonder that being separated, abandoned, or mistreated by a parent even momentarily can be experienced by the infant as a horrific loss. Infants experience intimate caregivers as an extension of their own being with no sense of distinction between the "self" and the "other." After months of relative safety within the mother's womb, birth becomes for the baby (who, in essence, is still a fetus) a rite of passage equal to death.

From an infant's perspective, the physical separation of mother and child at birth is bound to bear sorrow. Significant life-threatening change often does – whether it's acknowledged or ignored. Perhaps that's why healthy babies – who change at a monumental rate as they acquire the skills needed to survive on earth – cry so much. Perhaps that's why healthy babies learn to smile and laugh so easily. Babies can be as skillful at grieving and healing as any of us and during our infancy we have ample opportunity to put these skills into action.

Because bonding with an intimate caregiver in infancy is essential to our survival, health, and well-being, the greatest instinctual priority of the newly born is to foster that life-giving bond. In doing so, a healthy newborn's greatest power is its lungs. As infants, we cry, gurgle, and sound our way into the lives of our loved ones. Thus, a newborn's language begs attention, asks others to forsake the human fixation on words and enter into a baby's voice, eyes, facial expressions, sounds, and gestures. If you listen well, you'll find that the infant's language is rife with mantras of grieving and healing. So, whenever you're given the chance, hone in on that infant wisdom. Learn it and practice it with the babies and toddlers in your life. If you do, you may find that even the newest of the newly born can serve as gurus who offer healing enlightenment to all who seek it.

Guidepost 25

> But for the cry of a newborn, we may forget that grief is an angel who flies to earth with a message of healing on its wings.

For Crying Out Loud!
Lamenting in Infancy

The healthy newborn is a master at expressing pain and suffering – sometimes in monstrous proportions. Most babies lament easily, letting us know immediately when they're in distress. Needs and desires, anger, loneliness, and frustration are made apparent by an infant's wailing, screaming, moaning, vocalizations, facial expressions, and physical gestures. A healthy newborn laments so freely over life circumstances we adults fail to see as grief-striking for them that (despite a baby's obvious inclinations for lamenting) infant expressions of grief are often paid no mind.

In the 1940s, researcher Rene Spitz began looking more deeply into the infant psyche. Spitz's film, *Grief: A Peril in Infancy* (1947) documented the emotional and behavioral reactions of infants who were separated from their parents in what was once referred to as a "foundling home." When the film was shown to physicians and psychoanalysts at The New York Academy of Medicine, the viewers were devastated by image after image of babies pining away from grief. It was something the practitioners had never considered. According to Robert Karen in his book *Becoming Attached*, after viewing Spitz's film, one "prominent New York analyst approached Spitz with tears in his eyes, 'How could you do this to us,' he said."

It's complicated inhabiting a newborn body. Through all their senses, babies soak up an unending stream of internal and external stimuli from moment to moment. Physical, social, emotional, and mental cues help infants tune into their physical body, immediate environment, and the inner life of intimate companions. Being dependent on others for nourishment, mobility, communication, and protection makes an infant vulnerable to an array of grief-striking losses in the first few years of life – separation from an intimate caregiver (whether for minutes, hours, days, years, or a lifetime), physical pain or discomfort, illness, injury, abuse or neglect, being subject to an over-stimulating environment, conflictive relationships among other family members, fear, anxiety, or depression that a baby or toddler acquires from an intimate caregiver... The list goes on.

Aletha Solter, a developmental psychologist and author of *The Aware Baby*, is a vocal advocate for babies in need of lamenting. A one-time student of Jean Piaget, Solter says that babies all over the world cry for no apparent reason for an average of two hours a day. Solter believes that crying is a natural way for babies to express and release trauma, pain, anger, tension, and stress associated with birth and infancy.

According to Solter, well-meaning efforts to provide appropriate care and attention to an infant can be misguided when such "care" is used to repress a baby's need to cry. Silencing a baby's pain is not at all the same as healing their suffering. Herein lies one of the all-time challenges of healthy parenting and caregiving.

Showering a baby or toddler with the loving care and attention every infant deserves is a powerful preventative for helping babies and toddlers avoid grief-striking experiences in infancy. But no infant (no matter how well-cared-for) is exempt from grief. There are plenty of grief-striking loss experiences an infant may encounter that we parents and caregivers cannot magically vanquish for them, nor should we try.

Attempts to vanquish grief for infants and their birth mothers are reflected in our contemporary birthing practices in which we routinely aim to control and numb the pain of childbirth. Granted, conventional medicine has an honorable place in providing much-needed medical interventions to laboring mothers and infants whose medical and health needs require it. But our contemporary birth practices prompt questions for the discerning: How do we define a traumatic birth? A peaceful birth? In attempting to thwart the pain of labor in childbirth, have we made birthing more dysfunctional than ever? Pushing and resistance are a natural part of the passage of childbirth for mother and child. What happens to birth when we encourage fear of this natural biological process and routinely interfere with numbing medications, doctor-initiated birthing, and surgery? By making such interventions the norm rather than the exception and doing away with the natural life-shifting rite of passage that the labor of childbirth can be, do we strip mothers and babies of an essential experience of bonding as mother and child?

Beyond the birthing room, most parents and caregivers are unaware of our inhibiting behaviors to stifle an infant's experiences and expressions of grief, especially an infant's lamenting responses. After all, soothing a baby's cries can be as simple as changing a diaper, rocking a baby to sleep, or feeding a hungry infant. But, when we jiggle, jostle, feed, pacify, play with, ignore, or sedate a baby as a means of curbing the infant's needs to lament, we're setting up what Solter refers to as "control patterns" that teach babies to suppress their curative tears and outbursts.

Ask yourself: Is nursing a baby or giving an infant a pacifier every time they express discomfort, a precursor to the eating disorders and drug addictions so prevalent in our culture? If we feed babies when they aren't hungry, how will they ever learn the feeling of being sufficiently satisfied? If a pacifier is used to keep a baby from expressing personal pain, then why not drugs or alcohol as they meet the distress they encounter in their childhood, youthhood, and adulthood?

In truth, a baby's ability to express lamenting through crying is one of the most powerful sources of healing available to them. In the first few months of life, a newborn's cry is often the only language a baby has to let us know of their pain and distress. By the time a child can articulate their grief-related suffering accurately through words, most early experiences of grief have disappeared from conscious memory. So, after a baby's needs for physical wellness and nourishment, warmth and touch, activity and rest, companionship and soothing are fulfilled, parents and caregivers do well to simply hold a baby and let the tears and wailing roll. By doing so, we allow an infant to heal themselves the way babies know best.

By the way, has a baby in your life cried today? And when was the last time you let go a torrent of tears?

Guidepost 26

Eyes bereft a single tear are sadder still than those that weep.

Playing With Grief
Heartening in Infancy

Like lamenting, an infant's heartening responses to grief are staples of nourishment that infants can't live without. Usually, an infant can find a wellspring for heartening in the loving attention that an intimate caregiver provides. Alice Sterling Honig, in her paper, "What Are the Needs of Infants?" says it well:

> "The most important psychological need of the baby after the needs for physical care and comfort are secured is the need to mean something good to the special adults who provide the care... The baby seems to be learning, 'This person belongs to me for my good, my pleasure, my security. I feel cared for, cared about. I am delighted to be.'"

In the weeks and months after birth, healthy babies become natural comedians – smiling, laughing, joking, teasing us into grins and guffaws as only babies can. What fun to engage a baby in a simple game of peek-a-boo or in the "call-and-response" laughter games happy babies love. Such infant play may appear to be unexceptional, but humor is a social tool that allows a baby to assert their influence and responsiveness in relationship to others. What's more, laughter – like crying – can serve as a release for a baby's tension and stress, and may be a pacifying gesture used to convince the baby that all is well, despite a brush with grief-striking pain or anxiety.

The developmental psychologist Jean Piaget and others have noted that a baby's smiles and laughter often accompany moments of cognitive mastery. As babies learn to understand, manipulate, and negotiate their environment, they're prone to laughter, clapping, and other expressions of pride as they meet with success. Play and laughter reinforce a baby's confidence to adapt to their environment and take initiative. Conversely, a humorless baby is one likely to learn chronic helplessness and resignation to a life of depression or passivity.

In Rene Spitz's studies of infant grief (page 99), he observed babies and toddlers who had been separated from their mothers for months at a time. Significantly, these infants were not provided a surrogate primary caregiver. Typical behaviors for the babies and toddlers progressed from tearfulness after one month's separation to long screaming spells (up to three hours) after two months. Spitz observed infants refusing to crawl or walk after three months. During this time, infants were also prone to lying face down and refusing all social contact. In the fourth month, babies and toddlers took on dazed expressions and articulated their grief through whining moans.

Spitz found in his research another startling result. He observed that if the infant and mother were reunited sometime before the third to the fifth month of separation, an infant's social, emotional, and behavioral recovery took place within a period of twelve hours to fourteen days. For example, Baby Jane, who suffered a three-month separation from her mother had been distant and withdrawn during that time. But, after mother and child were reunited, Jane was soon laughing, clapping, and playing with the same zest she did before the separation occurred. Spitz found, however, that if reunification was made after a period of resilience for a particular child – sometime after the third to the fifth month of separation – full recovery for the baby appeared impossible. The lack of recovery that Spitz observed may be akin to what contemporary researchers call "Reactive Attachment Disorder" (RAD). RAD is thought to be a rare disorder that is caused by a lack of attachment to a specific caregiver in infancy, resulting in an inability to cultivate nurturing intimate relationships with others.

Although researchers today are identifying therapies that are successfully improving relationships for those suffering from Reactive Attachment Disorder, healing can be a long and difficult road. What's more, in recent decades families seeking help with attachment difficulties have been victims of some highly controversial therapies that involve coercive physical restraint and psychological abuse – in extreme cases, that led to the death of the child being "treated." Such misguided therapies raise alarming concern for infants who are denied the presence of an intimate caregiver past the point of an infant's tolerance for separation. Spitz's discoveries in this regard are an entreaty to continually improve care for orphaned, hospitalized, and fostered infants and children.

Equally noteworthy in Spitz's observations, however, is his conclusion that it is possible for a baby or toddler to recover quickly after three months and more of intense grief. In Spitz's studies, healing took place at an astounding rate when the delight of the mother-infant relationship was restored in time. Restoring or fostering a consistently trustworthy parent-child relationship is the foundation of effective therapies for Reactive Attachment Disorder. One such therapy for children two to seven years of age is "Parent-Child Interaction Therapy" (PCIT), an approach that earns a high rating from the California Evidence-Based Clearinghouse for Child Welfare. The program teaches parents positive attention strategies, effective and consistent discipline techniques, and communication tools that provide for a child's limited attention span; it helps to foster confidence, warmth, safety, and intimacy in the parent-child relationship. All of these PCIT intentions are hallmarks of healthy parenting – whether a baby or toddler displays reactive, secure, or insecure attachment responses.

The curative power of loving, consistent relationships is good news for caregivers everywhere who desire to assist grieving infants and it provides good reason for families to establish more than one intimate caregiver for every infant. Although a loving parent may serve as a baby's or toddler's primary caregiver, shared infant care among a small circle of elders – parents, grandparents, godparents, aunts, uncles, siblings, intimate friends, or childcare providers – can offer a net of protection and healing for grieving infants who suffer the physical or emotional loss of a caregiver, either long-term or temporarily. Such parenting partnerships are especially crucial for babies and toddlers being raised by a single parent.

Loving, attentive caregivers can easily provide the impetus for an infant's heartening responses. There are endless possibilities, depending on the little one's unique needs and preferences, including:

- affectionate conversation
- interactive smiling
- cooperative learning and doing
- singing
- pat-a-cake games
- laughter
- breastfeeding, holding while bottle-feeding, or sharing family mealtime
- expressing encouragement and pride for a baby's newfound skills and understanding
- rhythmic movements
- rocking
- dancing
- looking at picture books
- playing with interesting objects
- nurturing touch or infant massage

Assisting a grieving baby or toddler to experience and express heartening responses has its perks. In addition to helping an infant balance distressful aspects of grief experiences, such play and nurture can help you to access your own capacities for heartening. What's more, heartened infants often reciprocate the favor.

In *Stricken: The 5,000 Stages of Grief,* Owen Egerton beautifully describes in his essay, "The Holiest of Times," how his four-month-old daughter, Arden, becomes a healing presence at the death of Owen's grandfather. When "Poppa" finally slips away, Arden is nursing peacefully at her mother's breast. She stops momentarily to cry in tandem with her great-grandmother. Then, later that evening, after the family sheds many tears, Owen places Arden in her great-grandmother's arms. It is Arden who penetrates her elder's dazed expression with a smile. It is Arden whose laughter revives the laughter in her great-grandmother's heart.

Babies are like that. They can melt our pain with a smile.

Guidepost 27

How would your life be different if you regarded it as a warmhearted comedy from the beginning?

A Matter of Survival
Tempering in Infancy

Heartening interactions between an infant and their caregiver (page 103) can be useful in providing a baby or toddler with the reprieve from suffering that the infant psyche requires. But not always. Sometimes, a grief-striking loss is so consuming for an infant that pain is all there is. Suffering may demand the infant's attention at all waking hours. What's more, an infant's chronic lamenting responses can make it more difficult to maintain healthy attachments between an infant and their care providers. That's why learning to temper (avoid, suppress, relieve) the distress of grief is as crucial to an infant's health and well-being as any other grieving response.

Fortunately, nature provides the ultimate tempering mechanism that few babies can resist: deep, unencumbered sleep. But, during waking hours, most newborns rely on intimate caregivers to introduce them to modes for tempering: rocking, singing, cooing, playing, holding, and gentle bouncing, to name a few. In the first months of life, most infants are learning to engage in self-soothing behaviors on their own – through repetitive movements, vocalizing, or sucking a thumb, hand, foot, fingers, toes, or anything else a baby's mouth can get its built-in radar honed in on.

While most infants take their tempering cues from intimate caregivers, an infant may learn to temper their grief as a means of survival. For example, Sky, a dear friend of mine, grew up in a foster home for the first 18 months of her life. Sky's foster mother was one who methodically granted care to her favorite children but identified a select few whom she neglected. Eventually, Sky's foster mother was arrested and convicted for the gross neglect of a child in her care.

For the first several months of life, Sky spent hours alone in a crib set apart in a darkened basement room where she learned that crying for attention was not in her best interest. As Sky grew, she learned to observe everything in her environment: where things she needed were kept, who and what was around her, how her caregiver responded favorably or punitively to certain behaviors, needs, and desires. Sky's ability to temper her grief related to an infant's needs for nourishment and companionship was what kept Sky alive and fed for the first 18 months of her life.

No doubt, Sky could regard her infancy as a deep and debilitating scar of rejection and neglect. But after being rescued from that foster home by a loving family, Sky's recovery was miraculous. At two years old, she was athletic and agile. By the time she was three, she could tell you where every item in her house was stored. She made sure that the needs of her younger siblings were known and met – if not by herself, then by Mom or Dad or another caregiver. When she began grade school, in a matter of days she knew everyone's names – teachers, students, administrators, janitors. Sky's early challenges caused her to become an eagle-eye observer – gathering a wealth of information when it comes to the practical details of life. So, when I see her, I think, "Thank heavens she was able to temper her grief in infancy! Look at the strengths she embodies (and shares with those fortunate enough to know and love her) because of it."

Granted, Sky learned later than most to engage in the crying response that comes naturally to most infants and there are some lasting psychological ramifications from her less-than-ideal beginnings. I imagine healing from her traumatic infancy will be a life-long learning process as she expresses unmet needs and desires in ways that help her to mend her injured psyche and release frustration, anger, and pain – past and present. But my friend is also an expert at knowing when tears and outbursts don't serve her well. She has a sixth sense to know with whom she's safe enough to express her repressed grief without experiencing rejection or love lost.

The blessings of tempering for an infant are manifold: Tempering may serve as a bridge from suffering to heartening – allowing the pain of grief to subside long enough for the infant to rediscover joy, wonder, or companionship despite a significant loss. Tempering may be what helps an infant to sustain cherished relationships or keeps an infant safe and unharmed in the presence of an abusive or neglectful caregiver. Tempering intense pain or despair allows an infant to access a greater sense of equilibrium in body, heart, mind, and spirit. Moreover, a baby's or toddler's ability to temper their grief can be a boon for exhausted parents, sleep-deprived siblings, and fellow travelers, restaurant patrons, worshipers, or audience members. Tempering (in the context of four-dimensional grieving) can provide an infant and their loved ones an oasis from the sheer volume of pain and suffering that an infant can express. Amid family grief, thank heavens for that little miracle, too.

Guidepost 28

What we learn in infancy
is the doctoral course for survival.
Pray our instructors, at the very least,
do not bar our way.

You and Me, Baby
Integrating in Infancy

In his book, *The Boy Who Was Raised as a Dog*, child psychotherapist Bruce Perry tells the story of a group of infants raised in a Russian orphanage who received only a few minutes of adult interaction each day. Perry describes the orphanage as a "baby warehouse:"

> ". . . a big, bright room with sixty infants in seemingly endless, straight rows of perfectly sanitized cribs. The two caretakers on duty for each shift would work methodically from one bed to the next, feeding each child, changing his or her diaper, then moving on."

The infants received almost no touch or verbal interaction. They weren't rocked or held, cooed awake, or sung to sleep. The childcare workers didn't have enough time to consider any but the most essential of the babies' physical needs – that is, food and diapering. The infants were left alone in their cribs 24/7. But, even in these severely deprived circumstances, the infants were smart and resilient. Imprisoned in their cribs, they reached through the crib bars with their little hands to touch one another and play together. Deprived of any semblance of a mother's or father's companionship or guidance, these infants composed a common language by which to communicate!

Most of us don't begin life in such a stark environment. Many of those who do, aren't as adaptable or innovative. Some may carry the wounds of infant deprivation for life (as Rene Spitz's studies of babies and toddlers in the foundling home suggest). Yet, these Russian infants provide a remarkable example of the resilience of the human spirit in infancy, especially with integrating difficult changes that accompany grief-striking losses. What's more, these babies demonstrate one of the greatest instinctual skills of the healthy infant: seeking intimate connection and communication with significant others.

For better or worse, most babies are born into families where caregivers are available 24/7. So, for the vast majority, our abilities to integrate grief in infancy, particularly in ways that facilitate healing, are dependent upon the integrating abilities of those who provide our care. If an infant's intimate caregivers are suddenly unavailable due to death, estrangement, incarceration, injury, illness, or work responsibilities, there are a couple of pivotal questions that must be asked and answered immediately:

- How will the infant's daily needs for physical care, connection, and communication be provided and by whom?

- How will the caregiver's importance in the infant's life be maintained and honored in the caregiver's absence?

An interesting exploration of infant grief related to the sudden absence of a primary caregiver is presented in Kathryn Stockett's novel *The Help*. Stockett's story that inspired the movie by the same name, explores separation-related grief experienced by caregivers and their charges when the intimate caregiver is a housekeeper, maid, or nanny who is viewed by others as being subservient and not regarded as a valued member of the family. Such intimate caregivers often disappear from an infant's life with little fanfare. However, the healthy infant (whose intimate bond with a loving caregiver is oftentimes a bond for life) makes no distinction between those paid or unpaid, valued or not, for their services. Add to the relational equation the fact that an infant's sense of "self" and "other" is, as yet, undeveloped and it's easy to see how the disappearance of an intimate caregiver in infancy might be equivalent to losing an integral part of yourself. Such infant grief is often overlooked by those who fail to understand such loss experiences from an infant's perspective.

If a beloved parent or other intimate caregiver is estranged from the family, works long-distance, or moves away, painstaking efforts to establish and reestablish intimate connections are essential to maintain the infant-caregiver bond. If physical distance prevents immediate bodily contact, hearing a caregiver's voice often – on the phone, Zoom, FaceTime, or an audio or video recording may be a great comfort for an infant. You might also create a homemade picture book or "baby board" book using photographs of the caregiver interacting with the infant and glimpses of the caregiver's life apart. The book might conclude with a much-anticipated reunion between the infant and their cherished caregiver. Over the distance, such physical reminders of connection can foster an ongoing bond with the parent or caregiver, and provide a sense of continuity and security for the infant in the present moment.

If an infant is estranged from you for months on end, upon reuniting don't expect the infant to take up with you where you left off. Likewise, bonding with an adopted infant may take more time than you imagined. Some infants require weeks, months, or even years to reestablish the depths of old bonds or create new ones if need be. Don't take it personally. Moment-by-moment and day-by-day, simply find avenues of caring, connection, and communication to which the infant responds in ways that build intimacy between you. Make these intimate interactions a staple of daily life.

If you care for an infant, make an effort to imagine grief-striking losses from the infant's perspective. Imagine how the infant might perceive a particular loss in every aspect of their being – physically, emotionally, mentally, and spiritually. Take stock of the significant changes impacted by a loss that an infant might find to be particularly distressing. Day-to-day, how can you assist an infant to integrate these changes? Day-to-day, how might you encourage an infant to find the healing balance between lamenting a grief-striking loss and honing in on relationships with significant others that are heartening (comforting, uplifting, and pleasurable) for the infant?

Although abandoned and orphaned infants may do their best to adapt to grief-related changes, in an infant's life nothing takes the place of an attentive and loving caregiver. So, if you provide care for an infant, be the kind of caregiver who is willing to learn, at the infant's bidding, what the grieving infant requires, needs, and desires to heal the way babies know best.

Guidepost 29

When the bough breaks, pray to God someone's there to catch the baby.

The Great Imitator
Companionship Needs of the Grieving Infant

Babies and toddlers may be smarter than you think when it comes to healing grief-related suffering. Healthy babies and toddlers instinctively know how to lament their grief. What's more, babies are quick learners. When daily care needs are met in an environment in which cherished companionship is available, most babies develop remarkable abilities to hearten, temper, and integrate grief and loss. But, when it comes to striking a healing balance among the four types of dynamic grieving responses, infants are at the mercy of their intimate caregivers.

In infancy, we experience our sense of selfhood through those we depend upon for life – literally absorbing the emotional, psychological, and social content within a caregiver's being. Colwyn Trevarthan, professor of Child Psychology and Psychobiology at the University of Edinburgh, speaks of this infant inclination to share and engage in the inner life of intimate caregivers:

> "The Self (of the infant) is looking for the vital will and imagination of the Other, not just receiving bodily comfort in the rhythms and accents of immediate body contact. A new-born may imitate expressions of an adult's motives and emotions within minutes of birth. This 'mirroring' has been proven to be expectant, purposeful, and reciprocal . . ."

This intense infant-caregiver bond poses an interesting dilemma: We may be able to hide our emotions and inner gestures from everyone else in the family, but we can't hide from our babies and toddlers. They have a special radar for finding us out. For better or worse, our feelings become their feelings; our intentions become their intentions; our interest becomes their interest.

From two or two-and-a-half to around the age of nine or so, a child gradually receives the knowledge that the child is an individual apart from others, including intimate caregivers. But from an infant's perspective, during the first few years of life, your body is their body, your heart is their heart, your mind is their mind. So, a priority of healthy parenting and caregiving is, yes, to regard the infant as a unique and complete person aside from you – while you honor the infant's utter dependency on all you are and do. Primary caregivers are an infant's lifeline for learning to survive and thrive on planet earth. Thus, a parent or other intimate caregiver serves as an infant's inner homing device. Who you are is everything to an infant.

If only every parent were prepared for the depth of intimacy the newborn can achieve. An infant's well-being depends not only upon your physical behaviors and care. Get this: an infant is a seeker of your will, imagination, emotions, and motives! This reality, above all else, is what makes caring for an infant one of the most significant acts of humanity a person provides for another. Despite each newborn coming into the world with an essence that is the infant's own, an infant learns from its intimate caregivers how to be human. This potentially terrifying news may send a would-be-parent running for the hills or cause a veteran to reel into a tailspin of regret. Because, after all, how many new parents in our culture are well-prepared for the job? I have yet to meet a parent who makes such a claim. Of those who attempt to be prepared, how many of us come to the realities of parenting with the resources and support we need to be the sort of exemplary human being most of us desire to be for our children? For those of us falling short of this ideal, it's fortunate that caring parenting has little to do with perfection and everything to do with healing our wounds and helping our children to do the same.

When you're grieving, it may be difficult to offer yourself to an infant in ways that help an infant to heal. That's why it's crucial for grieving parents and caregivers who experience difficulties in their grieving process to be given a daily reprieve from caregiving responsibilities. Sharing an infant's care among a small, dependable circle of adults allows a primary caregiver time and space to tend to their own grieving and healing needs while providing a safety net of love and protection for the infant.

As a horse lover, I've learned that horses (like babies) are highly intuitive. At times when I'm riding, it appears that a horse can read my mind. My intention becomes the horse's intention. In the documentary, *Buck*, about Buck Brannaman, a real-life horse whisperer who "helps horses with people problems," Buck says, "Your horse is a mirror to your soul, and sometimes you may not like what you see." The same is true for aspiring baby whisperers everywhere. You have to be brave to give yourself to an infant because an infant will reflect back to you the best and worst of yourself, and everything between.

An infant's empathic nature can be a great motivator for intimate caregivers to carve out time, space, and intention to grieve and heal extravagantly. If you won't make the effort for your own sake, then do it for an infant in your care, because when you're special to an infant, you can't keep your grief from them. Your grief is their grief. Your grieving is their grieving. Your healing is their healing.

Guidepost 30

To teach an infant, learn yourself.

Do-It-Yourself

Self-Guided Contemplations for the Infant Within You

In Part I of *Doing Grief in Real Life*, you were provided with eleven full-blown contemplative activities to help you explore your intimate relationship with grief – past, present, and future. At the end of each chapter in Part II, you'll be provided with suggestions to create self-guided contemplations related to each stage of your life – some that you may want to enjoy with your loved ones. Choose what is most helpful to you. Use these ideas as they are, revise them, or let them inspire contemplations of your own making:

- ◆ **A Blessing for the Infant Within You:** Read Debra Frasier's picture book, *On the Day You Were Born*, or Nancy Tillman's, *On the Night You Were Born*. In a quiet place, close your eyes, relax, and create a self-guided meditation to bless your infant self. Begin by imagining yourself in a comforting place, encircled by your intimate loved ones. Held securely in that place of love and encouragement, as an adult, imagine attending your own birth. Envision your mother handing you to yourself. Hold yourself as a newborn – as each of your loved ones blesses your infant self and thanks you for making the journey to earth. Conclude the blessings with your own words and gestures of love and gratitude for yourself and the precious gift of your life. (*A guided audio version of this contemplation is available online at DoingGrief.com.*)

- ◆ **Take Stock of Your Infant Wisdom:** Reminisce through your grief-striking losses as an infant (and those of your parents in the months leading up to your birth or adoption) – perhaps losses that involved abandonment, illness, injury, family dysfunction, abuse, neglect, prolonged separation from or death of an intimate caregiver, etc. You may need to glean impressions of this time of your life from elders who journeyed with you in your early years. Imagine how your infant instincts, intuitions, and behaviors allowed you to heal the pain and suffering related to each loss. What help did you receive from others? As you consider each healing transformation, you may want to write a list, journal about your healing wisdom in infancy, create a photo album, or choose a small token or symbol that represents each healing strength or capacity you imagine displaying as an infant. Reflect on ways that the healing wisdom of infancy enlightens your present healing process.

- **Weaving an Adoption Story that Heals:** Once a mom approached me after a keynote talk I gave at a parenting conference to ask my advice about something her psychiatrist had encouraged her to do – to tell her preschool son (as soon as he could understand) that his birth parents literally abandoned him at birth. Unfortunately, this was the reality, but it wasn't the truth – at least not the whole truth and certainly not the adoptive mom's story to tell. I suggested that her story of her son's birth and infancy was about preparation and welcoming. Her story for her son was about the miraculous journey of being united with one another as mother and son, child and family. No doubt, at some point in the boy's life, the details of his abandonment by the parent/s who birthed him might be useful information for him to have, but not as a mantra of grief during his infancy and early childhood.

    Stories of abandonment can wait until children know their stories of welcoming by heart. If you or your child was abandoned or placed for adoption in infancy, rather than imagining and re-imagining the circumstances of abandonment or a birth parent "giving up" a child, consider weaving a birth or adoption story that emphasizes celebration and gratitude for a child's irreplaceable presence in a family that would, otherwise, be incomplete.

- **Make a Healing Map:** Along the lines of Contemplation 5, "Your Grieving Map: Picturing a Lifetime of Loss" (page 44), make a "healing map," comprised of the moments in your life in which you experienced potent healing and how you imagine healing in the future. As you're inspired, reflect on each phase of your life from infancy to elderhood. If there are interludes of your life that are difficult to recall in detail, then imagine how healing might have occurred – perhaps through physical comfort, tears, laughter, nature, music, spiritual nurture, physical release, intimate relationships, another's healing touch, etc. Create your healing map all at once or add to it a life stage at a time as you read through each chapter of Part II on infancy, childhood, youthhood, adulthood, and elderhood.

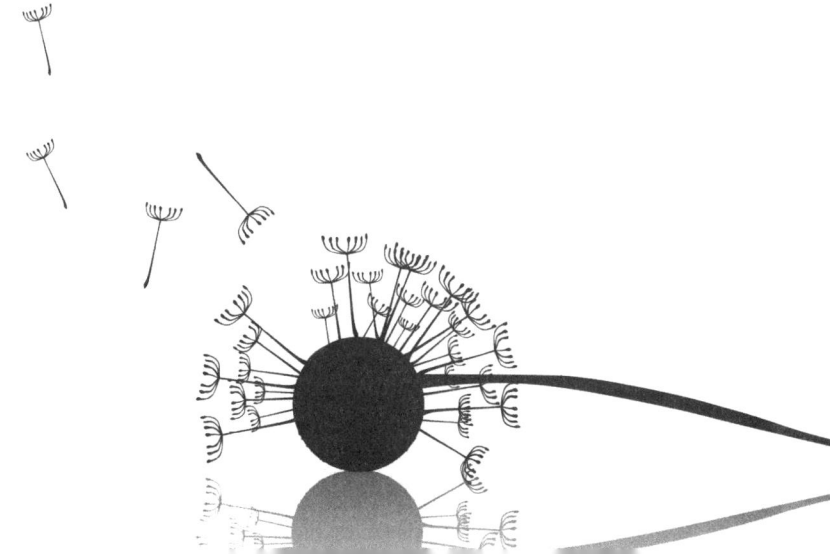

||||||||||||||||||||||||||||||||||||||||||||||||||||||||||||||||||||||||||||||||||||

An Infant's Healing Chest
Approaches to Grieving and Healing in Infancy

Look through the following list of approaches to grieving and healing from Part III, "The Healing Chest: Gathering Your Own Best Medicine." Which approaches might be especially useful to heal yourself for an infant's sake, care for a grieving infant, or revisit and heal grief from your infancy?

||||||||||||||||||||||||||||||||||||||||||||||||||||||||||||||||||||||||||||||||||||

- Abuse Awareness & Prevention
- Addiction Prevention & Recovery
- Apologies
- Art & Creativity
- Bibliotherapy
- Breathing & Relaxation
- Caregiving
- Ceremonies & Celebrations
- Cinematherapy
- Cognitive Healing
- Community-Building
- Conscious Eldering
- Crying
- Dance
- Death Care
- Dreaming & Visitations
- Dying a Good Death
- Emotional Healing & Expressing Feelings
- Exercise, Body Awareness & Physical Release
- Forgiveness
- Funeral Planning & Memorial Services
- Grieving & Healing Perspectives
- Habit-Building
- Helping Others
- Hope
- Illness Tending
- Integrative Care & Complementary Therapies
- Laughter & Humor
- Listening
- Massage, Reiki & Comforting Touch
- Meaning-Making
- Memoir & Autobiography
- Memorials & Remembrance
- Metaphors, Objects & Symbols
- Mindfulness & Meditation
- Movement, Yoga & Posture
- Music & Sound Therapy
- Nature
- Natural Remedies for Pain Relief
- Parenting Mindfully
- Pets & Animals
- Pilgrimages, Labyrinths & Hiking Treks
- Play, Fun & Games
- Poetry
- Prayer
- Repairing Broken Relationships
- Sanctuary & Sacred Space
- Self-Injury & Recovery
- Sexual Healing & Recovery
- Sleeping
- Stories & Storytelling
- Suicide Prevention & Survivor Support
- Talking Cures
- Theater & Speech
- Trauma Recovery
- Wonder
- Writing

5 ❧ Coming to Our Senses
Grieving & Healing in Childhood

> . . . and when all the wars are over,
> a butterfly will still be beautiful.
>
> Ruskin Bond

Childhood Smarts
A Child's Natural Genius for Grieving & Healing

An infant's ability to heal grief is liberating – after all, if a baby can do it. . . right? But as we roll, stand, walk, and talk our way into childhood, we experience grief through a kaleidoscope of changing perceptions, feelings, and ways of thinking. So, as children, we're required to learn and learn again what grieving and healing demand of us. We caregivers are also required to learn and learn again how to assist children to grieve and heal through the many changes and transitions of childhood.

Too often we expect children to act like pint-sized adults. We commonly use the phrases, "he's such a child," or "don't be so childish," as derogatory jabs at anyone who fails to meet our adult expectations of behavior. But childhood is an extraordinary embodiment of our humanity. For one thing, a child's imaginative thinking and attention to the present moment allow children to perceive the nuances of life and relationships in ways we adults find difficult to understand or emulate. In fact, as an adult, Albert Einstein attributed his intellectual achievements to his ability to see the world through the eyes of a child. Given this endorsement of childhood genius from Einstein himself, perhaps a child's potential for healing grief might soar astronomically if we simply quit asking children to "quit being so childish."

Grieving the Loss of Childhood

In *The Drama of the Gifted Child*, Alice Miller recounts the childhood of novelist and poet, Hermann Hesse, who at the age of three distressed his parents by what they referred to as Hesse's "violent temperament." Miller highlights letters and journal entries written by Hesse's parents concerning their grief over Hermann's spirited demeanor. When he was six, Hermann was sent to boarding school to gain some "discipline." After the first term, his mother wrote:

> ". . . he lived wholly in the boy's house and only spent Sundays with us. He behaved well there but came home pale, thin, and depressed. The effects are decidedly good and salutary. He is much easier to manage now."

Contrast this picture to his father's description of the boy before Hermann was sent away from home. He wrote that Hermann was:

> ". . . gifted for everything: he observes the moon, and the clouds, extemporizes for long periods on the harmonium, draws wonderful pictures with pencil or pen, can sing quite well when he wants to, and is never at a loss for a rhyme."

The father's description epitomizes the creative freedom of childhood, itself. It's telling that Mr. Hesse found that he and his wife were "too nervous and weak for (Hermann)," and that "the whole household (was) too undisciplined and irregular" to make room for the largeness of their young son's spirit.

Hermann's autobiographical story, "A Child's Heart" (about a child stealing figs from his father's study) reveals the depths of suffering the young Hermann encountered under his parents' punitive watch. In the story, Hesse describes the extinction of childhood bliss due to a chronic feeling of dread – "dread of punishment" and the soulful stirrings of conscience that he regarded to be "forbidden and criminal."

When a child is subject to adults who deny a child's worldview and natural ways of being and doing, a child's grief may erupt from within, where we parents and caregivers cannot see the havoc it spews. In the early 1980s, 100 years after Hesse's parents sent Hermann off to boarding school for his childish ways, psychologist and long-time Tufts professor David Elkind published a book called *The Hurried Child*. In his book that popularized the "Hurried Child Syndrome," Elkind identified a cultural phenomenon (that snowballed over the past several decades) in which children experience intense distress from the pressure put upon them by adults to grow up too fast. Elkind proposes that, collectively, parents, teachers, and the media

- Push children toward constant achievement that leads to a fear of failure
- Expect children to adapt to a quickly changing society without cracking emotionally
- Persuade or allow children to dress or act like adults in an overly-sexualized way
- Overschedule a child's day in ways that diminish play, leisure, and family time

Childhood breeds plenty of grief-striking losses without a child being inflicted with the loss of childhood, itself. Respecting childhood is a prerequisite for respecting the child.

Losses Born of Innocence

Even in environments in which "childish" behaviors are tolerated with compassion, a child's increasing mobility and initiative can lead a child to make glaring errors of judgment that cause grief-striking losses for the child and others. Such childish mistakes may fill a child with a deep sense of rejection, shame, guilt, or self-loathing. Think back to your childhood. Do you remember any childish mistakes that led to a grief-striking loss for you?

When I was three, I was enamored with the birdbath on our front lawn. Thinking how happy the birds were as they flitted in the fresh rainwater there, I filled my sand bucket with warm water (the way I liked it in the bath), decidedly grabbed our pet bird from its cage, took bird and bucket outside to "play" at the birdbath, and proceeded to hold the little bird underwater for a good and happy cleaning. But I was shocked out of my delight by my mother yelling panic across the yard. What I remember most was the devastation I felt when I pulled the dear little bird from the bucket, soaked and limp in my palm.

Then and there, I stared into the face of death for the first time, and although I had no name for it then, I was the "murderer." A deluge of shock and guilt flooded into the space within me where blissful innocence and ignorance dwelt only a moment before. Despite my mother's compassionate and attentive response to the event, in my three-year-old body and soul, I experienced the equivalent of the fall of Eden – a looming sense of "badness" that jarred me with self-doubt and shame.

The vast majority of children desire nothing more than to please those they love. So, berating a child for mistakes or spiritedness can be overkill for the child who desires to be accepted and loved, foibles and all. Dampening a child's active, inquisitive spirit or sense of wonder for the world is like giving an adult a lobotomy. Childhood requires spirit and initiative. It requires us to ride the edges of creativity and disaster, self-direction and conformity, fiery independence and caring relationship. Raising a perfectly-compliant or overly-cautious child ought never to be our ultimate parenting, teaching, or caregiving goal – despite our efforts to save a child, ourselves, or others (including unsuspecting birds) from a child's harmful actions and behaviors.

The Physicality of Childhood Grief

Let's be honest. Growing up isn't always a picnic and most of us have plenty of losses to grieve during childhood – whether these losses occur at our own hands, the hands of others, or due to grief-striking circumstances beyond our control. Pause for a few moments and take a journey back. Can you remember what it was like for you to suffer a grief-striking loss as a child – not just what you thought or felt about a loss, but how your whole body reacted to it? Back then, did you ever feel abandonment or anger in the cells of your skin? Did you ever become physically paralyzed or get a belly ache from guilt, shame, doubt, fear, or sadness? Or explode in an act of defiance? Were you ever shushed into powerlessness, or dazed by too much or too little information regarding a loss? Did you ever suffer the death of a doll or stuffed animal who, to your child self, was nothing less than a friend or hero? After all, how does one live without the presence of a cuddly companion who, day in and day out, closed the gap on loneliness, or night after windswept night, helped to ward off clanging, creaking monsters in the dark? Can you remember? And, if you can't remember, then imagine it. Imagine grief from a child's perspective.

As most caregivers of young children can attest, children are able imitators of all that we adults say and do. But don't let a child's sometimes uncanny impressions of us fool you. Children generally don't experience, think, or speak about grief as adults do. They're usually not about dissecting life and relationships through cognitive analysis or conversing about complex feelings. Most children come to know the world and their grief in a different way. They're prone to dive into grief headlong – walking, sitting, crawling, skipping, jumping, hitting, clinging, speaking, touching, biting, fidgeting, running, and rolling in and out of grief as a physical reality.

For example, one afternoon when my children were young, Willa came screaming through the back door as if the sky were falling. At the top of her lungs, she cried "I said sorry! But Morgan wouldn't listen to me!" When I asked why Willa had apologized, she yelled through her tears, "I accidentally opened my mouth and put my teeth on her arm, and I accidentally bit her!" Although I had to suppress a belly laugh at her comical explanation, I had little doubt that Willa's reaction was as unintentional as she professed. Willa was generally a joyful and congenial child, but when she was tired or angry, she often felt like a victim to her lack of self-restraint.

Although she was highly verbal from the time she was eighteen months old, intense feelings made her tongue-tied. Like many young children, Willa tended to express and process painful sensations, thoughts, and emotions physically. At such times, those likely to receive the brunt of Willa's pain and frustration were those she trusted most – her immediate family members. But we were also the last people on earth that Willa would purposely choose to alienate. So, the loss of Morgan's companionship (even for part of an afternoon) caused deep distress. There was no need to reprimand Willa for biting her sister. Morgan's initial rejection of her little sister's apology was consequence enough.

In the first several years of life, an immense amount of a child's focus and energy goes into negotiating physical relationships with people, places, and things in the child's immediate environment. Thus, a child experiences grief somewhere between physical pain and pleasure, comfort and discomfort, bodily ability and limitation, mobility and paralysis. It's defined by physical closeness or distance from what or who is desired, cherished, abhorred, or feared by a child.

What's more, a child is a sponge-like sensorium with a complex network of sensory receptors that are indiscriminately attuned. Whereas a healthy adult brain can instantaneously sift through and identify sensory input that is more or less relevant to our interest and well-being, a child's brain is less able to filter and prioritize in this way. For a child, an overstimulating home, school, or care environment that pummels the child's senses is likely to become a chronic source of stress.

In mainstream culture, we often categorize sensory perceptions by Aristotle's five well-known senses of sight, smell, taste, hearing, and touch. But, over the past century or so, various theorists have proposed that human beings possess somewhere between nine and twenty-one senses. In the early 1900s, the educational theorist, Rudolf Steiner, posited twelve senses at work in the human being, including sight, smell, taste, warmth, touch, hearing, speech, thought, movement, balance, life (a sense of well-being in the physical body), and ego (a sense of "self" and "other"). Steiner encouraged parents and teachers to keep these senses in mind when identifying and providing for a child's physical, emotional, intellectual, and spiritual needs.

However we choose to define and categorize the human senses, scientists today assert that the human brain receives, categorizes, and interprets billions of sensations every fleeting second. So, it's easy to understand how, in our often noisy, busy, adult-centered culture, the sensorially-attuned child might become overwhelmed with the scads of sensory stimuli the child receives. In fact, in our culture today, sensory overstimulation, in and of itself, can be an intensely debilitating (although mostly unrecognized) source of childhood grief. Our cultural tendency to expose young children to an overload of sensory stimuli is made evermore problematic by our commonly sedentary lifestyles.

It may seem counterintuitive, but as the sensate beings children are, bodily movement is an essential means by which a child processes and makes sense of their life and relationships, including grieving and healing loss-related pain and distress. As observant caregivers of young children can attest, and as many developmental theorists (Jean Piaget, Erik Erikson, Maria Montessori, John Dewey, Lev Vygotsky, and Howard Gardner, among others) have concluded, a child learns through active engagement. The grieving child is no exception. As children, we think about, express, and heal our grief by physicalizing it.

Unfortunately, in the United States and other countries following Western trends, physicalizing grief isn't easy for children today. Although our lives are generally busier than ever, most children spend countless hours sitting still – at desks in schools that have slashed recess, free play, P.E., and arts programs from the curriculum; engaging in online learning; riding in cars to school or daycare, errands, shopping, a quick trip through the drive-through for dinner; or being drawn into inactivity by the lure of the television, cell phone, or computer. So, just at the time in our cultural evolution when children commonly have countless grief-striking losses to heal and need to be more physically active than ever, the lives of many children are often devoid of meaningful movement. Some theorists and researchers are beginning to wonder if our current tendency to impoverish childhood of movement causes or exacerbates attention deficit disorders, mental and emotional disturbances, and depression in children.

Imagine how much repressed pain and suffering a child might avoid when they are provided with the time, space, and opportunity to move with their grief. Imagine how great the healing when children are encouraged to grieve in ingenious ways that come naturally during childhood. And imagine all that we adults might learn by taking a child's lead on their winding treasure hunt to healing.

Guidepost 31

Let childhood genius fall upon your brow like magic rain – to cure the soulful drought brought on by too much reasoning.

Mother (or Father) May I?
Lamenting in Childhood

In her essay, "Grief as a Gateway to Love in Teaching," from the book, *Teaching, Learning, and Loving*, Rachel Kessler shares the story of Richard, a psychologist whose brother died just before Richard started first grade. Unable to lament his grief at home among family members who didn't express grief openly, Richard was fortunate to find his healing in the arms of his first-grade teacher:

> "I can see her face, but I can't seem to remember her name . . . She had a rocking chair in the classroom and on the first day of school, she picked me up on her lap in the rocker and began to rock me. She rocked and I sobbed. And sobbed and sobbed . . . And you know, she did that for months, every day for minutes or sometimes what seemed like hours. She took me into the chair and rocked me for about five months, when the crying was done."

At home, Richard kept his need for lamenting his brother's death locked inside, as his family members taught him to do through their example. But, at school, with his teacher's non-verbal permission, Richard was able to rock and sob in the comforting presence of a caregiver who could see through his silent pain. The teacher didn't talk to Richard about his grief, she merely gave him the physical support and nurturing that allowed Richard to lament his sorrow related to his brother's death.

Adults who have difficulty expressing grief often give children direct and indirect cues to stifle their need to lament. A woman I know characterizes the day her mother died (when she was nine) as the day not a single adult relative or friend was willing to speak the awful truth. The daughter of the deceased was whisked away to an aunt's and uncle's house without anyone ever breathing the dreaded "D" word. Yet another griever recalls the day her brother died after being hit by a car. A neighboring farmer was sent to retrieve her from her grade school classroom to break the news. Upon hearing of her brother's death, tears rolled down the girl's face. In an awkward effort to comfort her, the farmer told her not to cry. So, she stopped. But the girl-turned-woman remembers pointedly, "I hated him for that."

One reason an adult may have an aversion to a child's lamenting – especially by way of a tangible expression of tears – is because tears are associated with pain, and most of us can't stand the idea of suffering, much less a child's suffering. As Aletha Solter claims in her book, *Helping Young Children Flourish*:

> "The meaning and purpose of tears has been greatly misunderstood. There is a cultural notion that equates crying with hurting, and parents are led to believe that their child will feel better if she would only stop crying. In reality, the opposite is true: crying is the process of becoming unhurt, and children will not feel better until they have been allowed the freedom of tears."

Tears can be therapeutic for grievers of all ages. But we who have left childhood behind may forget to tap into the curative relief and release from pain that crying can provide. What's more, there may be an empathy gap between adults and grieving children because a child's world is so much smaller than our own. Children are usually more adept than adults at focusing on the here and now. Most often, they focus their interest on the people, places, and things in the immediate vicinity. So, a child's experience of a present loss can (and often does) trump the child's awareness of losses that we adults define as more critical and traumatic. For example, a beloved grandparent's death who lives at a geographical distance may be less debilitating for a child than finding their threadbare doll or favorite toy in the trash bin. Of course, as a child's thinking and feeling life mature through the years and they gain a broader perspective of their childhood losses, the grandparent's death may become increasingly significant to the child and their grief over the doll's or toy's "death" less profound.

A bounty of grief literature today focuses on the effects of adult-defined trauma on children. That's well and good, as children do experience grief related to such adult-sized losses as death, divorce, natural disasters, war, abandonment, abuse, or illness. But what of the everyday childhood losses that are largely overlooked in our culture: rejection, social difficulties with friends or classmates, losing a treasured object, geographical moves, attending a new school, or "minor" family conflicts that may cause the child deep concern? And while we're on the subject, what about a child's fears of storms, strangers, the dark, dogs, clowns, or Santa Claus? What about a child wrestling with feelings of naughtiness, being scolded for uninhibited self-expression, being the brunt of a joke for demonstrating innocence or ignorance, or being taunted for being afraid to learn to swim or waterski? And what of a child's grief-striking losses for which a child has no name?

No Explanations Required

When my daughter Morgan was three or four, I was bowled over by her poignant and poetic description of a loss that weighed on her. She told me that when she felt angry at me, her daddy, or little sister, Willa, her anger made the love she usually felt for us "go away" in her heart. She was disturbed and saddened by the sensation and her confession was filled with grief due to the fickleness of her affection for each of us. At the time, I was grateful for Morgan's illuminating explanation so I could respond supportively. But throughout her childhood, Morgan's enlightening descriptions of her grief were few and far between compared to physical and emotional displays that communicated the grief-striking losses she encountered.

One of Morgan's most dramatic childhood memories of experiencing grief that she could not explain took place one day after school when she was seven or eight. She couldn't articulate then (and doesn't remember now) what grieved her, but she was pointedly taking her pain out on me and her younger sister, Willa. I was in the kitchen fixing dinner. After several failed attempts to engage Morgan in conversation and dinner preparations, I finally had a brainstorm that inspired me to take the paper recycling bin (which included an old phone book) with Morgan to her room. There, I invited her to take her pain and frustration out on the contents of the recycling paper. I told her that she could rip and tear all she wanted as long as she cleaned the paper up afterward. Morgan looked at me in disbelief as I left the room. I'd never given her permission to destroy something before. She was surprised and, more significantly, empowered by the opportunity.

As I finished cooking dinner, I heard tentative ripping coming from Morgan's bedroom, then enthusiastic tearing. After a while, bubbles of laughter erupted as the tearing became more pronounced. Morgan spent a good thirty minutes or so shredding the paper and phone book pages. When she re-emerged from her bedroom carrying the bin of shredded contents, her whole demeanor had changed. The black cloud that covered her earlier had dissipated – all because Morgan was able and willing to relate to her pain and frustration in a physical manner that harmed no one. No amount of talking with her about her grief could have accomplished that so instantaneously – even if she or I had been able to recognize or articulate its source.

The paper-tearing incident with Morgan taught me that, when assisting a grieving child, sometimes it's more important to understand and respond to the essence of a child's grief rather than the details. As much as I may hate to admit it, I'm not all-knowing when it comes to the personal pain of my children, and helping them to heal doesn't require me to be. Of course, there may be instances, as with bullying, illness, or abuse, when a child's health and well-being depend upon identifying the source of grief. But in every child's life, there will be other times when the source of the child's grief is nebulous. All we can do then is to support them in their suffering and encourage them in their healing – no explanations required.

Acting Out the Pain of Grief

Even if a child is tuned in to their grief and can verbalize its source, a child may not be aware of the connection between a grief-striking loss and the painful sensations, feelings, thoughts, and behaviors that such losses inspire. Thus, a child's expressions of grief may be triggered in random moments for seemingly unrelated reasons. A grieving child may have no clue why sensations of grief descend upon them or be able to describe what caused their negative behavior related to it. Providing an adult with a reason for their grief shouldn't be a prerequisite for a child to be granted our "permission" to express it. What's more, reasoning with a grieving child about thoughts and feelings can be confusing or infuriating for the child, because children don't always understand or care much about the connection between their feelings of grief and their reactions to it.

The movie *Kramer vs. Kramer* offers an intimate look at the separation and eventual divorce of Mr. and Mrs. Kramer (brilliantly played by Dustin Hoffman and Meryl Streep). At the beginning of the movie, Mrs. Kramer unexpectedly walks out on her career-focused husband and leaves him with their young son to raise. As father and son (played by Oscar-nominated seven-year-old, Justin Henry) negotiate life as a duo, there's a riveting scene between them at the dinner table when the boy decides he'll eat his ice cream *before* dinner. Despite his father's protests, the son drags his chair to the refrigerator, climbs onto it to dig the ice cream from the freezer, and brings the whole half gallon back to the table. As his father casts a final warning, the boy scoops up a big spoonful of ice cream from the container and takes a bite.

The son's act of defiance sets off fireworks between father and son, and the boy is physically carried and banished to his room without dinner. But, of course, the conflict isn't about ice cream. Through the lens of the film, it's about a little boy's anger at his father for not being able to set their lives aright and return his mother to him. It's a war-waging power play to find out just how adequately the boy's father can provide for him in his mother's absence. It's about a boy feeling abandoned by his mother and asking his father (in a physical way) if the boy is "bad enough" that his father will leave him, too.

A child may act out physically to release intense negative emotions that have built up around a loss. The child may sense that it's safer to react to people and circumstances that aren't directly related to the child's grief. It may be too scary for a child to respond directly to a loved one's grief-striking actions or to a loss that's confusing and difficult for the child to comprehend. For example, as the Kramers' son did in the film, a child may displace anger at a parent for leaving because the child senses that expressing anger to the absent parent might banish the parent forever. What the Kramer boy desired most was for his mother to return to him, his father, and their home together. Thus, the ice cream wars between father and son began.

Behavior that adults view as problematic may simply be a child expressing grief. Imagine how much more adept we parents, teachers, and caregivers might become at assisting a child to heal their suffering if we regarded behavioral problems as a child's attempt to identify, express, and heal their grief – whatever its source might be. What shift might take place in our relationships with the children in our care if we adults regarded a child's "misbehavior" as a call for help and guidance?

For the first six years of her life, a major source of grief for my daughter Willa was the necessity of succumbing to sleep. We can laugh about it now, but back then it was no laughing matter, especially to Willa. Extended relatives and family friends still talk about Willa's legendary tirades at naptime, bedtime, or whenever her eyes were heavy with sleep before she was ready. As a child, Willa engaged with such gusto in life and relationships that, despite her tendency to spend every last ounce of her energy interacting and playing with others, she despised her body's need to rest. Given the magnitude of her grieving response, it would have been easy to forego her tantrums and crying spells by giving up naptime or a regular bedtime altogether. But Andrew and I were convinced that Willa's well-being required more (not less) sleep. So, instead of loosening our expectations at naptime or bedtime, we created soothing rhythms and domestic rituals that invited sleep. Despite Willa's sometimes flailing legs and arms, we learned to hold her lovingly as she negotiated the inevitability of rest. The last few times Willa put up a fight at bedtime (which happened only sporadically by the time she was seven), she mumbled to Andrew who was holding her, "Thank you, Daddy. Thank you," as she drifted off to sleep.

Not every child will feel comfort or gratitude for being held physically during times of intense frustration or anger. In her younger years, my daughter Morgan despised being held when she was upset as much as Willa despised her need for sleep. Morgan was more apt to appreciate physical holding and comfort when she was sad or fearful.

A grieving child may leap, fight, or edge their way into your arms to seek quiet comfort or release grief-related pain by crying, wailing, or moaning within the stronghold of your embrace – no questions asked. But some young grievers may require an unequivocal invitation to find the courage to do so. Richard's first-grade teacher knew that. Making space in your arms that is large enough and strong enough to hold the weight of a child's suffering with intention and love can serve as a child's sacred portal of healing.

Guidepost 32

What a grieving child wants to know: that your love is stronger than their pain.

Gathering Wildflowers
Heartening in Childhood

Grieving children are often quick to rediscover that the sun still shines, love still flows, play and laughter can still ring true, and life with loss can still be full of hope and wonder. Most children come to heartening with their arms wide open – gravitating easily toward whatever is comforting, uplifting, or pleasurable within a loss experience. That's why, before a certain age, best friends can have a knock-down-drag-out fight one moment and make a beeline together for some great collaborative adventure the next. A young child may find comfort in the laughing arms of a parent who was drunken and violent the night before. A kindergartner may speak happily about a deceased family member despite the restrained silence of their elders.

Heartening means snooping around in the dark corners of our pain to find the lost treasures of joy, laughter, pleasure, and lightheartedness that are hidden in the nooks and crannies of our suffering. Granted, there are some childhood losses so heavy that they make heartening difficult at best – neglect, homelessness, hunger, abuse, abandonment, long-term illness, or injury. Such losses may fall on a child's demeanor like a heavy shroud. However, of all the life stages, as children we humans are masterful at heartening – that is, if the present moment gives us sufficient cause.

In my book, *Sanctuaries of Childhood: Nurturing a Child's Spiritual Life*, I share the story of a boy for whom Andrew and I provided occasional care. At 3-1/2, the boy had never been away from his mother for an extended time because, according to his mom, the boy had intense separation anxiety. But the boy's mother was determined to volunteer as a reading tutor and decided to leave her son with us for a few hours at a time during the tutoring sessions. Even though the boy enjoyed playing with our daughters (who were around his age), when his mother began to depart for the first time, he became upset and frightened. He screamed after his mother that he didn't want her to go. When she did, the boy threw himself into the middle of our living room floor – crying, kicking, and screaming with all his might.

Since I didn't know the child well, I chose not to touch him or pick him up to comfort him. I sat quietly and observed his sobbing heart-felt tantrum. Then, after the boy quieted down, I helped him to think about his separation from his mom in a different way. On our piano, I spied a clay whistle, shaped as four people standing together in a circle. Gently, I blew the whistle three times, which immediately got the boy's attention. As he lay on the floor listening, I told him a spontaneous story about a group of children whose mothers and fathers went off to work in the fields each day. The children were left in the care of their grandparents. Each morning as the parents went off to work, the children gathered at the well to draw water for the day's needs. One day, when a child became sad about being separated from their parents all day long, another child suggested that they sing to their parents as they walked off down the road, so their parents could carry the song with them in their hearts. Upon the story's cue for the children to sing, I blew the clay whistle again. The story ended with the parents reassuring their children that they would return home soon.

By the end of the story, my new friend was standing beside me, intrigued and no longer afraid. I handed him the whistle and invited him to blow it three times. After that, much to his mother's surprise, the story took the place of tears and tantrums whenever the boy's mother left him with us. He looked forward to the moment at the end of the story when he could blow the whistle for himself. Then, lickety-split, he was off and running to keep up with his playmates.

This blessing of separation and reunion comforted the boy. It helped him to trust that his mother's love would return to him in person. It offered both affirmation and resolution to his pain, celebrating the deep connection he and his mother shared. Such is the key to heartening grief. It doesn't make the reality of the loss go away; it simply allows a griever to see the loss in a different, more radiant light.

A child's magical thinking and playful spirit can lighten the burden of painful sensations, thoughts, and feelings that accompany grief. Moreover, a child can play with a grief-striking loss during expanses of free play, using dolls, objects, and playmates to stand in for real-life people and events related to a child's loss. A child may create stories, active metaphors, and playful symbols for their grief that help the child to better understand their loss and feel a sense of control over it. During solitary or parallel play, children may participate in lengthy monologues regarding their grief as a way of thinking about and processing their loss experience aloud.

The Italian film, *Life is Beautiful*, contains a poignant example of a child's imagination and playful spirit lending themselves to heartening amid tragedy. In the film, a young child is convinced that the concentration camp where he and his family landed is the location of a game in which the child must hide from guards, be uncomplaining, and bear up under hunger to gain points to win a life-size army tank. The game eventually saves the boy's life.

A little magical pretending can help to transform devastating grief-striking realities for a child. Many an imaginary playmate or pain-defying fantasy has been born out of a child's suffering. Playful activities may also suffice to balance the pain and suffering a child encounters when facing a grief-striking loss. For example,

- A child undergoing a painful medical procedure may find that a party whistle, stories, music, bubble-blowing, puppets, or massage can work wonders for easing fears and anxieties.

- A child who lives at a distance from a loved one after a geographical move can write letters, or make a daily or weekly habit of writing, drawing, or photographing entries in one of two journals or scrapbooks to pass back and forth – sharing stories, memories, anecdotes, expressions of affection, questions, and details about upcoming events that the two will enjoy together.

- After a child has been snapped at or bitten by a dog (and develops a frightful opinion of the creatures) healing might involve reading stories about dogs, looking at pictures of dogs, choosing a favorite breed, and gradually learning to befriend a gentle dog who lives in the neighborhood.

Once the friendship between child and dog is solid, the child might be allowed to adopt a dog of their own and raise it as a loving companion.

A child's penchant for play and laughter is a leg-up to celebrating the pleasures of life that continue to appeal to the child, despite a loss. So, a grieving child may not need much assistance when it comes to heartening. However, if a child experiences a lengthy interlude of lamenting and needs a reprieve, there are ways to gently encourage a child toward heartening behaviors and interactions; for example,

- Telling the child a curative story or reading a storybook together that provides an example of another child's approach to healing after a similar loss experience
- Providing time, space, and objects for unhindered free play
- Engaging in physical games or activities that are invigorating for the child;
- Offering physical comfort, nurturing touch, rocking, or holding
- Providing hands-on materials for artistic expression (drawing, painting, modeling with clay, dough or beeswax, etc.) that allow a child to express in pictures and symbols what the child may not have the ability or desire to express in words
- Laughing and acknowledging humorous aspects of a loss experience without disregarding the painful elements
- Discovering what continues to fill a child with a sense of love, hope, and delight (despite their loss) and helping the child to foster these healing relationships.

The poet, Robert Frost, once wrote, "We need something like a star to stay our minds on and be staid." At no time in our lives is this truer than during childhood. Children need something good and beautiful to believe in. That's why children often find heartening irresistible. That's why most children are unabashedly willing to wish on a star and believe that the wish will come true. We adults ought to be so wise, because wishes are full of hope, and hope is another name for healing.

Guidepost 33

There is a casket of treasure to be found within the darkness of childhood peril. It's filled with love, hope, play, laughter.

As If By Magic
Tempering in Childhood

When it comes to tempering grief, the magical thinking that is common for children in the first seven or eight years of life is an invaluable asset for healing. Magical thinking may be nature's way of protecting young children from the lasting consequences of harsh realities before a child's psyche or soul can bear them. So, if a child appears to be overly accepting and congenial while facing tragic circumstances, it may be that the child is viewing a loss through a rose-colored lens. Don't be too quick to snatch that lens away. A child may need to take the magnitude of a grief-striking loss into their being gradually over time. Magical thinking can help to soften the blow.

For example, regarding death, a child of four or five may understand that a loved one's body has "stopped working" and that family members and friends are greatly saddened by the loss. However, a young child often senses death as another place from which a loved one can return. In fact, during the first several years of life, children tend to be eternal optimists when it comes to reversing grief-striking losses. After a death, a child may believe that Mommy or Fido is waiting for them on a star, or that a beloved grandparent who died might wake up or come walking through the front door at any moment.

Just shy of my fifth birthday, my beloved "Pappaw" (as we grandkids affectionately called him) suddenly died of a heart attack. I didn't know then that I should be devastated by the loss. As a young child, I hadn't yet grasped the gravity of death. Looking into my grandfather's open casket, the magical thinking of early childhood had me believing that all I had to do was shake my grandpa awake. I leaned toward his face and whispered, "Wake up, Pappaw." I wanted him to open his eyes and tell me what all the crying was about.

It took me years to fully understand that I would never see my grandfather in the flesh again. He would never again slip me a little cup of coffee behind my mother's back, or rock me on the old rocking chair on his back porch, or read me stories. I would never watch him devour a whole jar of jam at the same breakfast or eat vegetables with him straight out of his garden. I would no longer be able to look into his beaming face – the personification of love for my almost five-year-old heart.

A child may begin to understand the finality of physical death around the age of six or seven when it dawns on the child that a deceased loved one cannot return to this earthly life. But a child may not fully comprehend death's inevitability (for oneself and one's loved ones) until sometime between the ages of eight and ten. All kinds of disillusionments (real or imagined) enter into our consciousness around this age: "I couldn't possibly have been born of these parents, so I must have been adopted," "Neither Peter Pan nor I can remain a child forever," "Sometimes an adult doesn't have a child's best interests at heart," etc. But younger children tend to believe in, well, magic, and if they don't like or approve of the realities of their loss, they may make something up. For example, that the people we love live forever; mom and dad are eternally destined to kiss and make up; a parent who abandoned a child as an infant will surely show up in all their glory one day; a lost, broken, or worn-out toy can be super-naturally restored; an abusive parent is by the very nature of parenthood deserving of a child's steadfast love and protection.

Until a child can make sense of a loss experience by way of reason as the child matures, a child's inclination for magic, fun, and play can shield the child's psyche from grief-striking realities that might otherwise overwhelm a child's sensibilities. So, even though the father in the film *Life is Beautiful* (page 125) has little power to free his son from the concentration camp where they are held prisoner, he can create a game with the boy that protects him from real-life danger and fear without his son being the wiser. Some people may deem the father's actions to be a lie. After all, the boy was never to win a life-size army tank. But the more important truth that the father desired for his son to understand was that the boy could hide from danger without panic or fear. Through symbolic metaphor, the father created for his son a sought-after prize that ultimately represented the gift of life, itself.

What a Child Needs to Know

Many childhood losses are not as life-or-death dramatic as being held prisoner in a concentration camp. But the example awakens us to the dilemma many parents and caregivers face as they figure out how much information a child needs to effectively integrate a grief-striking loss. What line is it that we parents toe between deception and magic when we translate grief experiences for our children into fanciful games and illusions? A child loses a tooth and the tooth fairy comes to temper the loss with gifts and magic fairy dust. A child breaks or loses a cherished toy and another materializes in its place. What happens when a child eventually sees through such fun and games? Some children may feign belief for the sake of the game. Others may be confused or angered at a parent's or caregiver's attempts to "trick" them. So, how honest is honest enough when it comes to revealing the details concerning a grief-striking loss? As always, answers seldom come in black and white.

When I was four and my beloved Pappaw died, it was helpful for me to know that my grandfather's physical body had stopped working. It was helpful to know that the body I was viewing at the funeral no longer contained the breath or heartbeat that allowed my grandpa to walk, talk, and move about in the world. What I did not need to hear was that God had "taken him" or to be told that death was like a "long sleep." What child cares to believe in a God who snatches loved ones away, or wants to go to sleep at night in fear of never waking up? Death is death, and children (of all people) have natural inclinations to integrate its impact on their lives. This is, in fact, the key to giving children the information they require regarding a loss: *to let them know, specifically, how the loss affects them and their loved ones in the immediate present and imminent future.*

With death-related losses, a child may or may not be inquisitive about the details of what happens to the loved one's body after death. Some families make the death process more transparent than others. Whatever is involved in death observances for your family and friends, affirm to a grieving child that the child's relationship with their loved one can continue even after death. The child may be searching for ways to relate to a deceased loved one – physically, emotionally, mentally, and/or spiritually. Let children know that when they're ready, it's possible to foster an ongoing sense of love and connection. For ideas, see my *Lilipoh* magazine article, "Forever After: Helping Children Re-connect with Loved Ones Who Die," listed in the "Memorials & Remembrance" section of Part III on page 331.

In attempting to be "honest enough" with a child experiencing a loss, please remember that children do not need to be apprised of the ins and outs of traumatic circumstances that do not directly involve them. For example, a child does not need to know the gory details of a loved one's violent death, the unedited version of the circumstances leading to mom's and dad's divorce, or disturbing stories about a playmate's abusive experiences. Even so, a child may be curious and have questions that will require some answers. Sometimes, answers can unfold as a child matures and discovers new insights and questions about their evolving understanding of a loss. Offer information as it becomes relevant to the child's changing perspective, questions asked, and immediate circumstances. If a child asks a question you're not comfortable answering at the moment, let the child know that their question is a good one and that you will explore answers with them in the days to come. Then, be sure to follow through and sort out what is needed so you'll be prepared to respond to the child's questions without letting too much time pass.

Years ago, when I served as a school administrator of a preschool and kindergarten program in Louisville, Kentucky (for 3-1/2 to 6-year-olds), there was news of a man in the vicinity approaching unattended children and tattooing them with a drug-laced tattoo. To avoid fostering fear and panic in the children who were in our care, the staff and faculty of the school chose not to share this information with the children firsthand. Rather, we made sure that all our teachers and parents knew of the predator and were ever more vigilant in keeping a protective eye open.

Teaching children age-appropriate guidelines that help to protect them from so-called "stranger danger" is essential as children mature and journey beyond the attentive presence of caregivers. Until then, take advantage of teachable moments that pop up as you interact with those beyond your intimate circles of family and community. Review safety rules now and then; communicate them calmly and comfortingly in ways that project a sense of security. But steer clear of fostering unnecessary fears and worries in children who don't yet have the physical strength to protect themselves or the social awareness to assess when they may be in danger. With young children, we adults carry the burden of protection. So, we needn't deprive children of their sense of innocence and well-being in the present moment because we're scared that they might be the victims of some random act of violence on our watch. If we impose such anticipatory fears and worries on children, the violence done to a few becomes the violence done to many, as children have their sense of security and innocence robbed from them.

Whatever you say or do to help a child grasp an age-appropriate understanding of a real-life loss, don't insist on pulling the veil of magic from a child's eyes unnecessarily. When there is no harm in it, let a child live in their dreamy, imaginative world where all is well. For example, if a child believes they will meet up with Mom or Fido on a star one day, instead of setting the child straight, regard the child's imaginings of such a meeting as a poetic metaphor. Let it represent a spiritual reunion in the child's dream life or the after-life upon death, or as an allusion to the scientific theory that we humans are made of star-dust and to the stars we will return. Such magical thinking lays the foundation for deeper spiritual beliefs and scientific investigations as the child matures. Seldom are such imaginations so complete as to bar a child from assimilating the pain and suffering that accompanies a grief-striking loss experience over time.

It may be that a child's magical thinking or idyllic worldview is insufficient to avoid grief-related thoughts, sensations, and feelings in the curative doses that help a child to find needed reprieve from their suffering. If so, a child is likely to call upon other tempering strategies to ease their pain. In their article, "Coping with Stress," Nancy Eisenberg, Richard Fabes, and Ivanna Guthrie cite several studies suggesting that children of different ages can do so expertly. The studies show that children under the age of seven generally temper their distress by physically removing themselves from the source of their pain and suffering. Older children – eight or nine and up – are apt to use their increasing cognitive abilities to limit thinking about distressful experiences and are also able to consciously use behavioral distractions to ease stressful situations. Depending on a child's tempering abilities and preferences, a child may temper their grief through engaging in

- Magical thinking and fantasy
- Play
- Laughter
- Daydreaming
- Sensory-pleasing activities and behaviors
- Sleep
- Behavioral distractions
- Limiting their thinking about a loss
- Moving away from the source of their pain

If you hope to encourage a child to temper their grief as a child knows best, in healthy cycles of avoidance and engagement, you do well to embrace childhood for what it is – a time for children to be children. Provide a grieving child with time and space to play, daydream, and fantasize their way to healing. If the process seems slow-going to you, be patient, pay attention, and remember: Toeing the line between deception and magic where children temper their grief can be a funny business. Keep your sense of humor along the way and don't take yourself too seriously. Laughter, leisure, and a playful spirit can work wonders to help temper grief.

Guidepost 34

Acting more like a child may be the wisest thing you do today.

Everyday Grieving, Everyday Healing
Integrating in Childhood

If we let them, children remind us that grief can show its colors, more or less, any day. How rich life can be for a child and their caregivers when we accept grief as a natural everyday experience. We do so not by making grief the center of a child's life or avoiding it like the plague. We do so by learning to embrace grief as a common human experience among other human experiences.

When my children were young, they made a habit of enlisting my participation to help patch up every scrape and bruise they garnered in their work and play. A box of band-aids didn't last long with my children around. Their band-aid fetish became an almost daily ritual to acknowledge, inspect, and heal their pain. Oh, they didn't dwell in my loving attention long. They were far too busy exploring childhood to dally. But healing their momentary pains became a touchstone for making their way back to the merriment and adventure of childhood.

Some grief experts discount distress associated with momentary everyday losses as being something other than grief. They say grief is more earth-shattering and complete. But anyone who is an observer of children knows how deep and riveting a child's momentary distress over everyday losses can be. What's more, learning to heal the "little losses" a child encounters in the daily round is some of the best preparation a child gains for meeting other more traumatic losses that have longer-lasting consequences in a child's life.

Since children generally focus on the physical realities of here and now, present losses are likely to cause the most suffering for a child. These child-size losses may seem inconsequential to a parent or caregiver: losing a treasured toy, being disappointed by a change of plans, having a bellyache, etc. As adults, we often perceive grief from a wider lens: the diagnosis of cancer a long-distance friend received two months ago, the pending foreclosure on the building that houses the family business, or a hurtful conversation with an intimate that happened long ago and far away. Thus, an adult caregiver may fail to see a child's momentary grief in the earth-shattering proportions the child does, and a child may appear to disregard major family losses – past, present, and future – that don't directly affect the child in the present moment.

We don't come into the world with ready-made perceptions of "now," and "then." During the first years of life, young children acquire only a vague sense of "the past," and (then) of "the future." Time constructs such as "yesterday, today, and tomorrow" and especially "past, present, and future" may be confusing for a young child. Given these differences in perception, time-related misunderstandings are apt to spring up between a child and their caregivers – sometimes, in ways that provoke a child's grief and provide an opportunity for the child to reconcile a loss.

For example, consider the loss I experienced at five when I was introduced to the conventions of kindergarten registration protocol: I was born the youngest of four children. My next oldest sibling, Rebecca, is four years my senior. By the time I was three-and-a-half, one of my most yearned-for aspirations was going to school like my big brothers and sister. Every time my siblings were carted off to their school-day adventures, I felt as if I was missing out on something monumental. My parents assured me that my school days would come soon enough. They told me I could attend when I was five. So, for months I patiently waited for my fifth birthday. The first school-day morning afterward (a wintry, January day in Iowa), I woke up like a light, put on the first-day-of-school clothes I laid out for myself the night before, and ran to the breakfast table for my first-day-of-school breakfast. To me, it felt like Christmas day, only better.

Imagine my five-year-old disappointment when I was told that I had to wait to go to school until an entirely new school year began. I was told it would be months before I would see the inside of my kindergarten classroom. To my child-brain, it may as well have been decades. All I knew was that I deserved a chance. Despite my mother's loving attention as the best-of-the-best at-home moms, I had been promised a whole new world. I had waited forever to be five. But as I stood behind our front storm door that fateful morning, watching my siblings march down the street to catch the school bus, my school-age fantasies dissolved in a flash. Sadness and anger poured through my body. I was confused that I had been "lied to," subjected to some cruel joke by my own flesh and blood.

Of course, the same here-and-now attentiveness that produced my first-day-of-kindergarten crisis is what makes holistic grieving for the young child so doable. Most children can fluidly and easily move from lamenting to heartening, or from tempering to integrating – depending on present circumstances. My recollection of the intense grief I encountered at being barred from school at the age of five, is that the earth-shattering aspects of my grief lasted but a good part of that day and into the next. Despite the intensity of my sadness, anger, and confusion at the "false" information I had been given, by the end of the following day I had already been lured back into the joy and comfort of my stay-at-home-with-mom-in-the-neighborhood daily routine.

A loving, dependable relationship has a way of dissolving the angst of a child's grief. Love may be the greatest catalyst of all in helping a grieving child to integrate the realities of a loss. That is, love and a home, school, or care environment that is built on love – love that accepts a child's unabashed expressions of grief and a child's need to temper their pain, love that allows a child to laugh in the face of devastation and get on with life despite a grief-striking loss.

As you provide a healing environment for a grieving child, it's possible to create physical spaces that encourage children to move with ease between integrating and tempering grief-related change as they see fit. The following story provides an example of how to help children orchestrate the balance:

Going In & Out the Window: A Child's Healing Space

When a long-distance friend died from cancer, I was unable to attend her memorial, so I went to visit Katrina's spouse Scott and their children, Emily and Devan, a few months later. The children were thrilled to share with me the altar they created with their father in a special room of their home to honor their dear mom. On the altar, they had gathered photographs, poems, treasured objects, and mementos. I was struck with the ingenious placement of the altar, not in the center of the home, but rather in a room on the periphery of their daily activities where the children could go whenever they chose. It was obvious they took great pride in the creation and their love for their mother was palpable in it. Yet, as I shared the day with this grieving family, it was clear that the altar was only one aspect of the children's animated daily discoveries that caused life to continue to overflow with joy and goodness – despite the sorrow of their excruciating loss. What made the memorial for their mother so ingenious was that the children could change and add to the altar whenever they chose, making it a living symbol of physical interaction. What's more, they could access the altar in a flash or beat a hasty retreat as they saw fit.

Scott understood that his children needed a physical expression of their ongoing relationship with their mother and he supported them in their creation. He was also aware that, at the ages of seven and five, his children were likely to encounter greater difficulties in integrating their mother's death as they matured. So, as the months and years unfolded, he continued to encourage his children to remember and reconnect with their mother in spirit.

※ ※ ※

Patience is a priority as a child gradually wraps their body, heart, mind, and spirit around a loss and all the changes a loss brings with it. As you provide touchstones of acknowledgment and remembrance, watch and listen carefully to a child's healing journey. A child may show you how grief breaks you and heals you in the course of a day or a moment. A child may reveal to you that loss can empty you of delight even as it makes room for joy to be born anew. A child may embody the wisdom that when love attends to your pain, all kinds of everyday miracles can light up the dark corners of your life, where despite everything, hope, faith, and magic still reside.

Guidepost 35

> Grieving children are often generous. If you're willing, they will gladly share their healing remedy without a thought of hoarding it for themselves.

Build It & They Will Come
Companionship Needs of the Grieving Child

There is a field of dreams called "childhood." In that field, imaginations run wild, time stands still, and life is for jumping into – body, heart, mind, and spirit. If you hope to accompany a child there, you'll need a boatload of courage, because happily-ever-after isn't all that's waiting for you in that field of dreams. No matter what your parents told you, childhood is full of monsters and dragons that can threaten your very existence.

The monsters and dragons of childhood are fears and worries made visible. They can show up in the dark or broad daylight, in your sleep or when you are widest awake. When a child is grieving a significant loss, monsters and dragons may come out in droves. Fears and worries that grow to such monstrous proportions in a grieving child's wild imagination may reveal some of the obstacles that block a child's path to healing. So, a child's healing quest is not to forever banish these scary creatures. Like Max in *Where the Wild Things Are* by Maurice Sendak or *A Monster Calls* by Patrick Ness, a child's quest for healing includes learning to live peaceably with the monsters and dragons that lurk within a child's being.

Pablo Neruda writes: "Everything is ceremony in the wild garden of childhood"— everything, even grieving. Grieving children often display expert know-how at making grief tangible and putting it into action in ways that acknowledge, release, resolve, and heal their suffering. Unfortunately, we adults don't always trust a child's grieving genius. Some of us find it difficult to resist the urge to throw ourselves as a shield between a child and their grief. Some claim a child's grief as our own or attempt to dictate a child's grieving process, imagining that children have no idea how to grieve or heal on their own. But running chronic interference between a child and their grief can weaken a child's natural instincts, intuitions, and abilities for grieving and healing. So, as you assist a child to become their own best grief expert, avoid these knee-jerk reactions that are all-too-common among adults:

- ⬥ **Resist the urge to temper a grief-striking loss for a child by ignoring, belittling, or denying a loss or the grief it causes.** Enforced tempering can increase a child's suffering, so when you find yourself negating a child's grief, ask yourself what is motivating you – fear, a desire to protect, your own need to temper, a lack of empathy for the child's perspective, or guilt for not shielding a child from a loss? There may be circumstances when helping a child to temper grief is appropriate and useful – in the throes of a life-threatening situation, undergoing a painful medical procedure, in social circumstances that call for some restraint, or after a child has experienced a long bout of lamenting and needs a reprieve. But repeated attempts to temper a child's grief for the child may make it difficult for a child to learn to trust their inclinations to meet and retreat from everyday grief and life-shifting losses on their own.

- ⬥ **Resist the urge to become overly-involved in a child's grieving experience.** When a child experiences a grief-striking loss, you may find yourself staking a claim in the child's suffering. Your enthusiastic ranting and raving about a child's grief experience may be born of love, but it can also cause a child to become overwhelmed, overinvested, or disinterested in lamenting a loss firsthand. A child may amplify their grief (to meet your intense emotionality) or hide it (to save themselves or you from the pain). Offer age-appropriate gestures of support and comfort without co-opting a child's grieving process. Then, seek out time and space to contemplate your empathic grieving responses in solitude or with a trusted listener who is more your age.

⬥ **Resist the urge to overlook grief that a child experiences from abuse or bullying that occurs in your intimate circles of relationship or from family dysfunction that you accept as "normal" behavior.** Unfortunately, most incidences of abuse that children endure occur within intimate relationships. A sibling, parent, extended family member, close friend, or mentor are among the most common perpetrators of child abuse and bullying. When physical or psychological violence happens between siblings, parents may adopt the attitude that "siblings will be siblings" and overlook its sometimes severe and lasting consequences. What's more, because of a caregiver's unhealthy relationship patterns or addictive behaviors (with alcohol, drugs, food, gambling, media, etc.), a caregiver may fail to observe or remember how their numbed presence or aggressive words or actions negatively impacted a child. Whether a caregiver is physically or verbally abusive or is absent, unresponsive, needy, or neglectful, a child may suffer wounds that are difficult to fully comprehend or heal. Be sure that anyone responsible to provide care and protection for your child (including you) is sober, trustworthy, and equipped to do the job. It will save you and any child who is entrusted to you a mountain of grief.

⬥ **Resist the urge to withhold pertinent information from a child regarding a loss.** Withholding information about a loss may seem like an age-appropriate solution to help a child temper grief. Perhaps you've been told that "what a child doesn't know won't hurt them." But withholding information may backfire. Many children are highly intuitive, so not being given pertinent information may confuse a young griever who absorbs a loss subconsciously. What's more, being denied information about a loss may play havoc with a child's natural and timely grieving process, robbing a child of the opportunity to grieve and heal alongside loved ones.

If information regarding a loss is reported to or discovered by a child in a raw or especially graphic form, it may cause added trauma for the child. Be sure to relay information to a child in a caring and supportive tone. If someone other than an intimate caregiver is the one to break heartbreaking news, significant others can follow up afterward. An intimate caregiver's willingness to acknowledge and speak about a loss creates an opening for a child to engage in conversation, ask questions, and seek comfort to allay fears and worries.

A child may get the wrong idea that a loss (such as a death or divorce) occurred because of something the child did or said, or a child may place blame on someone else for a loss that was beyond the person's control. If so, affirm relevant causal facts of the matter in words and pictures a child can easily understand. Sharing a picture book or story about a child suffering a similar loss can help a child to integrate the information that's needed without blaming themselves or others undeservingly. For ideas, see "Bibliotherapy" (page 320), "Stories & Storytelling" (page 339) and "Healing Through Novels & Picture Books" (page 341).

⬥ **Resist the urge to overwhelm a child with unnecessary information regarding a loss.** The key to sharing pertinent information with a child regarding a loss is to speak to a child in thoughtful age-appropriate ways, relaying information that is relevant to the child in their present circumstances. Observe a child's natural tendencies for curative doses of integrating and tempering throughout the grieving process so you can impart information at a time when the child can receive it. If you are one of the child's primary caregivers, let the child know that you will be there for them – to provide nurture and daily care, and to help the child explore answers to their questions as they arise. (For more on this subject, refer back to the section "What a Child Needs to Know" on page 128.)

⬥ **Resist the urge to cast a child's emotional outbursts in a negative light.** Being scolded by a beloved or domineering adult for emotional outbursts related to a loss can cause a child to deny or minimize their pain and suffering indefinitely. Throwing a genuine tantrum is not equivalent to being a "problem child," and crying is not the equivalent of a child "being a baby," or a boy "being a girl." Some babies and girls are terrifically efficient at having a rousing good cry, but they certainly don't have the market on it. Tears and supervised tantrums are far healthier in the long-run than suppressing or denying intense personal pain. Childhood is an ideal time of life to learn this wisdom – when tears and tantrums may come more easily.

⬥ **Resist the urge to scorn a child's playfulness and laughter as a sign of uncaring or denial.** A child being frowned upon for laughter and play while the rest of the family is lamenting a loss is no better than being scolded for tearful outbursts. A child's lighthearted activities may be a source of heartening, tempering, and integrating a loss in ways that lead to profound healing. So, when a child talks happily or banters playfully while everyone else is deep in the thick of suffering, learn to regard a child's upbeat presence as evidence that grief is born of more than pain.

⬥ **Resist the urge to repeatedly question a child about a loss or prod them to analyze their responses to it.** You may find it tempting to pepper a grieving child with questions or to guess what might be "wrong." But asking a child to assess a personal grief experience may call for mental and verbal abilities that the child hasn't yet acquired. What's more, your prodding may confuse a child about their genuine feelings, thoughts, memories, and physical sensations regarding a loss experience. Be patient, attentive, and supportive so a child can grieve in their own way and time. If you suspect a child is being abused or bullied, a few well-chosen, open-ended questions may be necessary to let a child know you are there for support and will listen to whatever a child is able and willing to share with you. If the child is reluctant to talk with you, you may need to wait and ask again, suggest that the child talk with another trusted adult, or call a reputable child abuse counselor or hotline for further guidance.

⬥ **Resist the urge to tell a child you know just how they feel.** Even when you have experienced a similar loss, it's important not to jump to conclusions about what aspects of a loss experience are distressing or uplifting for a grieving child. Give a child plenty of room to express their feelings – physically, emotionally, and verbally. If you need to identify the source or impact of a child's grief, it may be helpful to describe to a child what you observe. For example, saying to a child "Your face looks so sad (mad, worried, frustrated, relieved, or whatever feeling you sense) to me right now," "The way you're sitting makes me wonder if you're hurting inside," or "It seems to me like you may need a hug." After offering a brief description of what you observe, allow the child to respond. If a grieving child becomes withdrawn and uncommunicative, it may be helpful to find a capable counselor who specializes in childhood grief to help you think through your parenting, teaching, or caregiving approach with the child.

⬥ **Resist the urge to temper a child's childish ways.** Adult-centered rules and ageist attitudes that squelch a healthy child's active engagement, curiosity, or animated expressions can become a crushing source of childhood grief. Punitive or authoritarian parenting, teaching, or caregiving often gives a child the message that there is something inherently "bad" about the child that needs to be suppressed or denied. Because children have little recourse or know-how to directly protest such shaming adult behaviors, a child's resulting grief can twist itself into behavioral problems and emotional disturbances that feed on themselves. Respect a child's need to be a child. Of course, one of the greatest challenges of parenting and caregiving is to do so while also teaching a child to respect the needs and preferences of others.

Creating Lifelines of Healing

The best you can do to assist a grieving child is to provide opportunities for a child to grieve and heal in their own way and time. But when you're tending to your own pain and suffering, you may lose your motivation to provide care for a child, or you may become confused about what encouragement and support a grieving child requires. After all, if you are being swept downriver in your private riverbed of suffering how can you serve as a lifeline for a child in your care?

Fortunately, there are lifelines you can create for a child that don't depend on your continual effort and guidance. Creating an environment that fosters imagination, presence, and active engagement is key. Consider these practical ways to transform your home, school, classroom, or daycare into a sanctuary where healing can come naturally for a child (and you, by association):

◈ **Provide familiar daily rhythms and rituals.** Most children, especially those under the age of nine, thrive in care environments that offer familiar daily rhythms a child can count on – daily patterns that provide a balance of activity and rest, interaction and solitude, work and play, sufficient sleep, regular mealtimes and snack times, etc. Of course, there may be times you need to diverge from your usual daily rhythms, but when a child is facing undesirable changes, maintaining or creating rhythms and simple daily rituals of connection and nurturing can go a long way: a regular mealtime, nap or bedtime blessing, song or verse of greeting or parting, etc. Amid loss and change, such rhythms and rituals bring comfort to a child and deepen intimacy. For more ideas, see my books *Seven Times the Sun: Guiding Your Child Through the Rhythms of the Day* and *Sanctuaries of Childhood: Nurturing a Child's Spiritual Life*.

◈ **Create a child-friendly lifestyle that nurtures and protects a child's senses.** Creating a home, school, or childcare environment that balances the busyness of current cultural trends with a slower, gentler, simpler lifestyle, provides a child with the time and space to digest the overabundance of sensory stimuli that the child devours in a day, including grief-striking losses. Restricting a child's exposure to electronic media, including television shows, movies, computer games, and news reports can be especially helpful to reduce chronic sensory overload for young children. Interlacing more active periods of the day with quiet interludes for daydreaming, cloud-gazing, pleasure reading, a simple board game, or meditative arts or crafts may be just what a child's body, heart, mind, and spirit need for healing.

◈ **Provide sufficient opportunities for sleep.** Sleep offers a child tempering relief and release from painful thoughts, emotions, and physical sensations, and allows a child to subconsciously integrate a loss in the child's dream life. Sleep rejuvenates a child physically, emotionally, mentally, and spiritually so the child is more prepared to meet the realities of loss-related change upon waking.

Unfortunately, many children in our culture are sleep deprived due to busy schedules and over-stimulating, movement-deficient lifestyles that make it difficult for a child to settle themselves at bedtime. In the chapter on sleep from my book, *Sanctuaries of Childhood: Nurturing a Child's Spiritual Life*, I offer ideas for rearranging evening family time and creating bedtime rhythms and simple rituals to welcome a child to sleep. (More "Sleeping" resources are listed on page 338 of Part III, "The Healing Chest: Gathering Your Own Best Medicine.")

◈ **Allow a child to daydream.** Daydreaming may have gotten a bad rap when desk-centered learning for children became the norm, but daydreaming is a natural way that a child can assimilate, temper, and tolerate the grim realities of a grief-striking loss. Daydreaming can be a private means of lamenting without interruption or influence from others. It may help a child to integrate memories related to a grief-striking experience, clarify questions to ask regarding a loss, escape from grief-related suffering through pleasurable fantasies, or dwell on happier times. Daydreaming can also be a source of empowerment and hope as a child imagines better circumstances in the future or a wished-for resolution that might provide healing. In today's information-loving, hurry-up society, daydreaming is often a luxury a child isn't afforded, but it can serve as a soothing balm that heals a child silently from within.

❖ **Provide activities in which a child can take charge.** Engaging in activities that a child can control may help the child to overcome fears, transform a sense of powerlessness, and seek diversion from their pain – for example:

- *Role-playing:* Give hospitalized or bedridden children an opportunity to role-play being "the doctor" who is caring for the doctor, nurse, or another caregiver; it can help everyone see a child's illness or injury from a different perspective.

- *Shopping Around:* Invite a child who is poverty-stricken or the victim of a house fire or natural disaster to go shopping at a food or clothing bank, or at a private "store" set up by friends or neighbors to inspire the child with a needed sense of abundance. Likewise, a child might be given a list of needed items (food, clothing, school supplies, games, or toys) to buy and a gift card to shop at a local grocery, retail, or thrift store.

- *Staying Connected:* When a parent is absent from a child's daily life, if possible, provide various means for parent and child to stay connected – perhaps, through daily phone calls, ongoing letter writing (a sentence or paragraph a day can be added to a letter that is sent or given to one another regularly), or keeping a calendar with the best and worst thing that happened that day (so you can record ups and downs of daily life to share in more detail at a later time).

- *Buddying Up:* A young child and their primary caregiver/s may be able to experience a funeral or memorial service of an intimate loved one more meaningfully if a trusted and observant childcare provider is "buddied up" with the child during the service. Ideally, choose someone who can tune into the child's momentary needs to engage in the event and retreat from the service if need be – to play, take a walk, or tend to care needs. Of course, some children may want to stay close by your side and experience the service or memorial from start-to-finish with you and your intimates. Do your best to create an environment that is child-friendly and flexible to the momentary needs of the youngest family members and friends in attendance.

- *Making it Happen:* Invite a child to help plan or participate in a ceremony of healing – for example, creating a memorial celebration for a deceased or dying family member, pet, or cherished toy that is beyond repair, or offering a healing blessing to someone who is ill or injured. Such opportunities empower a child to "do something" about a loss and serve as a healer for others. One of my family's most memorable funeral services was for our family cat, Caspian – a service that my children helped to plan and lead.

Morgan penned and read a memorial poem, which she wrote on a "memory stone" in permanent marker for our garden. I wrote the eulogy and we all sang a song of blessing, dug the grave, shared memories, and buried our beloved Caspian with all the honor and love he deserved.

- **Let a child talk.** Some children process grief by talking about it in the presence of a caregiver, doll, toy, pet, real or imaginary playmate, stranger, or acquaintance, or by talking alone in private moments. A child may engage you as an active listener or may "talk it out" to no one in particular. If a child invites you to listen, be an encouraging presence, empathize, and if it seems helpful, reflect aloud what you see and hear – perhaps, "It sounds like you really miss grandpa," "If you need a hug, I'm right here," "It hurt your feelings when the kids yelled 'loser' to you after the contest," or "It can be sad and scary to see your mom at the hospital looking so sick." Let the child do most of the talking and if an open-ended question is asked, invite a child to explore answers with you: "I wonder about that…," "What do you think?" or "Let's put our ideas together and try to figure it out." Of course, coming up with answers may not be as important as listening to a child's questions, because sometimes having an opportunity to "talk out" their questions may be the only answer a child requires.

- **Model healthy grieving.** Children tend to view crisis, loss, and change through the lens of their intimate caregivers' responses. What's more, many children under the age of eight or so are kinesthetic learners (who learn through touch and movement) and have a strong tendency to imitate the actions of their adult caregivers. So, it helps when care providers model healthy grieving in physical ways that a child can emulate. You might reminisce about a deceased loved one as you plant a memorial garden, let tears or laughter related to a loss flow naturally, take a needed break from your pain by watching a funny movie or going for a bike ride, or ask your child for a hug or shoulder massage when you're feeling sad or distressed about a loss. In a child's presence, you can speak about your grief or loss simply and matter-of-factly as you engage in physical gestures of grieving and healing. For example, saying to a child as you draw (or write), "Sometimes when I'm mad (or sad) about the fight I had with Aunt Rita, it helps to draw a picture (or write a poem) about it." Of course, whatever gesture you choose ought to be meaningful for you. Perhaps you find comfort or diversion by swinging on a porch swing, exercising, taking a warm bath, playing a musical instrument, looking at old family photographs to remember better times with Aunt Rita, asking Aunt Rita to set aside some time to talk, or whatever soothes your soul, gives you hope, or helps you to express your suffering and need for healing.

- **Create nurturing environments that allow a child to grieve and heal in the activities of everyday life.** Children can grieve and heal through:
  - *Physical nurture* – receiving care and caring for others (a pet, doll, sibling, ill or injured friend or family member, etc.)

- *Pleasurable or therapeutic sensory experiences*: aromatherapy (dabbing a few drops of essential oil of lavender on a favorite toy, blanket, or pillow), rocking, swinging, laughing, crying, climbing, building, playing, wrestling, star-gazing, finger painting, dancing, puppetry, etc.
- *Nature walks, gardening, and outdoor play*
- *Movement songs and verses* that engage a child in daily rhythms and care routines that are re-created after a parent's or caregiver's death, divorce, move to a new home, etc.
- *Mutually enjoyable activities to re-establish an intimate relationship after conflict or separation:* cooking, painting, hiking, biking, etc.

◈ **Offer plenty of opportunities to engage in free play.** During expanses of free play, a child engages in the grieving and healing process as an adult might accomplish through grief counseling, journaling, creating a memorial, or participating in a religious ceremony. Encourage free play by making age-appropriate toys, art tools, and crafting materials easily accessible in a designated space or cabinet where a child can get to them and store them away afterward. You might include costumes, musical instruments, building or crafting materials, puppets, dolls, crayons, colored pencils, watercolor paints, beeswax, clay or dough for modeling, etc. A child's playful meanderings can tell you a great deal about the child's grieving and healing process, even if the message is simply that the child needs a break from focusing on the pain and suffering of grief.

Although you may prefer to grieve and heal without getting your knees and elbows dirty, it's crucial to provide grieving children with the time, space, and opportunity to move with their grief – to jump, run, and saunter in and out of the mud and muck of it. So, next time you want to grieve and heal alongside a child in your life, put on your play clothes and don't worry about the mess.

Guidepost 36

We humans can play at anything – even grief. Thank heavens, play is cheaper than therapy.

Do-It-Yourself

Self-Guided Contemplations for the Child Within You

These self-guided contemplations will help you to put the healing wisdom of childhood to good use for yourself. Use these ideas as they are, revise them, or let them inspire contemplations of your own making:

- **Play With Your Grief:** When you're grieving, commit yourself to at least one daily interlude of play. Discover the people, places, and activities that allow you to engage playfully and happily in life and relationships despite your suffering. Children tend to do this naturally. In her article, "Laughter and Healing: Humor in Hospitals Treating Children," Barbara Powell writes of the playful adventures of hospitalized children who turn a hospital room into a pirate's den that is off-limits to all adults who do not know the secret password to enter. Children have a way of finding fun even in grief-striking challenges. So, when you find it difficult to play on your own, enlist a child to join you and playfully cajole, tickle, or puzzle the secret password into play right out of them.

- **Forget It to Forgive It:** My brother Roger is one of the most forgiving adults I know. When I told him so one day, he laughed and said something like, "I'm forgiving because I can't remember what happened yesterday much less years ago." My brother's desire to be connected with the people he loves always trumps his need to make people pay for the harm they do to him – a quality that children often possess. Of course, as adults, there are times it behooves us to remember so we can identify harmful interactions and unhealthy patterns of relating – to address them before taking up where we left off. Unfortunately, a problematic relationship may be beyond repair. But when a relationship and circumstances allow, there is something to be said for being so present with a loved one in the moment that you simply forget to be mad.

  Try it for a moment, a day, a week: Let your grievance go and interact with a loved one who hurt you as if the wound that was inflicted is mended. Forgiving and forgetting can sometimes be the shortest road to healing. In your forgetful reprieve, you may remember all kinds of reasons to make an effort to bind up the wounds between you. For more on forgiveness, see the "Forgiveness" resources (pages 326) in Part III, "The Healing Chest: Gathering Your Own Best Medicine."

- **Get Physical:** Explore your physical relationship with grief. For inspiration, see the portion of Contemplation 4 – "Location, Location, Location" entitled, "Your Physical Body" on pages 28-29. Once you discover how grief lives in your physical body, identify physical activities and sensory experiences that allow you to process, relieve, and release the physical hold grief has on you. For example, you can physicalize your relationship with grief through:
    - Physical exercise
    - Movement, dance, games, or play
    - Drawing, painting, clay modeling, etc.
    - Creating physical memorials and rituals of remembrance
    - Designing and creating a sacred healing space
    - Engaging in light therapy, hydrotherapy, or aromatherapy
    - Praying or meditating
    - Laughing or crying
    - Storytelling or acting
    - Seeking out physical comfort, massage, or therapeutic touch
    - Singing, playing, or listening to music

    Use whatever approach to physical healing is most effective for you that allows you to express, release, process, or tolerate your grief more fully.

- **Claim a Child's Healing Powers:** Have you ever played the "blame game" with yourself or others about where the responsibility for your childhood grief lies? Playing the blame game may help you to make sense of a grief-striking loss experience from childhood, but it may also deepen the imprint grief made upon you once upon a time. Everyone suffers childhood grief, and you are no exception to that rule – whether you suffered at your own hands, the hands of others, or due to life circumstances beyond your control.

    As you discover unresolved grief from your childhood, rather than focusing indefinitely on who is to blame, take time to contemplate how your child self was able to discover, create, and receive healing – at your own hands, the hands of others, or due to life circumstances beyond your control. Express gratitude for these healing experiences, add them to your "Healing Map" (page 111) if you created one, and create similar opportunities for healing yourself now.

A Child's Healing Chest
Approaches to Grieving and Healing in Childhood

Look through the following list of approaches to grieving and healing from Part III, "The Healing Chest: Gathering Your Own Best Medicine." Which approaches might be especially useful to revisit and heal grief from your childhood or to grieve and heal alongside a child in your care?

- Abuse Awareness & Prevention
- Addiction Prevention & Recovery
- Apologies
- Art & Creativity
- Bibliotherapy
- Breathing & Relaxation
- Caregiving
- Ceremonies & Celebrations
- Cinematherapy
- Cognitive Healing
- Community-Building
- Conscious Eldering
- Crying
- Dance
- Death Care
- Dreaming & Visitations
- Dying a Good Death
- Emotional Healing & Expressing Feelings
- Exercise, Body Awareness & Physical Release
- Forgiveness
- Funeral Planning & Memorial Services
- Grieving & Healing Perspectives
- Habit-Building
- Helping Others
- Hope
- Illness Tending
- Integrative Care & Complementary Therapies
- Laughter & Humor
- Listening
- Massage, Reiki & Comforting Touch
- Meaning-Making
- Memoir & Autobiography
- Memorials & Remembrance
- Metaphors, Objects & Symbols
- Mindfulness & Meditation
- Movement, Yoga & Posture
- Music & Sound Therapy
- Nature
- Natural Remedies for Pain Relief
- Parenting Mindfully
- Pets & Animals
- Pilgrimages, Labyrinths & Hiking Treks
- Play, Fun & Games
- Poetry
- Prayer
- Repairing Broken Relationships
- Sanctuary & Sacred Space
- Self-Injury & Recovery
- Sexual Healing & Recovery
- Sleeping
- Stories & Storytelling
- Suicide Prevention & Survivor Support
- Talking Cures
- Theater & Speech
- Trauma Recovery
- Wonder
- Writing

6 ☙ Stressing Love & Intimacy
Grieving & Healing in Youthhood

> Do I contradict myself?
> Very well then, I contradict myself,
> I am large – I contain multitudes.
>
> Walt Whitman

Bridging the Gap Between Me, Myself & I
A Youth's Natural Genius for Grieving & Healing

You might think a youth has some advantages over a child when it comes to healing grief-related suffering. After all, a youth's rational thinking is more pronounced, the emotional functioning of a youth's brain is fully developed and engaged, and a youth has been around the block a few more times, so is likely to know grief's sting and live to tell about it. But that isn't the whole picture. For one thing, youthhood is the most rapid period of human development bar infancy. Whatever other loss-related changes a youth faces, developmental changes are happening faster than a youth can say "me, myself, and I."

To become better acquainted with a youth, forget everything you know about adolescence. Better yet, call it by a different name – one that doesn't sound like a dreaded disease every teenager wants to avoid. Adolescent, pubescent, juvenile – if there is a generation gap, I imagine it's forged with words like these. Our youth deserve to be called by a name that shows some respect. What's more, to get to know a youth more genuinely, you'll need to set aside your bias-laden stereotypes – those you've acquired about youths in general and those you've built up about a youth, specifically. Youths can be wonderfully complex and contradictory human beings who cannot easily be defined by age, gender, rank, or serial number. So, when you think you have a youth all figured out, get ready to be surprised.

Youthhood – a life passage that eventually opens the door to adulthood – may begin to show itself as early as age eight or nine and can create a trail of remnants well into the twenties. Cultural stereotypes pronounce youthhood as being all about puberty, romance, sex, trouble, defiance, drugs, drinking, and fast cars. But the common denominator of youthful becoming isn't any of these. What distinguishes youthhood is self-consciousness – developing a solid awareness of oneself as a unique individual apart from others. During youthhood, we wrestle with and learn to reconcile the powers and vulnerabilities that come with that emancipation. Youthhood is that time of life when it begins to dawn on a human being that it is not enough to belong to a parent, family, or people. You cannot trek the passage into adulthood until you learn what it is to belong to yourself.

Losing a Child, Gaining a Youth

There's an oft-repeated legend roaming the streets that says no cycle of parenting is as terrifying as when magical thinking fades and a young person breaks away from childhood. The story tells of parenting powers being drained away as a youth's sense of self-awareness, independence, and sexual identity grow stronger. It doesn't happen all at once. It usually comes in waves. A child is taken out to sea bit by bit, washed away alongside a sandcastle that's built of wonder and innocence. In the child's place there gradually appears a youthful stranger who is bold enough to throw off your protective cloak of affection and run off into the spray and fog alone.

So it goes: because the youth can do it, it is done. No need to take it personally. It's part of the developmental focus of youthhood – pulling away from the "we" and into the "me." In the quest for one's self, a youth is destined to slip away from time to time and get lost from anyone and everyone the youth holds dear. Intentional or not, it's a formidable move that may leave you as a parent or elder confused to know how to bridge the distance and wondering if your loved one will return to you in the guise of some demanding youthful ogre more powerful than yourself. But even that isn't the truly scary part of nurturing and guiding a young person at this stage of life; rather, it's knowing in your marrow that the youth's autonomy comes with a price.

Youthhood drives a hard bargain. It forces a young person to trade in a bag of childhood magic for a bag of disillusionments that cause a good bit of grief-striking pain. No longer can a youth depend upon magical thinking to promise that, even in the face of tragedy, all will be well. What's more, a young person's newfound sense of independence and personal power (to make individual choices and control one's destiny) is measured. Most youths continue to be largely at the mercy of adults who, based on developmental brain function, are supposed to be better decision makers and problem solvers. So, it's common during youthhood for more constant adult supervision to be gradually replaced with adult-imposed rules that may or may not be fairly chosen or applied. As a youth's social circles expand, a youth also discovers that personal power is not divvied up equally. If a youth is left wanting, social pressures and comparisons may lead to self-criticism, compromising behaviors, social rejection, or bullying. All of this at a time of life that many adults revere as being the most virile, memorable, and carefree – as it may well be for some. But no matter how generous the blessings of youthhood or how much personal power a young person acquires, no one escapes this cycle of life unscathed.

Youthhood packs a lethal punch that lets a young person know that each and every earthly relationship the youth enjoys (sooner or later) will end because death is irreversible and spares no one. A youth's knowledge of death's inexhaustible sting may be experienced with losses that are specific and personal or perceived (however consciously or subconsciously) as an unconquerable limitation of our human condition. Either way, there's no going back to Neverland.

What's a Parent to Be?

When a child morphs into a youth, the scepter of mortality is being passed on in earnest. So, for many parents, it is not so much the youth's power but rather the youth's vulnerability that slays us. We look into a youth's disillusioned eyes to see that we are no longer regarded as gods or guardians. We are but mortals who wish we did not have to see our children bleed. We are but mortals who wish our children did not have to watch us die. But there it is: the great secret is out – more volatile than the truth about Santa Claus or the tooth fairy. We cannot always and forever take the bullet for our children. If that's not cause for sorrow, then no sorrow ever was.

Yet it is so and since it is so, be glad that the human spirit looms large enough that even mortality cannot keep us from being one another's champions. For, on the playing field of mortality, we disperse annihilation, fear, and loneliness by way of compassion, courage, and companionship. When the enchantment of childhood fades, such is the new magic. On that playing field, we parents and elders are no longer regarded as all-powerful gods or ever-present guardians, but we can still serve as valued players, coaches, and referees – all three. We can be worthy role models, vibrant encouragers, and thoughtful rule keepers. Although we cannot save a youth at every turn from the jaws of harm, at least we can be someone they can depend upon. When it comes to grieving and healing, be sure a youth can depend on you to acknowledge, ease, tolerate, and heal your own grief-related suffering, support the youth's efforts to do the same, and collaborate to find ways to grieve and heal alone and together that are respectful and fair to everyone.

Of course, there are situations that make such efforts appear meaningless: Perhaps a youth died or is in a coma and unable to communicate with you, or perhaps you are estranged from one another due to custody battles, incarceration, conflict, hospitalization, or military service. If so, your self-healing becomes paramount. Despite a profound loss of intimacy, you may continue to negotiate and foster a loving relationship with a youth, even if you're able to do so in spirit only. Your self-healing can be an act of love that communicates your belief that life is still worth living despite profound grief-striking losses. If there is any saving to be done for our youth, this is it: We may spare them from piling our sorrows atop their own.

Little Self in a Big World

A youth's natural bent toward self-absorption may discourage you from inviting a youth to grieve and heal alongside you, especially when you're absorbed with your own suffering. As you learn to navigate around a youth's egoism, remember that youthful self-centeredness is not necessarily a liability. Self-centeredness, or centering on oneself, is part of a youth's job description. Self-awareness and self-definition are the meat and potatoes (or the tofu and greens, as you would have it) of a youth's development. Thankfully, that's not all, because self-awareness is not achieved by any of us solo. "Me" is known in relation to "you," "myself" to "yourself," and "I" (knowing oneself as an individual who is singularly complete) is known in contrast to an evolving perception of everyone and everything that exists – from a youth's widening social circles to contemplating the farthest reaches of the cosmos.

Curiosities about the larger world and what it means to live as a minuscule part of an immense universe may inspire mind-numbing questions for a youth (that even we adults and elders find difficult to unravel). If a youth can't get their words around these questions, it doesn't mean the questions don't exist; they may be rumbling around in a youth's subconscious, sensed more than spoken:

- How do I become my own person when I am so connected with another that separation (by death, conflict, rejection, or distance) seems unbearable?
- Where is the fine line between self-determination and interdependence that will ensure my survival, health, and well-being?
- Why should I assert personal power to impact life and relationships when others (intimates, peers, authorities, etc.) can negate my efforts instantaneously?
- Who am I as an inhabitant of planet earth – one little human among billions residing with every creature under the sun in a gargantuan universe that may contain other planets with remarkable life forms I can only imagine?

How do you suppose such ponderings might affect a youth's self-identity and relationships with others?

The wild terrain of youthhood is covered in land mines that can bury us in existential crises before we know the meaning of the term. When such massive philosophical riddles pound at the door of a youth's consciousness, they may cause anxiety, loneliness, confusion, and grief. But they may also serve to fuel a youth's soulful mission – to know and belong to oneself alone while seeking acceptance and belonging with others who give and receive encouragement, love, and support.

What's a Parent to Do?

When a child strides into youthhood, parents are told to let go and let go and let go. But we may resist by hanging on and on and on, so that if a land mine of loss is triggered, we can be one of the first responders. The cultural mandate for parents and elders to "cut the apron strings" when childhood fades and youthhood dawns for a young person is misleading. If we adults respect their needs for a measure of privacy, youths seldom require more solitude and aloneness than they can provide for themselves. A youth needs your loving attention and support every bit as much as a child, but differently. As a youth learns to live increasingly apart from you – whether retreating into the youth's private inner life, becoming more involved in school or work obligations, seeking intimacy outside your family circle, or due to a geographical move – parenting a youth often requires you to deliver support and affection from a distance. This realization may cause parental panic, because loving a youth from a distance is a learned skill most of us gain only from on-the-job training.

During youthhood, a recurring nightmare of anxious parents screams forth of the missing child – lost at the hands of evildoers or a mighty twist of fate. But a youth can be lost to troubles that are more subtle and silent. While abductions, fatal violence, and accidents happen, a youth in our 21st-century Western culture is more likely to be lost to depression, eating disorders, sexual exploits, mental illness, nursing the wounds of social rejection, drug or alcohol abuse, addictions to electronic media or pornography, and the list goes on. Indeed, a youth might be lost to trouble while standing right under your nose. So, a parent's nightmarish anxieties are justifiable. But the irony of such well-meaning concerns is that fixating on the myriad ways a youth can be lost to us is simply one more way to lose them. Worry doesn't bridge the distance or bring our children back to us, nor does regret. Worry and regret are diversions from seeking and finding a youth in the only place a lost youth can return to you – in the acceptance and belonging of relationship in the here and now.

Fortunately, the voyage of self-discovery requires intimacy as much as independence, and a youth's need for solitude and companionship outside the family circle doesn't negate the profound sense of acceptance and belonging a parent and family can provide. So, whenever a youth disappears, everyone who is anyone to the youth is free to join in the search party. As Robert Brault once wrote, "Sometimes it's worth getting lost to see who will come looking for us." It's also part of our job as parents and elders – to make that search long and often, and not to give up, not ever.

Guidepost 37

Sometimes searching for yourself takes a village.

Love, Love Me Do
Lamenting in Youthhood

When a child steps into youthhood there is plenty to lose. The question is, what losses is a youth likely to find distressing enough to lament – whether privately or in the presence of others? Answers to this question are as varied as there are youths who ever were, are, or will be. But even with vast differences in what is lost and lamented among youths, there is a recurring theme of grief-related pain that commonly strikes humans who are newly self-aware. The Greek myth of Echo and Narcissus offers insight:

Narcissus and Echo were each known for their incredible beauty. Yet, each had a fatal flaw. Echo was a mountain nymph who was notorious for mindless chatter. One too many times, she used her talk as a diversion to detain a rageful goddess whose god was out philandering among the nymphs. Echo's divine punishment for tampering was to have her willful voice taken from her, so she could only repeat the trails of speech uttered by others.

Narcissus was a youth whose beauty so set him apart that countless many desired the youth and sought his affection. But he spurned every admirer, every would-be paramour, every one. When one among the rejected entreated the deities to make Narcissus fall in love with someone who would never love him back, Narcissus was made to fall in love with his reflection. He happened upon it at the side of a pond one day in the forest where he was separated from his hunting companions. Narcissus became obsessed, desiring nothing more than for the gorgeous youth in his reflection to love him back. As he gazed into the pool, Echo happened upon Narcissus and she, too, fell incurably in love. But she had no voice to speak, so she hid out of sight.

As Narcissus gazed upon his image, at first, it appeared to him that the youth in the pool's reflection returned every nuance of his love. When Narcissus spoke of his admiration and desire for the youth (none other than himself), the hidden Echo repeated his vows of affection. Hearing this, Narcissus was overcome with passion and his hopes were fueled. But when

Echo jumped out from hiding to embrace the ravishing youth, Narcissus was appalled. This creature before him was not at all the one to whom he had professed his love! In his surprise and frustration, Narcissus yelled at Echo, "I would rather die than give myself to you!"

Despite Narcissus's sudden awakening to romantic desire, the youth's consuming love for himself could not be shared by two. In the end, each of the would-be lovers, Echo and Narcissus, pined away until their deaths. It is said that only Echo's voice and this story of warning was left behind.

From ancient times, this myth has been told as a cautionary tale: *Too much self-love can kill you with pain and loneliness!* But the story deserves a closer look and Narcissus (if ever such a youth lived and breathed) deserves to be cut some slack; because for Narcissus, too much self-love isn't the problem. As the story goes, Narcissus isn't narcissistic until he is punished, and for what – his devotion to his virginity and his unrelenting self-determination. Take another look at the story – Narcissus isn't some arrogant bastard who has no friends. Before the pond incident, Narcissus is out hunting with his buddies. It is the other self-absorbed youth who conjures the whole ordeal – the one who is steaming mad because Narcissus won't hook up. Yet, we have no iconic word for this self-serving avenger.

And what of Echo's part in the story? In contrast to Narcissus, Echo gives herself freely without ever being asked. She wants only what Narcissus wants and speaks only the words Narcissus speaks. Although she has no willful voice to make her intentions clear to Narcissus, Echo is willing to throw herself before the beautiful boy, hoping it will be enough to inspire his attention and affection. But she too becomes one of a long list of the rejected. Ironically, it's a list that ultimately includes Narcissus, who inflicts the pain of rejection on himself.

Look again at the story and you'll see not one tormented youth, but three (if nymphs count). All three, so intent to have Narcissus in body, heart, and mind that they can't see past their blazing desire. But each one is rejected, rejected, rejected. Indeed, it is rejection rather than self-love that spurs one of the three to conjure harm against another who will not be had, and rejection that spurs the other two to conjure harm against themselves for being denied the person they imagine they cannot live without. In the end, Echo and Narcissus suffer the selfsame fate: being hopelessly obsessed with and rejected by someone who will never love them back. From the opposing cliffs of self-absorption and self-abandonment, Narcissus and Echo jump simultaneously to their slow and painful deaths. So, the story warns that seeking love and companionship by way of either extreme can be fatal. But this is not the only moral of the story.

More cryptically, the myth of Echo and Narcissus points to the psychological death that accompanies youthful self-consciousness, whispering itself into a youth's soul like a powerfully crippling affirmation: "I am alone with myself." While this knowledge empowers a youth to stand apart as one, it also binds the youth to be forever separate from all others. In such a state, which is worse, being rejected by someone you adore or being divided against yourself?

One of the great developmental tasks of youthhood is learning to act upon intense desires for relationship with another without dishonoring yourself or losing yourself in the exchange. It's a tall order. At once, a youth is obliged to create and recreate a sense of self that the youth can accept, respect, and love, and must also forge a sense of self that others with whom a youth seeks belonging can accept, respect, and love.

We humans are social creatures, so without companionship, there is no such thing as a whole human being. But neither does companionship, in itself, make each of us complete. The holy grail of youthful camaraderie involves a search for relationships in which loving attention can be lavishly shared among intimates without diminishing a youth's efforts to also know and love oneself alone. Although such loving camaraderie may one day be found in the arms of a lover, a youth may also seek it in platonic relationships with friends and family members. Indeed, in a less fateful world than that of which the Greeks told, Echo and Narcissus might have pursued a different sort of companionship that didn't involve unrequited sexual passion or their untimely physical deaths. However, this woeful tale speaks of harboring desire for another that is unquenchable, yet unreciprocated. For a youth, there is no more foolproof recipe for unending grief.

Have you seen it – a youth so enamored with another that the youth cannot think, speak, or dream of anything else? The obsessed youth may seek companionship with a sense of life or death urgency – even sacrificing self-knowledge or self-identity, or risking health and well-being for the cause. When a youth so consumed is met with rejection, the blow can be experienced as a death worse than death. As the story goes, even Narcissus (the epitome of the Big Man on Campus) was not immune to rejection's venom. Has a youth ever lived that did not experience some form of personal rejection? Whether the biting blow is dealt from without or within, a youth so grieved has good reason to be self-absorbed and overly sensitive to criticism and disapproval. A youth's self-identity is at stake, and that's all a youth has to barter for love and companionship – in the best of times, the worst of times, and every moment between.

The Curse of Self-Scrutiny & Not Measuring Up

As any self-aware youth can tell you, there is a vast difference between self-love and the relentless self-scrutiny that usually hounds a person during youthhood. Youths spend a great deal of time thinking about themselves and, more pointedly, thinking about what others think of them – at least, the people from whom the youth seeks love, respect, advantage, or admiration. Generally, youths don't ruminate on themselves and the perceptions of others because they enjoy being perpetually self-centered. It can be a real burden caring so much about what everyone else thinks of you, but youths seem to have little choice. This is just how the youthful brain works.

Do you remember as a youth ever having a distinct feeling that you were being watched and scrutinized – even when there was no one else present? If so, you weren't being paranoid. There's a simple biological reason for it: a youth's brain is overly sensitive to the hormone, oxytocin. Although oxytocin is generally a "bonding" hormone, it causes a youth to feel self-conscious. So, if a youth suddenly becomes more introverted, shy, secretive, distant, or withdrawn, it may be that the youth is seeking a greater sense of privacy to escape this phenomenon of always being watched.

The youth who spends hours absorbed in self-centered thoughts and feelings may find (as Narcissus did) that self-perceptions come charging at one another like warriors vying for the throne of a youth's self-identity – causing a youth to be enamored and appalled by their reflection at once. So, it was for Narcissus and, in a roundabout way, for Echo, who served as a broken mirror to the tormented youth.

What makes the quest for approval and acceptance especially problematic during youthhood is that the intense emotional reactions youths experience toward themselves and others often generate an attitude of social judgmentalism. Think about it: how much of your time and energy during youthhood was focused on judging who was worthy or unworthy of affection and interest, who was ugly or beautiful, sexy or not, smart or stupid, good or evil, kind or cruel, admirable or inferior? Then, consider how keen you were to attract to you those who were considered (by yourself or others) to be worthy, interesting, beautiful, sexy, smart, good, kind, or admirable, and how much more attractive and appealing you suddenly became (to yourself or others) when you received attention or affection from someone perceived to be so.

Intense emotions of attraction and aversion among peers can cause a youth to feel as if their social destiny is out of their control – akin to the curse that Narcissus and Echo were said to have endured. Overt and subtle messages of rejection, disapproval or not measuring up, or messages of chronic self-criticism can feed on a youth's self-perceptions and become an excruciating source of grief. The youth may respond to their grief by turning feelings of rejection or self-loathing out toward others in acts of violence or bullying, or become angry, defensive, uncaring, or rebellious. The grief of rejection or self-loathing turned inward may present itself as social awkwardness, perfectionism, depression, drug or alcohol abuse, media addictions, eating disorders, or self-harming behaviors. No matter in whose direction it's turned, such unacknowledged grief can be lethal.

The paradoxical developmental challenge of youthhood is learning to live with yourself as you are and as you desire to be, at the same time you're learning to live in community with others as you are and as others desire for you to be. Reconciling these contrasting urges for individual freedom and social belonging can be a challenge. So, one of the trickiest riddles that young people must solve for themselves on their way to adulthood is this: *How far can I venture into solitude to discover myself without being hounded by loneliness, and how far can I venture into a relationship with another (or many others) without losing the integrity of myself?*

The Bigger Picture: Searching for the Whole Self

Youthful maturity hinges on the knowledge that relational wholeness cannot be found in the arms of another, nor within the private world in which you are your own universe. A genuine sense of relational completeness requires both.

A pair of picture books written by Shel Silverstein – *The Missing Piece* and *The Missing Piece Meets the Big O* – provide a humorous perspective of the human pursuit for relational wholeness that is not nearly as fatalistic as the myth of Echo and Narcissus. A synopsis of Silverstein's two-part series (that is playfully written and sketched out as simple line drawings) goes something like this:

In *The Missing Piece*, a circular creature realizes that it is missing a wedge of itself and it is not happy. So, it goes off looking for the piece of itself that is missing. Despite the unhappy search, as the creature rolls along it begins to sing a happy song. Because it is missing a piece, it cannot move swiftly, so has time to talk to a worm or smell a flower as it rolls slowly along.

The creature's quest for its missing piece brings it into contact with all kinds of pieces – some that are unwilling to fill the creature's empty space, others that are too big or too small, too sharp or not the right shape at all. Some pieces fit rather nicely but are accidentally let go or held too tightly and shattered. At long last, a piece is found that fills the creature's empty space perfectly and the two roll along blissfully for a while. But soon the creature realizes that carrying the corresponding missing piece that completes its circular shape makes it difficult to sing or to meander along slowly enough to talk to a worm or smell a flower. So, eventually, the creature lets go of the missing piece and rolls off perfectly happy in its imperfection.

That isn't the end of the story. In *The Missing Piece Meets the Big O*, the missing piece sits waiting for someone who has an empty space to match it, someone who can fit the missing piece and take it along somewhere. But as the missing piece searches for its companion, there is a downside to every possible pairing. At long last, the Big O (who has no missing piece) comes along and inspires the little creature to find wholeness within itself. Gradually, the missing piece learns to flop its wedge-like body over and over again until it smooths its rough edges and changes into a circle of its own. In the end, the Big O and the missing piece (who is now a smaller O) roll along side by side.

Silverstein's missing piece metaphor is a rousing good description of a youth's soulful journey to relational wholeness. But not every youth has such an easy go of it. When cherished parts of yourself go missing or when you feel like a misfit piece who doesn't fit in anywhere, relational wholeness may seem like a long-ago or faraway dream. Feelings of incompleteness can torment a youth, whether these feelings are due to unrequited love, the death of a loved one, a romantic breakup, divorce or family conflict, illness, injury, disapproval, rejection, abuse, depression, loneliness, existential anxieties and fears, or unrealized hopes and dreams. Feelings of incompleteness can badger a youth even if what the youth is missing is nothing less than perfection itself.

The Selfie Generation

Just as ancient Greeks criticized youths in their day, the present generation is criticized for being the most narcissistic generation ever. Selfies are the new greeting card and a youth's attempts at social networking often read like a litany of self-obsession – "Look at me! See what I look like now, see what I'm eating, see where I'm going, see what I'm feeling, thinking, doing, see who is with me now. . ." But spending time collecting "friends" online can be a ploy to fill the hole where real live companions ought to be. If you read between the lines, "incomplete," "imperfect," "lonely," and "isolated" may be written there in disappearing ink. Social networking is just another way of searching for your Missing Piece (or Big O as the case may be).

Rather than harp on a youth for thinking too much of themselves, adults and elders do well to capitalize on youthful self-absorption and encourage youths to use their self-focused tendencies to practice self-care in good times and bad. Learning to care for yourself is a first step to learn to care successfully for others – particularly during interludes of grief. For one thing, when a grieving youth engages in self-care, it frees the youth's caregivers from having to provide the youth's care in full.

Youthful independence gained through self-sufficiency is vastly more useful to a youth than acquiring a superficial set of "adultish" rights and responsibilities that most youths from middle and upper-income families in the U.S. have come to expect – gaining an arsenal of material possessions, driving and owning a car, attending college, making one's own choices about electronic media, curfews, nutrition, cell phone use, etc. These freedoms are often granted to young people in our culture without a youth putting forth concerted effort to earn these rights and responsibilities or being guided to consider the consequences of personal choices regarding them. Ideally, when a youth earns these freedoms and is asked to self-evaluate in relationship to them, a youth not only gains needed confidence to provide care and be responsible for oneself but also develops an ability to observe and care for the interpersonal and social needs of others.

There is no time that self-care skills are more vital to a youth than when the youth is lamenting a grief-striking loss. Unfortunately, our human curriculum of compassion often skips over self-compassion and self-respect (believing them to be narcissistic) and emphasizes compassion and respect for others. Despite these well-intended lessons to help make a human more humane, overemphasizing care for others to the neglect of self-care can derail a youth's journey toward self-love and self-acceptance.

There is nothing in a grieving youth's life that can substitute for a sense of relational wholeness and compatibility within oneself – not a good family or good friends, good health or good grades, athletic or artistic skills and achievements, adventures in risk-taking or pleasure-seeking, money or material possessions, sexual intimacy, physical beauty or strength, or even love and admiration given and received with a romantic partner. Surely, any of these can positively enhance a youth's self-esteem; however, personal wholeness and relational compatibility are qualities a youth must ultimately negotiate within the privacy of one's own being.

In the hidden contours of self-awareness, self-respect, and self-compassion, blows of grief can be softened, even (and especially) when one feels utterly alone. If parents and caregivers gauged our words and gestures toward a youth by the impact they have in helping a youth to love, know, and belong to oneself, then even when no one else is there for a youth (or a youth prefers to be alone with personal grief), they will already be well-versed in loving and supporting their self. It's called self-reliance and there's nothing narcissistic about it.

Guidepost 38

When you can be a friend to yourself, there's no such thing as lonely.

The Power to Change for Good
Heartening in Youthhood

It's Thanksgiving and my fifteen-year-old niece, Marin, sits with friends and family, holding hands around the dinner table. It's her turn to verbalize what she's thankful for from the year past – a year that included her 26-year-old brother Kyle's death. At the tail end of Kyle's winter holiday break from college, Marin and her dad were devastated to discover Kyle's body, lying lifeless on the bathroom floor of their home. The police told them later that Kyle died from a bad batch of heroin. No one close to Kyle saw it coming. The last any of his family members knew, he had been clean for over four years.

Ten months after Kyle's death, here we are, gathering to celebrate family and friends – our Thanksgiving round is nearly complete. A tender veil of compassion settles over us as we hold hands around the table. Then, Marin tells us simply that the year past held many new firsts for her, some good and some bad, but that every one of them helped her to grow. We know she is right. As awful and shocking as Kyle's death was for her, the tragedy inspired an unmistakably positive change in Marin. It was obvious to the rest of us from the day of Kyle's funeral. That day, after the memory-sharing portion of the funeral service ended, a sad-eyed Marin, known for her shy reticence, walked unbidden to the speaker's podium. Her mom and dad, who were sitting on either side of her in the front row, caught sideways glances at one another, silently expressing their awed and pleased surprise at Marin's bold move.

Before hundreds of mourners and without a glitch or a catch in her throat, Marin spoke of her love for Kyle. She admitted that if it hadn't been for so many (among the multitude of Kyle's friends) telling her one after another over the past few days, how much she meant to Kyle, how much he loved her and talked about her, she wouldn't have realized just how greatly he loved her back. She said it with a giggle and a smile that did not negate her sorrow, yet did profess her joy and love in the knowing. It was obvious that, to Marin, the knowledge of the profound love her brother harbored for her was a heartwarming salve that was helping her to negotiate the pain and distress of her loss. She shared it with us as if it might warm a bit of the hurt away from our hearts, too.

As surprising and inspiring as Marin's transformation was to those of us who love and admire her, such personal growth after loss is more common than you might think. Recent studies indicate that many youths perceive positive changes in themselves after a traumatic loss. Whether or not a youth is able or willing to articulate these changes to themselves or others in the course of everyday life (as Marin did), at least in research surveys and interviews, many youths view themselves as being stronger, wiser, more compassionate, and capable than they were before a grief-striking loss took place. Personal growth that shines with an "improved self" after a loss experience can be a potent source of heartening, particularly during youthhood when self-esteem and self-compassion are vital to a youth's healthy development.

The concept of human beings experiencing personal growth after a traumatic loss is an ancient concept that is foundational to many religious teachings and spiritual perspectives. However, the term Post-traumatic Growth (PTG) is one brought to life by psychologists Richard Tedeschi and Lawrence Calhoun, who have been researching and striving to define this phenomenon since the 1970s. In their article, "Posttraumatic Growth: Conceptual Foundations and Empirical Evidence" (2004), PTG is described as "positive psychological change experienced as a result of the struggle with highly challenging life circumstances." It's quite a broad definition; so, it may come in a variety of shapes and sizes. One way it came to Marin was through the realization that her brother loved her more than she knew. Somehow that love gave her the uncharacteristic and unapologetic confidence to voice the positive changes that had taken place in her and her relationships with others in the aftermath of her brother's death.

Somewhere along grief's bumpy road, a youth is likely to become privy to the knowledge that grief-striking loss can change a person for good. As a youth becomes more familiar with good things that arise out of a loss experience, the youth may learn to utilize heartening thoughts, feelings, and behaviors as a positive healing force. No doubt, there is something victorious, something crisp and clean about looking grief in the eye and single-handedly changing the substance of something as formidable as suffering. When a youth does so for oneself, such character qualities as resilience and self-confidence are born. When a youth does so for others, the act smacks of heroism, as the following family story illustrates.

Rejecting Rejection: Mean Girls Revisited

The summer before our children were going into fifth and seventh grades, Andrew and I moved our family to a small town in Wisconsin – thirty minutes northeast of Madison where Andrew was to attend the University of Wisconsin. It was our first move outside a large city, so we weren't prepared for the social culture of the town that other transplants told us, "can make you feel like an outsider for a good two years – if you're lucky." Despite the warning, many made us feel welcome right away, but the seventh-grade girls weren't having any of it. They worked overtime to ensure that Morgan knew she wasn't one of them and proceeded to make her life miserable.

Early in the school year, Morgan let one of the seventh-grade boys walk her home after school. That evening, she received an anonymous phone call from a group of girls who told her that if she did it again, they would beat her to a pulp. She was ostracized and gossiped about by classmates during the school day and shunned by teammates as a member of the seventh-grade girls basketball team. Although we kept a pulse on the situation and made sure Morgan wasn't vulnerable to the girls' threats, Morgan asked Andrew and me not to speak with her teachers or principal about the girls' behavior. She was determined to deal with it herself.

Morgan displayed strength and confidence in public, choosing not to let others see her inner pain, but occasionally at home, she crumbled into my arms and sobbed of her suffering. As she came to grips with the cruelty of her female classmates, she decided not to allow the rejection of these peers to define her world. Morgan methodically identified girls in the grades above and below her own to befriend. As an accomplished track and cross-country runner, she found friends and mentors in some of the high school athletes who became her after-school and weekend running partners. She continued to enjoy time with our family and her passions for running, acting, singing, and Irish dance.

Again and again, Morgan was victorious in her efforts to live happily despite her pain. Although she acknowledged the difficulties she faced, she told me more than once that something valuable was coming from it. She spoke of her deepening compassion for others, despite her firsthand experience with the dark side of human nature. She tried her best not to take it personally. Only it was personal. There was no getting around it. Rejection hurts – especially when you're the new girl in town.

In the fall of Morgan's eighth-grade year, the high school cross-country coach invited her to train with the high school team. A few weeks after practice started, Morgan received an anonymous hate letter in the mail. This time, the injury came from a parent of one of the high school athletes who told her that she should "go back to where she came from," that she wasn't welcome to train with the high school team, that her presence made others uncomfortable and insecure, and that acting like she was better than her middle school teammates was a sure recipe for further rejection. The letter also criticized me, as her mother, for not having the sense to keep Morgan in her place.

Morgan held on to the letter for a day before showing it to Andrew and me. When she came to us with the letter in hand, before she let us read it, she made us promise that we would allow her to be the one to take care of the situation. She said she would talk with the cross-country coaches about it – which she did (and they handled it beautifully). But that day, as we read the hateful letter for the first time, it took a massive amount of self-control to check our mounting anger.

The next day, I was on my way out the door to speak at a parenting conference in California. Before I left, I asked Morgan to read a quote from the book *Return to Love* by Marianne Williamson that was displayed on our bathroom wall. A portion of the passage reads:

> "It is our light, not our darkness that most frightens us. We ask ourselves, who am I to be brilliant, gorgeous, talented, and fabulous? Actually, who are you not to be? . . . Your playing small does not serve the world . . ."

I asked Morgan to memorize the entire passage as a mantra of self-encouragement. A few days later, we talked on the phone and Morgan told me proudly, "I did it, Mom! I know the whole thing by heart." To this day, Morgan regards these words as a sacred text, an old friend who saw her through a difficult time.

I didn't expect any greater resolution than that – Morgan using every scrap of courage and intelligence to face rejection in ways that increased her confidence and forged compassionate, meaningful relationships with others. So, it was a welcome surprise, toward the end of Morgan's eighth-grade year, when there was an unexpected turn of events. One of Morgan's peers who had participated in the cruel ploy against her, asked if it would be all right with Morgan for her to write her eighth-grade thesis paper (a required final English project) about the pact that she and the other eighth-grade girls made – to ostracize Morgan from the time she arrived in their little town.

According to her classmate's thesis paper (which she was required to present orally to the class as all the eighth graders were), at the beginning of seventh grade, several of Morgan's female classmates decided that she was too pretty. They were afraid that Morgan would turn all the boys' heads. This repentant classmate regretted taking part in the scheme, so she built her thesis paper around making a formal, public apology to Morgan. Talk about heroism. I was ready to give the girl a medal of honor. But the English teacher saw it differently. At the end-of-the-year awards assembly, he awarded Morgan his annual honor to the eighth grader who, in his estimation, displayed the greatest character and was an exemplary human being.

No doubt, the apology from her classmate and the award from an English teacher she admired deepened Morgan's sense of accomplishment in facing her grief with courage and grace. But it was also a dramatic victory for the singular classmate who admitted that she was as guilty as anyone in the wrong that had been done to Morgan. This classmate made her best attempt to change the substance of Morgan's suffering, just as she had watched Morgan do for herself day after day for almost two years. In mustering the courage and humility to make her valiant apology, the classmate gained something of great value for herself – nothing less than the integrity and sense of humanity she lost by participating in the hurtful scheme. That's better than a medal.

Personal growth is only one source of heartening that a youth might discover amid grief-related suffering. Other heartening pleasures can blossom from the dark and fertile earth of painful loss during youthhood – sweet remembrances, camaraderie, laughter, celebration. But, ultimately, the most heartening of all may be knowing that grief can coax you to become more compassionate, more humane. When you are, you take another step toward maturity and become privy to the knowledge that you need never be alone in your suffering again.

Guidepost 39

The grieving heart carves out a deep well of compassion. It's up to you to fill the bucket, do the hauling and be sure to take a dipperful of kindness for yourself.

Give Me a Break
Tempering in Youthhood

There's an old philosophical riddle: "If a tree falls in the forest and no one is around to hear it, does it still make a sound?" Here's another stumper: "If a youth grieves and no one knows it, does it still hurt?"

Parents and elders may pride ourselves on being eagle-eye observers and expert mind readers when it comes to knowing our children and grandchildren, but even those who know a youth longest and best may not catch wind of a youth's grief-related suffering. When they have a mind to, youths can bottle up their feelings and hide their pain even from those they love best. They don't do it to be cruel. Hiding grief may help a youth to seek shelter from their suffering, avoid others' attempts to tamper with their grieving responses, or dodge questions that pry into thoughts and feelings a youth imagines may be hurtful or unacceptable to those they love, respect, or admire. Despite your compassionate concern, a grieving youth might even convince you that nothing is amiss. So, while you're tending to the loudest trouble, you may not hear the silent grief that storms a youth behind your back.

When suffering is intense, a youth's unexpressed grief may cause inner turbulence that others don't detect until it's too late. Tragically, a youth might succumb to depression, run away, overdose on drugs or alcohol, engage in self-destructive or criminal behaviors, or die by suicide without loved ones realizing that there is a problem. If this is the case with a youth you love, faulting yourself or others mercilessly for failing to see it coming only adds insult to injury. Know this: Youths who are learning to "go it alone" can be expert actors when it comes to protecting their privacy. It isn't anyone's fault. Hiding private thoughts and feelings from others is what youths are built to do, and some learn to do it more completely than others.

In and of itself, a youth's genius for seeking diversion from grief isn't a bad thing; it's what tempering is all about. We all need to shelter ourselves from grief-related suffering now and then. However, there's a huge difference between holing up with grief and tempering the pain and distress of it. When a youth is keen at hiding grief, it may be impossible to tell these two grieving responses apart. With your own grief, the difference is unmistakable because private grief can still hurt like hell no matter how stiff you hold your upper lip. When you temper grief, you experience an easing of pain, disheartenment, and distress. Tempering may cause your grief to disappear altogether – for a moment, an hour, or an afternoon.

The good news is that tempering responses that help a grieving youth to ease, tolerate, and heal the sting of grief can be learned. The more difficult challenge is unlearning tempering responses that intensify the ache of grief or cause a pileup of hurtful losses – either immediately or in the long run. Attempting to keep emotional suffering in the dark indefinitely is like pouring water on a grease fire; it will only add fuel to the flame – a critical life lesson every grieving youth deserves to learn.

Scaling the Hidden Depths of Suffering

As an adult, my daughter Morgan tempers her grief like a pro. That's because she spent most of her youth learning to tell the difference between tempering responses that hurt and need to be unlearned, and tempering responses that heal and can be fostered into habits that serve as a salve for suffering.

Morgan is an artist (actor, singer, and writer) who isn't afraid to dig deep into the dark of grief to transform it. Since she was eight, she showed remarkable ability to reflect on human suffering without allowing it to rob her of joy and her love of life, but there have definitely been some rough patches.

Middle school rejection was only one of a pile of heart-wrenching losses Morgan suffered in her youth. Some of her losses were grief-striking developmental changes and mind-numbing existential crises. Others were physical and social losses that were more tangible. For Morgan, the losses that couldn't be seen or heard (and for the most part went unnoticed by others) were the most difficult of all to reconcile.

She can laugh about it now, but when the magic of childhood faded, it shook her world. She was devastated when she realized that Christmas stockings were not filled the world over by Santa's own hands and that she would never be able to fly like Peter Pan. Not so laughable still was her realization of death's inexhaustible sting. As a youth, integrating the far-reaching realities of death, she wondered how life would ever be worth living again. Although she seldom let on to others, the recurring question that pounded her young heart was a doozie, "If Neverland is only a fantasy and if everyone who is anyone to me is going to die anyway, what's the point?"

Even though Morgan recalls her life as a child and youth as pert near idyllic, her fear of dreadful losses (that included traumatic injury and death of her loved ones) hounded her. She had recurrent nightmares of having to save us all. These fears couldn't be blamed on too much television, as TV shows and movies were limited at our house and chosen with the utmost care. What's more, Morgan enjoyed a home and family where love was found in plenty. Back then, there were expanses of green space and time to play with her little sister, Willa, who brought a certain evenness and groundedness to Morgan's life. Willa was the kind of child and youth who took life as it came and was afraid of almost nothing (bar having to take her daily nap before she started grade school). The two conjured many happy childhood adventures together.

As with most families raising children, there were challenges and conflicts to attend, but in Morgan's estimation, life was good. The irony of it is that when life is that good, there is much to lose. So, when Morgan experienced the disillusionments that come to all children as they turn toward the years of their youth, she felt that she was brought up short and that somehow childhood had been a beautifully cruel joke. Although her youthful awareness told her otherwise, she couldn't imagine a world without magic or without the presence of any of the people or pets she adored.

Unbeknownst to anyone outside our immediate family circle and sometimes even hidden from the three of us who she loved best, Morgan grieved like a champion when there was seemingly nothing much to grieve. Except, in truth, there was plenty – nothing short of the losses of childhood invincibility and belief. To Morgan, perhaps the most lethal loss of all was the loss of her childish ability to live in the momentary present that knows nothing of losses yet to come.

As a youth, Morgan grieved deeply even before she had obvious reason to do so. She was familiar with grief's sting before she experienced the pain of social rejection in middle school or the deaths of cherished pets. Grief harangued Morgan's feelings and thoughts even before her friend and running partner, Dana, suddenly died of viral encephalitis (just after Morgan's fourteenth birthday) and before she succumbed to an overuse injury from years of Irish dance that forced her to give up her passion for track and field forever – a sport that could fly her away from all things scary or difficult. Morgan's grief was a heavy burden to her even before she watched her beloved Grandpa Chuck wither away from cancer, or before she experienced the murder of her larger-than-life Grandpa Jim and the resulting decade of court battles that punctuated a good portion of Morgan's youth.

As Morgan's pile of losses grew, her keen awareness of suffering could have done her in. Fortunately, she learned not to throw water on the grease fires of her grief. She learned to distract herself from her suffering and make good use of tempering responses that brought relief and release from her pain.

Putting a Lid on the Grief Fire

Whether consciously or unconsciously, the question that lives within a grieving youth's thoughts and behaviors is, *"What can I think or do to convince myself there is more to life than the parts of me that grief has lit on fire?"* Of course, the question can only be answered rightfully by the one who asks it.

Fortunately, alongside Morgan's "what's the point" question she asked herself the "what can I do or think" question in equal portion. She learned to answer both questions in ways that tempered her grief and she learned that sometimes the only answer that could save her was to forget that the questions existed at all.

Morgan tells me that her lowest point came when she was working and living by herself in Boston at the age of twenty. She was struggling with suicidal thoughts, wondering what it might be like to put herself out of her misery, when a simple change in the way she thought about her life became one of the most effective tempering techniques she discovered. She said that whenever she found herself wanting to leave this life behind, she would distract herself from the thought by clearly imagining her dad and me so happy together before she was born, hoping for her and awaiting her presence here with us. She envisioned herself, again and again, as our dream. So that in those dark times, when life seemed pointless, Morgan found her life purpose simply by continuing to fulfill our dream of a life with her in it.

As Morgan discovered other ways to temper the pain, disheartenment, and distress of her grief, she learned to tell the difference between tempering responses that ease and heal her pain progressively, and those that cause addictive behaviors that can lead to real trouble. She stopped drinking socially and stayed away from drugs, knowing our family history (on both sides) included alcoholism and drug abuse. But she sought solace in more subtle and culturally-accepted addictions, such as binge eating and excessive use of electronic media. She discovered firsthand that while these tempering approaches brought immediate diversion and comfort, the benefits were fleeting and caused her greater suffering in the long run. She recognized striking similarities between her addictive behaviors and the alcohol and drug-related addictions of several of her extended family members. So, as Morgan edged her way toward adulthood, she dedicated herself to untangling the addictive mess that plagued her thinking patterns and compromised her health and well-being. She admitted to her loved ones that her recovery was an imperative priority.

Morgan read recovery books, talked to counselors and eating disorder experts, and mostly journaled her way into insights that freed her from the unhealthy habits and thinking patterns, fatalism, depression, and self-criticism that created fertile ground for her addictive thoughts and behaviors. Ironically, in addition to facing what had to be faced for Morgan to change, she ultimately discovered that a good portion of her recovery came by finding ways to divert herself even from her intense efforts of recovery.

There were times that Morgan leaned heavily on her dad and me to help her sort out the nuances of her pain and the tempering behaviors that serve her best. At a crucial point, she asked to return home and engage in a year of recovery away from the daily grind of job responsibilities and peripheral social distractions. Andrew and I were happy to offer support and grateful that Morgan was willing to ask for it. We also reaped unexpected benefits as Morgan's daily presence in our home helped us to identify our own habitual attempts to relieve grief-related pain in ways that limit our health and happiness. We became increasingly motivated to temper grief in ways that were more life-giving and learned to speak freely with one another about our personal and family strengths, growing edges, needs, and preferences for tempering loss-related pain, disheartenment, and distress.

Talking with a youth about tempering responses to grief may seem counterintuitive. After all, tempering is all about diversion, right? But tempering is not the same thing as ignoring the elephant in the room who just dropped a stinking pile in the big middle of everything you hold dear. It is not pretending that your grief doesn't exist. Tempering is distracting yourself from your grief so completely from time to time that your suffering is not the motivation for what comes next.

Talk with the youths in your life about how you choose to temper grief (personally and socially) and ask about their needs and preferences. You might each make a list of your natural and preferred ways of tempering grief alone and together with others, then contemplate how each response affects you and your relationships by asking some pointed questions – for example:

- Is this tempering response effective to help me ease, tolerate, or heal my suffering – in the short term and long term?
- Is it fun, engaging, or highly interesting to me?

- Is it legal and age appropriate?
- Is it kind to myself and others?
- Is it something I can talk about with someone I trust (or something I keep hidden)?
- Is it a response that is effective in moderation, or is it likely to lead to addiction?
- Is there anything I am sacrificing to engage in this response? Is it worth it?

As an adult, Morgan continues to seek answers to these questions. Thankfully, the myriad go-to tempering responses that became lifelines for her as a youth are mainstays of her healing. Some of her favorites include reading engaging novels, watching funny movies and sitcoms (on a more limited basis), meditating and creating meaningful spiritual rituals for herself, and throwing herself into her passions – notably, acting and writing. But, selfishly, my favorite of Morgan's tempering responses is a daily habit she developed that she isn't able to keep to herself. At some point along the way, Morgan realized that humor was her greatest ally in tempering her grief, so she made it her mission each day to find every possible shred of humor that kindles a giggle or busts her open with a belly laugh. Among family and friends, Morgan is known as the guru of everyday comedy that helps make life worth living for all of us – even in the darkest times.

By making tempering a daily practice, Morgan became an expert on the tempering responses to grief that were likely to hurt or heal her. She forms her daily habits accordingly. But, of course, now that she embodies adulthood in earnest, that's a story for a different chapter – perhaps, one to be found in a recovery book that Morgan will write herself. You can be sure that I'll be the first one in line to buy it.

Guidepost 40

Sometimes healing is refusing to fuel the fire that burns you.

If a Youth Were a Feeling, What Feeling Would It Be?
Integrating in Youthhood

Leo Tolstoy wrote in his celebrated novel Anna Karenina, "Is it really possible to tell someone else what one feels?" That's the absolute challenge for a youth when attempting to convey the nuances of their grief. Youths tend to be all about feelings but feelings are impossible to communicate precisely. So, don't be surprised whenever a youth gives up the effort and stomps off with the trailing mantra, "You don't understand!"

Grieving or not, youths tend to experience a wide range of intense emotions – a developmental attribute that can be the salvation or bane of a youth's existence any moment of any day of the week. A youth's intense emotions can override rational thinking and cause a youth to make choices and behave in ways that are based purely on the emotion of the moment. Do you remember such a time in your youth? When fear, or joy, or desire filled your being so completely that there was no room in your brain to think about what came next. Whatever it was. . . just. . . happened.

Emotional reactivity is further complicated by the scourge of boredom that plagues a youth whenever nothing is happening that is especially engaging or interesting. This youthful bent towards boredom is due to a youth's body producing a lower baseline of dopamine (the hormone and neurotransmitter associated with pleasure and well-being). Remember Aesop's fable about "The Boy Who Cried Wolf?" Boredom is where that legendary mischief began. Whatever a youth can do to get immediate gratification (to raise dopamine levels) may become an obsessive priority: stirring up trouble, engaging in risky behaviors, indulging in self-pleasure or sex with a partner, seeking peer approval or a sense of belonging, getting a high from drugs, alcohol, food, electronic media, pornography, video games, or exercise, or becoming mono-focused on achieving personal goals in sports, arts, academics, or other areas of interest – anything to get that next fix of fun and pleasure to combat youthful boredom and angst.

Given the complexities of a youth's emotional life, it's understandable why a youth might struggle to identify and communicate their grief to others. A grieving youth will need to make peace with all sorts of emotions that can be overwhelming, intense, confusing, and changeable. So, it may seem futile to a youth to express to others what they can't explain to themselves. Authentic grieving is like signing up for a 900-level graduate course in emotional intelligence. And it's a course that will take a lifetime to complete. A grieving youth may wonder: Is it really worth the trouble?

The Complexities of Communicating Grief

Communicating and interpreting complex feelings isn't an exact science. Emotions border on the mysterious. Yet, they wield enormous power to change our self-identity and relationships. So, it's no wonder that researchers find human emotions to be a compelling subject to explore. One study published in 2014 suggests that there are only four basic human emotions. This conclusion was drawn because research participants who were shown examples of facial expressions representing six emotions – happy, sad, afraid, surprised, angry, and disgusted were unable to tell the difference between the faces that communicated anger or disgust and those that communicated fear or surprise. Based on this research, the "basic four" read something like "happy, sad, angry/disgusted, and afraid/surprised." But into which category might desire or love fall? And if we reduce our understanding of emotions into themselves, do we make it more (not less) difficult for people to communicate what's real for them?

In contrast to the "basic four" is the work of researcher and psychologist Paul Ekman. Ekman and his colleagues have identified 10,000 distinct human facial expressions. This body of work may indicate that humans find it easier to show our emotions rather than talk about or interpret them; otherwise, we might need thousands of "emotion words" to communicate our feelings to one another. We humans experience multiple (even contrasting) emotions in infinite combinations that give rise to the personal feelings of a lifetime.

Describing the nuances of personal grief with a few "emotion words" like "sad," "angry," "afraid," is like describing the many hues and shades of a brilliant landscape with three primary colors. A griever may feel at once sad and happy, angry and loving, afraid and interested. Yet, feelings are more than a combination of emotions. Feelings arise out of the interplay between your emotions, sensations, movements and gestures, physiological responses, beliefs, values, judgments, circumstances, self-identity, social relationships, and environment. What you perceive as feeling, thinking, being, and doing are so dynamically interwoven that it can be difficult to tell where one ends and another begins, and which is responsible for the other.

When someone asks, "How are you feeling?" an honest answer requires you to assess emotions, sensations, thoughts, and behaviors and decide which are particularly noteworthy to describe the present ambiance of yourself. Whether you can verbalize your feelings accurately or not is another matter. For example, when you cause irreparable harm to a dear friend or family member, and that person offers understanding and forgiveness, you might experience feelings surging through your being that are a combination of love, sorrow, shame, guilt, gratitude, hope, and awe. This instantaneous feeling may be difficult to communicate precisely no matter how many different words or facial expressions you use.

To communicate your feelings, you may hone in on whatever emotion is most obvious to you at the moment. But a singular emotion is hardly ever the whole story. Anger may be motivated by love as easily as it is motivated by hatred. Pride may have shame at its core. Wonder may be born of both fear and joy. The complexities of grief may be intertwined with a broad spectrum of emotions. A feeling is greater than the sum of its parts and grief can wrap its arms and legs around a mountain of feelings simultaneously. So, please be patient and gracious with a grieving youth who is willing to make an effort to communicate personal feelings that drive their thinking and actions, and ask the youth for a little patience and grace as you attempt to offer understanding and acceptance.

Skirting (or Slamming) Social Rules of Grief & Grieving

Spoken or unspoken social rules may discourage a youth from openly confiding their struggles with grief. When social rules forbid honest grieving responses, the youth is faced with a dilemma. Depending on a youth's temperamental tendencies and perceptions of social power, the youth may choose to acknowledge and integrate grief privately in ways that can be hidden from others, or a youth may choose to blast social decorum to smithereens so grief can be seen and heard. Sue Alexander's beautiful picture book *Nadia the Willful* portrays a youth's eloquent grieving efforts to buck social decorum. Perhaps you will recognize yourself or a loved one in the following synopsis of Alexander's bold and tender entreaty to acknowledge grief.

Fighting to Remember: A Story About Integrating Death & Love

Nadia the Willful is a Bedouin youth who is the daughter of a sheik. Nadia is known for her fiery temper. Whenever she strikes out defiantly, the sheik's oldest and favorite son, Hamed, is the only one Nadia allows to calm and tease her until she laughs. When Hamed dies unexpectedly, his father (the sheik) decrees that no one is to remind him of his grief by talking about his son or saying his name. Although Nadia is allowed to grieve on her own behind closed doors and during solitary walks in the desert oasis, in public, Nadia and everyone else (including her mother) abide by the sheik's wishes. Then, one day, the willful Nadia realizes that it is the very act of remembering and talking about her brother with others that relieves the pain related to her brother's death. So, against the sheik's decree, Nadia begins to tell stories of Hamed to anyone willing to listen.

At first, Nadia's brothers and mother, the crafting women, and the shepherds tending the flocks resist Nadia's stories and warn her of the trouble she is stirring up with the sheik. But Nadia is persistent. Those who hear her stories discover that Nadia's remembrances ease their pain, too. So, Nadia's recollections of Hamed's life and influence fill her daily conversations. Others begin to join in willingly, until one day a young shepherd forgets himself and in earshot of the sheik, he calls to Nadia to come and see how big and strong *Hamed's* favorite sheep has grown. The sheik is outraged to hear his son's name and the shepherd is banished. But, once again, Nadia protests. She goes to her grieving father and persuades the sheik that silencing Hamed's name forever only serves to increase his pain.

In 21st century Western culture, grieving the death of a loved one – especially in the first few months following the death date – is generally accepted and encouraged. But most of us don't fully conceive of grief as the ongoing process it is. What's more, there are types of loss in addition to death that aren't socially recognized. So, a youth may be able and willing to acknowledge grief related to a recent death or socially acknowledged life-threatening events (such as the spread of COVID-19 or being the victim of a natural disaster). But the youth may find it more difficult to confess grief related to losses that are not socially recognized or "approved," those for which a youth has no words, or those that inspire grief long after an initial loss event is past.

The self-conscious youth who values acceptance and belonging among intimates may be unwilling or unable to divulge grief related to:

- Grief-striking events that took place months or years ago
- Developmental, religious, spiritual, existential, or identity crises
- Physical, sexual, or emotional abuse
- Chronic self-criticism
- Empathic grief assimilated from the loss experiences of others
- Committing to or breaking up a romantic partnership
- A parent's divorce or remarriage, a divorced parent dating or experiencing a romantic break up, or moving in with a parent's romantic partner
- Physical or emotional separation from a parent due to neglect, mental illness, custody battles, incarceration, hospitalization, military service, etc.
- Oppression, rejection, or neglect due to ethnicity or nationality, gender, gender identity, sexual orientation, religion, or mental, emotional, physical, or social limitations
- Pregnancy, abortion, or miscarriage
- Poverty, homelessness, or unemployment of a family wage earner

Moreover, adults may trivialize losses that severely rattle a youth's self-esteem, self-compassion, or confidence in life and relationships – for example:

- Loss of supervision or protection
- Loss of childhood privileges and comforts (for example, sitting in an elder's lap, cuddling, holding hands, or being tucked into bed)
- Loss of virginity or innocence
- Loss of confidence in a parent's ability to parent
- Loss of respect from beloved elders or loss of self-respect after engaging in forbidden, cruel, or criminal behaviors
- Academic failure or losses in athletic, academic, or art competitions
- Nonfatal injuries or illnesses

Social expectations that obstruct grievers from confessing the sources of their grief to one another can be a double whammy for youths who are already developmentally inclined to integrate grief on the sly. So, beware turning expectations into blinders.

When A Youth Takes Their Grief Underground

Self-inflicted loneliness may descend on a youth who lets the sleeping dogs of unacknowledged grief lie. Some youths become so proficient at hiding grief that resilient appearances can be mistaken for healing and unnamed grief for depression that appears to have no loss-related source. Privately, a youth may express unbearable grief in self-destructive ways.

Over the past few decades, reports and studies show that a surprising number of youths engage in self-injury – intentionally cutting, scratching, bruising, burning, breaking bones, or otherwise doing harm to themselves physically. Self-injury may be a way to physicalize psychological pain, revive oneself from numbing depression, and provide momentary pleasure as endorphins (the body's natural painkillers) are released. Some young people who self-harm admit that they would rather feel physical pain than nothing at all and some report that the physical pain of self-harm provides temporary release and comfort from mental or emotional anguish. As Caroline Kettlewell writes in her memoir, *Skin Game*, that reveals her personal experiences with depression and cutting,

> "That's when I wanted to cut. I cut to quiet the cacophony. I cut to end this abstracted agony, to reel my selves back to one present and physical whole, whose blood was the proof of her tangibility."

A systematic meta-analysis on self-injury reports that less than 5% of adults engage in non-suicidal self-injury, but the numbers are higher among youth: 17.2% for youths 10-17 years old and 13.4% for youths 18-24.* According to the American Foundation for Suicide Prevention, suicidal behaviors not necessarily intended to kill are also more prevalent during youthhood. For youths, approximately 25 suicide attempts occur to every one suicidal death, as compared to the 4:1 ratio for adults. Among mental health professionals, suicidal behaviors are regarded as a call for help when psychological pain is overwhelming. It is not a huge leap to conclude that non-suicidal self-injury may have a similar motivation – an indirect admission that psychological distress has become greater than one can bear.

It's a good rule of thumb to assume that every youth who suffers a grief-striking loss will carry a pack of unacknowledged grief on their back from time to time. Assume, as well, that a youth will experience grief-striking losses that the youth is unable or unwilling to reveal to you. Then, do your best to respectfully discover whether or not your assumptions have merit. If not, no harm is done. Your assumptions will simply help you to create keener habits of observing, listening, and relating to a youth more intimately and honestly. These are social habits worth living (and modeling for a youth) whether the youth is grieving presently or not.

---

* "Prevalence of Non-suicidal Self-Injury in Nonclinical Samples," by Swannell, Martin, Page, Hasking, and St. John; *Suicide and Life-Threatening Behavior*, Volume 44(3), 2014.

A Youthful Curriculum for Integrating Loss-Related Changes

If you speak and live but one grief-related truth with a youth in your care, let it be this: *There is no grief-striking loss so little that it is insignificant and none so large that it is beyond the reach of love.* No matter the loss or how long ago it took place, it can be empowering for a youth to build a trusted repertoire of integrating responses to help the youth acknowledge and adjust to the changes that accompany loss. Effective integrating responses might include:

- Engaging in artistic endeavors that allow for self-expression (theater, music, writing, visual arts, crafts, woodworking, etc.)
- Creating or participating in meaningful daily or weekly domestic rituals and activities, for example:
  - Lighting a candle of remembrance at mealtime or bedtime
  - Cooking favorite foods or engaging in a cherished activity that was shared with a loved one who is deceased or absent
  - Taking a walk to look for signs and symbols of hope and healing
  - Planning a morning check-in for a youth to share what they are or are not looking forward to that day and an evening check-in to share what was difficult or uplifting about their day; at either check-in, needs for self-care and support from others might be revisited
- Creating a memory book or photo collage that incorporates images of what or who was lost and remembrances of one's healing journey, including memorial celebrations, personal growth, new beginnings, etc.
- Designing or choosing a tattoo as a memorial symbol for a loved one who dies, or getting a tattoo, ear or body piercing to symbolize surviving or enduring a particular loss experience
- Fictional or biographical storytelling that highlights both painful and uplifting aspects of a loss experience
- Talking about a loss with a trusted confidante who is a supportive listener
- Being held by a trusted and trustworthy elder who can provide comfort
- Praying about or meditating on a loss, or tending an altar in memory of a deceased or missing loved one
- Listening to music or reading stories that tell of others facing a similar loss
- Constructing a memorial symbol by hand
- Creating or participating in a ceremony intended to honor a loss experience
- Educating others about a particular type of loss experience or participating in an organization that assists those suffering a similar loss

Whether a youth is more comfortable integrating grief alone or together with others, a combination of private and social approaches to integrating will provide the greatest benefits. Integrating by oneself can help a youth gain confidence in going it alone. Social integrating provides evidence that a youth is grieving and healing in a company of others who are also affected by a loss – even if it is a youth's private loss that others experience only peripherally because they care.

Integrating a grief-striking loss is not a once-and-for-all endeavor. No matter how proficient you are at integrating a loss or encouraging a youth in your life to do so, there may come a time when grief from a loss revisited, plops itself into the big middle of everything, like an elephant in the room that no one wants to talk about. There's no need to worry if, at first, the words don't come. Grief doesn't always need words to be heard or felt among intimates. Sometimes, you can simply look into one another's faces and know more of grief than words can speak. You can acknowledge grief one smile, one tear, one silent hug at a time.

Guidepost 41

It isn't the volume of pain that determines its impact. Silent pain can kill just as noisy pain can heal. Attune yourself to the suffering that cannot be heard.

Feeling Your Way to Healing
Companionship Needs of the Grieving Youth

As a youth, becoming yourself is a full-time job because there's no expert hovering over your shoulder to tell you how it's done. Oh, there may be plenty of folks who try. When you step into youthhood, everyone who is anyone to you may have an opinion about who or what you ought to be or do, how you ought to dress, drive or wear your hair, what you ought to feel or think, who you ought to befriend or date, what sport, art, academic subject or job you ought to pursue, what you ought to believe or value, and how you ought to behave. As annoying as such social pressures may be for a youth, they are generally less annoying than being surrounded or abandoned by people who don't care what you feel, do, believe, or think.

It's a catch-22 for a youth – having people in your life who care enough to fight with you about who and what you are. Some youths will rise to the challenge, others will find it easier to blend in, and most will vacillate between the two – at times, walking boldly through the walls of others' expectations and, at times, shrinking into a dark corner or going along with the crowd. Either choice may cause anxiety for a youth who is learning to define themselves and take individual initiative during a stage of life when peer approval and family support are top social priorities. When disapproval or rejection raise their ugly heads, being true to yourself is a real accomplishment.

Rising to the youthful challenge of becoming, knowing, and declaring yourself to others can be difficult in the best of times. Imagine then, the trials of becoming oneself that a youth faces when layers of grief weigh heavily. How is a youth to unpack selfhood when one's self is knotted up with grief-related pain, disheartenment, or distress? This is where a loving and attentive adult (or two or three or ten) can come in handy. Encouragement from a circle of trusted elders can inspire a grieving youth to take advantage of the youth's self-focused tendencies – the seedbed of self-study. If given supportive opportunities, youths are poised to observe and untangle their relationship with grief and become familiar with how grief influences their feelings, thinking, and behaviors.

Unfortunately, among a youth's loving and attentive elders, there may be no adult who feels especially qualified to educate a youth on the topic of grief or support the youth in ways that help them to grieve and heal their suffering. If that's the case for you, you'll be glad to know that as a parent, teacher, counselor, or mentor, it isn't your job to tell a grieving youth how to grieve or how to heal. Rather, it's your job to offer a youth a bounty of compassion and respect as a youth discovers their unique path to healing. It is your job to help a youth to create emotional safe havens that the youth can return to time and again for support and encouragement during the grieving and healing process.

Creating Emotional Safe Havens

A youth's emotional safe havens are relationships, places, and activities that inspire a youth to express, explore, identify, and gain a sense of self-control over personal emotions, including emotions that dominate a youth's grief experiences. Safe havens may include:

- Loving and supportive relationships with others
- Curative spaces and activities
- Clear rules
- Healthy daily habits

Emotional safe havens that a youth can count on are imperative for healing, especially when loved ones are absent from a youth's daily life or need to attend to their own care needs or the care needs of others. Emotional safe havens provide time, space, and motivation for a youth to sort through grief-related feelings with confidence and grace, and make healthy choices as the youth adjusts to the internal and external changes a loss sets in motion. What's more, emotional safe havens are a rope up from the stormy sea of potential losses that a grieving youth might otherwise bring upon themselves as they find themselves flailing in rough waters.

The Safe Haven of Room 203

A poignant example of an emotional safe haven was built among 150 "low performing" youths at Woodrow Wilson High School in Long Beach, California between 1993 and 1998. The safe haven of room 203 was an English course taught by first-time teacher, Erin Gruwell. Many of Gruwell's students were gang members and most experienced violence in their neighborhoods regularly. Initially, when Gruwell began teaching, class dynamics were rife with the intense fear and hatred that students harbored for those with a different skin color or gang alliance from their own.

Gruwell's students had been written off by society and the educational system as being an unteachable bunch of "delinquents." But Gruwell believed in the essential goodness and academic capabilities of these youths. She worked diligently to gain her students' trust and help them unravel their feelings of vulnerability, defensiveness, and hatred toward her and one another. Gruwell changed her curriculum to focus on teaching racial tolerance, but her educational approach did more for her students than help them to overcome their racial prejudices and bigoted attitudes.

As the story is told through the film *Freedom Writers* (2007), Gruwell's students learned tolerance for one another (and for their teacher) that was more than skin deep. It may or may not have been Gruwell's initial intention, but her approach to teaching tolerance hinged upon students telling their grief stories – to their teacher, one another, and themselves. Gruwell gave each student a journal to write their personal stories – the good, the bad, and the ugly. She required the students to write in the journal every day, but each student could choose whether or not Gruwell read their entries. The vast majority wanted a reader. So, the journals became conduits through which the students shared with Gruwell their personal stories of pain and suffering.

In addition to journal writing and class conversations, Gruwell invited her students to share grief stories without ever speaking a word. It was through the "red line" game in which students stepped onto a red line to acknowledge their similarities. Sometimes, the similarity was sharing an interest or owning the latest album of a popular artist, and sometimes the similarity was having suffered a similar loss of safety or friendship, like being shot at or losing a friend (or three or more) to death by gang violence.

The opportunity that Gruwell gave these students to tell their grief stories set the wheels of compassion and respect in motion. The students began to realize that all of them had suffered grief-striking losses and that many of these losses were catalyzed by the same racist attitudes and behaviors that they espoused. This was what made these youths more similar to one another than different: Each one was equally vulnerable to suffering.

The personal and social transformations that made these students, at long last, claim to be "family" to one another didn't happen overnight. Gruwell was a warrior. She worked hard to create a curriculum and class atmosphere that was inviting and compelling to her students. She relentlessly advocated with administrators and other teachers for her students to get the education they deserved. She bought books for the students out of her own meager funds. She expected students to read diaries and novels that were challenging for some of them and to contemplate and journal about their lives on their own time. Students were allowed to be real rather than editing profane language or subject matter to impress their teacher or get good grades. Telling their stories meant telling their stories in their own words, in their own way.

Along with her efforts, Gruwell required her students to take initiative and to fight for their lives through self-awareness and social change rather than fighting one another with guns and knives. She challenged the students to reconsider feelings, attitudes, beliefs, and behaviors that were hurtful to themselves or others. She required students to make their own choices (within certain guidelines) and students were given ultimate control over what content and details about their personal lives and relationships were expressed and communicated (and to whom).

When Gruwell asked students to make a commitment to their schoolwork or personal transformation, she translated her invitation into a physical behavior or shared ritual that required students to take action. For example, she invited students to come to the front of the class one by one to receive their new journals and she created a "toast for change" in which students drank sparkling apple cider from champagne glasses and toasted to future visions of themselves. The students helped to raise funds for class trips and bring in guest speakers that included Miep Gies (who hid diarist Anne Frank and her family during the Holocaust), and Zlata Filipovic, who published diaries depicting her experiences surviving the war of Sarajevo from 1991-93.

Gruwell found ways to say "yes" to the momentum and enthusiasm the youths expressed regarding the hoped-for direction that their class studies, projects, and special events might take – because each one needed to believe that they could be a catalyst for positive change. The transformations that occurred in the youths' attitudes toward themselves and one another occurred largely because the students began to identify themselves, both individually and collectively, as survivors, thrivers, heroes, and co-creators whose inspirational influence was larger than the suffering they endured.

Ultimately, all 150 of Gruwell's students graduated from high school and many went on to college – the first in their families to do so. In 1999, they published a collection of their writings called, *The Freedom Writers Diary: How a Teacher and 150 Teens Changed Themselves and the World Around Them*. Many of Gruwell's former students now work with her at the Freedom Writers Foundation in Long Beach. The bridge that got them there was built in room 203 at Woodrow Wilson High School – where they created an emotional safe haven with one another that would reroute the direction of the rest of their lives.

For some of Gruwell's students, room 203 was their one and only emotional safe haven. Ideally, a youth will find emotional safe havens at home, school, work, in the neighborhood, at church, synagogue, temple, or mosque, and in larger circles of community. So, beyond your efforts to offer an emotional safe haven to the youths in your care, be sure to support the efforts of others who provide a trustworthy presence for a youth. Become familiar with the safe havens that a youth finds especially inviting and compelling – whether these safe havens are created solo, one on one, with family, friends, peers, mentors, or other community members.

One of the saddest scenes in the movie *Freedom Writers* is when Gruwell prepares excitedly for her first parent-teacher night and not a single parent shows up. Maybe that scene in the film is just Hollywood talking, but it does happen in real life and not just to teachers. Whether it's a teacher, parent, grandparent, administrator, counselor, healthcare provider, clergyperson, or another elder who is left standing alone in their efforts to provide for a youth's support needs, it is a sad day, indeed.

Building emotional safe havens with our youth, particularly those who are grieving, requires teamwork and collaboration. This effort doesn't ask you to be the alpha and omega of a youth's emotional healing. It only asks you to provide a youth with emotional support wherever and however a youth's life crosses your path.

Perhaps you don't have the influence or opportunity of a Ms. Gruwell, but you know how to look a youth in the eyes and ask their name or invite them to tell you what is noteworthy about their day or their life. You know how to pay attention to what motivates a youth and what emotions drive them. This isn't rocket science. You know how to listen to a youth's stories, just listen, and you know how to pay attention to the hard stuff. So, start wherever you are, wherever a youth will let you in.

Relationships as Safe Havens

Whether they tell you so or not, grieving youths depend upon tried-and-true relationships to provide emotional shelter and support following a loss. Some find these tried-and-true supporters in the family circle and some look beyond. At a time of life when peer group friendships are greatly valued, peers may gather during times of shared grief, but have no idea what to say or do to communicate grief-related feelings, support a friend, or pass the time together. With a little encouragement, some youths will jump at the chance to get involved with others in the grieving and healing process – perhaps, helping to plan and organize an event, make food, provide childcare or manual labor, engage in problem-solving or strategic planning (given the impact of a loss), or add to artistic or practical contributions for a memorial service, ceremony, or project that fosters a sense of healing.

When grief is fresh or fierce, youths may find that just being in the presence of friends and family who are huddling into the pain is enough. There is a purity of thought that can arise amid collective grief that humans share. Witnessing the animated suffering of a loved one or the aching stillness and silence that can pour into a person's soul after a loss experience may inspire a youth to find the courage to tend to another's pain, no matter how far a youth must fling open the door of their heart to do so.

In high school, when my best friend Sheri died in a car crash, it was Maggie, my other BFF who made the terrible nightmare seem bearable. While most of the adults in my life were painfully stumbling over their words and actions, Maggie stood beside me in a hospital chapel where we held vigil for the driver of the car who was still fighting for his life. All at once, I felt Maggie brace herself and then slice through the excruciating silence with a clear sense of purpose when she said, "I know I can never be the kind of friend Sheri was to you, but I am standing right here and I will be here for you. You can count on it." Ingeniously, in the same sentence, Maggie confirmed to me that there was no friendship like the one I had with Sheri and she also gave me evidence that the friendship I shared with her was equally exceptional. After that, whenever sorrow and loneliness threatened to fill up every inch of me, Maggie's words floated back into my memory like a comforting song.

Rather than seek a safe haven with friends and family members, some youths may prefer to explore grief-related emotions with people who are peripheral to their daily lives. Engaging in a confidential support group or talking with a counselor, therapist, clergyperson, or spiritual director can help to preserve a youth's privacy and encourage a youth to navigate grief-related emotions without having to worry about offending or burdening those that a youth knows and loves best. (For ideas and contacts, see "Healing Through Education & Support Groups" and "Healing Through Therapeutic Counseling & Spiritual Direction" on page 350.)

A youth might also seek relational support from a teacher, guidance counselor, coach, care provider, or mentor. An adult outside the family circle who shows special interest in a young person can be a lifesaver for a grieving youth and, indirectly, for a youth's parents or guardians who may be tending to grief-related challenges of their own. *But please be wary of adults and other youths who strategically prey upon a grieving youth's vulnerability and may take advantage of the youth's desire for caring companionship, especially during interludes when parental attention or family support is waning.* Whenever another person steps forward to provide emotional support for a youth in your care, become familiar with the person and their mode of operation. Be in conversation with that person and others who can verify the person's reputation and motivation for interest. Be able to account for the amount of time and the activities the two share.

A disturbing statistic on sexual abuse of a minor is that approximately 85-90% of perpetrators are known to their victims and some 60% include someone within a young person's intimate social circle. So, when someone steps in to assist a grieving youth in your care, don't be tempted to take leave of your responsibility to be the one who shows up quietly in the margins of a youth's life to witness what is taking place at the center of it. Be poised to offer your protection if a youth is being threatened or mistreated.

When a youth's loss is related to sexuality, a cultural taboo, or circumstances that make a youth appear weak or partly responsible (even if the youth isn't), it may be difficult for a young person to confide the loss – for example, date rape, pregnancy or abortion, an eating disorder, substance or media addiction, bullying, rejection, conflicted gender identity or sexual orientation, a consensual but painful sexual experience, contracting an STD, etc. In age-appropriate ways, confidently bring such topics into your conversations with a youth and demonstrate compassion and respect for yourself and others who have experienced such difficulties. These acknowledgments relay to a youth the message that if such troubles come, you will be there to offer support and help sort through alternatives as the youth seeks resolution and healing.

Private Spaces & Solo Activities as Safe Havens

Gonzo journalist, Hunter S. Thompson writes in one of his letters included in *The Proud Highway: Saga of a Desperate Southern Gentleman (1955-1967)*:

> "We are all alone, born alone, die alone, and—in spite of True Romance magazines—we shall all someday look back on our lives and see that, in spite of our company, we were alone the whole way. I do not say lonely—at least, not all the time—but essentially, and finally, alone. This is what makes your self-respect so important, and I don't see how you can respect yourself if you must look in the hearts and minds of others for your happiness."

Exactly. Thompson hits the nail on the head when it comes to one of the most important lessons a human being must learn if life is not to be a litany of grief. We must learn to be alone with ourselves without losing self-respect, and being alone with yourself is the very place where self-respect is grown.

Creating private spaces for contemplation and solo activities provide a youth with protected time alone to express, explore, and gain awareness and self-control over emotions and grieving responses. Such safe havens can foster healing for a youth without having to depend on the guidance or support of another, or feeling a need to censor potentially offensive or hurtful thoughts and feelings.

A solitary safe haven may be created in a bedroom, reading corner, treehouse, backyard tent, workshop, nearby green space, porch or gazebo, or even (as a dear friend of mine from a large, noisy family professes she did) in a spacious closet that serves as an emotional fortress to which a youth can retreat. Older youths may enjoy private retreats in nature – finding a quiet spot at a park or forest preserve, enjoying a meditative outdoor activity (hiking, biking, rock climbing, etc.), or going to a library or coffee shop regularly where there's a hidden nook away from the crowd. Ideally, private safe havens are free from distracting activities: TV, cell phone, computer, video games, etc. If music is a healing refuge, it can be played on an iPod, record player, or CD player to avoid needing an internet connection. Of course, the true test of any emotional safe haven that a youth enjoys in solitude is the reckoning of that moment when the youth emerges from a safe haven more relational, more emotionally balanced, and more compassionate toward oneself and others.

The Arts as Safe Havens

Georges Braque says it poignantly: "Art is a wound turned into light." The power of art to heal the whole person is remarkable. Artistic expression can bring emotional balance, reduce stress, build self-esteem, and help a griever to express creatively what they are unable or unwilling to express during interpersonal conversations. Recent studies claim that creative expression through art can even boost the immune system – which is good news for grievers, since grief weakens a body's ability to fight disease. What's more, the arts serve those of all ages as a form of play that can uplift a griever's spirits and ease the burden of grief. Art heals. It's as simple as that.

A youth's artistic safe havens may be found through visual arts, reading, journaling, creative writing, listening to or making music, dancing, woodworking, crafting, or creative prayer, visualization, or meditation practices. For a youth who seeks companionship with others, the performing arts – theater, dance, music, performance poetry, etc. – allow a youth to explore a spectrum of personal emotions and provide creative outlets for feelings that may be difficult for a youth to identify or express otherwise. The performing arts are a natural meeting place for those suffering and healing grief, as artists explore together the meaning of life and relationships, and strive to develop compassion for grievers from all walks of life.

As youths, both my children found theater and music to be two "therapies" that were effective to rediscover hope, cherished meaning, interest, and gratitude after devastating losses. Willa, the youngest, is an actor who can cry on a dime. Her ability to easily articulate human suffering without becoming overly attached to it is one source of strength that makes her as fearless as any five-foot-two-105-pound young woman ever was. Somewhere along the way, she also discovered that balancing the dramatic roles she plays with comedic roles and improv performances provides a healthy mix for her emotional well-being.

Curative art not only tells a vignette of our human story that is truthful and engaging; it also relays the story with a generous portion of compassion, humor, and hope. Indeed, curative art is the closest thing to a universal faith perspective that we earthlings can claim.

Rules as Safe Havens

Therese Anne Fowler writes in her novel, *Souvenir*, "Some rules are nothing but old habits that people are afraid to change." It's true, some rules are. And some rules are like an old friend you can count on. Some rules foster peace and integrity among people. They serve as agreements we make with one another so we can move through life more freely, knowing on which side of the road to drive or whose turn it is to bat. Some rules help to build congeniality and trust so you know that when someone gets angry, you don't have to fear for your safety or when someone asks for your dessert in the school lunch line, you have a right to say no. No matter that a rule-disparaging youth claims that "rules suck," youths generally depend on rules to provide comfort and protection, especially when facing a grief-striking loss.

When my daughter Willa transferred to a new middle school where a group of popular but unsupervised youths took her in, she consistently sought Andrew's and my blessing to give these new friends the message that whatever trouble they were drumming up, her parents wouldn't allow her to participate. As these "friends" got to know us and realized that we provided both supervision and rules for Willa, they lost interest in including her in their parties and after-school activities, and they shunned her at school. Although there was a bundle of grief involved and Willa needed a good bit of emotional nurturing and support to make the transition to a new set of friends, she was profoundly grateful that we were there to provide guidance and encouragement to help strengthen her resolve.

No doubt, rules can be a source of comfort and direction. Even so, during youthhood rules usually don't hold the same power as they did once upon a time. As children, we are inclined to follow rules that are kind and fair to everyone because "that's the way it's done." But when the bell of individual freedom rings loud and clear, the stealthy youth may find it increasingly difficult to follow a rule simply because it's a rule. Youths generally need to feel that a rule serves them better being kept than bent or broken. Even if a youth believes that a rule has been imposed for their own good and understands rationally why not to kick someone in the head, steal money from a parent's drawer, have unprotected sex, speed along a neighborhood street, or drink themselves silly, feelings can trump reason and a youth may give in to a desire to break a rule simply because the youth feels like it.

A youth's inclination to break rules may be unnerving to parents and elders who consider ourselves to be responsible for a youth's choices and behaviors. Breaking rules during youthhood can invite all kinds of grief-related trauma that we parents and elders harp on our youths to avoid – fatal accidents, unplanned pregnancy, addiction, foul play, being expelled from school or arrested. Despite the general intention of rules to keep youths safe and out of trouble, a youth's maturity is too often gauged by the youth's ability and willingness to follow adult-imposed rules unquestioningly. Here's the drawback with that kind of thinking: a youth can follow rules and still be devious and manipulative in ways that undermine cooperation and social equity. Conversely, a youth may break rules unwittingly or for a good cause and still keep integrity and a sense of duty intact.

True maturity is recognizing that even good rules have their limits. So, make an effort to help a youth figure out what rules are non-negotiable and what rules may warrant breaking or bending under exceptional circumstances – for example, refusing to follow rules that perpetuate violence or abuse, or not making it home on time because a friend is having suicidal thoughts and needs support. Life isn't always neat and tidy, and sometimes rules are limited in their usefulness to help clean up the mess.

Negotiating rules during youthhood isn't child's play. Rules can tread you into gray waters. Like when you have a right to speak freely but the truth of your words cuts someone else's integrity in two, like a knife. Or, when you break a "no fight" rule to punch a bully in the nose or yell at a teacher or parent who is rough handling a classmate or sibling. Or, when you know you're supposed to be home with your dad's car at midnight with no excuses, but there's a drunk friend who needs a ride home from a party and your dad's cell phone is off. Or, when you choose to lie because telling the truth is too dangerous, or you break an unjust law.

There in the gray waters where questions of morality and good sense reside is where a good portion of a youth's self-identity and personal character emerge in earnest. Not necessarily all at once. Every once in a while, or more often than not, a youth's intense emotions may blur good sense and fiery desires may burn a hole in a youth's morality. Some mistakes and regrets are to be expected. But sooner or later, without bowing to any "fool-you-better-listen-to-me" rule-maker or going along with any "come-on-let's-do-it-just-for-the-fun-of-it" rule-breaker, a youth can become familiar with the leeway between dogmatic dictums and careless nonsense. There in that space between the two, a youth can choose to take a stand neither in the black nor the white, but in a place that is as right as any rule ever was. Arriving in that place of "rightness" beyond rules is the destination every parent and elder ought to have in mind when setting rules with a youth in the first place.

Ironically, the path to get to that place beyond rules is lined with the rules a youth embraces along the way that foster cooperation, courage, and compassion. Such rules may define details of practical daily life – like what chores a youth is responsible to carry out each day, when a youth is expected to share family time, or how and when a youth may use a cell phone, play video games, use a computer, watch TV, or access the internet at home or school. A rule may set limits on curfews, a youth's readiness to drive, date, or socialize with friends unsupervised, or it may attend to healthy communication, such as no punching or name-calling, actively listening when another is talking, or having an approach for conflict resolution that requires the active participation of everyone involved.

Moral sensibilities and strength of character are often grown at that five-way intersection where a youth must decide whether to follow, bend, break, question, or fight to change a rule. Some of my proudest moments as a parent have been when my children (in their teens and early twenties) each stood up to me and my rules, or to their dad, or a teacher, coach, or administrator who couldn't justify the rightness of a rule in a particular circumstance. As our family fought the decade-long battle to settle their grandfather's probate case, Willa and Morgan each had moments at the court-assigned mediation hearings when they clearly and respectfully articulated protest or suggested a plan of action to work toward a resolution. In each of these instances, the youthful timbre of their voices defending fairness and justice (that a given set of rules didn't provide for them or their loved ones) easily commanded adult respect and attention.

There may be times when a grieving youth is so overwhelmed with pain that they feel as if nothing they do or say much matters. A youth may be tempted to act out unthinkingly to relieve emotional distress. At such times, a cherished set of rules can serve as a curative intervention. For example, if rules are created to enhance intimacy, cooperation, and community-building among a youth's loved ones, then upholding such rules when grief strikes can foster compassionate social connections that balance feelings of despair and loneliness. Showing up for family dinnertime, resolving conflicts civilly, participating in domestic chores or community cleanup days, keeping an eye out for the neighborhood children at play when driving down the street, putting electronic devices away for family time or a class session, balancing one's conversational talk with listening to others – these are the types of social rules that can motivate a grieving youth to foster and sustain respect and intimacy despite feeling like hell.

Not all rules are created equally. If a rule is devoid of compassion and respect, it is a rule begging to be broken, especially when a youth is in the throes of grief. Rules that are charged with love, empathy, courage, joy, comfort, confidence, or relief are rules that a youth is more likely to keep because positive emotions ingrain the rightness of a rule in the youth's emotional memory. Take an inventory of the rules you keep and be sure they are rules that invite a youth's emotional investment – not by shaming or threatening a youth with punishment for breaking a rule, but by creating a kind and thoughtful set of rules that the youth believes in and knows how to keep – whether they feel like it at the moment, or not.

Healthy Daily Habits as Safe Havens

While some rules may be "nothing but old habits that people are afraid to change" (as Therese Anne Fowler puts it), there is something at least as problematic as fear that enslaves human beings to old patterns of behavior, including the ways we grieve and heal our suffering. It's something called the "habit loop," explained in Charles Duhigg's book, *The Power of Habit*. The habit loop is your automatic answers to cravings for food, emotional relief, companionship, achievement, power, etc., in which an internal cue (such as hunger pangs, anxiety, loneliness, boredom, sexual desire, a yearning for achievement, victory, or praise, etc.) or an external cue (such as break time at school or work, a television commercial promoting beer, beauty, food, fast cars, cleanliness, etc., or reminders of behavioral expectations from a parent, boss, mentor, or teacher) sets off a habitual routine to achieve a desired reward. The reward can be anything from satisfying hunger or relieving emotional distress, to coming one step closer to achieving a personal goal or grabbing a few minutes to socialize with a family member, friend, peer, or co-worker. But whatever it is, the reward will be sought by way of least resistance – that is, the habitual routine that gets you there.

According to Duhigg, some 40% of our human behaviors are comprised of habits that come so naturally to us that we are not aware of our automatic responses. So, if there is one safe haven that will help a grieving youth to thrive above all others, it is forging a set of healthy daily habits by which to live and heal the suffering of grief. More than rules, healthy habits can take over a youth's thinking, feeling, and doing even when grief strikes a blow and disorients a youth from life as usual. Habits live deep in the human brain, so whatever a person usually does to relieve emotional distress will be the response most accessible when the chaos of a loss event recedes into the patterns of everyday life.

A child's daily habits during the first several years of life are often bestowed on the child by adults – parents, teachers, caregivers – who take a child by the hand and say "here, this is the way we do it." But a youth's habit life becomes more and more driven by individual choices and preferences due to a youth's increasing autonomy and a more relaxed approach to supervision by adult caregivers. Unfortunately, many adults fail to recognize the dramatic effect personal habits can have on a youth's happiness, health, and well-being. Moreover, when we acknowledge the power of habits in a youth's life, we come face to face with the fact that our own daily habits greatly influence the daily habits of the youths in our care – for better or worse and whether we intend for them to or not.

Stephanie Soechtig's documentary *Fed Up* demonstrates the power of habits, particularly when it comes to something as basic as the foods we eat. The film, which is narrated and co-produced by Katie Couric, exposes the malnutrition epidemic that is sweeping through 21st-century culture. The type of malnutrition that the film highlights is nutritional starvation experienced not from a lack of food in general or even a lack of food with nutritional benefits, but from the creation, promotion, and marketing of foods to which human beings are habitually drawn that fail to nourish a human body effectively and that cause chronic disease.

According to the film, over the past several decades we have created generations of sugar addicts by allowing big food corporations to successfully market sugar-filled foods to children and youths, in particular. The result is skyrocketing rates of obesity and diabetes among children, youths, and adults, alike. In the film, erroneous ideas about dieting and exercise are revealed – most grippingly in the stories of youths who have attempted unsuccessfully to fight obesity by way of the old "calories in and calories out" model. Through the voices of multiple researchers and reporters, the theme of *Fed Up* resounds loud and clear: The processed food products we habitually buy and consume in contemporary culture are addictive and are making our young people fat and sick. Unfortunately, purchasing and consumption habits can easily overpower a parent's well-intentioned efforts to help a youth find a cure for food-induced illnesses. Thus, the very definition of "youth" – revered for centuries as the time of life when health and vitality reign supreme – is in jeopardy.

The loss of health and vitality among our youth is a major source of grief for the millions affected. Ironically, this grief-striking loss may increase a youth's unhealthy food habits and addictions as food is used to relieve emotional suffering. Just watch this film – you can't miss it. Grief is written all over the faces and lives of the youths who are interviewed and the faces and lives of the parents who love them.

Changing a bad rule is easy enough if you have the information and know-how that's needed to do so, but changing a bad habit is more complicated because to eradicate a bad habit you have to replace it with a new habit that often takes days, months, years, or a lifetime to keep. Old habits are addictive; they live within your brain just waiting for an opening, so between the craving and the reward of relief, joy, pleasure, love, companionship, satisfaction, etc., a new routine of behaviors must be set in motion again and again – until it becomes so automatic that the old habit has no chance for revival.

Resistances to changing a habit can be systemic as well as personal. For example, the youths highlighted in *Fed Up* who are suffering from obesity and malnutrition not only have to work hard to change personal patterns of behavior; they must fight against cultural beliefs, practices, and marketing illusions created by big food corporations (and the political machines that serve them); they must fight against unhealthy family habits that reel them back into old patterns of behavior without giving it a second thought.

For a youth to create and sustain new healthier habits, the youth will need support from friends and family members who are willing to change their own habits, and they will need support from those who do their bidding in the educational, political, and civic institutions that serve them. Supporting a youth to make such changes in their habit life is no small task. Sometimes, it really does take a village.

When grief strikes, help a grieving youth to consider which "old habits" serve to heal their grief-related suffering and which "old habits" intensify grief. If a habit needs to be overhauled, take a team approach to change so loved ones are ready to support any new habit of self-healing that a youth sets out to build for themselves. For inspiration that includes a doable approach to habit change, see the book, *One Small Step Can Change Your Life: The Kaizen Way* by Robert Mauer, mentioned in the adulthood chapter on pages 247-48 and 258.

Shannon L. Alder wrote, "The best kind of happiness is a habit you're passionate about." This adage holds true even while grieving. Unmistakable happiness arises whenever healing becomes a daily habit that transforms loss into something remarkable and life-giving. As much as anything else, that's what Erin Gruwell provided for her 150 Freedom Writers – a safe haven in which to grieve, heal, and live with hope that happiness can become a habit, too.

❀ ❀ ❀

    There is no greater gift you can give to a youth than the know-how to create lifelines by which to pull their battered and aching soul from the stormy river of suffering without your assistance. Emotional safe havens that include loving and supportive relationships, curative spaces and activities, a good set of rules, and healthy daily habits provide the learning ground. Ultimately, a youth will need to maintain and strengthen the integrity of each of their lifelines; then, to grab hold and hang on when the going gets rough. No matter how great their strength or fortitude, the most important learning of all for a youth is knowing when to call for help when help is what's needed most. So, keep your ears attuned and your eyes peeled for a youth's S.O.S. signals. Asking for help is a habit that may take some practice, too.

Guidepost 42

You know the generation gap is bridged when an elder says to a youth, "I trust you will use your own best judgment" and the youth replies, "Then, first, may I ask: If you were me, what would you do?"

Do-It-Yourself

Self-Guided Contemplations for the Youth Within You

Choose among these self-guided contemplations that focus on the healing wisdom of youthhood. You may want to engage in a contemplation by yourself, with a youth in your life, or with a circle of friends or family. Use these ideas as they are, revise them, or create contemplations of your own:

◈ **Listen to the Music:** Victor Hugo once wrote, "Music expresses that which cannot be said and on which it is impossible to be silent." Music can be a powerful catalyst for expressing and changing grief-related moods and emotions. Consider your favorite songs or genres of music to listen to, sing, or play on an instrument. Brainstorm titles of songs to include on four separate playlists – lamenting, heartening, tempering, and integrating. When you need to engage more fully in any one of these types of grieving responses, listen to, play, or sing the type of music that inspires your needed response:

- *Lamenting songs* are those that help you to ponder, express, and release the pain of grief. If a song causes you to cry or feel a tender sorrow, it is a good candidate for this list. Blues are an obvious choice for lamenting.

- *Heartening songs* are those that help you to discover the goodness that is hidden in the pain of grief – love, hope, a new beginning.

- *Tempering songs* are fun, happy, upbeat, or beautiful songs that transport you and help you to forget your troubles.

- *Integrating songs* are those that inspire courage and clarity for making needed changes and tell stories in which love and joy reside right alongside death and sorrow.

Next time you need healing inspiration, let music be the source.

- **Safe Havens by the Dozen:** No matter what a griever's age, everyone needs safe havens to express and explore grief-related emotions and feelings. Reflect on the safe havens explored on pages 174-185; as you do, identify people, places, activities, beneficial rules, and healthy habits that open the door to healing for you. Make a list and post it somewhere you'll see it. Revisit one or more of your chosen safe havens every day. If it's difficult for you to think of a safe haven that is especially inviting for you, then it's time to create a new relationship with a person, place, activity, rule, or habit in your life that fosters healing. Build your personal and social safe havens one at a time and tend to them faithfully. Before you know it, safe havens will welcome you at every turn.

- **Draw a Circle 'Round Your Sorrow:** Youths aren't the only ones who can become self-absorbed during times of grief. At any age, whenever you become overly focused on your troubles, draw an imaginary circle around your family members, friends, neighbors, or community members. Take stock of the grief-striking losses represented in this circle and reach out to someone in need to let them know you're thinking of them. Invite someone to dinner or to go for a walk, offer to pick up groceries or do yard work, bring a meal or be on call to talk whenever a listening ear is needed, or volunteer at a nearby homeless shelter or girl's or boy's club. Sometimes, looking beyond your own sorrow is the surest way to lighten your burden of grief.

- **Smile the Blues Away:** It may seem corny or shallow to some, but a simple daily habit you can develop that may ease your sorrow is to smile more. According to research, it appears that our facial expressions do more than communicate our feelings, they also promote the feelings that they represent. While some researchers assert that any smile will increase feelings of happiness, others say that only a Duchenne smile will do – one so big that it gets your eye muscles involved. So, try it – for a minute, or two, or ten. Find reasons to break out a big smile every time you look at yourself in the mirror, gather for a family meal, or greet a stranger on the street. Once you make it a habit to smile more, it may lighten the load of your grief and someone else's burden, too. Fortunately, smiles can be contagious.

A Youth's Healing Chest
Approaches to Grieving and Healing in Youthhood

Look through the following list of approaches to grieving and healing from Part III, "The Healing Chest: Gathering Your Own Best Medicine." Which approaches might be especially useful to revisit and heal grief from your youthhood or to grieve and heal alongside a youth in your care?

- Abuse Awareness & Prevention
- Addiction Prevention & Recovery
- Apologies
- Art & Creativity
- Bibliotherapy
- Breathing & Relaxation
- Caregiving
- Ceremonies & Celebrations
- Cinematherapy
- Cognitive Healing
- Community-Building
- Conscious Eldering
- Crying
- Dance
- Death Care
- Dreaming & Visitations
- Dying a Good Death
- Emotional Healing & Expressing Feelings
- Exercise, Body Awareness & Physical Release
- Forgiveness
- Funeral Planning & Memorial Services
- Grieving & Healing Perspectives
- Habit-Building
- Helping Others
- Hope
- Illness Tending
- Integrative Care & Complementary Therapies
- Laughter & Humor
- Listening
- Massage, Reiki & Comforting Touch
- Meaning-Making
- Memoir & Autobiography
- Memorials & Remembrance
- Metaphors, Objects & Symbols
- Mindfulness & Meditation
- Movement, Yoga & Posture
- Music & Sound Therapy
- Nature
- Natural Remedies for Pain Relief
- Parenting Mindfully
- Pets & Animals
- Pilgrimages, Labyrinths & Hiking Treks
- Play, Fun & Games
- Poetry
- Prayer
- Repairing Broken Relationships
- Sanctuary & Sacred Space
- Self-Injury & Recovery
- Sexual Healing & Recovery
- Sleeping
- Stories & Storytelling
- Suicide Prevention & Survivor Support
- Talking Cures
- Theater & Speech
- Trauma Recovery
- Wonder
- Writing

7 ❧ Mi dolor es su dolor*

Grieving & Healing in Adulthood

We are accustomed to repeating the cliché, and to believing, that "our most precious resource is our children." But we have plenty of children to go around. The true scarcity we face is practicing adults, of people who know how marginal, how fragile, how finite their lives and their stories and their ambitions really are . . . who find value in this knowledge, even a sense of strange comfort, because they know their condition is universal, is shared.

Michael Chabon

*English translation: "My grief is your grief."

Serving the Greater Good
An Adult's Natural Genius for Grieving & Healing

If you want to grieve and heal like an adult, first you have to learn how to be one. But in our 21st-century Western culture being an adult is a bit of a mystery. Think about it: What does "being an adult" mean to you?

When I pose this question to grownups in my family education workshops, I'm often met with blank stares and twinges of fear or embarrassment in the faces of some who are surprised that they don't have a ready answer. Haltingly, one participant after another attempts (with difficulty) to reply to this looming question.

What does it mean to be an adult? The question begs an answer in a society painfully confused by the concept of adult maturity. After all, if you don't know what it means to be an adult, how can you aspire to become one? And if you aren't able or willing to wrestle with the question until you find some satisfactory answers for yourself, how can you hope to steer a young person in the right direction as they grow toward adult status?

As young people, we're led to believe that we become adults by passing through a number of age-related or educational milestones, or by earning enough money to pay our own way. But being an adult isn't that simple. When you arrive at the trailhead of adult-becoming, you realize that the challenge of youthful maturity – reconciling a craving for independence with a hunger for belonging together with others – doesn't let up, but rather deepens with complexity. As soon as you step onto the trail of adulthood, you can't shake the dawning realization that it's not enough to be older, more educated, or wealthier. It isn't even enough to belong to yourself and "your people," as it may have been once upon a time. The mind-blowing adult-making truth is that you are *a citizen of the world*. You realize that you belong to all of it. And that as an adult, belonging to anything – a relationship, family, school, company, community, world – means being at least partially responsible for it.

Grieving or not, adult-becoming hinges upon your willingness to belong to yourself and be your own person among your own people, while simultaneously cultivating an enlightened sense of social responsibility that takes the whole world into account. Hence, being an adult griever and healer means grieving and healing for your own sake and the sake of your loved ones, and it means grieving and healing in socially responsible ways for the sake of everyone and everything else.

The Making of an Adult

It's tough to become a self-assured, socially-responsible adult, particularly for those of us in the United States. Our U.S. culture was built from the ground up on such age-old concepts as manifest destiny and survival of the fittest. Striving for such brazen independence may be the pride of our nation and a central developmental task of youthhood, but in adulthood, it can encourage a false sense of self-sufficiency and a never-ending attachment to youthful self-absorption.

Some adults achieve sleek independence in public life but are startlingly dependent upon others in private relationships. Others attain hard-won independence in both professional and personal relationships but wake up one day to the reeking stink of loneliness or isolation. Absolute self-rule and self-sufficiency rob a person (or a people) of the surest assets we possess to foster true self-actualization, life satisfaction, and the evolution of our species – our human capacities for interdependence, cooperation, and collaboration. These three assets are vital to developing any socially responsible relationship.

Growing Your Way to Adulthood: A Rite of Passage

In *Stories for Free Children*, edited by Letty Cottin Pogrebin, there is a story within a story included in "Sun Stones" by Dawn Eng. The embedded story tells of an ancient people of Western Africa who celebrated an adult rite of passage that plants interdependence, cooperation, and collaboration at its core. The rite of passage Eng includes in her story is a tale of its own, retold in the following synopsis:

Once there was a tribe of farmers, musicians, and sculptors who had no sense of time and were the better for it. They didn't obsess over age or follow a tight schedule. Babies were born, grew, learned much, and were well-loved.

Whenever the villagers needed to make decisions about life and relationships in the village, they called all of the adults together to speak and listen to one another. But, because time had no meaning for these people, adulthood had nothing to do with age. It had to do with being responsive to the needs of the village and its people. So, adulthood was determined in a different way.

In this village, the fruit-ladened kula tree was an important resource, so every time a baby was born, a kula tree was planted in their honor. When the child was an infant, the parents cared for the tree. Then, when a child was up and walking, the parents thoughtfully guided the child to tend to the tree's needs for nurture and nourishment. Some children took better care of their tree than others did and were delighted to see their Kula tree grow tall and strong.

As soon as a child's tree reached a certain height, the villagers celebrated because they knew that its nurturer was ready to join in decision-making for the village. Some trees died from lack of care and the gardener had to begin again by planting a new seed. But, sooner or later, each villager became an adult when the kula tree that was theirs to nurture was tall and thriving.

❧ ❧ ❧

The first time I told this story to my (then) almost twenty-year-old daughter Morgan, she objected, "That's unfair! What if the seed was no good? Or, what if an animal came along and ate the seedling, or someone didn't like you and uprooted the tree? Or, what if a storm came along or lightning split it in two?" I shrugged. How is that unlike life? In our striving to become powerful and responsible adults, it's in facing losses that we learn humility, courage, and persistence to tend unflinchingly to our personal care needs and the care needs of others.

Unlike the kula tree people, in our culture, we have no well-thought-out passage of instruction by which young people evolve into adult ways of being. Even so, adult expectations in our culture abound and are oftentimes at odds with the undertone of gritty independence that we as a nation traditionally promote. As an adult, you're not only expected to be fiercely self-reliant, you're also expected to take care of the needs of others – infants, children, youths, dependent adults, your elders. Grieving or not, you're expected to earn an income, make your own way, and share your resources with intimates, acquaintances, sometimes even strangers who need shelter, food, protection. Grieving or not, you're expected to know the answers when it comes to resolving problematic circumstances and relationships, to think of others before yourself, and to sacrifice your own desires and needs for the good of the family, the company, the community. No confusion here, and no pressure at all.

Adulting: A Perpetual Process

With the conflicting expectations of adulthood and no formal training on how to achieve them, is it any wonder that there is so much confusion in our culture about what it means to be an adult? Most of us are handed "adult" status symbols without a great deal of fanfare and whether we are ready for them or not. So, the true meaning of adulthood gets buried under random (mostly age-acquired) "adult" rights to get a job, drive a car, have consensual sex, marry, raise a child, purchase cigarettes or pornography, vote, take a first "legal" drink, graduate from high school or college, buy a handgun, join the military, drive a rental car, buy a house, and the list goes on. Of course, adult maturity so defined is wildly off the mark and whether or not we are conscious of it, our adult sensibilities tell us so. But if we strip age-related rites from our definition of adulthood, what might persuade us to view ourselves as adults, and view one another and the world around us from an adult perspective?

There is a term coined by Alexandra Robbins and Abby Wilner in the title of their co-authored book, *Quarterlife Crisis: The Unique Challenges of Life in Your Twenties*, that describes the sense of loss that those in their mid twenties and into their thirties experience when they reach full adult status yet fail to already be "living the dream" that includes career, financial stability, fearless independence and a life partner with whom to share it. The authors assert that after a decade or two of schooling in which most young people had each step of their lives marked out for them, being faced in young adulthood with a flurry of important life decisions (that you're expected to make for yourself) can cause overwhelming anxiety and a prospect of gloom for the future. In the 21st century, as the cost of living becomes ever less affordable and as school loans and credit debt pile up, more and more young people are initiated into adulthood with the devastating recognition of all they lack in the way of adult-related resources.

A certain irony abounds when one considers the quarterlife crisis from the vantage point of the midlife crisis that occurs for many adults in our forties, fifties, or sixties. The midlife crisis comes bearing the message that the aspirations one desired to achieve once upon a time – career, financial stability, marriage, parenting, vocational achievements, etc. – in the long run just aren't enough to ensure a contented, happy, or fulfilled existence. Somewhere along the way, such "successes" may leave a person cold and, yes, grieving in disillusionment.

For many among the ranks of the divorced, separated, or unhappily married, it is a broken-hearted reality that personal ideals of what marriage, parenting, or family life "ought to be" never did come to fruition and that do-overs are not possible. There is no way to turn back the clock for ourselves, our partners, or our children. So, some of us in middle age find ourselves sitting helplessly among our broken dreams of "family," wondering how in the world we got here. As the "perfect life" fades into a sea of lost hopes, how do you continue your quest for adult maturity – particularly, being an adult who is contented and (dare I say) happy to meet life's losses and disappointments without giving up on yourself or others, or forsaking a quest for love, hope, or meaning?

Becoming a bona fide adult and continually striving to be one, whatever hard knocks or disillusionments come your way, requires monumental effort that may go undetected by others. Since much of one's striving to be an adult takes place in the privacy of one's inner life, it's often difficult to tell the practicing adults from the pretenders. Past a certain age, all but a few parade around in conspicuously adult-like bodies doing conspicuously adult-like things like earning paychecks and having children (either of which can be achieved long before you genuinely think of yourself as being "mature").

Kelly Williams Brown, in her book, *Adulting: How to Become a Grown-up in 468 Easy(ish) Steps*, writes:

> "One of the most jolting days of adulthood comes the first time you run out of toilet paper. Toilet paper up to this point, always just existed. And now it's a finite resource, constantly in danger of extinction. . ."

But it's not just toilet paper that can suddenly disappear when you cross that imaginary line into adulthood. It's the extinction of that feeling that there is always someone there for you who has your back – not only anticipating the timely purchase of toilet paper but forever helping you to banish the inner knowledge that, sooner or later, you will have to go it alone. Sooner or later, there will come a time when you will be required not only to buy your own toilet paper before it runs out, but also dry your own tears, call forth inner wisdom to counsel yourself, and find the inner strength to heal your aching soul when darkness descends and you are out on the trails of life scared and alone.

No matter how many adult status symbols, rights, or responsibilities you acquire, if you're like most adults, you're likely to experience a nagging feeling in the core of your being that you will never quite have it all together when it comes to being an adult. Here's why: *adulthood is not a destination; adulthood is a state of being.* To be an adult (not just in appearance but in truth as you relate to yourself and others), you have to practice at it and keep practicing.

Anaïs Nin wrote:

"We do not grow absolutely, chronologically. We grow sometimes in one dimension, and not in another; unevenly. We grow partially. We are relative. We are mature in one realm, childish in another. The past, present, and future mingle and pull us backward, forward, or fix us in the present."

Although "adult" may be defined as a person who is physically, emotionally, and mentally mature, a practicing adult is one who makes good use of maturity to grow personally and socially. Throughout your life, you'll never be finished growing into your full human potential – no, not even if you are an adult for whom the title fits like a glove. For one thing, as you face grief-striking losses, there will likely come a time when you question every adult sensibility you've acquired: physical prowess, emotional stability, mental clarity, mature spiritual belief. When it happens, your only viable option is to acknowledge your deficiencies and grow some more.

The Power of a Healing Perspective

The fully developed thinking powers that we humans commonly acquire by the age of 25 provide an invaluable asset for grieving adults: *the power of perspective.* As a practicing adult, perspective allows you to crawl out from under such self-inflicted tortures as being a victim to your pain, or spitefully blaming yourself or others, even God, for a grief-striking loss. Your keen analytical thinking skills allow you to differentiate your thoughts about grief from your feelings, and your feelings from your actions. If you will, you can observe your physical, emotional, mental, and spiritual responses to grief, reasonably assess them for their curative value or destructive force and choose to feed them or not.

When you face monumental losses, this self-reflective process may be one of the heaviest burdens of adulthood. You may take one baby step toward healing and then two giant steps back toward pain. But the bottom line is that when you experience life as a practicing adult, you not only come to realize once and for all that you are responsible for healing your relationship with your grief (and that there is no one but you to blame if you fail to do so), you also realize that your healing is not for your sake only.

As the saying goes, "No one is an island." An infant knows that, if only instinctually. People depending upon one another is integral to the human experience. But, for a practicing adult, the real stinger embedded in the inevitability of human relationship is that as an adult, your youthful desire to love and be loved must be yielded for something that extends beyond your singular existence. That's how love deepens into mutual respect and compassion for yourself and others. When this occurs, you no longer exchange love as a commodity by which you control another's actions, beliefs, values, thoughts, or feelings, or allow another to use love to control you.

The big enchilada of adult becoming is building adult relationships on mutual respect and compassion that frees you to love extravagantly – without sacrificing an iota of self-identity or self-determination, or asking another to do so. So, practice at it and keep practicing because, oh my, is it ever easier to talk about mutual respect and compassion among adults than it is to accomplish it. Unfortunately, many adult relationships function upon the premise that there is never enough love, attention, respect, or resources to go around. That's what happens when we allow loss to define us and our relationships with one another. Nobody wants to be a loser and it's easy to get panicky when you feel as if you're not getting your fair share of whatever it is you desire. When it happens, you may respond (even subconsciously) by foiling the successes or good fortune of another or justifying a move to take more than your fair share to compensate. The other may follow suit and so it goes. Soon you are grasping at straws and wondering how you got there.

Social responsibility in adulthood begins within yourself. It requires you to reflect on your gains and losses, and how your stewardship of your gains and losses not only affects you for good or ill but also affects other family members, friends, co-workers, even acquaintances or strangers who live next door or in a country you don't even know exists on the other side of the planet. As a practicing adult, you no longer have the privilege or torture (as it may seem) of viewing your grief or healing in isolation, because healing (or failing to heal) changes the way you love, care, hope, believe, work, play, and go about your business in the world.

As an adult healer, you are in the service of feeding the human spirit with a fine and sure sense that every person matters and that together we can face any trouble that life presents. To be a healer, you have to be willing to change your relationship with grief-related pain. Otherwise, personal and communal suffering become perpetual habits that play havoc with your mental health and well-being. It's like the wisdom attributed to Einstein tells us, "Insanity is doing the same thing over and over again, and expecting different results." As an adult, if you want to change your relationship with grief to heal yourself and help others to heal, you have to figure out what you can do differently to encourage healing – and then, quite simply, to do it and keep doing it until you get it right. If the kula tree dies, you have to be willing to start over again, as many times as it takes, with a new seed.

Guidepost 43

Each time you grow, a part of you has to die a little.
    Rest assured, with this death,
        you will become more than you are.

Bringing the Lessons of Dying to Life
The Practice of Breaking Down Your Grief

The tenets of adaptive grieving for the practicing adult read something like this: *Griever, know thyself, heal thyself, and make of thy grief something useful and life-giving.* These tenets are simple enough, but achieving them isn't always easy, especially when love and pain are involved. That's why as a practicing adult, you're obliged to reflect on what you know about yourself, your grief, and your healing process, and figure out how to put that knowledge to good use.

My Model of Adaptive Grieving Dynamics provides a map of the grieving process that can help you to accomplish what the tenets of adaptive grieving ask of you. It isn't the only map; there are others. So, as you reflect on the best path by which to heal and transform your grief, it may be helpful to cross-reference.

One map that may provide needed direction to heal your grief-related suffering is espoused by Richard Groves – hospice chaplain, death educator, and co-author of *The American Book of Living and Dying*. In his studies of various cultures, Groves discovered a common understanding among death and dying practitioners the world over: *Impending death spawns existential suffering that causes spiritual pain; spiritual pain, in turn, intensifies physical suffering.* For some, "spiritual pain" is synonymous with grief, plain and simple. But, no matter what words we use, there is wisdom in creating a shared understanding of our common sources of suffering.

Groves with his spouse, Mary, synthesized four dimensions of spiritual pain into a Spiritual Health Assessment (SHA) tool that is used by care providers and care receivers in hundreds of healthcare facilities around the world. The SHA (available at SacredArtofLiving.org) measures four common types of existential suffering:

- **Relatedness Pain** – losing or being alienated from a person, pet, place, thing, social role, or aspect of self-identity that you love, value, cherish

- **Forgiveness Pain** – the "common cold" of spiritual pain that involves harboring anger, blame, shame, guilt, hatred, etc. toward yourself or others in relationship to past mistakes or hurtful words and actions

- **Hopelessness Pain** – the "terminal illness" of spiritual pain that often involves a loss of will or reason to live, sometimes due to a belief that problematic circumstances or unbearable suffering will never subside

- **Meaning Pain** – a crisis of faith or identity that may include a struggle to make sense of a loss experience, your significance and purpose in life, or the purpose of human existence and creation as a whole; facing death, you may wrestle with the question, "Who (or what) am I as I disappear into death?"

⋏⋏⋏

As you contemplate these four types of spiritual pain, take a moment to ask yourself: *"How might my life and relationships be different if I attended to these four types of spiritual pain not only on my death bed or at the deathbed of a loved one, but whenever and however grief comes knocking at the door of my spirit?*

As you explore the four dimensions of spiritual pain and your relationship with each of them in the bulk of this chapter, hone in on the type/s of spiritual pain most relevant to you. In your grief experiences, there may be times when one type of spiritual pain comes through loud and clear above the others. With complex losses, however, it may be that two, three, or even all four dimensions of spiritual pain press down hard on you or someone you love. For example, if you suffer from a debilitating addiction that wreaks havoc in your life and relationships, you might experience *relatedness pain* due to obsessively hiding your addiction from your loved ones or otherwise creating barriers to intimacy; *forgiveness pain* as you struggle with shame and blame related to how you and others feed your addiction; *hopelessness pain* as you see no way out of your addictive patterns and the harm they cause to yourself and others; and *meaning pain* as you lose hold of your life purpose related to career goals or creating cohesive family relationships in which your identity as a beloved spouse, parent, child, sibling, grandparent, etc. is highly valued. Sometimes, one type of pain is so intertwined with another it is difficult to untangle the mess.

Knowing the source of your spiritual pain whenever and however it hurts is as crucial as correctly diagnosing a physical ailment. What might happen if you were offered conventional treatments for a stroke when suffering from diabetes, or given an appendectomy when food poisoning is the problem? Irrelevant remedies to ease a particular type of spiritual pain that is not problematic at the moment may divert a griever from addressing the real problem and cause suffering to worsen.

As you become more familiar with the sources of your spiritual pain, you may notice that when one type of spiritual pain resolves, another type surfaces. What's more, the interplay between complementary adaptive grieving responses (lamenting and heartening; tempering and integrating) is likely to cause your spiritual pain to intensify and subside in waves. Sometimes your pain will be noisy and sometimes silent even to you. Listen beyond the noise and into the silence, so your spiritual pain can reveal to you what your healing requires. If you're willing and able to do what needs doing to heal your ailing spirit, your spiritual pain can become your strength.

Setting Your Spiritual Pain & Spiritual Strengths Side by Side

When you're drowning in an ocean of grief, you may be too preoccupied with staying afloat to notice the lifeboat circling around you. You may grow so familiar (or even strangely comfortable) with your burdens that your suffering becomes a defining motivator for all you think, feel, say, believe, and do. However, as the Model of Adaptive Grieving Dynamics proposes, suffering is not all there is to grieving, nowhere near all of it.

Focusing solely on your spiritual pain without recognizing your spiritual strengths is like a surgeon performing an emergency procedure during a power outage and refusing to turn on the generator or battery-operated lighting that is there for the doctor's generous use. So, when you're suffering, be sure to turn on the power of your spiritual strengths that shed light on your healing path. Heartening yourself with your strengths is every bit as imperative as identifying the type of pain that is likely to pull you down into the undertow of your grief.

For some grievers, horrific sorrow creates a repulsion even for what is uplifting, pleasurable, or promising in a loss experience. So, when you suffer an agonizing loss, you may dig in your heels and hang on to your spiritual pain with a vengeance. Perhaps you stuff it inside where others cannot meddle with it or build a public altar of suffering that you tend 24/7. If your grief so consumes you, you may even be willing to forsake other cherished relationships or refuse to forgive yourself or others for past mistakes. You may lose hope and meaning on purpose because your suffering screams at you that hope and meaning are nothing but big fat lies.

In 21st-century Western culture, a griever's healing is often measured by the griever's willingness to make peace with the *pain* of grief. However, equally challenging can be making peace with the fact that grief often resides at the intersection of sorrow and joy, loneliness and intimacy, anger and mercy, despair and hope, insignificance and meaning. It is the *juxtaposition of pain and pleasure* in the human experience that often gives rise to suffering and also encourages healing.

Imagine the complexity of pain and pleasure one might encounter when a loved one awakens from a coma with brain damage or a long-awaited baby is born with Down syndrome. Imagine the layers of despair and relief that must be sorted through when a beloved soldier who was a prisoner of war (in a war long-ended) is finally confirmed as deceased, or a parent of three who was erroneously incarcerated for years wins a court appeal and is exonerated and released. The pain or promise of each outcome is a matter of perspective. With the evolution of each loss experience, an adult griever repeatedly bumps up against the question: "How are relationships, forgiveness, hope, or meaning redefined for me now, and now, and now again?

You may be motivated to face your grief head-on and transform your suffering by focusing on the type of spiritual pain that stings most. However, when grief overwhelms you, it may be more helpful to fortify yourself with spiritual strengths that come naturally to you before tackling the type of spiritual pain that is especially problematic. Perhaps you're a meaning seeker who easily recognizes the life-giving significance of a loss, or you uncover hope at every turn. Perhaps you're a natural at fostering intimacy with others, you easily fulfill roles of leadership or duty in horrific circumstances, or you forgive yourself or others when grievous errors are made.

Whatever your healing strengths, make good use of them as you transform the spiritual pain you suffer. Then, no matter what type of pain you encounter, you'll be poised to make the most of your suffering. After all, that's what the give-and-take between lamenting, heartening, tempering, and integrating grief is all about.

The next time your spiritual pain screams at you so loudly that you want to shut it up once and for all or it belabors a silent mantra that your life will be nothing but unbearable anguish forevermore, be proactive with your grief. Take a deep breath (or two, or three, or ten) and repeat to yourself:

> "*I am the one who determines how to be in relationship with my grief. I have the power to adjust my thinking, feelings, or physical behaviors to ease or ignore my pain, to see my suffering for what it is, or to grow and learn from it; I determine how, when and*

with whom I will or will not confide the pains and pleasures of my grieving and healing process; I determine if and when I will or will not forgive myself or others; I choose how I will or will not reimagine hope when my hopes are shattered and if I will or will not search for meaning where there is none."

Once you let your eyes adjust in that dark pit of despair that is your grief, you will see that it is teeming with choices and that you are making choices even when you are unaware of it. Of course, your choices are limited given the circumstances of your loss and the particulars of your spiritual pain, but they are choices all the same. So, be vigilant. Reflect upon and reason with the choices you make and the choices you don't – to know yourself, heal yourself, and make of your grief something useful and life-giving. Then, be willing to let it all go. Because, even when you aren't paying attention, you can take another step toward healing, and even when you get it wrong, you can always change your mind. As long as you're living, willing, and able, you can always choose a different path to healing.

Guidepost 44

Spiritual pain is the fuel that propels you to the heart of healing and you are the only driver who can get you there.

Bridging the Great Divide
The Practice of Healing Relatedness Pain

Relatedness pain: You know it as well as I do. It all started as an infant, crying alone in your crib or watching your favorite person disappear from view. Life is riddled with moments of harsh separation from the people, pets, places, possessions, and aspects of your self-identity that you hold dear. It can be spurred by death, divorce, conflict, injury, amputation, hospitalization, job loss, being deployed for military service, placing a child for adoption, growing up, growing old, being a victim of violence, theft, or a natural disaster that takes your land, home, possessions, people. . . Relatedness pain can pile up in a heap of brokenness and suffering.

Take a moment to imagine a person who is at once betrayed by a spouse, gets a divorce, struggles with addiction, loses parental custody, is shunned or avoided by family friends and in-laws, and is forced to move to a new place of residence without taking Fido, who is the eternal bearer of unconditional everyday affection. This jumble of relatedness pain doesn't easily quit.

Relatedness pain can loom when you or a loved one experiences a significant change in personality, attitudes, beliefs, or ways of relating. When this happens, you or your loved one may yearn for the person who used to be. For example, years ago when my spouse, Andrew, suffered a stroke as a rare complication to Lyme disease, he lost partial vision and his fairly exceptional short-term memory. We were grateful that the permanent damage was not so extensive that his professional work as a teacher or his ability to drive was hampered, but his relationship with his "new self" and mine with him after his recovery, took some adjustment. Until we each could fully appreciate the positive changes that came along with the negative – such as Andrew living more fully in the present moment – to varying degrees we both grieved for his former self.

Relatedness pain may rear its head even in times of celebration: a child going off to college, retirement, marriage, getting a new job, buying a new home, adopting a child, or giving birth. In such "happy times," you may feel alienated from a loved one, cherished aspects of self-identity, or a place of belonging, especially when less valued relationships take priority status in the day-to-day rhythms of life.

⋏ ⋏ ⋏

Take a moment to consider your cherished relationships with the people, pets, places, possessions, and social roles or aspects of self-identity that you value. If it's helpful, make a list of these relationships and ask yourself:

- Are any of these relationships especially life-giving at present? Do they inspire me with a sense that all is right in my little corner of the world?

- Am I experiencing separation, displacement, or alienation in any of these cherished relationships?

Acknowledging a relationship that needs tending is a first step toward healing and transforming your relatedness pain at its source.

Bridging the Separation of Death & Other Losses

The most studied type of relatedness pain is the suffering that arises with death-related losses. Few mortals are experts at bridging the great divide between life and death, earthly existence and the great beyond. Mostly, we create symbolic imaginings of a heaven in which we will be reunited with our loved ones one day. But, even if such a reunion is real in whatever form it might be, that vision may not quell your insatiable longing for the ongoing physical presence of a deceased loved one. The following story bears witness.

Reclaiming the Priceless Value of Little Things
A Family's Story of Transforming Relatedness Pain

The most poignant expression of relatedness pain I have witnessed firsthand came in the aftermath of the death of sixteen-year-old, Dana Waddell – a star athlete and all-around-great human being from Marshall, Wisconsin. Dana died suddenly of viral encephalitis in January 2002. Her funeral was held in the gymnasium of the high school she attended – to fit the hundreds of mourners who came.

There was a moment after the visitation and before the funeral service began, when Dana's casket was closed and Dana's mother, Sally, was struck with the realization that she would never see her daughter's face in the flesh again. A moment before, Sally was thoughtfully and lovingly receiving gestures and sentiments of sympathy and support from the endless line of grievers who came. But, as the casket lid was shut, Sally threw herself on top of it and wailed with a yowl of torment unlike any I ever heard. At once, the sound split me in two – with a heartfelt agony on one hand and an unexpected and resounding sense of sheer relief on the other. The enormity of Sally's grief could not be hidden behind social decorum. A sacred cord between mother and daughter had been severed and there was no reason to pretend otherwise. Sally's unabashed proclamation of anguish bounced off the walls of the gymnasium like a perfect song of suffering. Suddenly, I could breathe again. It felt as if everyone could. Sally had given voice to the abyss of unspeakable separation for all of us.

After Dana's funeral, there were days Sally told me she felt like packing it in. She might have lost her will to go on if it wasn't for her spouse David and younger daughter Danielle walking beside her every step of the way. Moment by moment, day by day, the family found numerous ways to comfort one another and continue to be close to Dana despite their ongoing grief over her physical absence. The real beauty in their efforts is their generosity to invite others to accompany them as they continue to reestablish and foster sacred bonds with their precious daughter and sister.

A few weeks before Dana fell ill, she wrote a tribute to her parents for Christmas and gave them a penny as a symbolic token. This bittersweet declaration of love and gratitude became a sacred text for Sally and David – words so perfectly chosen that the message radiates like a protective blessing of affection between daughter and parents that transcends death. Dana wrote:

"Mom and Dad ~ Merry, Merry Christmas! I tried to think of something creative to get you both or do for you . . . but I went blank. What do I get for two such important people in my life? I thought and thought, and then for some odd reason I thought of a penny. Isn't that crazy? . . . I mean, a penny is something not expensive at all . . . the least amount . . . next to nothing.

"Pennies are special though, just like you two. What do people usually throw into wishing wells – pennies. When you see a penny on the ground, what do you do with it? – pick it up and make a wish . . . Pennies have so many important meanings in our lives that many of us overlook . . . You see, a penny is like the cherry on ice cream, the sun shining on a rainy day, the snow falling on Christmas, the love two parents can give their children. You two have taught me the value of a penny, and how much something so small can mean . . . You, Mom and Dad, have given me everything I could ever want or need. You two . . . helped to develop who I am, the kind of person I want to become, and what I want to accomplish in life. Although I may not always show how much you two mean to me, words can't describe how much I love you.

"In a way, a penny has helped me through life. When I was born, I sure must have thrown in the right penny to have gotten you two as my mom and dad. I must have thrown in the right penny throughout my whole life to have both of you by my side, there for me . . . Thank you! Thank you for the love you have given me, the time you share with me, the comfort you give me when I'm sad, for everything! I would give my life for you two . . . just as you have given me life . . . Thank you for . . . sticking by me through thick and thin. When I was born, a penny was thrown in a wishing well, and my wish came true – I received the best parents that anyone could ever have . . . and I thank you! Love, Always and Forever, Your oldest daughter, *Dana Lynn*"

Following her funeral, David and Sally handed out pennies as a symbol of remembrance for Dana, made chain necklaces with a penny charm, had two pennies engraved on her tombstone, and left a penny box at her gravesite for people to take one or leave one. The place Dana's body was laid to rest became a living tribute to her, an interactive cemetery plot with symbols of life, hope, love – angel statues, mobile butterfly ornaments, a lantern, windsocks, a mailbox for notes of affection left by friends and family. On Dana's tombstone, her shining photograph is accompanied by a quote from one of her high school assignments, which reads, "I want to be remembered for making people laugh and for being happy. Also, for being there for people when they need me."

Ironically, this living testament of love was criticized by a few in that community in the months after Dana's death – as an overindulgent spectacle of endless grief. But, thankfully, David and Sally persevere even now, years later. They continue to make this public memorial for their daughter available in a place where friends and family members are inspired to grieve, heal, remember, and reconnect with Dana. The family started an annual fun-run and they also sponsor high school track and cross-country invitationals in Dana's name, where her mom and dad are on hand to award medals on her behalf. Thus, Dana's legacy of laughter, happiness, and encouragement continue; because, despite their never-ending grief, Dana's family courageously makes room for her illuminating ongoing presence.

What does Dana's story stir up in you? Ponder it a moment.

⋏⋏⋏

The death of a child or spouse, divorce, abandonment, alienation, incarceration, or the disappearance of a loved one may cause suffering that is so pervasive it overwhelms your sensibilities and causes your whole life to feel ill at ease. When such a severe break in an intimate relationship occurs, identify the specific sources of your relatedness pain. A mother lode of suffering may be due to a loved one's physical absence; however, relatedness pain may come from a different source.

If a loved one's death is expected and you experience it as a welcome relief from terminal illness, a long-term coma, or mental anguish, you may be well-prepared for it. Rather, your relatedness pain may be ignited by the shift that other relationships take after the death. Friends, blood relatives, step-relatives, or in-laws may treat you differently or suddenly withdraw into a cocoon of grief where you are not welcome. Perhaps you are thrust into family or community roles as breadwinner, spiritual leader, comforter, problem solver, motivator, primary parent, eldest child, or head of the family business that your deceased loved one filled, and for which you are ill-prepared or resent that the responsibility has fallen to you. Perhaps your new role makes it difficult for you to engage in other valued roles you fulfill in the family, at work, or in the larger community.

Losses other than death may present even fewer cultural protocols for bridging the great divide than death-related losses. Consider the woman who falls seriously ill and must have her leg amputated. Unable to move back home, she is put into a nursing home where her only companion, a beloved cat that was given to her by her late spouse, cannot accompany her. To this woman, it is not the illness, amputation, or move to the nursing home that is the most painful aspect of the changes happening to her, but the loss of her cat. When such nuances of relatedness pain are identified and addressed, effective approaches to healing become more obvious. In this case, the most devastating loss might be avoided altogether by finding a pet-friendly care facility or arranging foster care for the cat that includes visits to the nursing home. In this way, the woman's ongoing relationship with her cat might become a source of healing more valuable than anything her caregivers provide.

With my friend, Sally, her spontaneous outburst of lamenting at her daughter Dana's funeral was a response to the physical separation between mother and daughter that shook her to the core. It is no coincidence that Sally (and her family with her) find profound healing through physical remembrances that bring Dana's ongoing spiritual presence to life: a physical memorial site that includes a photograph of Dana, hosting a fun run, creating and wearing penny charms, awarding medals at memorial track and cross-country meets. Dana's family continues to find profound ways to cherish Dana's earthly life by allowing her influence to continue to make an impact in the here and now.

One error we humans often make in assessing our relatedness pain is thinking of our relationships in all-or-nothing terms. A person is alive and then that person dies. You share a home with a loved one and then you don't. You are married and then divorced. You give birth to a child and then you lose custody. You are successful and then you fail. You are respected, then rejected. You are loved, then hated. You are a professional athlete, artist, CEO, teacher, pilot, or carpenter, and you retire from your field, are fired, or can't get work in your area of expertise. When people ask about your line of work, you don't know what to call yourself. Despite your loss, these relationships are never fully severed because the people, pets, places, possessions, and personal roles and identities that you cherish are forever part of you – they live deeply in your psyche and soul. Intimate relationships with yourself and others are not simply there one moment and gone the next. They evolve with circumstances, life experience, developmental transformations, the passage of time.

Beware the excessive tendency to let go of a relationship completely because you can't have it the way you desire. When a loved one dies or disappears from your life, you must let go of that person's physical presence, but you can still relate to the person's essence – emotionally, mentally, spiritually, socially, and sometimes physically as the Waddell family does so eloquently in their ongoing relationship with Dana. Ask yourself what aspects of a severed relationship might still be fostered in ways that provide a heartening sense of life-giving connection and healing?

When a chasm of emptiness fills the space where a cherished or hoped-for relationship once resided, take heart. That excruciating void doesn't need to be a permanent fixture of your life. As an adult, you can fill that dark abyss with relationships that matter most to you – even if these relationships are changed or broken and you are changed and broken with them.

In her poem, "Wild Geese," Mary Oliver comforts the lonely by imagining the world calling to us, like a flock of geese across the distance, coaxing those who are absent to find our place of belonging once again. Finding that place is key to transforming relatedness pain. When a relationship is broken, how will you rediscover your cherished place of belonging?

Practical Ideas for Healing Relatedness Pain

Recreating an old relationship is never easy, especially in the absence of a loved one who is missing from your world. As you grieve losses of relationship, reimagine old relationships and establish new ones in your own way and time:

◈ **Reestablishing Bonds Across Time and Distance:** Discover ways to bridge the distance between here-and-there and now-and-then with a loved one. Even when a physical reunion or reconciliation is impossible, you can use your imagination and intuition to create portals of reconnection:

- **Envision It:** When you are separated by death, distance, or conflict, use prayer, visualization, or lovingkindness meditation (see *Lovingkindness* in "Mindfulness & Meditation" listings on page 332) to reestablish a healing connection, and pay attention to reunions that take place in your dreams (see "Dreaming & Visitations," page 324). Take note of symbols or messages you receive in your dreams and meditations that may inspire your journaling or an artistic creation.

- **Read the Signs:** Identify metaphors, symbols, and objects that reconnect you with your loved one – an animal, song, word, smell, food, place, photograph, poem, activity, etc. that renews a feeling of intimacy. For example, my father was a baseball player and lifetime St. Louis Cardinals fan. When I see a cardinal, I'm reminded of his ongoing presence in my life. When I play catch with my children, I'm transported back to the rounds of catch I played with my dad as he passed his athletic wisdom on to me. Symbolic interactions can nurture an ongoing bond of intimacy.

- **Long-Distance Celebrations:** Even from a distance, you can create meaningful celebrations and memorials for meeting dates, birthdays, holidays, and anniversaries. With friends and family members who are scattered far and yon, you might share the same menu for dinner, light a candle at a specific time and speak or sing familiar words of blessing or remembrance, send or give a gift in memory of a deceased loved one, or write a birthday card to someone as if from the "voice" of one who is absent.

- **Holding Someone's Place:** Keep a ritual of relationship going in a loved one's absence. For example, if you ate breakfast with your adult child every Sunday morning before they were deployed overseas, then do something special on Sunday mornings to bridge the distance. You might write a letter or send an email to your child as a mealtime blessing, or invite your child's spouse, family, or best friend to join you for breakfast instead.

- **Reaping the Leftovers:** With an irreconcilable relationship, practice selective remembrance. For example, if you're alienated from a family member or friend who is chronically abusive, resists recovery help for addiction, or is unwilling to mend a broken relationship, you may still carry fond memories of earlier times with your loved one that enriched your life. Find a way to honor what you cherish. You might create a scrapbook or write a collection of heartwarming stories and memories, or write a list of lessons you learned from the relationship that inspire you to embrace the gifts of the past. If need be, let that be enough.

- **Lasting Legacy:** Leave a spiritual legacy for those left behind when you die. There is a therapeutic intervention for the dying called "Dignity Therapy" that allows the chronically ill to dictate their memories, words of wisdom, and heartfelt sentiments to their loved ones as a lasting gift. A brilliant example of such a legacy gift is the book, *The Last Lecture* by Randy Pausch – a Carnegie-Melon professor and father of three who was diagnosed with terminal pancreatic cancer at the age of 46. In the academic tradition of a farewell speech (usually upon retirement), Pausch was asked to deliver a final lecture that contained the wisdom that mattered most to him. Later, the lecture was published as a series of essays and became a New York Times bestseller. More than that, the book continues to be an entryway of reconnection for Pausch's students, colleagues, friends, and most importantly, his spouse and his children who were all under the age of seven when their father died.

◈ **Release the Old Relationship as It Used to Be:** It may take time and be more easily said than done, but finding ways to gradually let go of a relationship (or your yearning for a relationship) as it once was is imperative. This doesn't mean you need to let go altogether or all at once, it just means disinvesting your time and energy from wishing for what can no longer be. With some losses, this happens naturally due to circumstances – you clean out your office before you retire or leave a job you cherish, remember (for the tenth time) not to pick up the phone to call a deceased love one or a romantic interest who isn't interested, pull out of the driveway with the moving van after being forced out of your home, or take off your wedding ring when a divorce is final. In addition to naturally occurring circumstances, creative acts or rituals of release can help you adjust to relationship changes and transform your relatedness pain into something useful. Keep it simple or make it elaborate. Go solo, invite one or two others, or create a larger gathering with those who are grieving and healing alongside you. For example:

- **Changing Spaces:** Remove or rearrange objects or furniture in your home or redecorate to symbolize a change in your environment
- **Fashion Statement:** Cut your hair to represent an inward change or buy a new pair of shoes to symbolize taking a new path
- **Making Room for Yourself:** Transform the bedroom of a family member who died or moved out by changing it into a creative workspace or prayer/meditation room
- **Parting Blessings:** Create a blessing ceremony for a baby you miscarried, child placed for adoption, home before a move, loved one going away to college or moving for a new job, ex-partner before you each embark upon your separate paths, a part of your body that was surgically removed, etc.

In the movie, *Fried Green Tomatoes*, a boy loses his arm in a railroad accident. After he heals, his family and friends put on a funeral for the boy to say goodbye to his arm and bury it. The funeral is thrown a bit tongue-in-cheek; even so, what a powerful ritual to honor the severing of a part of yourself! Without fear or embarrassment, family and friends gather at the arm's funeral to acknowledge the truth in the open air, and they manage to do it with a sense of humor.

- **Re-imagine a New Relationship With What or Who Is Lost:** While you are letting go of the old, you can also re-imagine the new. Although there may be a ripping separation between you and what or who is missing, there may also be ways to preserve the goodness of what was. Imagine these possibilities:
  - **Everyday Kinship:** Think of ways that an absent loved one can be a special part of your day through simple remembrances such as offering a morning, evening, or mealtime blessing for your loved one, tending to your loved one's unfinished business, or utilizing skills your loved one taught you.
  - **Consorting With Care:** Renegotiate an invigorating parenting partnership with an ex-partner that allows your child/ren to feel protected and supported by both parents despite divorce or separation.
  - **Passing It Forward:** After retirement from your job, consult or mentor others in your areas of expertise.
  - **A New Play:** If you are permanently injured and can't participate in a sport, art form, or other activity you love, identify another sport or special competition, new approaches to your art, or another activity you enjoy.
  - **For the Time Being:** When you're bedridden or homebound with an injury or illness, make a list of things you can do for yourself or others from where you are. You might identify work you can continue (with or without assistance), write or dictate cards or letters, listen to your favorite playlist, create art, call, email, or text friends and family members to offer love and encouragement, express gratitude and affirmation to your care providers, or whatever helps you to foster a cherished sense of identity and caring.

Relatedness pain is a trumpet call to recreate meaningful connections. Find ways to do so that gently coax you to accept the fact that every beautiful person or thing that you cherish, in one way or another at one time or another, will go missing. As I once wrote on a greeting card for a dear one, "What excruciating fortune! – that we love well enough for my heart to break upon your parting." So it is with love that lasts, and so it will always be.

Guidepost 45

All you cherish becomes a part of you. Anything or anyone missing from your world can be found just beneath your breastbone – in the beating of your heart.

Beyond Shame & Blame
The Practice of Healing Forgiveness Pain

There isn't anything easy about forgiving someone who does irreparable harm to you or someone you love. Harder still, it seems, is for we humans to forgive ourselves. According to a report issued by the Sacred Art of Living Center (SALC) – of 500 dying patients 66% experienced forgiveness pain for their own past mistakes, 17% were hurt by others, and 6% reported being hurt by God. (11% suffered all three.)

The world's great religions and philosophies tell us that forgiveness is a profound virtue, even a divine commandment. As well, in popular culture, the ability to forgive is viewed as a good and necessary human characteristic. But when, where, and how do we acquire the interpersonal tools to practice the art of genuine forgiveness?

As children, we are sometimes forced to apologize for our harmful actions against others even when we feel that our actions were justified. As well, we're expected to accept neat and tidy apologies from those who wrong us. But who among us ever learned (as a child or otherwise) what to do with residual anger, guilt, blame, shame, or hatred that lingers even after you or the one who hurt you apologizes or shows remorse, and even after you make amends? Who among us was taught to look at conflicts and misunderstandings through the lens of mutual responsibility or create new patterns of relationship in which the same old hurts will not become an everyday occurrence? If you are so fortunate, count yourself among an enlightened minority.

In *for colored girls who have considered suicide when the rainbow is enuf*, Ntozake Shange writes,

> "one thing I don't need
> is any more apologies
> i got sorry greetin me at my front door
> you can keep yrs"

Healing forgiveness pain takes more than wrongdoings being routinely admitted and freely forgiven without addressing the lasting ramifications of the harm done or the hard-edged relational habits that need changing. Whenever pain runs deep, genuine forgiveness requires self-reflection and purposeful action:

- Taking an honest look at the harm you do to others and others do to you (whether ignorantly or knowingly)
- Identifying patterns of abuse and dysfunction
- Confessing to yourself and others the hurtful mistakes, wounds, and betrayals you have inflicted, perpetuated, or endured
- Releasing toxic emotions such as anger, blame, shame, bitterness, hatred, etc.
- Imagining a new, life-giving relationship with one you harmed or who harmed you that fosters integrity, peace, and compassion – *even if it is a relationship you intend to create only within yourself because reconciliation with another who is involved in the wrongdoing isn't helpful, possible, or preferred*

- Making an effort to sustain this new life-giving relationship and to modify it as needed to foster continued healing

You may be one among the fortunate who is well-versed in forgiveness. Perhaps you can rightfully claim a "willingness to forgive" as a characteristic trait. But, even for the best-of-the-best forgivers among us, some grievances and mistakes are more difficult to pardon than others. . . like when a friend or relative betrays your trust beyond belief, or someone abuses your child, spreads lies that ruin your reputation or cause your business to fail, or drives drunk and causes an accident that kills or injures a loved one. As well, you may be a pro at forgiving yourself until you fail to reach out to a loved one who dies by suicide, cause your family to go in debt due to a gambling problem, or (in a moment of inebriated misjudgment) cheat on your spouse. At such times, finding ways to transform forgiveness pain is more imperative than ever. As Catherynne Valente writes in *The Girl Who Fell Beneath Fairyland and Led the Revels There*:

> ". . . there are two kinds of forgiveness in the world: the one you practice because everything really is all right, and what went before is mended. The other kind of forgiveness you practice because someone needs desperately to be forgiven, or because you need just as badly to forgive them, for a heart can grab hold of old wounds and go sour as milk over them."

The real challenge with forgiving yourself and others for causing deep wounds that ooze with grief and do lasting harm is that genuine forgiveness seldom happens once and for all or comes true by saying the magic words; however, repeatedly opening up old wounds to seek healing can also be re-traumatizing. It can be tempting for some of us to put off healing our forgiveness pain until the eleventh hour when deathbed apologies tend to proliferate. Although such last-ditch efforts at healing forgiveness pain may do you and your loved ones some good, the healing process for the living may continue long after a death occurs. So, whenever possible, it's wise to heal forgiveness pain while you still have plenty of time to do it in person.

When forgiveness pain is intense, pay attention to what is comforting, uplifting, and pleasurable in your forgiveness process. If your grief becomes overwhelming, take a break from it now and then through a captivating diversion or much-needed sleep. You can come back to the forgiveness process with renewed energy and a fresh perspective that allows you to clear your way to healing a step at a time.

Tracing the History of Hurt

Every hurtful act has a history, whether that history is based in reality or lives only in the perceptions of the person, family, or community who is hurt. Sometimes, the history is relevant to both the offender and the offended, such as those attacking one another on either side of a war or business partners who look out only for their personal interests. A shared history of a hurt might include living for years with someone who seldom listens when you speak, or who is unwilling or unable to reciprocate for the immense physical, emotional, financial, or psychological support you routinely give, and you are tired, oh so tired.

Sometimes, the history of a hurt is brought into a relationship from elsewhere – for example, when an abused child grows up to become an abusive parent or spouse, or when a baby who is abandoned for weeks and months on end develops sociopathic tendencies devoid of empathy or compassion for others. Perhaps the history of wrongdoing is fueled by oppression or social injustice, addiction, jealousy, cruelty, a chemical imbalance, injury, physical or mental illness, loneliness, or low self-esteem. Whatever it is, the history of a hurt and how you have and have not contributed to that history can give you the insight you need to transform your forgiveness pain.

If you desire to heal your forgiveness pain and keep on healing it, it's crucial to gain some understanding of what part of the hurt is yours to transform, what part of the hurt is yours to let be, and what part of the hurt is yours to let go. Forgiveness can't conjure miracles to undo what cannot be undone, nor can it transform the forgiveness pain that is someone else's burden. That is the hard truth. But it is also true that when you transform the forgiveness pain that is yours to transform, there is a softening of the heart, a mercy of the mind, a peace within the soul that allows compassion to walk through the walls of pain and misunderstanding.

Honoring the Mother & Father of Forgiveness Pain

In my mid twenties, I was in a women's group with others who were in their thirties, forties, and fifties. They were a gathering of intelligent feminists who came together to support one another and converse about various personal and social issues of importance to them. One evening, someone in the group confessed that she felt abandoned by her mother. Soon, almost every one of the ten or twelve others agreed that they too experienced this mother-daughter wound. There was a listing of the transgressions they had experienced due to their mother's abuse, neglect, self-absorption, or misunderstanding. Although I might have added examples of my own, instead I wondered aloud, "Where were your fathers in all of this?" There was an awkward silence, then slowly it dawned on the group that they felt abandoned by their fathers too. Even so, they all agreed it was the mother-wound that festered.

Perhaps these women were giving voice to a gender wound between mother and daughter, or perhaps as a culture, we expect more from our mothers in way of nurture and being there for us. Or, perhaps it's safer for us to blame our mothers for our feelings of abandonment because we sense that genuine bonds of mother-love are difficult to annihilate no matter how much we rail against them.

If you're like most adults, you can probably recall a time when a parent or guardian left you standing alone just when you needed their support and protection most. The more dependable a parent is, the more devastating the blow can be when they don't come through for you. What's more, even a committed parent's job includes knowing when the time is best to allow a child, youth, or young adult to go it alone. So, it's rare for a young person to grow to adulthood without experiencing at least one blow of abandonment from a parent. Such blows have a way of sticking with us. That's why some experts on forgiveness pain say that (no matter what the painful forgiveness issue or conflict of the moment or with whom) practicing forgiveness often begins with forgiving our parents for their flaws and mistakes, particularly those that continue to cause pain for us in the here and now.

Even if you were fortunate to draw the long straw when it comes to the quality of parenting provided for you, no parent is perfect and the job is impossibly complex. What's more, as a child matures, it may become unclear who is abandoning whom. The following story reveals a time when my mother and I stood on opposite sides of the parent-child abandonment chasm:

Going to the Source: A Personal Story of Healing Abandonment Pain

Throughout my parents' child-raising years, my mom was almost solely responsible for the day-to-day well-being of us children. Granted, my dad was usually the one to bring home the big bucks and he was never short on his love for us. But from the time my mom became pregnant at seventeen and quickly found herself the mother of three by the age of 21 (and four by the age of 25), my mom was the one who wiped noses, changed diapers, cooked, cleaned, clothed, and fed us while also helping to earn income for our family and run the family business. All of this in addition to protecting her children from my father's excesses – his periods of heavy drinking, carousing, workaholism, depression, self-harm, violent outbursts, and sometimes biting criticism. If Dad were still alive, he would be the first to admit it, albeit, not proudly.

Despite an incurable ornery streak or two, ultimately Dad's limitations didn't define him. He was successful in his work, deeply compassionate, and full of integrity when it came to helping those in need. In his later years, particularly after he and my mom divorced after 38 years of marriage, my dad capitalized on his best qualities and became an exemplary father and elder I greatly admire. He confessed many regrets and gave my mom generous credit for her commitment and persistence to nurture their children despite his periods of emotional and physical absence in our younger years. Even so, there was no getting around the fact that he wasn't the best spouse or dad when he started out or during his cycles of depression when we were growing up.

My mom did her best to hold the family together through good times and bad. She wielded a tenacious love as she attempted to transform and transcend all family difficulties. What's more, Mom protected Dad from being the "bad guy," the boundary setter, the disciplinarian. Even as we matured into adulthood, she was the buffer when Dad sought time apart from his children and grandchildren (so we wouldn't feel unloved or pushed away by him). But when my dad was present and wasn't blowing up the house or crawling into a cocoon of introversion or depression, he was as charming, fun-loving, and attentive as a father could be.

For most of my growing up through middle school, our family life was a Jekyll-and-Hyde existence with the good times wiping out the bad from our family consciousness. . . until the bad times returned. So, perhaps it's no surprise that despite my dad's offenses and given my mom's herculean efforts to foster love and respect between my dad and his children, oftentimes my mom was scapegoated as the troublemaker. Whenever her anger and resentment erupted and was displaced on us rather than our dad, Mom appeared to be the one who fell short of providing the unconditional love and acceptance we each craved from both our parents. Looking back, I am astounded that my mom survived the worst of those years without walking out the door and leaving us all to fend for ourselves, or suffering a nervous breakdown (or two or three or ten).

In my early years, my mom and I shared a golden bond that I thought could never be broken. We continue to cultivate a deep affection for one another now at my sixty-something to her eighty-something. But it wasn't always that way. During my elementary and middle school years, at times we struggled to understand one another – as many parents and children do. We also weathered many turbulent chapters of our family life together that seemed to cycle back around like the seasons. We were survivors, and by the time I was in high school, we were more than mother and daughter. We were confidantes, counselors, and "girlfriends" to one another. We'd always be there for each other. . . well, at least until I went away to college.

There was a rip that happened in my mother's heart then. She filled it with the thought that I was angry with her. I must have been angry because I didn't call enough or send letters (we didn't have email, texting, or FaceTime in the late '70s). But I wasn't angry. Mostly I was just a kid-becoming-adult and while time passed slowly for my mom, it passed quickly for me. Before I knew it, she was getting a divorce from my dad, striking out on her own, feeling vulnerable and alone. By then, I was in grad school and to my surprise falling in love and becoming engaged to be married – something I told myself that I'd never do.

Between my mom and me, it was the best of times and the worst of times. My mom wanted me to share her bitter anguish and I wanted her to celebrate my unbelievable good fortune. We did neither for one another, not really. We went through the motions now and then, but our hearts weren't in it. When we spoke to one another, we seemed to speak different languages. We fought about things that didn't matter and the subtext of every word in every fight was, "Why can't you just be there for me, love me completely, accept me warts and all." At one point, I suggested going to a counselor together. We never did. Instead over the next few decades, we made it a habit to come close and then suddenly abandon one another at times when our undivided presence was needed most. Once the silence between us lasted for two years or more without a phone call or letter.

When Dad died in January 2005, Mom and I were on speaking terms again, but not for long. My father's death represented monstrous grief for my mom, who felt a longing to speak to him before he died and to attend his memorial. But these opportunities came and went. Although I filled her in on the details of dad's illness and passing, our conversations were like a bed of hot coals that she so wanted to walk across but as she did, she couldn't avoid the searing burn. It was as if every atom of my mother's being was contorted by the painful fire of her unconditional affection and heart-breaking bitterness for a man she would always love like no other – a man she felt was not there for her at crucial moments, did not love her completely, did not accept her warts and all.

Caring for my father in his last months of life and experiencing his beautiful, yes *beautiful*, death with a circle of loved ones who came together generously and courageously to be there with Dad as he slipped away are awe-inspiring memories that I will treasure always. But for my mom that period of separation, not only from the man with whom she shared 38 years of her life but also from their four children who were present there without her, was horrifyingly symbolic of her feelings of abandonment by every person who ever mattered to her. I believe that chronic feeling of abandonment ignited my mom's recurring rage at my father and me. I can't remember how our conversation went after his death, but suddenly Mom was telling me that she never wanted to speak to me again. Once more, she wanted me to share her bitter anguish and I wanted her to celebrate my unbelievable good fortune. But we were like ships passing in the night and the distance rolled out and out like an ocean between us.

Not knowing what to do and not wanting to repeat the past, for a while I did nothing. The wounds of abandonment my mother and I shared were nothing new. These wounds lived in my mom before she married my dad, could be traced back to her mother and her grandmother before her, and back and back through a family history of incest, suicide, and mental illness. Our wounds of abandonment were like a generational tradition. But it had to stop somewhere and whether my mom had ever really abandoned me or not, I didn't care to live the rest of my days feeling like a motherless child as she and her mother and her grandmother did before me. So, rather than repeat our relational patterns that included me blaming my mom for her inability to be there for me when I needed her most and shaming myself for not being the daughter or friend she desired as she nursed her wounds, I decided to heal this mother-daughter wound without her.

Many months later, I was training to be a spiritual director. One assignment included the practice of centering prayer, an ancient meditation form that I had never tried before. It involves using a single word as a silent mantra of focus to let go of distracting thoughts, feelings, and sensations. In that focused and silent place within, there is a soulful connection, an energetic expansion that can occur in which one can access and converse with a spiritual thread of consciousness within and beyond the self. I was skeptical that it would be effective for me, but I decided to give it a try.

There I was, sitting in an airplane with my spouse, Andrew, on one side and our daughter Willa on the other; they were engrossed in the in-flight movie. I put on noise-reducing headphones and committed myself to twenty minutes of silently repeating my mantra, "Amma" (an Aramaic word for "mother" or "mama") – that I chose with the healing of my mother-daughter wound in mind.

It took a few minutes to give myself over to breathing and speaking my mantra within. Then, suddenly, I sensed a spiritual presence in and around my body, an energetic life force communicating to me that this spiritual presence had always been, would always be, all the mother I would ever need. Instantaneously, I experienced healing at a cellular level, as if this spiritual experience was changing the imprint of my DNA, healing not only my personal mother-daughter wound but also the familial wounds that had been passed from mother to daughter from generation to generation. In that moment, I felt that my personal and family biography was forever changed.

There in the middle of the airplane, I quietly wept with the knowledge of this inexplicable healing. Then a week or so later from out of the blue, my mother called me. Her voice was peaceful and tender on the other end of the line. She asked if we might begin again. She said she was sorry for anything she said or did to hurt me. We didn't review the details of the hurt that transpired between us. We simply agreed to wipe the slate clean and see what we could make of our relationship aside from blaming one another or shaming ourselves. That was over a decade ago. Since then, my mom and I have experienced conflicts now and then, but we have not abandoned the effort it takes to talk them through when we're able or to move past them when we're not. We don't always see eye to eye when it comes to recounting past family history or assessing interpersonal circumstances or social interactions; but, when we butt heads, we take a step back and generously agree to disagree. We're able to give one another room to be ourselves, to be human, make mistakes, and eventually come back together again in a spirit of humility, understanding, and forgiveness.

Sometimes, healing forgiveness pain can free you from the burden of perpetually yearning for more than a parent, child, or any loved one can give.

Practicing Reconciliation in More Ways Than One

Reconciliation with someone you hurt or who hurt you can be positively transformative. Equally true: it can do more damage than good. It may be that you or someone you hurt doesn't have the desire, energy, know-how, or resources to seek reconciliation without creating further trauma or sacrificing a hard-won sense of health and well-being. The relational dynamics or emotional chemistry between you and another, even someone you love greatly, may not work after repeated attempts. Finally, you admit it and go your separate ways. But don't let that separation keep you from healing forgiveness pain and making peace with yourself. If you fail to do so, the hurt is likely to fester and seep into other intimate relationships.

Whether you choose to heal your forgiveness pain solo or together with others, reconciliation can happen by:

- *Reconciling with what is*: accepting the changed reality caused by the harm done that cannot be undone
- *Reconciling with what is required for restitution*: identifying what desirable change can be changed, deciding how specific changes will be made, and putting forth the effort to make it happen
- *Reconciling differences in perspective*: after conflict, creating a full picture of what transpired that includes the perspectives of each person or group involved before negotiating a resolution that is acceptable and fair to everyone
- *Reconciling with the one you harmed or who harmed you*: whether reconciliation happens between intimates regarding day-to-day hurts that need

tending or regarding grave offenses inflicted by intimates, acquaintances, or strangers that involve lasting harm

- *Reconciling with yourself:* making peace with yourself after inflicting or enduring harm in ways that allow you to acknowledge, transform, and heal your forgiveness pain

Reconciling with yourself after you inflict harm on another may be more difficult than reconciling with those who harm you – especially if you harmed a loved one you're obliged to protect and honor. Self-forgiveness demands self-awareness, self-respect, and self-compassion that allows you to admit your mistakes, offer recompense however you're able, and mercifully free yourself from defining your relationships with yourself and others by past errors.

When you experience remorse for a wrongdoing, you may find yourself denying or justifying your harmful words or actions because they are too reprehensible to face, or you may punish yourself indefinitely for a harm done that can't be retracted – even when you or a loved one is overtly violated by another person or circumstances beyond your control. Yes, even when you are from every angle an innocent victim, you may experience a need to forgive that part of you that feels responsible for allowing harm to find its way to you or someone you love. Wallowing in regrets or blaming yourself for another's actions when you were not able to protect yourself or a loved one from harm is just another way to perpetuate the hurt. No matter what the offense or who is at fault, the harm done has to stop somewhere. Let it stop with you.

Forgiving others is like a sacred ritual that balances your own need for mercy, and forgiving yourself is a lesson in humility like no other. To practice genuine forgiveness, you have to find that crack in human consciousness where grace and mercy can slip through. So, don't let a day go by without admitting to yourself that you depend upon forgiveness to help right your wrongdoings and overhaul your mistakes as much as the next fool. Forgive yourself and others, not only for past mistakes, but also for being human and fallible. Loosen your grip on your biased perceptions and beliefs about yourself and others, and imagine for a moment – yes, at least for a moment – that all of us are doing the best we can do.

Taking Stock of Your Forgiveness Pain

If it's relevant for you, take an honest look at your present forgiveness pain, making sure that you only review past hurts to the extent that it's helpful. If your forgiveness pain is problematic for you, seek out a counselor or trusted confidante for support. Go slowly and nurture a bounty of compassion for yourself and others as you untangle your suffering. Whether solo or in the company of others, the following reflective practice may be a good place to start:

1) Identify a personal wound inflicted upon you that is a source of ongoing physical, emotional, social, psychological, or spiritual pain.

2) Identify a wound you inflicted on another that is a source of ongoing suffering for you and/or for the one you harmed.

3) When you're ready, able, and willing, explore your perceptions of responsibility, guilt, shame, and blame related to each of these hurtful acts, perhaps by asking yourself one or more of the following questions:
   - Who is responsible for the harm done? Is there a clear culprit who was the offender, or do those involved share mutual responsibility?
   - Has the hurtful outcome been minimized or exaggerated by you or others?
   - What was the extent of the damage done?
   - Is the harm done to you worth being offended over?
   - Was the one who was hurt disempowered or victimized – for example, a child or youth mistreated by an adult, a victim of abuse or violence, or one who was bullied, oppressed, or subject to the power or authority of another?
   - Are there any similarities between the harm inflicted upon you and harm you inflicted on another?
   - Was the hurt you endured or inflicted acted out vengefully or accidentally, knowingly or ignorantly? Was the offender influenced by abuse or addiction, mental illness, family, social or institutional dysfunction, emotional disturbance, or distress?
   - Was the wrongdoing a one-time occurrence or was it the result of dysfunctional relationship patterns or systemic injustice?

Once you explore the sources of your forgiveness pain, consider how your grieving responses have intensified or transformed your suffering:

4) In the past, what made your forgiveness pain worse – perhaps, ruminating on a loss, unrelenting emotions of shame, guilt, blame, anger, bitterness, etc., being in the presence of someone you harmed or who harmed you, experiencing melancholy or depression after a drinking or eating binge, engaging in activities or being in a situation that you associate with a loss, or being pressured to forgive someone you aren't able or willing to forgive, etc.?

5) In the past, what or who helped you to ease and transform your forgiveness pain in lasting ways that did no further harm to you or another?

ᚼ ᚼ ᚼ

A real difficulty with healing forgiveness pain is that many of the wounds we humans inflict upon one another are not obvious to the naked eye. We often hurt each other simultaneously, sometimes without even knowing of the pain our words or actions caused another, or understanding how some commonplace interaction managed to offend. Patterns of assumption or avoidance may blind you from seeing any part you play in the harm done. To resolve forgiveness pain, it's crucial to acknowledge our shared human capacities to hurt others and be hurt by others. None of us has a market on shame or blame.

Can You Forgive the Unrepentant?

There is an anonymous quote making the rounds on the internet these days that says, "I never knew how strong I was until I had to forgive someone who wasn't sorry and accept an apology I never received." Yes, there may be times, for your own good and that of your loved ones, that you will seek to forgive those who are ignorant of the pain they cause you or who know of it and show no remorse. Such injuries may be inflicted by a person or social group, an entire family or community, or an institution.

In your family, there may be festering wounds that ache with forgiveness pain but go unaddressed for years – if ever they are acknowledged. When long-ago hurts are finally brought to light, each person involved may remember completely different versions of the same event or may not remember the incident at all. That's how human memory works – it is selective and oftentimes biased toward our beliefs and perceptions of ourselves and others. Becoming eternally bitter or vengeful over hurts that are played over and over again in your mind without addressing them promptly or sufficiently when they occur, may only serve to make your forgiveness pain worse.

Despite bearing the burden of intangible proof, there may be instances when healing requires you to stand up for yourself or a loved one to seek retribution or justice for unacknowledged suffering of the past. Those who were abused as a child, or attacked or raped without therapeutic or legal support at the time, may find that the road back to health includes confronting a victimizer or going public with a past story of abuse. Such efforts may be an essential part of the healing process.

There is much debate concerning whether or not some offenses are forgivable (murder, rape, domestic violence, child abuse, terrorism, infidelity, etc.) and if so, whether any sense of pardon or reconciliation is beneficial – either for the one who was harmed (or their loved ones) or the one who did the harming. Some people believe that some offenders don't deserve mercy, especially those who fail to acknowledge the hurt they inflicted. However, genuine forgiveness is a process by which anger, blame, shame, hatred, and a seeking of vengeance are given up, sacrificed for the sake of peace within yourself above all else. So, the real beauty of forgiving yourself and others is the commitment you make not to perpetuate the harm that is already done. That is all that forgiveness will ever ask of you. If you choose to give more by way of pardoning yourself or another, reconciling with one who harmed you, or even condoning the hurtful act as justifiable once all the details of the circumstances are known, then that is up to you.

Heroic examples of forgiveness reconciliation and pardoning abound. There are astounding stories – one of a mother adopting the young man who murdered her son. There is a father who befriended the grandfather and guardian of the fourteen-year-old boy who shot and killed his son (who was a college student and pizza delivery man) for not giving up the pizza that the boy and his friends ordered and planned to steal. Father and grandfather travel around together, talking with young people about the power of forgiveness. There are stories of children forgiving their parents for unthinkable abuse and exploitation, and whole countries adopting post-genocide processes of reconciliation by which those who raped, pillaged, killed, and tortured are pardoned for their wrongdoings. Such stories are examples of our human capacities for mercy.

But just as heroic are the efforts of grievers who heal forgiveness pain without granting a pardon or reconciling with an offender:

- The young adult who was the victim of repeated beatings as a child who, once separated from the abuser, builds a life and relationships with others in which the intense anger, fear, and bitterness driven into the young person's soul are courageously transformed
- The sex trafficking victim who finally escapes their torture and becomes a vocal advocate for other victims of sexual exploitation or the inmate who is unjustly incarcerated and (after a successful appeal and release) becomes a champion for prisoners' rights and a proponent for those appealing unjust convictions
- The wounded war veteran who, with the help of loved ones and those providing post-combat mental health care, recovers from post-traumatic stress – so that capacities for inner peace, intimacy, cherished meaning, and hope in daily life are gradually restored
- The ex-spouse who finds joy and trust again in a romantic partnership after being betrayed by their "one and only"
- The person chronically scapegoated by their family of origin who, instead of going back for more mistreatment to prove themselves worthy of love and empathy, creates a new "family" – one that is not defined by blood or name, but by a handshake of the heart, an echo in the soul that says, "I know you. Kick off your shoes and make yourself at home"

When you struggle with forgiveness pain that seems to be never-ending, pray at last there comes a time when you realize that hoarding your anger, shame, blame, guilt, fear, bitterness, or hatred requires far more effort over the long haul than the effort it takes to transform it and let it go. Even after you do, remnants of forgiveness pain may float back to you in the winds of memory or circumstance, slapping you with the hurt once again. A renewed need for forgiveness may return. On top of that, there will always be new opportunities to forgive yourself and others, because we humans are often clumsy in our relationships with one another, even (or perhaps, especially) with the people we love best.

Practical Ideas for Healing Forgiveness Pain

Depending on your present needs for lamenting, heartening, tempering, or integrating, seek out approaches to healing forgiveness pain that are authentic and effective for you. Practice what works and keep practicing – perhaps through one or more of the following approaches:

- **Acknowledging the Hurt:** Acknowledging the hurt at the root of forgiveness pain involves more than lamenting the reasons for your suffering. It requires a good look through the lens of objectivity to size up the circumstances and people wrapped up with your pain. This may be a private undertaking or it may call for the supportive presence of a trusted counselor, friend or family member. Either way, a certain vulnerability is required to integrate the circumstances that fuel your forgiveness pain. Such integrating efforts may include:

    - **Confessing to Yourself & Others:** When you suffer forgiveness pain, find a tangible way to confess it to yourself or a trusted confidante. If your forgiveness pain is shrouded in silence, you may find that confessing the harm you inflicted or endured helps you to lament, hearten, and integrate your grief and the loss at the center of your suffering. There are endless ways to make your confession: express it in an artistic form – prose or poetry, songwriting, painting, journaling, sculpting, building, collaging, etc.; tell a trustworthy friend, spiritual director, or counselor who can listen without judgment; or seek out a support group to explore the nuances of your forgiveness pain.

    - **Saying Sorry:** Whether you're solely to blame for a conflict or wrongdoing or not, assessing your remorse for your words and actions that added to a hurtful situation can be liberating. Practice saying sorry to those you harm even for little offenses and do it without expectations for the other's mercy, empathy, or reciprocal apology. Refrain from using your apology to justify your hurtful words or actions, or blame the other for causing you to say or do something you regret. Genuinely expressing that you're sorry is different from asking for someone's forgiveness. You don't need anyone's permission to do it and you can offer an apology with no strings attached. Of course, the best apologies include reflecting on how you can do things differently next time, then doing it when the time comes.

    - **Braving a Broader View:** If you're willing and able, trace the history of a wrongdoing from the perspective of a person you hurt or someone who hurt you. Building empathy for others can help you trace harmful words and actions to the source of the pain that caused them. For example, a friend of a friend was once accosted by a man as she took her daily jog. The man literally picked the woman up and started running down the street with her. Of course, the woman was frightened, but she found herself saying to her offender, "Who hurt you, who is it that hurt you?" After she asked the question several times, the man finally set her down. Amazingly, the woman ended up inviting him to her home that day to help him out, and then never heard from him again.

Perhaps it was a naive gesture and one that ought to be qualified: "Caution – don't try this at home." However, the story demonstrates that empathy can be a powerful shield when it comes to protecting ourselves and others from perpetuating harms of the past.

- **Releasing the Hurt:** For a heartening sense of release from hurtful memories, emotions, thinking patterns, and sensations caused by forgiveness pain, it may be helpful to engage in activities that help you to purge your pain. For example,

  - **Letting It Go:** Create a ritual of release. It may be as simple as giving away, recycling, shredding, or safely burning objects, photographs, letters, newspaper articles, or other memorabilia that fuel your negative feelings and memories. Or, you might create a simple ceremony by painting a symbol of past hurts on a flat rock, then tossing it into a large body of water or taking it on a long hike and leaving it somewhere in nature. When my mom and dad got divorced, my mom melted their wedding rings into a gold necklace charm as a symbol of her new beginning, letting go of past hurts, and carrying the gifts she gained from their relationship with her into the future. Create whatever ritual of release is most meaningful for you.

  - **Re-imagining the Hurt:** Use daily prayer, visualization, or lovingkindness meditation (see *Lovingkindness* in "Mindfulness & Meditation" listings on page 332) to imagine yourself or another person free from forgiveness pain and filled with healing energy. To release anger, hatred, or yearning for vengeance toward someone who hurt you, you might visualize the offender being healed of the pain that fueled the offense in the first place and wish the person well. To release forgiveness pain within yourself, breathe naturally; as you exhale, imagine all the suffering you experience in your body, heart, mind, and spirit being released; as you inhale, imagine being filled with peace, light, and a sense of levity until every trace of your suffering vanishes. Memorize this way of being and practice it often.

  - **Exorcising the Pain:** Physical movements can help to purge your forgiveness pain (or any physical grief you harbor). Several years ago, when I was struggling with forgiveness pain, I found myself sighing many times a day and realized that this was my body's way of attempting to release the grip that my suffering had on me. Try releasing your grief-related pain through sighing, laughing, crying, orgasm, sports and exercise, dancing, shaking out your legs and arms, gently tapping over an area of the body where suffering lodged itself, massage, energy work, or whatever physical release helps you to rid your body of toxic feelings and sensations. For a more formalized approach to the physical release of forgiveness pain, check out Eye Movement Desensitization and Reprocessing (EMDR) therapy that is guided by a trained practitioner (see "Emotional Healing," on page 325) or learn Trauma Release Exercise (TRE) that involves physical tremoring techniques you can do on your own (see "Exercise, Body Awareness & Physical Release" on page 326.)

- **Re-thinking the Harm Done**: Forgiveness expert, Fred Luskin, suggests a tempering approach to forgiveness pain that involves deciding not to be offended by another's wrongdoing. Luskin says this approach can minimize harm that a potential offense does to you. Using this technique is misguided if the offense calls for radical interpersonal or social change – domestic abuse, violence, terrorism, date rape, or hate crimes; but it may be useful with lesser offenses. Luskin talks about the application of this technique in response to infidelity or rejection in romantic relationships. Being the victim of romantic infidelity or rejection can be painful. But Luskin claims that if you see the experience as an opportunity to reassess your relational commitments rather than as a failure, it may inspire a change that leads to a more meaningful, contented, and happy life.

- **Putting Remorse Into Action:** Brooding over your mistakes is the surest way to defeat yourself when it comes to forgiving yourself for wrongdoings of the past. Putting your remorse into action can help to integrate the source of your forgiveness pain in ways that are heartening for you and others. A poignant example of making things right in the broader scheme of things, is illustrated in the movie *Gandhi* when a Hindu man named Nahari laments to Gandhi of his simultaneous rage and remorse at being both victim and murderer in the ongoing conflict between the Muslims and Hindus in India:

    Nahari: I'm going to Hell! I killed a child! I smashed his head against a wall.

    Gandhi: Why?

    Nahari: Because they killed my son! The Muslims killed my son!

    Gandhi: I know a way out of Hell. Find a child, a child whose mother and father have been killed, and raise him as your own. Only be sure that he is a Muslim and that you raise him as one.

    Your need for forgiveness may seem mundane in comparison to Nahari's story, but if you hope to forgive yourself and make a change to avoid making the same old mistakes that caused harm to another, it can be remarkably helpful to clarify what positive change may be possible and take action to make it so.

- **Listening to the Hurt:** In your intimate relationships, integrating forgiveness pain to make it useful includes speaking and listening to one another in a spirit of compassion whenever someone is hurt by the words or actions of another. Pay attention to what transpires when the hurt is acknowledged: Does the offender withdraw, quickly apologize to avoid further conflict, or become defensive and begin to list all the ways they were wronged by another to avoid taking responsibility? Unless you're one of the fully enlightened, hurting one another in intimate relationships is inevitable, even if the hurt inflicted is simply misunderstanding another's words or actions when it matters. So, it's useful to have a familiar listening process in place to hear one another out and focus on fostering understanding rather than "one-upping" each other with who committed the greatest offense. If you use it wisely, conflict can improve your relationships for the better. (See "Listening" resources on page 329.)

※ ※ ※

If you hope for a good death that is free from forgiveness pain, live your life as if forgiveness matters. Everyday, we can grasp opportunities to forgive ourselves and others. We can seek understanding for those we misunderstand and who misunderstand us, love those who seem unlovable, and show compassion to those who appear to be undeserving, including ourselves. It is the only way we will keep from blowing up the house we live in.

Once upon a time in the U.S., during the politically turbulent times of the mid to late 1960s, the title of a Hal David song became a mantra of popular culture: "What the world needs now is love." But more than love, what the world needs now is forgiveness. Because, without forgiveness, love is likely to strangle itself.

Guidepost 46

Try this: measure out a cup of forgiveness to pass around every day, and don't be surprised when it comes back to you empty — sometimes, even before it leaves your hands.

Hope Against Hope
The Practice of Healing Hopelessness Pain

For some, hopelessness pain is the "terminal illness" of spiritual pain. It is strongly related to depression and suicide, and may be the most difficult type of spiritual pain to transform. As William Styron aptly puts it, "It is hopelessness even more than pain that crushes the soul." When a person is without hope, words of comfort are likely to fall flat and a person's spiritual or philosophical beliefs may shed no light on what some call "the dark night of the soul." In that empty place where hope is absent, a griever will likely be repelled by well-meaning attempts from others to raise the curtains of hopelessness even a little to let some light in.

Perhaps you (or a loved one) know the desolate wasteland of hopelessness pain where your spirit is pounded over and over again with the message that there is nothing to be done about your current state of suffering. When there is no hope, there is no seeing a future in which life will ever get any better. For the hopeless, life becomes an endless trek upon which the thirsty will never find water, the hungry will never be fed. The hopeless believe that whatever is needed to spark one's imagination for a better future, simply does not exist.

Any grief-striking loss that causes a person to feel utterly out of control may foster a sense of hopelessness that makes "keeping on with it" seem pointless – for example, losses involving terminal illness, life-threatening violence, death or disappearance of a loved one, abandonment, chronic abuse, being permanently debilitated by an injury or illness, experiencing a critical failure, depression, powerlessness, chronic loneliness, or being marginalized or rejected, and the list goes on. Whether one acts upon it or not, a griever who is without hope may ruminate upon death as an escape from unbearable physical or psychological pain.

Take a moment to consider your current state of hope:

- Do you generally feel optimistic or pessimistic about the future?
- Can you name a handful of reasons you are grateful to be alive or do you often find life to be a drudgery that promises only continued suffering?
- On a scale of one to ten, with one being least hopeful and ten being most hopeful, how would you rate your sense of hope at present?

Once you assess your present state of hopefulness, contemplate a time in your life when hope eluded you or was at an all-time low:

- Was there a situation that precipitated your experience of hopelessness?
- Was it at a time in your life when you were feeling depressed, alone, misunderstood, or helpless?
- What, if anything, moved you out of hopelessness into hope?

Maria Edgeworth wrote, "Those who are animated by hope can perform what would seem impossibilities to those who are under the depressing influence of fear." Add to fear, the depressing influence of injury, illness, self-doubt, anger, hunger, loneliness, despair, or any number of hope-thieving ogres that may accompany grief. The "depressing influence" of disparaging words or actions that strip you of the self-confidence you need to achieve a goal or invest in your future happiness may also cause hope to flee. The worst kind of thieves are those who make it a business to rob hope from those who grieve and the greatest benefactors are those who help to restore it. Consider the story of Clara Juden:

Clara-fying Hope: A Teacher Transforms Hopelessness Pain

Clara Juden was born in Missouri in 1929 at the beginning of the Great Depression. An only child to her mother and father, Clara's childhood home was situated near the Frisco Railroad line that ran between St. Louis and Memphis, Tennessee. As Clara grew and began to speak, it became apparent that a birth defect caused a severe speech impediment. Her garbled speech made it difficult to communicate with others. Clara noticed that people looked at her dumbfounded whenever she tried to engage with them or offer directions to someone who was lost. Children at school were often unkind. It took Clara some time to realize that her speech impediment was like a foreign language to others and that the vast majority were unwilling to learn it.

To make matters worse, Clara's second-grade teacher was a hope thief. Clara clearly remembers the moment she and her classmates were asked to write about the goals they imagined accomplishing by earning an education. Clara wrote about her desire to become a teacher. However, her hopes were quickly smashed when in front of the whole class her teacher announced by way of a rhetorical question, "Now Clara, how do you ever expect to be a teacher when you can't even speak properly?" The same message resounded again and again throughout her grade school education. That message caused Clara a bundle of grief as her sense of self-worth was battered again and again. But in her heart's core, she knew that she was destined to be a teacher. She studied hard and hoped that her efforts would be sufficient to overcome her liabilities.

Clara spent long hours on her own and sometimes played near the railroad tracks, watching the trains go by. Perhaps she imagined how she might hop on a train one day and travel far away from the people in her little town who had no idea of Clara's capabilities or her bright and active mind. Perhaps she imagined a train taking her to the school she pictured in her imagination where she would teach one day.

There was a freight engineer on the Frisco line, Ed Cable, who was acquainted with Clara's family and often came to hunt on their land. He talked with Clara and soon recognized both her difficulties and her intelligence. So, each time the train came through, Ed yelled to Clara from his locomotive perch and threw her the latest newspaper so she could practice reading and learn of important events taking place in the world beyond.

By the time Clara reached high school, her grades were impeccable. But there were yet other obstacles to overcome. The family home was flooded and a few years later both of Clara's parents died. So, her friend Ed Cable invited Clara to live with him and his sister in Chaffee, Missouri. There she was provided a stable and loving home in the wake of her tragic losses. What's more, Ed became her educational advocate in earnest, making sure that Clara received the education she deserved so she would be well-prepared to attend college. Although Clara had enough credits to graduate by her senior year, she was told by the vice-principal that her valedictorian status was compromised by the fact that she had only been in the school system since her junior year. She was encouraged to take another year of classes so that she could claim her well-deserved academic award. However, Clara saw it differently. To her, others' perceptions of her abilities were less important than becoming a teacher. So, Clara chose to graduate without the honor and went on to enroll in Southeast Missouri (SEMO) Teacher's College in Cape Girardeau.

Again, at SEMO on the first day of Speech class, Clara was asked by the professor to write about her goals. Again Clara expressed her passion to become a teacher. After class the next day, her professor asked her to stay behind when the others were dismissed. Clara thought she was in trouble. She imagined that she would be told that her dream to be a teacher was unrealistic and she would need to choose another path. Instead, the Speech teacher kindly asked Clara to come by the window where there was more light so she could take a look into Clara's open mouth. As she did, she said, "Just as I thought." The next time Clara was asked to stay after class, two professors were looking into her mouth! Then, they told her what she was to do.

The professors provided Clara with a recipe for a special thick milkshake that she was to drink through a straw. Three times a week, Clara walked from campus, uphill about a mile, to Sunny Hill Dairy to order the milkshake. The first time she sat to drink it, it took her a good 2-1/2 hours to finish. The professors worked with Clara throughout her college years to teach her to speak slowly and accurately. They taught her to form words in her mind before she spoke them. Under their tutelage, Clara made monumental progress. After graduation, she not only became a successful first-grade teacher and continued at it for 34 years, she was also chosen to be president of her school district's Parent-Teacher Association (PTA).

Clara's parting act as PTA president was giving an outgoing speech at the Missouri PTA Convention. As fate would have it, in the audience that day was the second-grade teacher who told Clara that her dream of becoming an educator was impossible. After the speech, as Clara walked off the stage, the teacher approached her and exclaimed, "Well, you could have knocked me over with a feather!" Clara smiled and thanked this woman who represented to her every naysayer who had ever doubted her. But Clara's gracious response did not deprive her of an inward dance for joy, reveling in the serendipitous event when this antagonist from her childhood was a witness to a pinnacle moment of her teaching career.

Perhaps Clara's graciousness toward this hope thief came from the habit she formed throughout her life to take wise advantage of every opportunity she was provided by those who fanned the flames of her hope. These gifts, she paid forward. After Clara retired from teaching, the school district continued to send students who struggled in school (whether academically or socially) to Clara's home so they could blossom under her wise tutelage. As a teacher and a tutor, Clara taught her students that they could always improve their life circumstances and she was there for them to help make it so. But perhaps the greatest lesson Clara bestowed through her life's work was that improbabilities are not life sentences, and of that, she was living proof.

(This retelling of Clara Juden's story was inspired by the recollections of Clara's high school classmate, Demetra Anne Woodyard.)

Once upon a time, what unlikely person, activity, place, or event served as a harbinger of hope for you when you needed it most?

As Clara's story demonstrates, hope can come in many forms. Although speech therapists and researchers today may question the efficacy of a "milkshake treatment plan" for those who suffer as Clara did, for Clara the prescribed milkshake trips were a symbol of hope that propelled an unlikely would-be teacher toward achieving the dream she carried with her from childhood.

Being a conduit of hope for yourself and others is easier if you possess a naturally optimistic temperament as Clara did. Jane Austen wrote in her novel *Emma*,

> ". . . but a sanguine temper(ament), forever expecting more good than occurs, does not always pay for its hopes by any proportion of depression. It soon flies over the present failure, and begins to hope again."

This temperamental inequity may seem unfair to those who find hope to be generally elusive even in good times. But grief has a way of leveling the playing field. Under the weight of grief-ladened burdens, the levity that we optimists depend upon may buckle. Grief can smother every bit of hope you once took for granted.

We all have times in our lives when we are less hopeful than at others. So, before you get there, it's essential to stock up on personal approaches to healing that create openings for renewed hope, motivation, and belief in a better future. Waiting until you're stuck in the quicksand of hopelessness to identify activities, people, places, and things that offer you a hand up to hope can be a dangerous play. Generating hope takes practice. So, if you forgot how it's done, you'd best get to it, because without hope, healing becomes irrelevant.

Practical Ideas for Healing Hopelessness Pain

Fortunately, hopefulness can be learned and is a useful habit when grief-burdening circumstances justify having no hope at all. To make hope a habit:

- **Identify and Disinvest in Hopelessness**: Think of hopelessness as junk food for the mind, an addictive substance that once you devour it, can trick you into thinking that you can't get enough – like the motto of a famous potato chip brand, "You won't be able to eat just one." One thought of hopelessness can easily lead to another, robbing you of every good memory of your past, every reason to celebrate the present, every imagination of a better tomorrow and the means to get there. So, make it a habit to assess the influences in your life that act as hope thieves. Hopelessness may be generated by your repetitive thoughts, feelings, and actions, or may be imposed upon you by hopeless circumstances, a dysfunctional relationship, or a sense of powerlessness to change what needs changing. Identify the sources of your hopelessness and learn to temper hopelessness pain by disinvesting your time and energy from feeding it. Here are a few practical ideas to get you started:

  - **Thoughts Matter:** If you keep telling yourself that a situation will never get better, it probably won't (at least in your perception). Take stock of messages you replay to yourself that perpetuate hopelessness; find ways to disrupt negative self-talk and thinking patterns that rob you of hope. For example, after a divorce or death of a spouse, you might tell yourself, "I will never trust another partner," or "I will never find true love again." After a child dies, night and day you may tell yourself, "My life has no purpose." After a personal failure or romantic infidelity, you may lament, "My partner will never be able to respect, forgive, or trust me again." After a business goes belly up, your mantra may be, "I am ruined." Whatever the hopeless message, change your relationship to it in a tangible way that makes room for hope – for example:

    - **A Powerful Act:** Write the negative message on a slip of paper and say aloud: "I refuse to let this message dominate my life." Then, tear the message to shreds. Do this every time you think or speak the negative message to remind yourself that you can assert some power over how you think about yourself, your loss, or the grief related to it.

    - **A Subtle Change in Perspective:** Write your negative message on a slip of paper. Turn the slip of paper over and write the statement as a wonderment or question. For example, if your message is, "I will never find true love again," write "I wonder if I will ever find true love again," or "Will I ever find true love again?" If you can muster a bit more courage, ask, "How might I seek true love again?" Your thoughts create your realities, so changing your phraseology can change your perspective and help to keep the door of possibility open, even if it is only a crack.

    - **Refocus the Message:** Write your negative message on one small section of a full sheet of paper. Then as you contemplate the message, ask yourself what alternate realities permit you to hope. For example, if your negative message is "My life has no purpose," write other messages around this message that propose how your life still has purpose. If your negative message is "I am ruined" due to a business failure, alter your message to state specifically what aspect of your life is ruined – for example, "My business is bankrupt," "My biggest client moved to another company," or "My business partner ran off with all our assets and the blueprints for my new invention." Then, around this foreboding message, write down a brainstorm of messages that reflect aspects of your life that are not ruined and may be thriving. Perhaps an intimate relationship is solid or you are looking forward to a visit from a long-time friend. Perhaps you enjoy exercising each day, playing a sport you love, or walking in nature. Perhaps you have a keen mind for strategizing solutions to your problems or can liquidate assets to get you through some thin times financially.

If you can't think of any positive aspects of your life and relationships, ask a trusted counselor or confidante to help you. Whenever you find yourself dwelling on your negative message, return to your collection of alternate realities that promote a more hopeful perspective.

- **Under the Influence:** If a friend or loved one is depressed or suicidal, you may find yourself lending an ear to their hopelessness or empathically absorbing their sense of despondency or despair without them ever saying a word. It's crucial not to allow your loved one's chronic hopelessness to become your own. When a friend or family member digs a hole of hopelessness and refuses to come out for sunshine and fresh air, it's time to help your loved one identify a counselor or other support person who is expert at getting to the root of hopelessness to help transform it.

There may be others you know who are not depressed or suicidal, but who characteristically thrive on hopelessness and negativity and subject you constantly to their moaning and groaning. If need be, find ways to gracefully set limits on conversations around negative topics. If you are subject to someone in a position of authority who lords hopelessness over you, someone you can't avoid or don't want to risk holding accountable (a boss, teacher, judge, etc.), seek out a healthy source of hope each time you're subject to the person's influence to balance its negative effects.

- **When Hope Is Out of Place:** Be aware of places and objects that feed your hopelessness. Avoid them whenever hope is difficult for you to muster. Put away or get rid of objects in your home that hold negative memories that rob you of hope. If the objects might be cherished at a later time or by others, ask a trusted confidante to keep them for you or give objects away to someone who will cherish them.

- **Identify and Reinvest in Hope:** Hope is a gamble. The more often you hope, the more often you may be disappointed in hopes that don't come true. That's why it's a good idea to sow more seeds of hope than are likely to grow. Nurture your ability to hope beyond hope as you might learn a new language. You will know you are fluent in hope when you not only speak of hope but also think and dream in that language. You'll be an expert at flipping your hopelessness on its head to jostle remnants of hope from the pockets of your despair.

  An earnest quest for hope reveals that even hopelessness has its uses. For one thing, hopelessness can foster an acceptance of "what is." Accepting the hopelessness of a grief-striking circumstance creates a stark backdrop for detecting the light-filled hope that can save you.

  There is a story about a boy who was badly burned and lying in a hospital bed covered in bandages, unable to speak, and without a shred of hope that his life would ever get any better. . . until a rookie teacher came in to tutor the boy in his school work. Although the teaching process was tedious and the teacher felt for days and weeks that she made no progress with the injured boy, the nursing staff saw an immediate change in the boy's demeanor. Later when the boy was able to speak again, he admitted that when he was lying in that hospital bed day after day with his burns and bandages, he thought all was lost. Then his new teacher came and he knew he would live because, in his mind, a teacher wouldn't take the time or make the effort to teach a child who was dying.

  When you're in need of hope, try one of the following:

  - **Taking Note of Hope:** Keep a running log of every source of hope you can wrap your mind around in a day, week, or month – every person, activity, daily routine, aspect of your work or play, encouraging words, place in nature, a particular time of day, etc. that inspires you to believe that your life has a purpose and that your reasons to keep "keeping on" will be made clear in time. Whenever hopelessness knocks you down, revisit this list of hopes you can usually count on to lift your spirits. Focus on the sources of hope that speak to you in your present circumstances.

  - **Daily Gratitude:** Every day, upon waking or preparing for sleep, at breakfast or dinner, pause to remember one good thing for which you are grateful. Perhaps that one good thing is an inspiring relationship you share with another, an activity you enjoy, a delicious meal someone cooked for you (or you for yourself), a special event you're anticipating, the sun shining through the window, a refreshing breeze on a warm day, your ability to support yourself or your loved ones emotionally and/or financially, etc.

    If gratitude is difficult for you, you might want to start with something you usually take for granted. For example, when my daughter Morgan began to transform her eating disorder, she engaged in a daily exercise from the *Fitspiration Journal* (getfitbook.com) in which she was to list one thing she appreciated about her "strong body." At first, it was uncomfortable to imagine something she genuinely appreciated, so she started with such expressions of gratitude as, "I am grateful for my ten fingers," "my ten toes," "my heart pumping blood through my body," "my skin holding me together." These expressions of gratitude kept her going until she was able to accept and love her body more completely.

Acknowledge a different source of gratitude each day for a whole week. Even when you're suffering, you may be surprised how many good things in your life inspire gratitude. Thankfully, gratitude is a harbor for hope.

- **Hopers Unite:** Even when it seems there is nothing to be done to improve on a situation, making an effort to build a sense of community, collaboration, and cooperation with others can inspire hope and belief in a better tomorrow. The documentary, *Reason for Hope: A Spiritual Journey* (1999), is an example. The film offers a glimpse into the life of scientist, conservationist, and humanitarian Jane Goodall. Goodall studied and communed with the chimpanzees in Tanzania for a good thirty years with few other humans around her in that natural rainforest habitat. However, when abduction and deforestation threatened her chimpanzee companions, Goodall decided to leave her home with the chimps to travel around the world, persuading others that there is much that can be done together in the name of peace and humanity to make the earth a better dwelling place for ourselves and other creatures. Goodall offers inspiration to live with integrity and spread hope for the future. Take Goodall's lead – imagine a better future, seek out others who are willing to believe in a better future with you, and most importantly, work together toward actualizing it. If you need encouragement and well, yes, hope that your efforts can make a difference, read a biography or watch a film about someone like Goodall who has been there and done that.

- **Recognize the Usefulness of False Hopes:** What sense is there in rationalizing against hope? Hope is not a promise. Often, it is but a flimsy thing that can burst like a thin-skinned balloon against your fervent wishes. However, even a flimsy hope may temper your hopelessness pain and help get you where you desire to go. Hope, like love, can "bear all things, believe all things" (I Cor. 13:7) – if only it is a little scrap of irrationality that convinces you that you can endure what is hopeless. So, as long as your hope doesn't harm anyone, be slow to dash it. Your little bit of hope may be just the thing that is needed to get you on to the next hope that has a bit more substance to it, and that hope may propel you to a greater hope again. At last, one hope may prop itself on the back of another and another – until it grows fat with possibility, like the swell of a perfect wave that a surfer has waited a lifetime to ride. There is nothing false about hope if it keeps you afloat.

- **Put Hope into Action and See Where It Leads You**: Twenty-some odd years ago, when I was a young minister, I was on a mission to bring a deeper sense of spirituality to what I experienced as the sterile, lifeless, and sedentary worship forms I often encountered in the institutional mainstream church. In my mind's eye, I saw myself as a minister through the arts, enlivening worship with meaningful drama, speech, music, dance, movement, participatory ritual, and the visual arts. Back then, there were few churches diverging from conventional forms of worship. So, I visited my denominational district superintendent and told her of my ideas and my desire to work as a minister through the arts, hoping she could help me to identify possible venues for my work. Without hesitation, she told me that no church was going to hire me as a worship artist. Our meeting was brief: she said what she had to say and then curtly dismissed me. I left her office that day dejected and without hope.

  As I drove home, sadness welled up in me and lodged itself in my chest. I imagined that there was no place for me to do the work I desired to do. All too willingly, I let the weight of the superintendent's words sink into that hopeless, hapless place in my mind. Her negativity was profound and authoritative and I let it get to me. I wondered if it was time to leave church ministry for good before it robbed me of my sense of purpose and integrity. However, as I grieved that possibility and let go of my hope that the superintendent would offer a hand in helping me to actualize my artistic vision, I caught a glimpse of a dead tree along the road that had not one leaf or sprout of growth. Oh, but the tree's old gnarled branches were brilliantly decorated with potted flowers that appeared to me at that moment to shine forth with every color under the sun! That sparkling image became my rainbow of promise, my symbol of hope that soon had me writing letters to every church in the district about my vision of worship and the work I desired to do. A few months later, I landed (what was then) my dream job. My artistic vision and I were welcomed with open arms. Later, when I moved to another city, I landed a similar job in the same way for a second time.

  Hopes are oftentimes irrational and may go against the flow of convention. Your hopes may even propel you into grief because it seems they are impossible to make real. As Nell Gwyn put it, "My hope, although its greenness cost me dear is watered by my eyes."

  Make hope an aspiration and when it comes to you as it surely will, allow its promise to settle in your soul. Recognize the gifts of hope that demand action, then step by step, do what needs to be done to either make your hopes real or trade your hopes in for an upgrade.

- **Sensing Hope Beyond the Silence:** Hopelessness can be intensified by an inability to communicate. So, when communication is difficult or impossible, build a bridge of hope that can span the silence:
    - **The Language of Art:** Choose a form of artistic expression to relay your thoughts and feelings – writing, dancing, creating visual art, collaging, etc.

- **In the Blink of an Eye:** With someone unable to speak or write, develop a language by using Morse code with the eyelids or communicating through eye contact and facial expressions, point-to-communicate booklets, or an eye gaze computer.

- **Making It Physical:** Reconnect with hope indirectly by engaging in a pleasurable sensory experience – comforting physical touch, sunlight, beauty, nature, lighting a candle, massaging the body with scented oil, taking a warm bath, partner or small group meditation, pain management approaches such as biofeedback, acupuncture, or guided meditation, empowerment through information-sharing or education, engaging in tai chi, qigong, yoga, hiking, biking, dance, or some other form of exercise, or enjoying poetry, film, literature, or music that serves as a gentle harbinger of hope.

- **Coma-Communicate:** If a loved one or someone in your care is in a coma, remember that communication may still be taking place. In *The American Book of Living and Dying*, Richard Groves and Henriette Klauser relay a riveting story about Henry, a music teacher who was the driver in a car accident that took the life of his young, promising music protege. After the accident, Henry fell into a deep coma for months. Although friends and family consulted coma experts from all over the country and attempted to bring Henry out of his coma through extraordinary means, they finally decided that their efforts were hopeless and took him off of life support, but Henry remained alive. One night, shortly thereafter, as he lay in his hospital bed, the old gospel song "Wade in the Water" played softly on the radio of a woman who was cleaning the hospital. It was that song that reached through to Henry to bring him back to full consciousness for a few weeks before he died. During that time, he was able to relate his feelings of grief and self-blame, and his memories of his interactions with others, observations, and sensory perceptions he experienced when he was comatose.

When a griever is helpless and uncommunicative, all hope is not lost. The trick is to discover languages of hope that can speak through the silence.

※ ※ ※

What cherished companion, place, perspective, or activity might one day keep you from digging a living grave filled with hopelessness? Know before you get to that dark night of the soul (whether for the first time or a return visit) what or who is likely to be a harbinger of hope for you – even if it is only some small pleasure that might relieve your suffering for a moment.

Hope is the harbinger of a better tomorrow that refuses to forsake the hard lessons of today. It is a generous lover that comes willingly to those who believe that the memory of a beautiful sunset can transform the darkest night that falls. Hope cannot thrive unless it is fed, clothed, and given a bed in which to rest. It needs your care and a little time and space, now and then, to rejuvenate itself. Be assured, a little ray of hope can grow into the sunrise of yet another day.

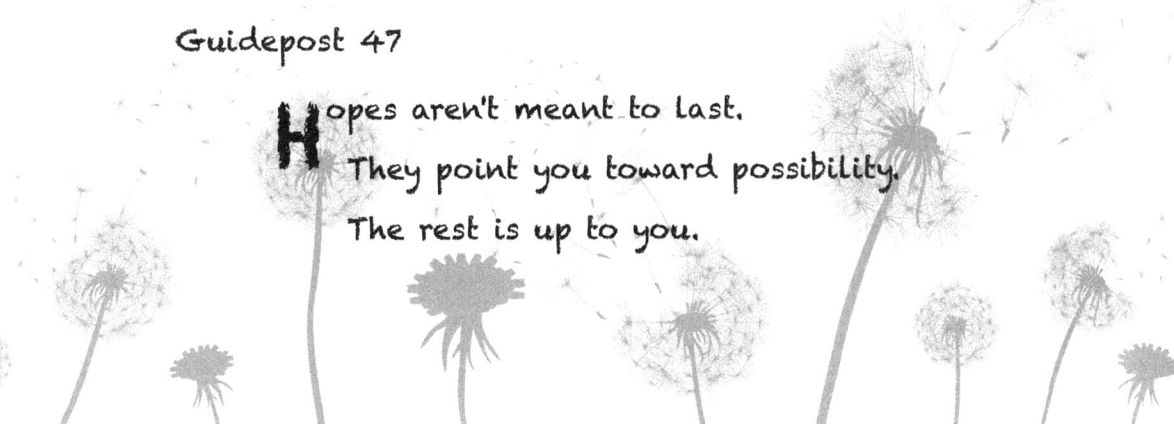

Guidepost 47

Hopes aren't meant to last.
They point you toward possibility.
The rest is up to you.

Grasping the Meaning of Meaning
The Practice of Healing Meaning Pain

What is the meaning of "meaning?" Oftentimes, meaning is thought to be positive, purposeful, or redeeming by definition, but meaning can also be negative, aimless, or vile. Meaning is what you make of it. It is a mental reckoning of how you interpret, explain, represent, or make sense of the nature and worth of life in general, your own life in particular, or any aspect of your life – a relationship, task, conflict, character trait, loss. . .

When you suffer a grief-striking loss, you may ascribe meaning to the loss that brings you a heartening sense of promise or relief, or you may hit upon meaning that results in excruciating pain or hostile negativity that is difficult to shake. When a family tragedy strikes, it may be viewed as a catalyst for cooperation, compassion, and resolution of conflict, or regarded as a fatal blow that tears a family apart. Just as meaning can be a source of pleasure, so too can it be a source of pain. Surprisingly, the etymological origin of the word "meaning" comes from the Old English, "maenan," which goes beyond familiar present-day definitions such as "signify" to include additional meanings such as "complain" and "lament."

There is no human thought devoid of meaning, which is why your life and relationships are full of it. But, if meaning is a given in all human experience, then what do we earthlings define as "meaningful," especially in comparison to what we deem "meaningless?" Commonly, "meaningful" refers to positive, uplifting, or purposeful perceptions of meaning, while "meaningless" is perceived to be negative, painful, confusing, ambiguous, or inconsequential meaning. This being the case, there is not more or less meaning in your "meaningful" or "meaningless" experiences, but rather more or less meaning that you consciously value.

After her husband's death, the Medieval Frenchwoman, Valentine Visconti is quoted as saying, "There is nothing more for me, nothing matters more." Shortly thereafter, she died. Cherished meaning is as vital to human accomplishment and contentment as love. It is difficult for most of us to believe in one without the other. Consequently, we humans are meaning-makers to the core. Each of us decides by what meaning we will live and with what meaning we will die.

Some educators believe that meaning-making is central to all transformational learning. What is more transformational than learning to grieve and heal your loss-related suffering? David Kessler who worked with Elizabeth Kübler-Ross on her final book, *On Grief and Grieving*, added "meaning" as a sixth stage of grief in his 2019 book, *Finding Meaning*. Some of our foremost grief experts today, including Robert Neimeyer and Crystal Park propose that a search for meaning is the crux of a griever's healing process. Before them, Viktor Frankl advanced the same idea, aptly put forth by Gordon Allport in the preface of Frankl's *Man's Search for Meaning:* "To live is to suffer, to survive is to find some meaning in the suffering."

As you transform your grief into something useful and life-giving, you're likely to discover a mother lode of meaning buried beneath the rubble of your pain. But, beware in your search for meaning: There may be losses you experience that make absolutely no sense to you no matter how diligently you scavenge. It is then that you may choose to suspend your meaning-making efforts for a time to seek reprieve from your suffering, or you may decide to expand your repertoire of strategies that help you to reconstruct the valued meaning you lost. For example, in *The American Book of Living and Dying,* Groves and Klauser propose that to reconstruct meaning beyond a loss, a griever might ask questions like:

"What is it that I am still willing to live and die for?"

"Is there something beyond the familiar world that I know and love?"

If these questions are pertinent, take a few moments to answer them for yourself. You might also ask:

- What aspects of my life (relationships, work, identity, beliefs, daily activities, etc.) are teeming with meaning that I value?

- What aspects of my life seem senseless, inconsequential, or devoid of purpose?

- How can I better attend to the most meaningful aspects of my life and identity?

- How can I discover what is meaningful in what causes suffering or strikes me as being senseless or worthless?

After being liberated from his imprisonment at Turkheim and discovering that all but one family member was exterminated by the Nazis during World War II, psychologist and holocaust survivor Viktor Frankl wrote his classic memoir, *Man's Search for Meaning* (1946). In his memoir, Frankl suggests that finding cherished meaning within and beyond oneself is the human being's foremost endeavor. From his personal experiences and observations of other prisoners at Auschwitz and Dachau concentration camps where he was imprisoned for three years, Frankl concludes that

- A meaningful sense of purpose and relationship can be found amid the most horrific circumstances.

- Suffering is a transformative source of meaning, particularly when you adopt an attitude of "tragic optimism" by which to respond to life's difficulties.
- A genuine search for meaning is active and experiential rather than being merely reflective.
- A human's search for meaning is at once self-defining and self-transcendent – a process by which meaning can be found within your individual experiences and initiative, and also in your encounters with something or someone that matters beyond yourself.

During his imprisonment, Frankl witnessed prisoners who adopted an optimistic, active, self-transcendent approach to transforming meaning pain. In the psychologist's estimation, this allowed for a sense of victory in their suffering, even unto death. For example, he relates the story of a young woman in her final days:

> "It is a simple story. There is little to tell and it may sound as if I had invented it; but to me it seems like a poem. This young woman knew that she would die in the next few days. But when I talked to her she was cheerful in spite of this knowledge. 'I am grateful that fate has hit me so hard,' she told me. 'In my former life I was spoiled and did not take spiritual accomplishments seriously.' Pointing through the window of the hut, she said, 'This tree here is the only friend I have in my loneliness.' Through that window she could see just one branch of a chestnut tree, and on the branch were two blossoms. 'I often talk to this tree,' she said to me. I was startled and didn't quite know how to take her words. Was she delirious? Did she have occasional hallucinations? Anxiously I asked her if the tree replied. 'Yes.' What did it say to her? She answered, 'It said to me, 'I am here-I am here-I am life, eternal life.' '"

A search for meaning may involve making peace with mystery and ambiguity. Our human knowledge is limited concerning the origins of the universe and what, if anything, lies beyond the material world. So, we earthlings are compelled to wonder about the purpose of our existence and the individual part we each play in this dramedy called "life." A search for meaning forms our cherished beliefs and gives rise to faith communities in which we bind ourselves to other like-minded devotees and to spiritual entities who accompany us in life and death. Some rally around a divine calling to actualize human potential for a higher purpose. Others put faith in philosophy, science, art, nature, or increasing compassionate regard for ourselves and others. Some find value in all of these approaches to meaning-making and some find value in none. For some, creation is little more than a cosmic accident that we, as a species, are somehow obligated to live out to its eventual promise or demise.

In addition to making sense of the cosmos and our existence within it, a valuable sense of meaning can be discovered within the rhythms and details of daily life – in work and play, solitude and community, waking and sleeping, cooking and cleaning, being and doing, grieving and healing. In *The Pocket Pema Chodron*, Chodron describes this experience of meaning well:

> "The key is to be here, fully connected with the moment, paying attention to the details of ordinary life. By taking care of ordinary things – our pots and pans, our clothing, our teeth – we rejoice in them. When we scrub a vegetable or brush our hair, we are expressing appreciation, friendship toward ourselves and toward the living quality that is found in everything."

There is no aspect of life or relationship that is meaningless without your say-so. If you desire a more meaningful existence, you are the only one who can create it for yourself. As Joseph Campbell puts it, "Life has no meaning. Each of us has meaning and we bring it to life. It is a waste to be asking the question when you are the answer."

If you are willing to uncover the nuances of meaning in your loss experience, you may find that even aspects of a loss that at first appear to be dreadful or gruesome can inspire meaningful insights and relationships. The following story and poem regarding a significant loss my family experienced serve as stark examples.

Hidden Peace: A Personal Story of Transforming Meaning Pain

After my father-in-law, Jim, and his wife, Martha, were murdered by Martha's son, Tom, my spouse Andrew and I were hounded by a stream of "what ifs." What if we had said "yes" to Jim's invitation for us and our children to meet up with them that Labor Day weekend at Jim's lakeside vacation home in North Carolina where the crime took place? What if our presence had deterred the killer or brought the paramedics in time, or what if our presence put all of us in jeopardy? What if I had listened more keenly to Martha's fears about her son's troubled psychological state, his feelings that he was not "really" her son, and her concerns about never having bonded with him after she adopted him as an infant from a birth mother whose family kept the birth a secret. What if we had helped her and Jim think through how to better protect themselves from Tom's access to Jim's property and them? There were a hundred ways and more we wished we had been there for them, but it was not to be.

After Jim's and Martha's double funeral and police investigations were complete, we were finally given access to Jim's lakeside home. Andrew, as his father's executor, had the responsibility of seeing to the repair and cleaning of the property – yes, even the spilled blood of our dear ones. The estate lawyer at the time (among others) told us vehemently that we should not enter the property until all signs of the murder were erased by a crime scene cleanup crew. Andrew and I were unsure about this. It was surreal. We didn't know what was right because we had never been faced with such a decision. Certainly, it struck us as horrific to see the aftermath of Jim and Martha's murders, but we also sensed that there was something else there for us and decided that whatever it was, we needed to experience it before others came to wipe out the evidence of their deaths. The following poem that I wrote afterward is a testament to the meaning we discovered there that helped to ease our suffering:

Going In

I.

We were told not to go in.
We were told to wait for the ones
Who were used to cleaning up
After a bloodbath.
But those who told us didn't understand:
It was all we had left of them.

II.

Divided by a continent,
It took three days for us
To hear the hush of insanity
That tripped the trigger.

A son who was never born,
A son who was not a son
On fire with crazy mixed-up metaphors:
A birth wish to kill his death parents.

It took three days before state troopers
Could catch the son of a bitch
For contorting himself back
Into a wretched orphan again.

III.

When the bullets ripped through
Their bodies – a wind storm
Came crashing in like an omen.
We bounded from our bed
To stifle the cacophony of chimes.
But failing to heed the alarm,
We slept again into the silence.

IV.

It took three days for us to know:
We weren't there to catch their falling bodies,
Protect their heads from the unforgiving
Surface of things, bid the screeching pain away.
We weren't there to pray over their trembling.

Dried up puddles
Were all we had left
Before all evidence of them was
Wiped from the face of the earth.

> V.
> We were told not to go in
> Through that door of fury where
> The invisible man desecrated
> Their bodies – that place
> Where their lives drained away
> Into the floor boards.
>
> But it was the only place
> We could be with them
> When time stopped.
> It was the only place
> We could catch
> Their final breath.
>
> So, against all advice,
> We went in unafraid
> To touch the blood.
>
> VI.
> It was all we had left of them.
> Their death was our death.
> Their blood was our blood.
> And the story we found
> Written in dark crimson
> Was a prayer for peace.

During that visit, Andrew and I lingered in the room where Jim and Martha died to somberly relive what the police and coroner's reports and the physical space told us of what took place. Then, we got busy cleaning up the fingerprint dust and the mess Tom left from his time staying in the house (while awaiting Jim and Martha's arrival). We sorted and packed up their belongings and secured a construction crew to replace the floorboards where their blood was soaked and stained.

After the room where Jim and Martha died was clean and repaired, we created a peace blessing for them and the home that was Jim's favorite place to relax and enjoy the little things in life. We recalled our happiest memories in that lake home. In subsequent visits, Morgan and Willa went with us. The first time, they chose not to enter the house but helped with yard work and outdoor cleanup. Afterward, we recalled our favorite stories of time spent with Jim and Martha there and offered a blessing for the home and the land upon which it sits. During our final trip to clean and do repairs, we were able to stay in the house with Morgan and Willa to enjoy a peaceful and fun visit on the lake. It was during that visit we all agreed, at last, that the home felt like one of the safest, most relaxing, and blessed places on earth.

Some grievers who suffer the violent deaths of loved ones choose not to experience the aftermath and cleanup of the death firsthand. Each of us is wired differently and find cherished meaning wherever and however it exists for us, wherever and however we claim it for ourselves. Some might find such an experience to be disturbing or grotesque and may desire to focus on more gratifying memories of a loved one. But, if there is even a little doubt with which to wrestle, don't quickly give in to conventional practices or cultural biases. If you do, you may miss a crucial encounter with healing simply because you fold into what someone else expects of you. Decide for yourself.

Discovering Grief-Striking Meaning Your Way

How you choose to think about and respond to a loss defines its meaning for you. Sometimes, a loss experience becomes more meaningful simply by having a singular word to articulate your grief in a way that is commonly acknowledged or understood by others: In the movie *Demolition*, written by Brian Sipe, a bereaved father whose adult daughter dies in a car accident speaks of the grief he encounters because there is no word for his breed of pain. He says,

> "Man loses his wife, he's a widower. Child loses a parent, they're an orphan. But losing a child . . . there is no word for this. And it shouldn't be."

It is a piercing sentiment for those who can relate firsthand or those who take on secondhand grief due to a loved one's experience of child loss.

Serendipitously, after I watched *Demolition*, I came across an insightful article on the subject, published in *Duke Today* (May 26, 2009) in which Karla FC Holloway suggests that just as "widow" is a Sanskrit word meaning "empty," so the Sanskrit language offers a word for a bereaved parent. It is the word "vilomah," meaning "against a natural order." Holloway writes to those who suffer the death of a child:

> "Vilomah is a name for the grief we represent . . . A parent whose child has died is a vilomah. Watch the evening news and you will see a vilomah. Scan the news on the web and you will read about a vilomah. Walk through your neighborhood, there are homes with vilomahs inside."

It is only a word, but sometimes a single word can speak volumes and is more expressive of the contours of a loss than a lifetime of unending discourse on the subject. So, yes, it matters what we call ourselves: "vilomah" "widow," orphan," "victim," "survivor," "griever," "healer." If you're willing, go ahead and ask yourself: "By what names do I relate to my grief?" Choose each word wisely for each is filled with meanings so ancient and intoxicating, they will not only change how you think about yourself and your loss, they will change how you live and love.

Beyond words, there are myriad ways to access meaning as you grieve. Perhaps, like me, you're grateful for the meaning you find in the beauty and wonder of the natural world. When all seems lost, I make it a habit to look at the moon and stars each night and I am consistently awed by this reminder that I am a living, breathing part of this planet so magnificently suspended within an ever-expanding universe. Here we are, the earth and its creatures, hanging vulnerably and resiliently in the balance! Whether you view it from a creationist or scientific perspective, it is difficult to name a greater miracle by which meaningful relationships can be forged.

Meaning is everywhere. You look at a wilted flower and there is meaning in it. You hear a cry for help and meaning follows. Whatever you perceive, experience, or imagine is filled with meaning that is positive or negative, significant or inconsequential, uplifting or painful. Meaning that matters most when you're grieving is the meaning that eases, heals, and transforms your suffering. So, make it a habit to assess and reassess what meaning matters most in your suffering – what meaning is valuable, useful, and heartening. Then, in your thinking, living, and being, devote yourself to it wholeheartedly.

Practical Ideas for Healing Meaning Pain

Meaning pain is the single greatest motivator to fuel a quest for meaning that matters most to you. In the academic literature on grief, popular approaches to integrate and transform meaning pain in the wake of a loss typically emphasize talking to a counselor, therapist, support group, or loved one about your loss; telling grief stories through spoken narratives or the written word; or participating in religious, philosophical, or spiritual communities striving to embody experiences of meaning that are believed to be worthy of attention, devotion, or willful effort. Each of these approaches works for some, but not a single approach works for everyone. Sometimes, cherished meaning is greatly personal and difficult to recount even to a trusted confidante. What's more, as you grieve and heal your suffering, your cherished sources of meaning may change as you and your perceptions do – from moment to moment and day to day. Meaning that matters to you may be elusive for stretches of time. Be patient. Pace yourself. Meaning-making is never-ending.

When you need inspiration to rediscover valuable meaning, you may find one of the following explorations helpful:

- **Create a Personal Book of Meaning:** Most religions, philosophies, and spiritual paths identify cherished beliefs, creeds, writings, ideas, rites, or symbols that help devotees to define the meaning of life and relationships. Whether you advocate such a belief system or not, it can be heartening to create a personal book of meaning that reflects the meaning that matters most to you.

  Your book of meaning might include:

  - *Your cherished beliefs and personal creeds*: Perhaps you uphold a guiding principle, marriage or partnership vows, a parenting covenant, personal mission statement, and/or your "top three (or five, or ten) rules to live by." If so, include these in your book of meaning.

  - *A listing of the earthly and/or spiritual companions with whom you enjoy meaningful relationships*: These might include people, pets, significant communities or small groups, God or a higher power (by whatever name), deceased loved ones, awe-inspiring places or elements in nature, or spiritual guardians or energetic entities that you experience as sustaining, accompanying, or protecting you.

  - *Your sacred texts*: These may or may not come from a bona fide "holy book." Whenever you come across a quote, poem, passage, proverb, anecdote, or story that strikes you as being particularly insightful or enlightening in relationship to the meaning that matters most to you, you may want to add it to your meaning book with a date and reference. You might also include personal stories, contemplative insights, and significant dreams that provide needed wisdom or answers to your questions of meaning.

- *Your cherished rites and symbols*: These may come from your chosen religion, philosophy, or spiritual perspective, or arise in your daily rhythms of waking, sleeping, work, play, home, and family.

Perhaps you participate in a religious or spiritual community that celebrates rites such as worship, prayer, communion, sabbath meals, seasonal holidays and special celebrations, rites of passage or initiation, marriage, ordination, blessingways, death rituals, or anointing the sick. Perhaps you find meaning in the symbol of the cross, star, yin-yang, interlacing circles, chalice, the four elements of nature, Dharma wheel, or the star and crescent, among others.

Or, perhaps the rites and symbols most meaningful for you can be found in your home and family.

Your domestic rites might include:

- Setting the table and offering a mealtime blessing
- Bedtime prayers
- Birthday, holiday, and anniversary traditions
- Gestures of affection that are reenacted often (welcome-home hug, after-dinner massage, kiss goodnight, morning song, parting blessing, etc.)
- Daily meditation, prayer, or exercise that clears your mind, balances your emotions, enlivens your body, or reconnects you with a loved one

Your cherished domestic symbols may include a work of art, song, memorial object, family crest, or chosen family symbol. For example, when Andrew and I were married we chose a heart shaped by its two separate adjoining sides (to represent both individuality and unity) as a symbol of our family name "Darian" that means "heart of wisdom, compassion, and grace."

Once you identify the rites and symbols that matter to you, you might include them in your book by name, photo, sketch, or description, and add notes, reflections, or stories about how each rite or symbol continues to enrich your life and relationships.

- *Your questions, fears, doubts, or disbelief related to your cherished sources of meaning:* Write these in your book as you experience them in your everyday life. Don't worry about answering or resolving them overnight, but don't forget about them indefinitely or entertain them only when grief strikes either. Use your uncertainties as clues to help you decipher where cherished meaning resides for you and in what ways meaning that you value might be further developed. As Frederick Buechner wrote in *Wishful Thinking: A Theological ABC*:

> "If you don't have doubts, you're either kidding yourself or you're asleep. Doubts are the ants-in-the-pants of faith. They keep it alive and moving."

Courage only becomes meaningful in light of fear, belief in light of doubt, and finding meaningful answers is only possible when you're willing to ask meaningful questions. Embrace your uncertainties.

Your book of meaning can serve as a testament for how meaning evolves, diminishes, and expands for you. In time, it may become a treasured memoir that helps your loved ones know you better even after you depart the earth.

⬥ **Forging Future Meaning:** What future loss do you imagine will be problematic for you or your loved ones? Imagine how you might find cherished meaning in this dreaded loss. Look to others who met similar losses in meaningful ways – perhaps someone who suffered a terrible divorce and embraced it as an opportunity to make desired changes, or a family who created cherished meaning in response to a shared traumatic experience that you think might overwhelm you or your loved ones. If it isn't obvious to you how someone you know was able to transform their meaning pain, don't be afraid to ask. Inviting others to confide to you the meaning that matters most to them in the healing process can be every bit as therapeutic as divulging the contours of their suffering.

If it's helpful, imagine a loss you dread in your future and ask yourself:

- How can I reconcile my fears and doubts about it now?
- When (or if) this loss occurs, how do I imagine life will be worth living despite the loss?

Look for cherished meaning related to your dreaded loss in biographies or memoirs, movies, novels, or your intimate circles of community. Your discoveries may persuade you to worry less and enjoy the present moment more because you know that even if cherished aspects of your life fade away, what is meaningful to you has a future.

⬥ **Find the Good in What Is Not:** Rudolf Steiner, an Austrian philosopher and founder of anthroposophy (a spiritual philosophy of inner development intended to foster imagination, inspiration, and intuition), offered six exercises to balance clarity of thinking, harmony of feeling, and strength of will. One of these exercises includes finding what is positive in the negative. Such a practice can be effective to balance lamenting and heartening responses to a grief-striking loss. Although you may find it impossible to do when at first sorrow breaks you open, it is crucial at some juncture of the grieving and healing process (and as often as needed) to revisit a loss experience to discover in it some uplifting insight or usefulness you did not see before. Grief-related suffering is nigh impossible to heal without deriving a sense of heartening meaning from it. Steiner's "observing the positive" exercise is laid out in these excerpts from Tom van Gelder's English Translation (2011) of *The Six Basic Exercises* by Rudolf Steiner:

> "Always try to see the positive aspects of something negative."
>
> "In many situations you encounter, you see the negative and ugly aspects quite clearly. In this exercise the aim is that you always see something positive, too, without denying the negative. When something is negative, you can emphasize the positive within or besides that. There is always something beautiful or good that lies concealed in everything. The exercise should not lead to an uncritical attitude and a vague 'everything is good and beautiful' or to denying the negative."
>
> " . . . to see the positive or good in the negative, you have to overcome your reactions, opinions, and prejudices. The circumstances become more interesting. Questions like 'What does this tell me?', 'What can I learn from this?'. . . may help in this exercise."

Depending on your temperament or personality, timing, or the type of loss you suffer, this exercise may be more or less difficult for you to practice or accomplish than for others. If it doesn't come easily to you, it may be helpful to try it out first with a grief-striking loss from the distant past that isn't all that problematic for you now, perhaps a wound experienced in your childhood or youth that engendered grief for you once upon a time.

For example, as a youth and young adult, I found this way of thinking about the "positives in a negative" useful to heal grief I experienced from feeling as if I were an only child in a family of four siblings. My older siblings are close in age, me trailing four years behind the youngest of them. By the time they hit grade school, I saw them as an intimate band of adventurers. Although there was an unmistakable family bond between us, I often felt like a lone wolf on the periphery of the pack. But eventually, as a teenager and young adult, I realized there were plenty of upsides to what I previously perceived to be a rift between me and these beloved and admired childhood companions.

The heartening meaning I found in my sibling position and family roles included: (1) benefiting from my parents' improved parenting skills (my eldest brother was born when they were 18 and 22), (2) enjoying luxurious family time with my parents in the years after my siblings left home, (3) having wider reign to become my own person apart from the "peer pressure" of being part of a tight-knit sibling group, and (4) observing my siblings' relationships, accomplishments, choices, and challenges, and learning from them. All of this was in addition to the fun and adventure of being part of a family who did our best to love each other and stick together through tough times. Despite often feeling like the "odd person out," transforming the way I saw these relationships helped me to appreciate the many valuable ways my siblings impacted and inspired me to become the person I am.

This practice of finding the positive within the negative continues to help me ease the pain of more recent losses. For example, a few months after my father-in-law, Jim, was murdered, I realized one benefit of his quick death was that he did not have to endure a slow and painful demise from his worsening emphysema. Jim was a feisty thrill seeker and world traveler who would not bow graciously to a slow, painful death. Amid our family sorrow, this recognition helped us to ease our pain and to identify other "positives" within this mind-numbing loss experience.

- **Tell a Meaningful Version of Your Loss Story:** Grief stories are told and retold, and sometimes we who tell them forget that the details of our stories are never written in stone. As you tell and retell your grief stories, be sure to integrate heartening insights and the positive outcomes that arise.

One of my foremost teachers in this regard is my brother, Roger. After experiencing the greatest tragedy of his life in the death of his twenty-six-year-old son Kyle who died from a bad batch of heroin, Roger gave the most meaningful and heartfelt eulogy I have ever heard. Roger didn't tell the story of Kyle's life without being vividly honest about his son's troubled youth and his relapse after four-plus years of recovery from drug addiction. Roger didn't fail to use Kyle's story as an opportunity to inform others of drug awareness and abuse. But my brother knew that Kyle's addiction and relapse did not define who Kyle was to the hundreds of mourners who came to his funeral and sent a pile of cards and letters telling Roger what a life-changing influence Kyle was to them. Those close to him knew Kyle as a fun-loving, articulate, intelligent, well-loved, and respected young man who was courageous enough to beat his drug addiction for over four years. In that time, he earned a college degree, became a loving father, served as an intern for the athletic department at Iowa State University, and was planning to marry the woman of his dreams. Kyle's untimely death at his own hands did not change the timbre of pride in Roger's voice as he spoke of his son's broad-reaching compassion, influence, and courage. Roger was well aware that the four-year reprieve from the troubled times he saw Kyle through during his youth might never have happened had his son not become the exceptional man he was. That fact was cause for celebration amid Roger's nightmarish grief. Because he could celebrate, so could the rest of us. Along with our grief, we could carry with us Kyle's legacy in the lessons and victories of his life and relationships.

When you tell your stories of loss, listen to yourself. Be sure you're telling the whole story as it unfolds within you, a story that includes meaningful insights, observations, outcomes, and memories that can serve to ease, heal, and transform your grief and the grief of those who mourn with you.

◈ **Take a Turn Towards Fun & Adventure:** Sometimes, no matter how hard you search, there is no good meaning to be found. Give up the search now and then, and find a way to divert yourself from your meaning pain. In dark times, making room for fun and adventure can temper your pain, allowing your body, psyche, and soul to get a needed break from your suffering. A poignant example of this approach to tempering can be found in the surfing programs that are popping up in response to the healing needs of war veterans. Many military veterans have difficulty finding valued meaning after returning from war. The Department of Veteran Affairs reports that, on average, 17 to 18 U.S. veterans die by suicide every day. In recent years, the Jimmy Miller Memorial Foundation, Surf Action, Warrior Surf, Waves of Impact, and Operation Surf (see page 350) have responded to this mental health crisis by offering surfing programs as an effective tempering therapy that brings cherished meaning to veterans who are suffering from physical wounds, amputations, PTSD, and depression. (A few organizations also offer programs for at-risk youth and family members of all ages.) Research shows that physically-absorbing activities like surfing can rewire the brain and heal past trauma.

Imagine how you might temper your meaning pain in an engaging way that works for you. Ask yourself, What brings me great pleasure? Who makes me laugh? What fun-filled adventure might distract me from the meaninglessness that weighs on me? What am I willing to check off my bucket list? Where can I find an uplifting sense of meaning other than the meaningless void where I keep looking for it? Ask a question and follow where it leads you. . .

※ ※ ※

As an adult, you can create meaning however and wherever you choose. What's more, when you become an expert at creating meaning that matters to you, enlightenment itself may be your recompense. The great novelist, Nikos Kazantzakis put it like this: "The real meaning of enlightenment is to gaze with undimmed eyes on all darkness."

Guidepost 48

Sit with your meaning pain as you would an enlightened teacher. Ask it a bucketload of questions.

You will know when you hit upon the right one: It will be the question that compels you to arise, dump out your bucket, and go fill it with some answers.

If Not You, Who?
Companionship Needs of the Grieving Adult

Please note: *The following section focuses on ways to become your own best grieving companion. If you need immediate suggestions on how to effectively serve as a grieving companion for other adults, jump to the section, "Polaris: Serving as a North Star for Grieving Adults of all Ages" (page 307) in the elderhood chapter.*

In a world of perfectly practicing adults, each of us is our own best grieving companion. In that illusive world, we each know on any given day at any given moment in the grieving process whether lamenting, heartening, tempering, or integrating is needed to translate our grief into something useful and life-giving. We know what type of spiritual pain we need to transform and how to get it done. We know when to go it alone and when to reach out for help, what help to enlist and who to ask for it. We not only know it for ourselves, we know it for anyone and everyone in our care. In a world of perfectly practicing adults, we know ourselves and others that well.

But the reality is that, even as a practicing adult, there will be times that your grief-related suffering causes you to lose hold of what you know about yourself and others. Healing may seem like an irrelevant distraction as you brace yourself to bear the burden of your loss. What's more, each of your loss experiences is unique so it is often impossible to predict with certainty what your healing will require or what your intimate relationships will depend upon to keep them intact, or better yet, increasing in love and wisdom. Grief changes you and your relationships. So, you may only be able to identify how the heck healing happens for you in retrospect. Whatever it took last time to heal your suffering may or may not work again this time around.

When grief strikes hard, the best you can do is to learn something new about yourself and your relationships. The hardest lesson of all is learning how to bear unbearable suffering. Fortunately, when that lesson seems unbearable for you too, other grievers and healers can come to your aid – to help steady you as you learn to steady yourself. That is, if they're able and willing. That is, if you're able and willing to let them. It may be that letting them is the first "something new" that you learn. Relax. Practicing adults do it for one another all the time.

As an adult healer, there's a hitch in letting others come to your aid as you grieve and heal your suffering: *Your companions are only able to help you to the extent that you are able and willing to help yourself.* There are no saviors here. No one will ever be as imperative to your grieving and healing process as you are. No one will be able to attend to the ins and outs of your suffering or healing as you do. You're the only one with a front-row seat to your psyche and soul. So, no matter who else you depend upon to help you grieve each loss experience and heal each pang of grief, dedicate yourself to being your own best grieving companion and encouraging other adults to do the same.

As an adult healer, you engage in a curative triage to prioritize and negotiate needs that include:

- Being responsible for your own grieving and healing process
- Being responsive to the grieving and healing needs and preferences of others
- Welcoming others to be equally responsive to you

The following story offers a poignant example of a griever's triaging efforts:

Cancer to Kaizen: How A Patient Triaged One Step at a Time

In the book, *One Small Step Can Change Your Life: The Kaizen Way,* author Robert Mauer, a clinical professor at UCLA School of Medicine, tells the story of Becky, a fifty-five-year-old woman who was diagnosed with cancer. The diagnosis came just as Becky was planning an early retirement from her corporate job to follow her long-held dream of becoming a visual artist. By the time she came to Mauer for help, Becky was overwhelmed with her diagnosis, making life-or-death choices about her healthcare, and keeping up with the demands of her job. In her state of crisis, Becky cut off all communications with friends and family, those people who were apt to support and encourage her most.

Mauer knew from his work with those facing similar crises that focusing on fixing the biggest problem looming (in this case, Becky's cancer) would be counterproductive. Research shows that humans resist change, even positive change that is likely to fix a looming problem. This resistance is biological: *The human midbrain is petrified of change in any form.* So, Mauer developed an extraordinarily simple approach to embracing change that is based on the practice of Kaizen, a strategy that incorporates changes so small and seemingly inconsequential that the brain's natural resistance to change is not activated.

The Kaizen Way that Mauer advocates and suggested to Becky to transform her despair, was originally a manufacturing strategy used to improve the quality and quantity of production. The strategy was first introduced in the U.S. during World War II, then developed and improved upon by the Japanese who used it to rebuild their devastated country and economy after the war. The improvement came by way of attending to small details, identifying any needed improvement that could be made by small efforts. The practice of Kaizen is built upon the idea that many small changes eventually add up to impressive results. The approach proved to be an ideal strategy for Becky because she only reluctantly agreed to Mauer's help if it would take no more than a few minutes of effort a day.

To assist Becky to change her responses to her cancer diagnosis and her resulting grief, Mauer asked her to set some goals for herself – primarily, to be rid of her cancer. However, since the disease process was beyond Becky's control, she was asked to list two additional goals. These goals included, 1) "to make the best of each day that I have" and 2) "to get more chores done." Although these goals were less of a challenge to conquer than her cancer, Mauer knew that given her work schedule and health needs, Becky would need help from others. So, he encouraged her to reconnect with friends and make a chore list that included which chores required assistance from a friend and the specific help she sought.

Becky's daily chore list worked wonders. It helped her to stay focused on her daily objectives, and it invited her to engage in wishful thinking as she imagined creative ways others could help her. Mauer writes:

> "The list at first was brief, with items such as 'I wish a friend would just say, 'You are so brave' or 'I wish a friend would do my laundry.' Within a week, the list became more detailed and emotional. 'I wish a friend would sit with me while I deal on the phone with the HMO or fill out their paperwork,' she wrote. 'I wish a friend would go to the Wellness Community [a local support group for people coping with cancer] . . . I wish a friend would hold me when I am crying.'"

The chore list was motivation for Becky to reconnect with friends and family. It served to calm the storm that raged within her. As she faced her cancer treatments and diminished energy, her list gave her a sense of control with the smaller aspects of daily life. Long after Becky's treatments ended, Mauer saw her one day and she told him that her cancer was in remission. They conversed for a while about her health and then she whispered to Mauer, "Thanks for the gift of Kaizen."

※ ※ ※

The real beauty of Becky's simple, doable approach to embracing change after her diagnosis with cancer was that it allowed her to attend to her own needs even as she welcomed the support and encouragement of others in ways she specifically desired. Over time, if you are persistent in attending to small changes that help you heal your grief-related suffering, you may be surprised when these small changes morph into big changes that your brain would never willingly endorse.

No one and nothing can provide for you continually (or perfectly) throughout your grieving process – most likely, not even you. So, if there is a person, community, activity or place that provides even a small part of what is needed, cherish that small part. It may be that many little things together make a big difference.

Guidepost 49

The practicing adult knows:
The old adage "practice makes perfect" is an illusion of those who don't practice.

Practice isn't about perfection.
It's about changing old habits and learning something new.

Do-It-Yourself

Self-Guided Contemplations for the Adult Within You

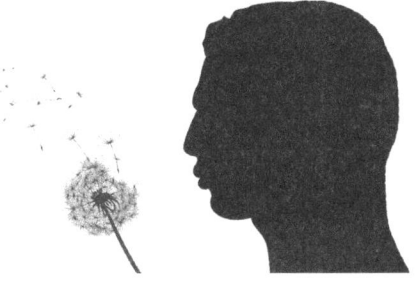

The following ideas for self-guided contemplations focus on giving and receiving mutual support among adults who are grieving together and supporting yourself as you grieve and heal solo. Choose what's helpful to you. Use these ideas as they are, revise them, or create contemplations of your own.

- ◈ **Giving & Receiving Loving Attention:** As practicing adults, genuine companionship is a two-way street built upon mutual exchanges of energy, interest, and affection. To make this intention more obvious, it may be helpful to create gestures of mutual care and support, such as

  - ◆ **A Gesture of Giving and Receiving:** When you hold hands for a mealtime blessing, prayer, or meditation, hold right hands down in a gesture of giving and left hands up in a gesture of receiving; if loved ones are distant or deceased, do this by yourself and imagine your dear ones present with you.

  - ◆ **Speaking & Listening:** In the tradition of indigenous North Americans, denote a "talking stick" or another object for family members or group participants to hold during a conversation or sharing time. The person holding the object can talk uninterrupted while others listen intently; then, pass the object around the circle so everyone has an opportunity to talk.

  - ◆ **Nurturing Living Relationships:** Think of your relationship with a home, job, nature, etc. as a living relationship in which the other gives and receives love and care. You may become aware that some places or types of work you do generate life, enthusiasm, and love for you more than others. Make it a priority to tend to these life-giving relationships and express your gratitude for the healing blessings each relationship provides.

  - ◆ **Breathing Together**: With someone who is in a coma or fading into death, or as a silent meditation with an intimate companion, practice what is called "a mingling of breaths" – an age-old tradition in which companions sit together and breathe in sync with one another as a form of physical and spiritual communion. With deceased loved ones, you might also close your eyes and envision them sitting before you as you "breathe together" in spirit.

  - ◆ **Honorary Gifts:** When you are feeling low after the death of a loved one, reach out to do something for someone else who may need encouragement in a way that also feeds your spirit. I know of one family whose basketball-loving son and brother died in a car accident. On the young man's birthday, the parents enlisted friends and family members to scatter all over town to anonymously leave donated basketballs (that were marked with a message in memory of him) at neighborhood basketball courts, parks, and school playgrounds. Imagine the possibilities in your circles of community.

- **Care for the Caregiver:** Providing long-term care for a loved one who is injured, ill, or dying requires tremendous effort, especially while grieving the loss of a relationship with your loved one as it once was. This can be a double whammy for your body, heart, mind, and spirit. Create daily habits to renew your inner resources each day. Seek out the support you need from others. Practice self-care: get plenty of sleep and exercise, eat foods that are nourishing, and preserve interludes of personal time as a necessity. As you provide care, engage in activities, domestic rituals, and routines with your loved one that you each find meaningful and life-giving. (See "Caregiving" resources on page 321.)

   If you're the receiver of care, do whatever you can to offer gestures of gratitude to those providing your care. Even simple gestures can go a long way – written or spoken words of thanks, gifts that promote self-nurture (certificate for a massage, coffee or dinner out, bath salts or shower tablets, etc.), inspirational or entertaining book or movie, homemade gift or artistic creation, or whatever might be meaningful for the one who cares for you.

- **Give Yourself a Hug:** In the absence or incapacitation of someone who generally provides physical nurture for you, think of ways to create physical comfort for yourself. You might wear a piece of clothing from your loved one, make or buy a prayer shawl or blanket for cozying up, create spaces in your home that give you a sense of being held – a woodworking shop or art studio, prayer/meditation corner, comfy reading chair, crafting space, or a photographic display of loved ones where you can see it each day to connect in spirit. You might practice self-nurture by listening to your favorite music, preparing a special meal for yourself, enjoying a soothing bath, practicing self-massage, doing yoga, singing or playing an instrument, or seeking out a massage therapist, craniosacral practitioner, therapeutic touch provider, or reiki master.

◈ **Rituals of Reconciliation:** To heal a relationship after separation or conflict, a simple ceremony of reconciliation can be transformative. You might use it as a symbol of mutual commitment to make a fresh start – for example,

- Renew your marriage vows after recovering from the wounds of betrayal or recommit to a harmonious relationship after separation, absence, or conflict
- Engage in a ceremony of apology or forgiveness
- Create a collaborative work of art in a community that has been divided or experienced collective loss
- Share a tea ceremony with a friend or family member after a hurtful situation is resolved or to come back together after a separation

As you prepare for your ceremony or co-creation, consider what will be meaningful for each participant and do your best to create a ritual of healing that is memorable for everyone. You might incorporate symbols of renewed companionship, songs or words of unity, a special meal, or handmade gifts.

To heal grief related to betrayal or severe conflict in a significant relationship, it may be helpful to create a recurring ritual of healing or check in with one another periodically to identify ongoing sources of grief, challenge, growth, and positive change that result from your efforts to reconcile and forgive one another. If it's helpful, schedule an appointment with a counselor every month or two, or share a weekly or monthly meditative practice to contemplate the joys and challenges of fostering ongoing healing and trust in your relationship.

◈ **Silent Presence:** If you can't find the right words to express your grief, another's silent presence may be the gentle balm you need. Engaging in silent prayer or meditation with another griever can be transformative. Choose a method that is meaningful for you. You might sit across from one another and silently imagine your prayers for one another or engage together in a lovingkindness meditation (see *Lovingkindness* in "Mindfulness & Meditation" listings on page 332). Silent presence may be especially effective when your grief-related suffering involves private confidences or grisly details that you choose not to speak aloud. An invisible bond of companionship can be created without requiring anyone to explain themselves or struggle to verbalize the traumatic complexities of a loss experience.

An Adult's Healing Chest
Approaches to Grieving and Healing in Adulthood

Look through the following list of approaches to grieving and healing from Part III, "The Healing Chest: Gathering Your Own Best Medicine." Which approaches might be especially useful at present to grieve and heal solo or alongside others?

- Abuse Awareness & Prevention
- Addiction Prevention & Recovery
- Apologies
- Art & Creativity
- Bibliotherapy
- Breathing & Relaxation
- Caregiving
- Ceremonies & Celebrations
- Cinematherapy
- Cognitive Healing
- Community-Building
- Conscious Eldering
- Crying
- Dance
- Death Care
- Dreaming & Visitations
- Dying a Good Death
- Emotional Healing & Expressing Feelings
- Exercise, Body Awareness & Physical Release
- Forgiveness
- Funeral Planning & Memorial Services
- Grieving & Healing Perspectives
- Habit-Building
- Helping Others
- Hope
- Illness Tending
- Integrative Care & Complementary Therapies
- Laughter & Humor
- Listening
- Massage, Reiki & Comforting Touch
- Meaning-Making
- Memoir & Autobiography
- Memorials & Remembrance
- Metaphors, Objects & Symbols
- Mindfulness & Meditation
- Movement, Yoga & Posture
- Music & Sound Therapy
- Nature
- Natural Remedies for Pain Relief
- Parenting Mindfully
- Pets & Animals
- Pilgrimages, Labyrinths & Hiking Treks
- Play, Fun & Games
- Poetry
- Prayer
- Repairing Broken Relationships
- Sanctuary & Sacred Space
- Self-Injury & Recovery
- Sexual Healing & Recovery
- Sleeping
- Stories & Storytelling
- Suicide Prevention & Survivor Support
- Talking Cures
- Theater & Speech
- Trauma Recovery
- Wonder
- Writing

8 ❧ Harvesting Curative Wisdom
Grieving & Healing in Elderhood

One loses, as one grows older, something of the lightness
of one's dreams; one begins to take life up in both hands,
and to care more for the fruit than the flower. . .

        W. B. Yeats

Making Good Use of Old Age
An Elder's Natural Genius for Grieving & Healing

In my twenties, I met an old man who told me that "life only gets better and better and better" with age. He had a twinkle in his eye that was convincing and I believed him. I still do, despite taking some hard knocks over the past few decades. I'm aging into old as an optimist and grateful for it because not everyone's life affords such hopeful confidence. There is no foolproof formula to be healthy and happy in old age. As a lifetime of losses pile up, aging into old can be one of life's heaviest burdens. But on the flip side of old burdens is the mounting wisdom from a lifetime of experience with grief. Ask yourself: *Who is better off attending to grief – one who faced grief at every turn or one who knows nothing of suffering?* In old age, vast experience with grief can be useful if you make it so.

There's a well-known, politically-incorrect adage among the old that affirms "old age isn't for sissies." Despite the slur against the sisterhood, it's hard to argue with the sentiment. Old age is riddled with the deaths of peers and partners, increasing incidents of disease and injury, and diminishing serotonin and dopamine – chemical messengers in the body that are key to your sense of well-being and motivation.

In old age, your hope and joy may be sapped from you due to chronic pain, elder abuse, poverty, life-or-death medical decisions, dependency, forced retirement, immobility, impotence, or loneliness. You may experience an increase in depression, regret, pining for the past, frustration or dissatisfaction with present circumstances, or anxiety about the future. In old age, the most painful of all losses may be the loss of authority and respect due to ageist discrimination that portrays the old as ugly, silly, ignorant, or useless – as reflected (and corrected) in this Romanian folktale:

Harvesting Elder Wisdom

Once upon a time, old people were killed because they were seen by the young as little more than a nuisance, forever giving advice, retelling the same old stories, and promoting old-fashioned ideas. So, when a person reached a ripe age, the time of death was set. "This one is old," came the complaint, "what good are they now? Why should we feed them bread for nothing?" The elder was taken away from the village and killed without regret. But one son took pity on his father. Defying the law of the land, the son hid his father in the cellar. Famine caused widespread hunger, but the son continued to feed his father and visit with him at night.

All too soon, the last of the stored grain was eaten, even the seed to plant the crops for the coming season. But the one surviving elder told his son to thresh seed from the straw on the roof of the house. The son did and the seed grew, yielding a timely harvest that saved the people. When they learned the source of their good fortune, the elder was celebrated as a hero. After that, old people lived until they died and the young learned to listen to an elder's advice. . . and keep listening – even when the advice is out of fashion.

When old people are regarded as a valuable resource, it becomes more obvious how elders can serve the larger community in good times and bad. But not all old people are as wise or resourceful as the father in this folktale. There is a massive difference between growing old and growing as an elder who actively contributes to the health and well-being of the family, community, nation, and world.

Old age doesn't guarantee elder status. Aging into *old* is a physical process; *elderhood* is a state of being and a social relationship. You don't reach old age and suddenly become wise, knowledgeable, compassionate, courageous, widely influential, deeply spiritual, or greatly respected. Just as adulting takes practice, so does eldering. It requires you to cultivate an elder consciousness, envision the purpose and intentions of your elderhood, and take action to make your visions real.

There are indigenous peoples and Black communities, among others, who continue to honor and redefine traditional roles for elders. But the majority of old people in contemporary U.S. society are given little motivation or sense of honor and duty to embody elderhood in socially significant ways. Mostly, we idealize the age of retirement as a reward for those who work long and hard enough (and sock away enough of a nest egg) to kick back and enjoy their final years of life in leisure. For many who get that far, such leisure is short-lived. Research suggests that among retirees there is a significant increase in depression, divorce, drug and alcohol abuse, poverty (especially among women), and suicidal thoughts and behaviors. Retirement isn't always what it's cracked up to be. That's reason enough to rethink our priorities for the "golden years" of old age.

What are your notions about what old age has to offer you and what you have to offer old age? Have you ever envisioned an ancient version of yourself? If you're willing, do it now. Imagine yourself in the far away or not-so-distant future as the eldest of elders. If you are young think very old; if you are old think older still. Close your eyes for a moment and imagine who and what you will be if you get that far.

What do you make of your ancient self? Are you happy to be so old? Are there others who celebrate your weathered presence? Or, does your old age fall heavy on you and those around you? Perhaps it's hard for you to think past your fears of old age – wrinkled face, sagging skin, crippling arthritis, loneliness, injury, illness, forgetfulness, hearing loss, failing eyesight, impending death. . . Fears of growing old are common in a culture in which we broadcast the losses and complaints of old age without building a collective vision of the purpose and usefulness of elderhood. Without such a vision, how can you measure what your old age is worth to you? How can you see your way to becoming an elder who is worthy of the title?

Changing the Face of Old Age

Fortunately, on the horizon, there is a small but growing swell of elders who are consciously giving the face of old age a makeover. This burgeoning revolution isn't powered by anti-aging doctors, pharmaceutical companies, or beauty product lines that tempt you to fake your age or mask your disease. This crusade is powered by old people who desire to be, quite simply and unadulteratedly, ourselves. We are those who are not disturbed overly much by a slower pace, graying hairs or balding heads, sunspots, wrinkles, or sagging skin. We are those who have given up the quest for the fountain of youth and discovered a certain poetic beauty in all that is old.

Embracing the possibilities of old age is one way to transform stereotypes commonly promoted in mainstream media and popular culture of old folks who are inevitably decrepit, forgetful, forgotten, useless, burdensome, angry, sad, pessimistic, infantile, close-minded, ignorant, or unwilling to change. People of all ages display these characteristics and emotions, including old people who do so on a continuum from not-at-all to all-the-time. According to a telling treatise on the subject, *The Owner's Manual for the Brain* by Pierce J. Howard, many of our negative cultural attitudes about old people and old age can be dispelled by better understanding brain development. We each age into old at a different rate, experiencing the losses of old age in varying intensities. What's more, if you are free from any type of significant cognitive impairment due to brain damage or disease (as the vast majority of old people are), you may continue to develop your brain and grow new capacities for creativity, learning, retention, spatial reasoning, and critical thinking. Of course, general wellness has everything to do with brain health, so caring for your physical, emotional, and spiritual needs and using your brain in ways that support healthy cognitive functioning is essential.

In addition to brainpower, researchers tell us that old people commonly display increased capacities for empathy, the ability to imagine multiple points of view, diminishing self-interest, living more fully in the present (rather than the future), and utilizing a breadth of experience to see the bigger picture and cultivate patience, foresight, and needed caution. Such characteristics heighten an old person's abilities for creative innovation, critical thinking, and strategizing solutions to promote the well-being of others. Given these potential assets of old age, elders are far from useless and may be the most underused and underdeveloped resource in contemporary U.S. society.

In his later years, Walt Whitman called himself the "good gray poet" and celebrated old age as "the estuary that enlarges and spreads itself grandly as it pours into the Great Sea." In *Leaves of Grass*, Whitman writes:

> "Youth, large, lusty, loving – youth full of
> grace, force, fascination;
> Do you know that Old Age may come after you
> with equal grace, force, fascination?"

Whitman's words dare me to believe that old people may discover beauty, wonder, power, innovation, resilience, and companionship in the last decades of the human life cycle in massive proportions. It may be that the awakening to elderhood that Whitman describes results from old people facing their suffering in ways that strengthen their constitution for living larger than their grief – this, and the hovering knowledge that earthly life is fleeting. Encountering the losses of old age can make a person fiercely genuine. Such authenticity can inspire people to live as never before.

Here's the thing about reigniting your passion for life in old age: it requires you to invest in your happiness in more ways than one – and I'm not referring to diversifying your financial investment portfolio. In our culture, when we think of preparing ourselves for old age, financial assets are usually a hot topic – social security, retirement funds, investment decisions, health and life insurance, and housing, to name some. But, if you desire to live a good long life and (when the time comes) to die a good and peaceful death, financial security isn't enough. As a practicing elder, you invest in yourself – namely, attuning your brainpower, emotional intelligence, physical health, and spiritual well-being. Think of it as loving yourself for all the right reasons, so you can live your life as the wise old healer you have the potential to be and so you can die with no regrets.

As an elder, becoming yourself takes on cosmic undertones: If you're able and willing to foster an elder's sensibilities – heightened empathy, diminishing self-interest, and an ability to see the bigger picture – you're likely to experience a boundless sense of yourself that connects you to "all that is." Some call this expanding sense of self a "unity of being."

In her now-famous Ted Talk about a stroke experience that put her left brain hemisphere temporarily out of commission, brain researcher and mental health advocate Jill Bolte Taylor describes this unity of being as "stepping to the right of our left hemisphere" to experience "the life-force power of the universe." Philosophers Viktor Frankl and Abraham Maslow referred to it as "self-transcendence." Frankl writes in his 1946 book, *Man's Search for Meaning*:

> ". . . being human always points, and is directed, to something or someone, other than oneself–be it a meaning to fulfill or another human being to encounter. The more one forgets himself–by giving himself to a cause to serve or another person to love–the more human he is and the more he actualizes himself . . . self-actualization is possible only as a side-effect of self-transcendence."

Of course, many feminist philosophers argue that to transcend yourself, you need a "sense of self" to begin. In the final line of her poem, "To Begin With, the Sweet Grass," Mary Oliver suggests that we begin with self-love (harbored quietly within) before setting out to love others. Heed her wise counsel, because forgetting yourself (as Frankl suggests) without loving yourself first can lead to self-loathing and self-destruction as easily as it leads to self-transcendence and self-actualization.

Self-actualization and self-transcendence are like the roots and branches of an elder's development that ideally grow in balance to one another. As practicing elders, we know there is little difference between healing ourselves, helping others to heal, or receiving healing support from another. It is all one and the same. Every instance of healing that matters, matters for all. In the grander scheme of things, there is no "healing you" or "healing me," there is only healing the "we" that resides within everyone.

Changing Our Elder Ways

There is a long-standing myth that tells of old people becoming more and more set in our ways as we age. But Nikolas Westerhoff sets us straight in his article "Set in Our Ways" from the journal *Scientific American* (Vol. 19). Westerhoff asserts that across cultures we humans generally become more open to change in our twenties and then again after 60. Between 30 and 60 most adults are maintaining careers and raising families, and familiar habits and conventional choices may support these efforts. So, a more truthful version of the well-known adage "You can't teach an old dog new tricks," is "Middle-aged dogs become less open to learning new tricks, thank heavens for old dogs."

An increasing openness to change is a precious asset for those sidling up to or past the 60 mark; because, for better or worse, old age is chock-full of big changes that include big losses. What's more, most of us have no clue how to be an elder for ourselves and others in ways that matter. To learn how, we're forced to change. Fortunately, most old people are open to that. That's the good news. On the flip side of the coin is this: *being open to change is not the same thing as changing*. Instinctive fears of change and habitual behaviors and routines can play havoc with the best intentions to change even in good times. When grief strikes hard, you may feel a loss of control or motivation that causes the changes that you desire to make appear impossible to achieve.

If you desire to make changes to transform the pain of grief, a doable practice to change can be a real game changer. One such practice is Dr. Robert Mauer's approach to the practice of Kaizen (introduced on pages 247-48). In Mauer's book, *One Small Step Can Change Your Life*, he offers an everyday approach to creating habits of change one little step at a time. The change habits Mauer advocates are:

1) Asking small questions that welcome creativity and playfulness

2) Thinking small thoughts that allow you to imagine a change before making it

3) Taking small actions that are doable and build confidence to make changes

4) Solving small problems to avoid accumulating big ones

5) Bestowing small rewards to provide internal motivation for change

6) Slowing your pace to enjoy small moments

After 60, when we are generally more open to change, is an ideal time to learn new strategies of change such as the Kaizen practice (or any small part of it). Elders who parent, grandparent, teach, mentor, coach, counsel, or guide can impart lessons on the art of change by our example. So, go slow. Ask small questions. Think small thoughts. Solve small problems. Bestow small rewards. Then, take a step back and see how every little effort comes together in a big way. As James Clear, author of *Atomic Habits*, reminds us:

> "Rome wasn't built in a day, but they were laying bricks every hour. . . it can be really easy to underestimate the importance of laying another brick."

Dreaming Your Elder Self into Being

Do you remember as a child or youth being asked: "What do you want to be when you grow up?" For me back then, the question thrilled my young mind like a magic parable. Each time I heard it, I believed that whatever I could imagine as the best of all things to be, I had only to say it and my wish would be granted: Olympic athlete, singer, actor, writer, dancer, speaker, coach, teacher, doctor, lawyer; but, somewhere along the way, such questions stopped being asked. (Was it in college or grad school, when I became a parent, or took my first "real job" with benefits and a monthly salary?) At some point, I no longer heard, "What do you plan to do, to be, to make of yourself?" It was as if, once I had chosen a path, the curiosities about me and my dreams were answered once and for all. Maybe you have been there too. Maybe there was a time when you (or others) stopped dreaming you into the future. If so, it is never too late to begin again.

⋏⋏⋏

Consider this: how might your life be different if along with the question from your early years, "What do you want to be when you grow up?" yet another question was asked: *"What do you want to be when you grow old, and older, and older still?"* What if you learned early to regard elderhood not as a time of demise but one of harvest, not as the end of adulthood, but as the expansion of it, a chance to take the lasting lessons and assets of a lifetime and make the most of them – especially your abilities to heal yourself and help others to heal? What if, as an elder, you became the quintessential healer among your family members, co-workers, and friends? What if, rather than viewing yourself in old age as a burden and a drain on the young, you saw yourself more completely as a valued and healing presence?

⋏⋏⋏

Becoming a wise elder who cultivates healing for yourself and others requires more than knowledge and experience. It requires a way of living that is defined by thoughtful actions. Consider the etymological origin and evolution of the word "wisdom."

> *Wisdom:* a way of seeing, a way of knowing and using the best means to attain the best end for the greatest good.

Imagine the shift in cultural consciousness that might occur if enough of us among the old took up this deeper meaning of wisdom as an everyday mantra of healing intention. I don't mean we have to save the world. But we do our part, in whatever ways we're able, to heal and minimize suffering and encourage others to do the same.

Old age is not a disease. It is a stage of life that provides an opportunity to fulfill and complete a human life cycle. For most of us (and in growing numbers), old age lasts for decades. What if we made it our mission to reclaim our elder years from the snatches of retirement to create old age as a time of "protirement" or "refirement," as a friend of mine calls it? Why not aspire to become a more intentional and resourceful person, partner, friend, family member, neighbor, contributor, collaborator, or community leader as long as ever you live? Do it for yourself and for everyone whose life intercepts your own, even if such a meeting takes place after you depart the earth – in that part of you that lives on in spirit or your contributions and the remembrances of others.

Life calls every able old person to embody elderhood in ways that matter. Grief calls every able elder to grieve and heal in ways that allow us to see, know, and use "the best means to attain the best end for the greatest good." The bulk of this chapter highlights the lives and contributions of elders who can claim such a legacy. All of these elders – some who are household names and some who serve quietly in their own little corner of the world – discovered how to transform their grieving responses into something useful. They are activists, advocates, mindfulness practitioners, strategists and problem solvers, believers, educators, athletes, soldiers, grandparents, visionaries, storytellers, mediators, and artists who served, or are serving, as philanthropists of the soul.

It is never too early or too late to dream your elder self into being or to harness the healing powers by which to live a good long life or (when the time comes) to die a good and peaceful death. So, go ahead. Dare. Dare to dream it. Ask yourself every day if you have a mind to: "What do I want to be when I grow old and older, and older still?" Let this question guide you to think one small thought, take one small action, solve one small problem, bestow one small reward, enjoy one small moment that brings you one step closer to making your dream of your elder self come true.

Guidepost 50

> When you grow old, waste no time slowing the clock or straightening the creases. Even if you are ancient, the rest of your life is calling.

Making Good of a Bad Thing
Lamenting in Elderhood

Despite the banquet of human emotions, most of us in 21st-century Western culture are gluttons of happiness. Trouble is, getting fat on happiness is as risky as undergoing a lobotomy for mental illness. A lobotomy, that severs connections to and from the prefrontal cortex in a person's brain, may delete an obvious problem but may also obliviate one's personality, intellect, initiative, and interpersonal connectedness, or may cause death. When a person continually devours happiness as their emotion of choice, happiness can be blunted into a monotony of pleasantries. In fact, research gathered in *The Positive Side of Negative Emotions*, edited by Gerrod W. Parrott, suggests that if you buy into Western culture's bias for perpetual happiness, it can backfire on you. "Unhappy" emotions such as sadness, anger, and regret can enhance your self-knowledge, empathy, self-compassion, intellectual prowess, motivation, sense of freedom, strategic planning, observation skills, and interpersonal connectedness in ways that one-dimensional happiness cannot.

Popular culture often tells us that happiness is its own end. We are harangued with the falsehood that, no matter our losses or difficulties, all we need to do is *choose* to be happy. But happiness is more complex than being a singular choice for cheerfulness or detachment from pain. No doubt, feeling cheery or being detached may create a bit of happiness for a griever who needs to hearten or temper grief-related suffering. But without the broader spectrum of unhappy emotions, happiness cannot reside in all its glory as some promise that it will.

You can't merely choose to be happy by way of happiness itself. Happiness is ironic: the more happiness is your ultimate emotional obsession, the more difficult happiness can be to maintain. A human being isn't built to experience a monotonous emotional life – not even one comprised of the various hues of happiness as we define them by way of joy, luck, contentment, prosperity, pleasure, and the like. In Western culture, we need to forge a broader definition of happiness to increase the influence of happiness and maintain its benefits.

Try this: Imagine happiness as the "white light" of emotions. Just as white light contains a complete spectrum of color, so too does happiness contain a complete spectrum of emotion. Or, perhaps more accurately, each emotion contains an element of happiness; yes, even those emotions that make us feel "bad." Here's why: Every "bad" emotion that ever came to be in our evolutionary history as humans, came to be because in some way each one increases the health and well-being of a person or a people. So, painful emotions can be every bit as useful as pleasant ones to help you secure your happiness. Indeed, each contains a piece of the puzzle from which your happiness is made. As Parrot writes,

> ". . . the choice between positive and negative emotions involves much more than feeling good or feeling bad. Emotions have the potential to be useful, but whether this potential is realized requires a variety of skills and intelligence in order to produce the emotion in the right manner. The trick . . . is to find the right tool for the right job."

As you age into old, you may experience grief-related emotions more frequently due to cumulative losses, loneliness, increasing capacities for empathy, facing mortality, and decreasing dopamine and serotonin levels that function to lift our spirits and increase joy, pleasure, and a general sense of well-being. Sometimes, in old age, your increasing familiarity with grief may make you feel bad even on a good day. If so, a happy challenge you face is figuring out how to utilize lamenting responses to your grief wisely – to allow them to lead you to "the best means to attain the best end for the greatest good." Embrace the challenge. Your sadness, anger, loneliness, regret, fear, anxiety, or pessimism may be just what is needed to heal your grief-related wounds and help others to heal theirs.

Do this: Call to mind an elder you respect who makes good use of their lamenting responses – whether in intimate relationships or larger community endeavors. Elders who do so tend to be activists, advocates, mindfulness practitioners, and problem-solving strategists. So, perhaps the elder you call to mind is one among the famous elders on the national or international stage who are humanitarians, or political or spiritual leaders – Jane Goodall, Nelson Mandela, Maya Angelou, Maggie Kuhn, Mother Theresa, Helen Keller, Cesar Chavez, Delores Huerta, Mahatma Gandhi, Dr. Martin Luther King, Jr., Eleanor Roosevelt, the Dalai Lama, Pope Francis, Desmond Tutu, Harvey Milk, Ruth Bader Ginsberg, Harriet Tubman, Oskar Schindler, or Kim Bok-dong, to name some.

In your more intimate circles, perhaps you call to mind an elder who raises a child who is parentless, one who teaches children who are economically, physically, mentally, emotionally, or academically challenged, or one who is a local politician or activist who works to resource vulnerable groups in your community – wounded veterans or those who are homeless, impoverished, illiterate, or suffer domestic abuse. Perhaps you know an elder who simply tells their story of loss in a way that allows other grievers to know they are not alone, or who sits patiently and listens or serves as a quiet presence to another griever who is suffering. Lamenting responses to grief can be made useful for the greatest good in all these ways and more.

We elders become truly wise with grief when we learn to make the most of every "unhappy" emotion that draws our attention and energy. The elders included in the following sections pay homage to this wisdom.

Making Use of Sadness for the Greatest Good

In Western culture, chronic sadness is known to be a sure recipe for depression, isolation, self-absorption, immobility, and low self-esteem. But research also shows that if you know how to use sadness as it's useful, this often-misunderstood emotion can be a seedbed for mindfulness, self-compassion, self-knowledge, humility, heightened memory, and improved analytical thinking. Turn sadness inside out and you will see that it can become a gathering place of connectivity between you and others. Beyond its obvious function as a signal to others that you may need help or emotional support, sadness can also increase your empathy and sensitivity to others, and motivate you to practice patience, politeness, and a generous sharing of resources. If you use sadness as it's useful, sadness can promote more accurate social judgments and less stereotyping with strangers; it can improve your ability to argue more persuasively (using vivid details) to coax others to change their minds. So, next time you want to push away your grief-related sadness before it "gets to you," you may want to put your sadness to work for you.

The serenity prayer, attributed to the theologian Reinhold Niebuhr and made famous by its use in Alcoholics Anonymous and other 12-step recovery programs, highlights the hoped-for outcomes that sadness fosters: "*serenity to accept the things I cannot change, courage to change the things I can, and wisdom to know the difference."* Sadness slows us down, gives us pause to:

1) Accept grief-striking realities that are beyond our control
2) Find motivation and confidence to make needed changes
3) Acquire wisdom to know when it's best to simply be with a loss (and the grief it engenders) and when to do something about it

The usefulness of sadness is evident in the biography of Abraham Lincoln who suffered a number of grief-striking losses in adulthood and was prone to melancholy. Mental health experts suggest that Lincoln's great sadness lent itself to the characteristic leadership quality that served as a foundation for his political genius – his empathy. In her biography about Lincoln entitled, *Team of Rivals*, Doris Kearns Goodwin writes:

> "The melancholy stamped on Lincoln's nature derived in large part from an acute sensitivity to the pains and injustices he perceived in the world. He was uncommonly tenderhearted. He once stopped and tracked back half a mile to rescue a pig caught in a mire–not because he loved the pig, recollected a friend, 'just to take a pain out of his own mind. . .'

> "Lincoln's abhorrence of hurting another was born of more than simple compassion. He possessed extraordinary empathy–the gift or curse of putting himself in the place of another, to experience what they were feeling, to understand their motives and desires. . .

> "In a world environed by cruelty and injustice, Lincoln's remarkable empathy was inevitably a source of pain."

So, too, was Lincoln's melancholy a source of remarkable empathy that made him a strategic diplomat who could forecast the actions of his opponents and plan ahead. Lincoln's empathy inspired him to surround himself with those who were willing to question his decisions and opinions so he could learn from another's perspective what might be his potential pitfalls as a leader and strategist. According to historians, Lincoln's melancholy led to depression and he contemplated suicide more than once; but, ultimately he was able to make use of his great sadness by becoming an empathic and capable leader who guided a conflicted nation through one of our most problematic moments of reckoning.

You don't need to possess the political clout of Abraham Lincoln to put sadness to good use as an elder. Whenever sadness overtakes you, ask yourself, "What use can I make of my sadness?" Keep asking the question until an answer comes, and perhaps another and another. It may be that you know how to sing or play the blues, create visual art or a building project, craft, or write a poem or story that expresses sadness in a beautiful or enriching way. Perhaps your sadness motivates you to relieve the sadness of another by offering your time, talents, or expertise to help solve family, neighborhood, work-related, or community problems. How you carry your sadness may strike a chord with others in ways you never anticipated. Consider the story of Itaru Sasaki relayed in an NHK documentary, *The Phone of the Wind*:

The Wind Phone: One Elder's Sad Offering

In 2010, at the age of sixty-three, Itaru Sasaki made a curious addition to his home garden in Otsuchi, Japan. On a hill overlooking the sea, Sasaki set up an old public phone booth with a black rotary phone in it. The phone was disconnected and Sasaki had the idea that it would be an ideal way of talking with his cousin who died from cancer. He later told reporters from NHK (a Japanese broadcasting channel), "Because my thoughts couldn't be relayed over a regular phone line, I wanted them to be carried on the wind." Sasaki named the phone, "Kaze no denwa" (the wind phone). It was an unconventional altar of remembrance that helped Sasaki remain connected to his loved one and offered him a little sanctuary for his grief. When he set it up, Sasaki had no idea that the phone booth would one day attract a stream of visitors or garner international attention.

When a tsunami hit Japan in 2011, killing over 15,000, the small fishing village of Otsuchi was one of the coastal towns that was devastated. According to *USA Today*, most of the homes and buildings were demolished and nearly 10% of the town's population died or are still missing. It took more than a year for the town to come up with a recovery plan because almost all the government administrators were killed in the disaster. It was in the aftermath of such devastation that Sasaki thought to invite other grievers to come to his "wind phone" to call on their deceased and missing loved ones. Come they did. In the NHK documentary that honors this unorthodox memorial site, we are introduced to some of the grievers who use the wind phone: chattering grandchildren with their grandmother who catch grandpa up on the latest news, bereaved spouses, parents, children who ask heart-wrenching questions, "Why you?" "Why me?" Some make requests of their dear ones, "Come home soon." Others stand silently listening into the receiver because "there are no words" and some cry of their sorrow for the first time since the tsunami hit and a loved one disappeared.

It used to be just another discarded phone booth that had seen its day. But in his sadness, Sasaki was wise enough to clean it up, set it up in a place where it could do some good, and make of it something useful, something that speaks of the sacred – for the villagers of Otsuchi and for those who come from afar whose thoughts and words to their loved ones are now "carried on the wind."

As you grieve in creative ways that offer refuge, you may be surprised who joins you there. Sometimes sadness is waiting to be expressed in a place already visited by others who mourn. As an elder, you can lead the way to healing simply by grieving "outside the box," or inside the phone booth as the case may be. So, pause with your sorrow from time to time and ask: "How can I make good use of my sadness?"

Making Use of Anger for the Greatest Good

Many spiritual and religious leaders consider anger to be an enemy of virtue. It's no wonder since out-of-control anger can fragment your integrity, cloud your thinking, and cause you to fly off the handle without an intelligent plan of action. At its worst, anger can be wielded as a weapon to invade, injure, and destroy. But research also shows that a good measure of anger can be used as a tool to protect and persuade. What's more, sadness and anger together can be mighty allies for a griever when it comes to the balance of introspection and willful action that a griever needs to heal what needs healing. Whereas sadness is especially potent to promote clearer thinking, anger is an effective fuel for decisive doing. Anger can be used to energize a griever to get moving, confront a problem head-on, and overcome the difficulties that a grief-striking loss presents.

Gray Panthers founder, Maggie Kuhn, decided that "old age is an excellent time for outrage." After being forced to retire from a job she loved in the Presbyterian Church in 1970, Kuhn put her anger into action. From the age of 65 until she died at 89, Kuhn invited young and old to organize and address ageist laws and cultural practices. In an interview with Connie Goldman, included in the book *The Ageless Spirit*, Kuhn pronounces:

> "There's a fear of old people in this country. Gerontophobia is an epidemic; the fear of old people and the fear of growing old, the two are combined. It goes back, I think, to the fact that we've made a fetish of being young. We pride ourselves on being a youthful nation, and yet a growing percentage of our population has achieved a great old age. . ."

During the final 25 years of her life, Kuhn helped establish an intergenerational network that advocates for elder rights, nursing home reform, shared housing opportunities, and the preservation of Medicare and Social Security. Kuhn's efforts are all the more impressive because her work was accomplished while caring for a mother with a physical disability and a brother who suffered mental illness. In her later years, severe arthritis crippled her hands and made it "difficult to open things or turn off a light switch." So says Kuhn,

> "Old age . . . is strength and survivorship, triumph over all kinds of vicissitudes and disappointments, trials and illness."

That's what a little outrage will do for you. It lights a fire in your belly. It demands to be seen and heard for what it is – a shout-out for change.

Those who band together to fight for the rights of old people (or any oppressed or forgotten sector of society) are, in essence, a grieving support group with a mission. Expressing sadness over a social problem usually won't change what needs changing.

It is an angry sort of sorrow that propels people to action. Anger is the emotion that all of our great civil rights movements are built upon – which is why nonviolent protest and civil disobedience are central to their success. Research shows that a constructive expression of anger serves to reduce violence rather than amplify it. As practicing elders, we wisely take action to grieve and heal the social ills that enrage us without becoming the victimizer as well as the victim.

Anger can be as virtuous as love, but it takes a bit of genius to use this powerful emotion as a curative rather than a curse. As Aristotle wrote in *The Art of Rhetoric*,

> "Anybody can become angry – that is easy, but to be angry with the right person and to the right degree and at the right time and for the right purpose, and in the right way – that is not within everybody's power and is not easy."

Hitting upon just the "right anger" can be a complex puzzle for a griever. There may be moments when your angry grief rumbles up and out of you as fierce as it is painful and no harm is done, no innocent stands in your path. Your anger may save you or another from harm because you respond in a flash of anger-driven protection. Heroes are made for such moments. But, more often, as you grieve a problematic death, divorce, legal proceeding, conflict, or social injustice, your intense anger will require you to check yourself before going off half-cocked. It will require you to take some deep breaths, breathing vengeful rage out and breathing caring strength in, before blame, shame, or vengeance takes you somewhere you do not intend to go.

The question of "right anger" is one that grieving family members and friends may need to revisit often, because when you are grieving angry, you may inadvertently take your anger out on those closest to you. Intimates do well to give one another a balance of grace and constructive feedback in this regard. Let the following Hindu fable serve as food for thought:

> Once there was a Hindu saint gathered with a group of disciples when one asked, "Why is it that angry people shout at each other, even as they stand right next to one another?" The saint replied, "When two people are angry, their hearts are at a great distance, and so they shout so they can hear one another." The saint continued, "When people fall in love, they talk softly to one another because their hearts are very close, and when love deepens, they have only to whisper to one another and finally only to look into one another's eyes."

This story prompts the question: Does anger subside as love increases or does love make anger more easily heard? As for my spouse Andrew and me, we continue to deepen our love after thirty-plus years of grieving and healing our losses together. Yet, there are still times I spout my anger at him and he does the same for me. No love is lost in the exchange. He is a kind, fun-loving soul with a half-Irish temper. I am a born feminist with a sense of humor, so we are well-matched. We discovered long ago that whether our anger speaks loudly, softly, or silently, this potentially constructive emotion can protect and deepen our love if we use it to bridge the distance between us. Once we bridge the distance, there is no need to shout, yet there may be a lingering need to unravel the anger that persuaded us to sit up and pay attention in the first place.

Anger doesn't necessarily need to be loud to get the job done. But for anger to be of use, it needs to be communicated and explored. According to brain research, most of us get better at expressing "right anger" as we age into old because our brains become less reactive to volatile emotions. We also tend to remember more positive than negative memories in old age, so anger from the past may diminish as we focus on what brings us joy and pleasure in the present. However, traumatic memories may take years to release their iron hold.

Eva Mozes Kor, a Romanian survivor of the Holocaust, found that it took decades of peripheral healing after her release from Auschwitz to finally be able to speak the worst of her anger concerning the torments she and her family endured there. Eva's desire to be free from the tortures of her past led her to a place of reconciliation that other Holocaust survivors may not choose to go:

A Loud & Private Anger

During World War II, Eva's parents and two older sisters were murdered by the Nazis at Auschwitz. Eva and her twin sister Miriam were among thousands of children who became "Mengele Twins." The project was named after Joseph Mengele, a Nazi doctor known as the Angel of Death. Mengele was on a mission to discover how to increase the birthrate of a master Aryan race. Although twins were spared the gas chamber, they were also subjected to torturous experiments that caused severe illness, injury, and death.

Eva revealed in an interview with Buzzfeed Videos (*The Power to Live and Forgive*) that it was almost fifty years after her physical liberation from Auschwitz that she discovered the means for a second liberation. Through a series of coincidences, Eva made the acquaintance of Dr. Munch, a reluctant and remorseful colleague of Mengele's, who (at Eva's request to dispute revisionist claims) documented atrocities he witnessed, including mass murders in the gas chambers of Auschwitz that Munch supervised through a peephole and that remained in his memory like a living nightmare. Afterward, Eva wanted to thank the doctor for providing the requested evidence, but she did not know how to do it. Ten months later, Eva had the idea to offer Dr. Munch a letter of forgiveness. It took her another four months to write the letter as she continued to process her pain. Even then, the fact remained that the real ogre of Eva's suffering was Joseph Mengele who was already dead. When a friend suggested to Eva that it was Mengele that she might yet seek to forgive, Eva balked at the idea. She wasn't sure if she was ready for that. Eva remembers,

> ". . . when I got home, actually, I did something else. I picked up a dictionary and wrote down 20 nasty words which I read clear and loud to that make-believe Mengele in the room. And at the end, I said 'In spite of all that I forgive you.' Made me feel very good. That I, the little guinea pig of fifty years, even had the power over the Angel of Death of Auschwitz."

Speaking her anger loud and clear, Eva chose to stand bravely over her pain.

Until her death in 2019 at the age of 85, Eva continued to speak out as a historian and founder of CANDLES Holocaust Museum and Education Center in Terra Haute, Indiana. Eva was well aware that for many Holocaust survivors and their family members, the wounds are still gaping. So, she told and retold her story as a shout-out for personal and cultural healing – believing that anger, as much as compassion, can lead a griever to the door of forgiveness.

Justified anger can be a holy thing. Rabbi Abraham Joshua Heschel, who marched on the front lines of the civil rights movement with Dr. Martin Luther King Jr., says it best: "When I marched in Selma, I felt like my legs were praying."

Making Use of Loneliness for the Greatest Good

Loneliness is a barren emotion that may appear to be useless. But at its best, the solitude of loneliness can lead to artistic creation and a more liberated sense of self; it can inspire compassion and empathy. In fact, preschool programs in Japan encourage loneliness because it is believed that once a child stands apart and embodies the experience of loneliness, the child becomes more aware of others' lonely experiences and is more apt to invite a lonely child to join the group.

Unfortunately, when you suffer a devastating loss of relationship, a shroud of loneliness may envelop you even when you are surrounded by others who care greatly. For example, my adopted grandmom, Polly, repeatedly told me how devastating it was in the last decade of her life to watch her spouse and most of her age group peers die off one by one. She felt as if she was being left behind. That type of loneliness is difficult to shake. Despite being a bubbly dynamo who adored her close-knit family and slew of friends, Polly so immersed herself in the love she felt for her dear ones, that every death gave rise to sorrowful loneliness for those no longer with her. That loneliness hovered over Polly's bright shine like a dark and unrelenting cloud of grief that was often invisible to others.

The deaths of cherished loved ones may lead an elder into a deep pit of grief. So, it is imperative for elders to learn to put such loneliness to good use. Consider two old men who harbored the loneliness of grief following the death of a spouse:

The first man is in his eighties. He is legally blind (blindness that descended in his late sixties). He suffers from COPD from many years of smoking, so he lives with an oxygen machine constantly at his side. His spouse suffers from hearing loss, but she can still drive. She serves as the man's eyes; he serves as her ears. Despite these burdens, between the two of them, they get along well – visiting with family and friends, enjoying their country home, gathering with family on birthdays and holidays. Over the years, the man's beloved companion suffers a heart condition that worsens. She becomes severely depressed. The man cares for her in her final years as best he can. When she dies, the man is heartbroken and the loneliness that descends is almost unbearable. Years later, the man remembers the details of his wife's death as if it were yesterday. He still cannot speak of her without tears in his eyes and a crack in his throat. Despite weekly visits from caring friends, it appears at times that the man's loneliness will break him.

The second man's wife also dies of heart failure; his grief and loneliness are immense. This man celebrates his ninetieth birthday with a slew of family and friends. One after another, they speak of his influential and inspiring presence, his legacy of care. This man is physically strong and slender with a mind as sharp as they come. A gifted chiropractor and healer, the man continues to work part-time, keeping his medical license up to date and seeing patients in his home office most mornings. He continues to study and learn, keeping up on the latest chiropractic, nutritional, and physical therapy research. He talks to friends and relatives long-distance to help them heal physical ailments and illnesses that baffle other medical doctors who see their patients in person. This wonder of a man is my Uncle Bill. He died unexpectedly from pneumonia at the age of 93, and until then, served as my oldest living role model. He was a father figure to me after my father (his younger brother) died several years before. Paradoxically, so is the man I first described. These two men are one and the same, and each description is as accurate as the other.

My uncle's undying mission to help others to heal gave him sufficient reprieve from his overwhelming loneliness. Uncle Bill was legally blind for 25 years and used an oxygen machine 24/7 for the final 15, but his healing contributions and care for others drove him to stay strong and healthy enough to continue his studies and offer his services until a few weeks before he died.

In contrast to my Uncle Bill, there are some among the old who make good use of loneliness to create cherished solitude rather than connection – my mother, for example, who divorced my father after 38 years of marriage. Now, in her eighties, she has been on her own for three decades and prefers it. For my mom and others like her, choosing to live alone helps to keep a more painful experience of loneliness at bay. My mom is an introvert who paraded as an extrovert for most of her life, so despite her winning charm, she can feel awkwardly lonely in a crowd. When she goes out in public, a stranger can easily become an instant friend, but she also relishes her solitude without having to adjust her schedule, momentary desires, or personal habits to appease a live-in partner or housemate.

Like my friend, Polly, many of my mom's closest friends died over the past few decades. My mom suffers from COPD and chronic pain, so it's hard for her to socialize with any regularity. When she downsized from her house to an apartment in a 55 and older independent living community, it was quite an adjustment to get used to phone calls and knocks on the door from neighbors. My mom would rather be playing her grand piano (in her pajamas if she chooses), watching a St. Louis Cardinals game on TV (she's a die-hard lifelong fan), texting her children and grandchildren (as the queen of emojis), or reading a good book rather than entertaining an unexpected guest or negotiating a new relationship that imposes on the precious time she enjoys with herself. She claims that in her old age, her goal is to be who she is, unapologetically, and to do what she desires to do when she desires to do it. If that includes attending a doll-making class, visiting with family members who live nearby, having lunch with a friend, accompanying a sing-along, or joining other residents for a movie or coffee, you can bet she's there because she wants to be and feels up to it.

Loneliness can be made useful in old age on a broad continuum from prompting elders to seek compassionate community to braving creative solitude. Imagine how loneliness might serve you best. For my uncle, it was through imparting his gift of healing, and for my mom, it is by continuing to create the life she chooses for herself that strikes just the right balance of togetherness and solitude.

When a grieving elder finds it difficult to navigate through a thick fog of loneliness, a gesture of connection and support may need to come from outside oneself. Fortunately, that's what happened for Dan Peterson, who became the subject of an unusual love story reported by CBS News in November of 2016:

Buried in Grief: An Old Man's Story of Resurrection

After 82-year-old Dan Peterson's spouse Mary died, he was "buried in grief." He spent days staring out the window and fell into a deep depression, just waiting to die. But one day six months after the funeral, something happened. Dan claims he was visited by an angel while he was grocery shopping at the local supermarket.

Dan hates shopping and was the epitome of the grumpy old man as he wheeled his cart down the canned vegetable aisle. Just then, a mother with her four-year-old daughter Norah in her cart came around the corner into the aisle where Dan was shopping. Norah immediately piped up at the sight of him, "Hi old person, it's my birthday today!" As Dan tells it, Norah then asked him for a hug. "A hug!" he mused behind a deceptively grumpy expression, "Absolutely!" Needless to say, Norah got her birthday hug. The rest is history.

Norah and Dan became fast friends from that day forward. Norah and her mom began to visit Dan weekly and Norah cherished a large framed picture of the two on the day they met, sometimes falling asleep with the giant frame in her arms. In their first year as friends, Dan and Norah went trick-or-treating together and he shared in her family's Thanksgiving dinner. The love story went on with more of the same.

Norah's mom, Tara Wood, says the special bond between Dan and Norah defies explanation. In an online post she wrote about the remarkable event, "That Time My Daughter Talked to a Stranger," Wood says that the day before her birthday, Norah foreshadowed the meeting with a bit of no-nonsense childlike wisdom. Wood writes:

> "I'd just picked (Norah) up from preschool when she cautioned me to mind the elderly person walking across the parking lot at a glacier's pace. (Norah) went on to explain that she has a soft spot for mature folks: 'I like old peoples the best 'cos they walk slow like I walk slow and they has soft skin like I has soft skin. They all gonna die soon so I'm gonna love 'em all up before they is died.'"

Dan didn't mind Norah calling him an "old man" when first they met or any day before he died at the age of 86, four years after Dan and Norah met. Lucky for him, he was one. To Dan, being loved "all up" by Norah was an unbelievable miracle that he willingly embraced as the proof he needed that his life still had a purpose: "Watching Norah grow up!" Dan claimed that his little grocery store angel inspired him to make "room in (his) heart for a lot more."

Using loneliness for the greater good is sometimes accomplished by a little hand reaching out and a little cherub asking, "Come play?" Of course, someone has to receive and say yes to the invitation. For Dan, it was as easy as giving a four-year-old a birthday hug. With that hug, Dan realized, he was saying yes to life beyond loneliness, too.

Making Use of Remorse, Guilt & Shame for the Greatest Good

A lifetime of losses can be humbling, especially when remorse, guilt, or shame is at the core of your grief. You make a mistake, choose wrongly, or lose morality or virtue (even for a moment). You stop paying attention, blow your top, let bad habits snowball, or develop relationship patterns that bear losses continually. Even if you did nothing to cause a loss, you may find fault in yourself for failing to prevent it or for adding loss to loss by your response.

Remorse, guilt, or shame can be especially complicated when they are mixed up with virtue. Some wrongdoings are born out of brave and well-intentioned choices: You enlist for military combat, refuse to work for an unethical company that provides for your family's abundance, set a firm curfew for a teenager who gets into a car accident rushing home, report a family friend for child neglect, or admit you are an addict or struggling with mental illness. With some losses, there is no one (or everyone) to blame. Even so, you may find yourself wishing you could turn back time to reverse something you did (or did not do) to set another course and avoid a life-shifting loss. If so, you're in good company. Few of us make it to elderhood without a measure of self-blame for some of the losses we bear.

Making peace with remorse, guilt, and shame requires you to pay attention to how each fault-finding emotion can be vital to your healing and how each is likely to trip you up and make matters worse. This startling picture of remorse found in Tiffany Watt Smith's *The Book of Human Emotions* provides a harsh example:

> "A young man sits on a carpenter's bench, blood pooling on the floor beneath him. Overcome with emotion after kicking his mother, he has cut off his own leg. In the painting by the Venetian artist Antonio Vivarini, dated to the 1450s...Saint Peter kneels over the severed leg attempting to heal it, while two women – perhaps one is the boy's mother – wring their hands anxiously in the background."

Unchecked remorse can cause you to rage at yourself and demand payment that is out of whack with the harm you committed. But at its best, remorse can urge you to take action to right a wrong or better a situation. Remorse is a kind of urgent guilt or shame that comes with a clear sense of self-blame and an inner demand for some sort of penitent action. The challenge, of course, is determining how to use your remorse to make things right (or at least better, if "right" is out of reach) without doing further damage to yourself or others.

Remorse assumes guilt, but guilt can stand alone. Guilt can be a haunting or sporadic emotion that stirs up questions in you about where responsibility lies. Depending on how you apportion blame to yourself and others, you may talk yourself into and out of guilty feelings and what you do or don't regret.

Guilt encourages you to reflect on the responsibility that rests in your hands. It can promote empathy for others who were harmed by your behavior and foster humility, virtue, and caring action. Guilt helps you to reflect on a situation and develop higher-quality solutions to relationship problems. Like remorse, guilt can urge you to apologize, make amends, and avoid repeating the same harmful action.

Shame may be intertwined with guilt, but many emotion experts consider guilt to be an emotion related to *bad behavior*, while shame is related to viewing yourself as a *bad or defective person*. Thus, the same behavior – for example, spreading gossip, purchasing pornography, lying to a loved one, or binge eating – might cause one person to feel guilty about having done so and another person to feel shame for being the kind of person who would do it.

Because shame is intimately connected with self-identity, it can breed self-loathing. Shame may be self-imposed or arise when someone else judges you or your behavior to be unkind, unfair, cowardly, immoral, or unethical. It may be that a loved one discovers a trail of your indiscretions or you become the target of social humiliation for "bad behavior" or "bad character" that goes viral.

Shame may be a warranted emotion that fuels self-scrutiny. However, it may be projected wrongfully by those who spread slanted or untrue information about you or impose discriminatory moral standards or social codes. Unfortunately, social shaming can be used as a weapon to preserve social norms that are unkind, unfair, cowardly, immoral, or unethical, just as shame can indict a person from within. In some loss-related circumstances, it may be difficult to identify who ought to bear the brunt of shame – the one who is shamed or the one who does the shaming.

Shame is an emotion closely related to embarrassment, but it is an intense embarrassment that can lead to hiding or denying severe problems. Shame often accompanies addictions, including substance abuse that, according to the Addiction Center, affects approximately 17% of the U.S. population over 60 (and this number is on the rise). For those who suffer from addiction in the 60-and-over population, alcohol and the overuse of prescription medications are common go-to forms for numbing physical, emotional, mental, and spiritual pain.

Among the old, shame can also result from elder abuse, a mostly hidden cultural problem. According to the National Center for Elder Abuse, in the U.S. alone, one out of ten people 60 or older suffer physical, sexual, emotional, or financial victimization. Most of these cases go unreported and shame is a major contributor to that trend. Victimized elders may be ashamed to admit that a family member does them harm, or that they aren't strong enough to protect themselves or smart enough to avoid being conned by a scam artist, relative, or unethical financial investor.

Despite the damage that shame can do to your self-respect and self-compassion, it can also inspire self-assessment and self-improvement – particularly when you believe that constructive changes in behavior are possible. Shame can help you to develop greater compassion for yourself and others by inspiring you to transform a source of shame into a strength. For example, a person who is a recovering addict might choose to become an addictions counselor, or a person who is an ex-convict might become a prison chaplain to help others transform shameful suffering that they know firsthand.

As you explore your remorse, guilt, or shame, ask yourself "How can I use this emotion for the greatest good?" Be patient with yourself as you unravel memories and circumstances that breed each emotion and as you figure out if your fault-finding emotions are proportionate to the sense of responsibility you carry for a loss.

At some point in your life, you may encounter a situation in which you're forced to make a split-second decision that haunts you. Sometimes, the "right thing to do" may be a choice that smacks of unkindness, unfairness, cowardice, immorality, or a lack of ethics, even if it appears to be your only viable option at the time. Consider such a moment of reckoning and its aftereffects in the life of war veteran, Rich Luttrell, who shared his story in a 2008 interview with NBC news correspondent, Keith Morrison:

A Soldier's Journey of Healing

The year is 1967. Rich is a young soldier in the Vietnam War, serving in the 101st airborne. He is barely of age to fight a war, but chose to volunteer and is proud to serve his country. As soon as he and his platoon arrive in Vietnam, Rich is filled with a foreboding sense of death and devastation. It is a horrific war – steamy with heat and nowhere to rest. Just moving through the jungle, constantly in fear, in an endless maze of not knowing – not knowing when or where the next shot will be fired, not knowing when or where the enemy will materialize. Sometimes, Rich chokes back tears, sometimes he prays for the exhausting mix of paranoia and sleep deprivation to end. He dreads the moment of his first firefight. Then, in the blink of an eye, everything changes.

In that death trap of a jungle, Rich finally glimpses his first North Vietnamese soldier who is suddenly just a few short feet away, squatting with his AK47 rifle in hand. Rich freezes. He looks the NVA soldier in the eyes for what seems a good long while. Then something in him (training, fear, instinct) pulls the trigger. It all happens in slow motion. The pull of the trigger. . . the NVA soldier falls to the ground. . . the heavy firefight riddles on both sides. . . he is tackled by a fellow soldier who knows enough to hit the ground and take Rich with him.

The firefight ends. After the panic of adrenaline subsides and Rich's legs are weak with an ironic sense of relief, the horrible reality floods in – he just ended a human life, and it wasn't just any human life. The life Rich ended was that of an "enemy" who chose not to pull the trigger on him. More difficult still is what Rich discovers there on the jungle path – a post-stamp-sized photo of an NVA soldier and a little girl. Rich squats next to the soldier he just killed, looks from the photo to the face of the soldier, to the photo to the soldier. It is him and with him, a little girl looking so sad. Is this little girl a daughter seeing her father off to war?

Rich slips the photo into his wallet and his platoon quickly moves out again into that jungle of not knowing. Rich sets his mind to survive. He soon becomes a skilled soldier with extraordinary combat abilities who is passionate about his duty to his country and the U.S. soldiers with whom he serves. Rich survives the war, but not without taking a bullet to his back 20 days before his tour ends. It is the bullet that sends him home, but it isn't the only bullet he takes. There is that invisible bullet to his heart that shattered his sense of humanity on the day of his first firefight. It is a bullet he carried with him throughout his tour of duty and carries still, a bullet that doctors who heal his body can do nothing about.

Rich comes home as a decorated war hero. He marries his childhood sweetheart. They have children. Rich never talks about the war. He keeps his feelings hidden, along with the picture of a father and a girl who Rich imagines to be the man's daughter. Rich never forgets the soldier's face looking at him before he fired. But what haunts him most is the little girl in the picture. Who is she? Where is she? Rich is tormented by the thought that he killed this man who is so precious to her.

Years pass and finally Rich knows he must do something, anything to express his remorse and conjure some forgiveness for himself. So, he takes the photograph with him to Washington D.C. to visit the Vietnam War Memorial. Sitting in his hotel room the night before his visit, he scribbles a quick note to leave at the wall with the worn picture he kept close to him all these years. He writes,

> "Dear Sir, For 22 years, I've carried your picture in my wallet. I was only 18 years old that day we faced one another on that trail in Chu Lai, Vietnam. Forgive me for taking your life. So many times over the years, I've stared at your picture and your daughter, I suspect. Each time, my heart and guts would burn with the pain of guilt. Forgive me sir."

At the wall the next day, the gesture is made anonymously. Rich places the photo and note at the wall where the names of some 58,000 U.S. soldiers who died in Vietnam are inscribed. He feels a heavy weight lift from him. But that isn't the end of it, because that note and picture are collected with all the other offerings made at the wall, discovered by the curator of the Vietnam Veterans Memorial Collection, Duery Felton, and included in a book published in 1995, *Offerings at the Wall* by Thomas B. Allen. Rich, who now works for Veterans Affairs, picks up the book one day. As he leafs through it, he stops short: Staring up at him from one of the pages is the little girl in the photo, accusing him of abandonment. Later Rich says, "For me, that moment was, it was almost a nightmare. It was like, you know, 'Little girl, what do you want from me . . . what do you want from me?' "

Rich decides to find out. He contacts Felton to get the photograph back. The curator personally flies the photograph from Washington D.C. to Illinois to hand it to Rich. It is a photograph both men treasure and have mourned over. After that, Rich is obsessed with finding the girl in the photo. He contacts a reporter for the St. Louis Dispatch who prints an article about the picture. Rich sends a copy of the article to the Vietnamese ambassador in Washington D.C. who then forwards it to Hanoi where another article is printed along with the appeal, "Does anyone know these people?" A man buys the paper and uses it to wrap a care package he is sending to his mother in a rural village north of Hanoi. The old woman sees the photograph, recognizes the man, and takes it to a woman, a mother named Lan, and says, "This is your father."

Soon letters are exchanged between Lan and Rich, and Rich explains to Lan and her family the complicated feelings he wrestles with: He does not regret serving as a soldier but does experience deep-seated guilt for taking the lives of other human beings, particularly the life of a young father, Lan's father. Then, despite Rich's promise to himself that he will never go back to that land where he saw and did so much killing, endured and had a hand in so many horrors, Rich returns to Vietnam. Fear sets in as soon as he steps off the plane and takes in the smell of the place. It seems to him that he is more equipped to endure another firefight than to do what he came here to do. But, along with his guilt and fear to face Lan and her family, Rich makes the trip to their village, brings flowers, stands in awkward silence as he and Lan look into one another's faces for the first time with a circle of her family and friends looking on. Then, in Vietnamese, Rich speaks the words he practiced and came to impart: "Today," he says, "I return the photo of you and your father, which I have kept for 33 years. Please forgive me."

Lan and Rich embrace. She weeps into his arms, his chest, his heart. Her sobs speak of long years of pain for Lan, for Rich. He holds her, patting her back in comfort. Lan's brother tells Rich that they believe their father lives on in him, that they regard this meeting as their father's spirit coming back to them. So, the sacrifice comes full circle: a father gives a young soldier his life and a young soldier grown old gives the father's spirit back again.

※ ※ ※

Whatever cure that meeting held for Rich, whatever guilt he released or continues to carry, it is guilt that Rich was brave enough to acknowledge and use for the greater good – for his own sake, the sake of Lan and her family, and peripherally for all those who must reconcile the horrors of war. It was Rich's guilt that got him to that moment of reckoning in which great and far-reaching healing was possible.

As the saying goes, "all is fair in love and war," but the truth is that within each of us who enjoy a healthy, mature psyche and soul, there resides a moral code that will hound us to no end if we break it. What is confusing about this inner moral code is that it is based upon personal, family, and cultural beliefs and values that are prioritized differently for each of us.

A few decades back, when I was serving as a youth minister, a student approached me with a moral puzzle known as the "Heinz dilemma" that was posed in one of her high school classes. The Heinz dilemma is based upon the moral development work of theorist, Lawrence Kohlberg. Perhaps you've heard of it:

As the story goes, a man is faced with a moral choice when his wife falls gravely ill and will surely die. A druggist in the couple's hometown discovers an expensive drug that may save the woman's life. However, the druggist is charging ten times what the drug costs and Heinz is unable to raise enough money to buy it. The druggist will not budge on the price, and Heinz decides to break into the laboratory to steal the drug.

Take a moment to consider what you would choose to do if you were in Heinz's shoes. Was it right for Heinz to break in and steal the medication?

When this moral dilemma was proposed to me, I imagined my spouse, Andrew, in the place of Heinz's loved one and decided that rather than going to prison for stealing a drug that may or may not work, I would rather spend time caring for Andrew and helping to create a good death for him, if that came. I imagined that if the tables were turned, Andrew would be willing to do the same for me. But, after I told the student I would not choose to steal the drug if I were Heinz, she told me that if I were more morally evolved, I would know that saving a life ought to trump obedience to the law.

Upon further investigation, I discovered that the student's explanation of the moral exercise was oversimplified because the point of the Heinz dilemma is not to grade moral depth based upon whether or not you condone Heinz's thievery, but to reflect upon the reasons for your conclusion. A person might choose to steal or not steal the drug based on immoral or highly moral reasons. However, a basic flaw in the setup of this moral exercise and its analysis are the assumptions that highly evolved moral development primarily includes (1) a desire to preserve human life at all costs and (2) an understanding that preserving one's life is a fundamental human right. What the moral test fails to consider is that humans also have a fundamental right to choose to be ill and to die in their own way at their own time and among the people they love. In fact, at the other far end of this moral dilemma, the debate becomes: *What is a doctor to do – medically-induce the prolongation of an unhealthy, painful existence for one who desires death, or assist in medically-supported euthanasia?* With such moral complexities, loss is often certain whatever choice is made.

What the Heinz dilemma highlights beautifully is the process of reasoning by which a person feels justified, ambivalent, right, wrong, guilty, innocent, ashamed, courageous, or remorseful concerning choices that impact a grief-striking loss. Today, even choosing whether or not to go to the hospital when one is gravely ill or to remain home in the care of loved ones, or whether to follow conventional, experimental, or natural healing regimens, can generate remorse, guilt, or shame whatever choice is made. The stakes are even higher when an illness intensifies or results in death or injury, or when societal expectations are contrary to personal beliefs and values.

Whatever fault-finding you do in the midst of your grief, there may be instances when your remorse, guilt, or shame are interwoven with the remorse, guilt, or shame of another. Do your best not to make it a competition to see who can bear or dole out the greatest blame. Practice self-scrutiny, self-compassion, and self-forgiveness as generously as you offer encouragement, compassion, and forgiveness to others.

Making Use of Fear, Worry & Pessimism for the Greatest Good

Anxiety – some say it's rampant in the U.S., hounding us in epidemic proportions. Anxiety gone wild can paralyze or impair our thinking, being, and doing. It can lead to panic, paranoia, catastrophizing, or general nervousness that plagues our relationships, health, and well-being. However, anxiety-related emotions such as fear and worry can also literally spare our lives and keep us safe. In chapter 11 of *The Positive Side of Negative Emotions* – "The Right Tool for the Right Job," Julie K. Norem highlights the potential benefits of anxiety. Norem points out that anxiety can be useful if we channel it into problem-solving strategies. She asserts that when we can harness anxiety and use it to prepare ahead or psych ourselves up for necessary action, the discomfort of anxiety can be a catalyst to increase self-esteem, self-control, academic achievement, the pursuit of self-improvement, and even our physical health in old age.

Interestingly, anxiety paired with an attitude of pessimism can be a potent combination for improving upon a worrisome or fear-provoking situation. Research indicates that those who prefer to reflect on what could possibly go wrong in the future and strategically take action to avoid undesirable outcomes usually fare better than they would if they adopted a more optimistic, "all will be well" mindset. So, for all the research that claims that optimists achieve more and live longer, happier lives than pessimists, there are contrasting studies claiming that those who prefer to use pessimism as a problem-solving strategy, may see equal benefits. The key, of course, is to mindfully use fear, worry, and pessimism as goal-oriented motivators that inspire you to think ahead and prepare for the troubles that may come.

Today, there is a growing library of hopeful, optimistic self-help books that are written on the topic of successful "old aging" in the 21st century. However, on a far shelf, separated from the others, there is a book of another kind by the freethinking rationalist, Susan Jacoby, entitled *Never Say Die: The Myth and Marketing of the New Old Age*. Admittedly, I was put off at first by the pessimism that groans from every page. At times, I had out-loud arguments with Jacoby as I read certain passages that struck me as being especially slanted toward doom. It wasn't that I disagreed with any of Jacoby's well-thought-out conclusions, it was the lack of buoyancy with which she laid out her dark realities that caused my resistance. Even she admits in her conclusion that several well-meaning writer friends advised her to end the book on an optimistic note. Jacoby attempts it in her signature Eeyore style, but it is a bit awkward because Jacoby's thorough lamenting of the real and potential losses of old age is what her book is about. Her willingness to see her message through to its rather depressing end is noble, although annoying to hopers and dreamers like me.

In a book that is described as being both heretical and compassionate, Jacoby exposes our youth-obsessed, death-denying, old-age defying culture. She demonstrates the irony of our sworn allegiance to the omniscient magic of "modern medicine" and destroys our delusions about *Money* magazine's annual list of "best places in America to retire." (It seems that for the oldest among us, what's "best" may not be so ideal when it comes to real-life experience.) Jacoby claims that irrational expectations of old age lead to a demise in the quality of life and health for many in old age who find little joy, companionship, mobility, accessibility, pleasure, or passion there. Strangely, as I slogged through her unending cultural criticisms and negativity, I realized at last that Jacoby is offering the best a pessimist can offer: a warning of all that may go wrong as we age into the future of old, so we can get busy and do something about it before it's too late.

What's more, Jacoby believes there is redemption in facing one's despair about death and old age. She offers an excerpt of Susan Sontag's journal (quoted in David Rieff's memoir of his mother's illness and death from cancer):

> "Despair shall set you free. I can't write because I don't (won't) give myself permission to voice the despair I feel. Always the will. My refusal of despair is blocking my energies."

Jacoby tells us that in facing illness and death in old age, there is no room for

> ". . . psychobabbling optimism that sees unimaginable pain and sorrow as an opportunity for personal growth. Laying claim to the right to feel rotten about what is happening can free up energy for the fight to live as well as possible, through whatever life hands out as we grow older."

Cunningly, then, Jacoby laces her criticism of our culture's "psychobabbling optimism" with a little optimism of her own. She challenges us to face our despair so we may "free up energy" to "live as well as possible" whatever grief-striking losses we endure as we age into old. Hm. It sounds like Jacoby may be suggesting that even the despairing pain and sorrow of old age has an "opportunity for personal growth" in it.

Jacoby offers several suggestions for social and personal growth as we face the hardships of old age. She argues that we need to quit peddling today's ninety as the new fifty, but rather focus our energies on creating a "better ninety." Jacoby challenges her readers to grow intellectually, emotionally, personally, and socially by:

- Accepting "old" as an accurate descriptor of age rather than an insult
- Creating a cultural picture of old age that incorporates the worst problems some of our oldest citizens face, rather than giving our undivided attention to the "young old" or the healthiest and most resilient of the oldest old among us who make "old" appear keen, sexy, and problem-free
- Recognizing the challenges of retirement for many who experience cultural isolation, marital strife, or a sense of uselessness
- Admitting the suffering caused by our cultural obsession with longevity and our delusional medical practices that attempt to cure old age as a disease

- Redistributing funds for costly and unnecessary medical interventions (that do nothing to improve the quality of life for an old person) to resource the old among us who are "ill-clothed, ill-housed, and ill-fed"
- Refusing to use "the power of positive thinking" to mask the real problems of old age or put pressure on the old to be cheery and optimistic
- Increasing efforts to understand the hardships experienced among old people who are financially insecure or disadvantaged rather than defining the "new old age" from a financially secure, socially privileged perspective; Jacoby writes:

  "Many of the diseases that create the poorest health outlook for the old—including diabetes, chronic pulmonary illnesses, and some of the most common types of cancer—are directly linked to the poor education, poor nutrition, and poor medical care that are part of the culture of poverty in this country."

- Reconciling the inevitability of death so we are better able to assess when life-saving interventions interfere with living a full life or dying a dignified death
- Ultimately, ennobling the idea that making the "best of things" in old age "involves an unsparing candor about the vicissitudes of old, old age," because if we don't know what the problems are, it's difficult to fix them

Only if we are willing to face our fears, worries, and pessimistic attitudes about old age – as Jacoby does so generously and eloquently – will we become privy to the information we need to forge a better future for ourselves and others who suffer great loss in old age. Strategic worriers have a unique vantage point from which to contribute insights, imagine new solutions, and find motivation to make changes for the good of our oldest citizens, including ourselves – whenever and if ever we make it that far.

∧ ∧ ∧

If you're willing, pause and ask yourself: *What hardships are presently experienced among the old in my family, neighborhood, school or workplace, community, town, city, county, state, nation, or the world-at-large?"*

Start with your inner circle of intimates and see how far you get in your expanding rings of relationship before you encounter an old person who struggles with hardship – grief-striking loss, poverty, illness, injury, depression, abuse, addiction, isolation, etc.

Zero in on that person and imagine life from their perspective. Ask yourself, *"What is the cause of the difficulty?"* Trace the hardship to its source; for example, if isolation is a problem, what are its causes? Put yourself in the other person's shoes and contemplate what it is that might make life more pleasurable, meaningful, connected, purposeful, or whole from the other's perspective.

How is this old person transforming fears, worries, and pessimism into strategies of healing? How are they transforming anxieties into human connectivity, purposeful collaboration, and resource-building to solve a problem? What support from others might the person need to do so more effectively?

An Old Woman's Response to Fear & Worry

The first time I met Polly Hamann in 1998, I knew she was precious and one of a kind. For one thing, she wore her silver locks in a tall beehive hairdo that readily announced her nostalgia for a time past and her commitment to be herself (if not unapologetically, then at least courageously). Polly was a flag-flying patriot whose motto was The Four F's: Faith, Family, Friends, and Flag.

Despite her show of cheery optimism, in her later years Polly housed a bounty of fears and worries within the massive inner sanctum of her caring heart. She feared the illnesses and deaths of friends and family members before her own and worried about everyone else's personal and family troubles. She was anxious about the effectiveness of her faith community to attend to the downhearted and isolated, and she feared the consequences of all of us trying to keep up in a "hurry up" society that played havoc with family life, friendships, and caring for those in need. She feared the increasing violence in her home city of Milwaukee and worried about the degradation of U.S. society as a whole. However, rather than simply bow to her depression and disappointment over the loss of community as she once enjoyed it, Polly found it in herself to provide an oasis of faith, friendship, family, and flag-flying patriotism in her little corner of the world – at least, as long as she had the stamina and health for it.

Through Polly's creative embrace of life and relationships, she used her fears and worries as motivation to extend her role as mother and grandmother. Polly was known to take into her heart and under her wing every stray child or grandchild she found in her neighborhood, church community, or anywhere else she happened to meet someone who needed to be fed from her surplus of love. Her gestures of affection were like lifelines that kept her fears and worries from weighing down her spirit or the spirit of another.

Polly's expressions of care included sending out hundreds upon hundreds of handmade cards she created to cheer someone who was sick or grieving, celebrate holidays or personal accomplishments, or tell her never-ending circle of family members how greatly she cherished each one of us. Her card-making was a continual event at her house. When she wasn't cooking or entertaining family, her dining table was often covered with her card-making projects. I cherish a giant box filled with the cards she sent to me between 1998 and 2009 (the year before she died at age 86). I'm sure there are scads of others who can say the same. As my dear friend succumbed to health problems in the last few years of her life, this is how I knew she was fading. Her brilliant cards came less often, then not at all. A few months later she died.

She left this earth as the most prolific unpublished writer I ever knew who made a remarkable difference with the words she penned.

Transforming Fears & Worries into Community Resilience

Not every old person has the ingenuity, resources, or stamina that Polly did to transform fears and worries for the greater good. Sometimes, it takes a village of elders strategizing together to get the job done. What's more, elders working together on a cause can build a formidable sense of purpose that is larger than ourselves and extends far beyond a locale or lifetime.

Consider those highlighted in the film, *Elders Leading Resilience* directed by Mathan Ratinam. These elders work together in the Ibasho Cafe in the city of Ofunato, Japan. The Ibasho Cafe came into being to combat the isolation of Japan's elder population after the devastating earthquake and tsunami hit Japan in 2011. In a World Bank Group report by Kiyota, Tanaka, Arnold, and Aldrich (2015), the authors write:

> "(Ibasho) refers to a physical place where a person feels at home, is accepted and can be oneself, and to the social relationships associated with that place. The critical element of ibasho is that it involves sharing a physical place in an informal manner . . . It is a place that provides a sense of belonging . . . allows people to pursue their own interests and gives them opportunities to talk to others (Sumita 2003).

> "Further, an ibasho allows participants to select their role and use their skills and experience as they like, without imposing strong expectations on participants (Tanaka 2007).

> "Since the cafe was completed in June 2013, all generations have connected in the space, with children coming to read books in the English library, older people teaching young people, younger people helping elders navigate technology, and so on. In the first year, elders organized approximately 70 events and welcomed more than 5,500 visitors."

In the film, elders garden, cook, eat, laugh, and converse together. They welcome all ages to come together to learn about Japanese traditions and cooking, share stories, play, and socialize. They speak of their great losses and their renewed sense of purpose and community. One woman who donated the home structure from which the Ibasho Cafe was rebuilt, tells of the deaths of her mother and sister in the 2011 disaster. The donor imagines that the Ibasho is providing needed support for other elders in a way that she was unable to provide for her mother before her death.

In 2014, five months after typhoon Yolanda hit the Philippines, elders from the Ofunato Ibasho began trips to exchange ideas on community restoration, elder resourcefulness, and elder care with Filipino elders; they got busy helping to resource an Ibasho project in Barangay Bagong Buhay and another in Nepal. The mayor of Ofunato, Kimiaki Toda, says,

> "Ibasho is a community that is created by everyone. From children to elders, anyone can feel free to hang out. It's not an elder care facility, or community center, or social service center. It is a wonderful and innovative place that we had never seen . . . As the world's population is growing older, I'd like to see places like Ibasho spread worldwide."

May our anxiety about the future lead us all to the same conclusion. May it inspire us to build an elder community of healers across the face of the planet – elders whose presence and industry are at the center of solutions to the problems we face. May we ask ourselves often in elderhood: *What is it that we might create for the greater good from our collective suffering?*

As you grieve, all kinds of painful emotions or mental attitudes can live at the heart of your grief. Take a good look at yours now and then. Identify which grief-related emotions and attitudes are especially potent for you. Figure out how each one can be used in your life and relationships to do some good for yourself and others.

Each grief-related emotion can be planted as a seed to grow a greater yield of wisdom, health, and happiness. The task and the choice is yours.

Guidepost 51

Don't let a smiley face fool you. Happiness is a hybrid emotion.

The Silver Lining
Heartening in Elderhood

When grief strikes hard, there is nothing more healing than the presence of an elder who knows how to provide comfort, wisdom, love, courage, or laughter even in difficult times. Perhaps you are fortunate to enjoy the presence of such an elder in your life or perhaps you are one – a parent, grandparent, teacher, mentor, or friend who knows the art of spinning suffering into gold. Perhaps you are an elder who knows how to grieve and heal from a place of abundant hope.

Some elders age into old like it's the next big adventure. Come what may, these torchbearers inspire us to believe that what we have and who we are is enough and more than enough to get us through hard times. They show us how to meet grief, loss, and death with a generous heart. According to Anthony Scioli and Henry B. Biller in their book, *Hope in the Age of Anxiety,* an elder generation of hope providers (who can hook us up to an endless supply of the stuff) may be exactly the salve that is needed in today's anxiety-laden world.

Imagine it: *In your old age, how would your life and relationships be different if you regarded yourself as a provider of hope?* Perhaps you already do, or perhaps the idea of serving as a hope provider is foreign to you. Maybe you're a pessimist at the core and it's hard enough to provide hope for yourself, much less for others. Or, maybe you're a realist who only deals in the here and now.

One common zapper of hope as you age into old is that, at some point, you become increasingly aware of your mortality that allows only a temporary stay on planet earth. The reality of death appears to be more agreeable to some than others; but, as a species, death is regarded as one of humanity's greatest fears. The fear of death may be experienced as a vague sense of dread or, more specifically, a fear of pain, the unknown, spiritual or religious failings, punishment, losing the ability to communicate with loved ones, a sense of annihilation, or being forgotten after death.

While old age may come with messages of death, it also provides time and opportunity to make peace with mortality and your limited time on earth. Epicurus once wrote: "The art of living well and dying well are one." The Irish affirm this sentiment with a popular blessing of parting, "Bos Sona," meaning, "May you have a good death," a sentiment that also implies, "May you live a good life."

In *Hope in the Age of Anxiety*, Scioli and Biller suggest that when we embrace the present moment and also build our hopes for the future, we create a "double-life prescription" of hope that transcends death. This double life prescription relies on the "wisdom of here and now" and the "wisdom of there and then."

Here and now wisdom requires a willingness to give yourself to the joys and contentment of the present moment and to let go of past and future attachments. It's akin to what Eckart Tolle (in his book by the same name) calls *The Power of Now*. As Tolle puts it, in the "power of now…you are free to enjoy and appreciate (things, people, conditions)–while they last . . . Life flows with ease."

However, in addition to the "power of now," Scioli and Biller suggest that to be a hope provider, it is equally important to cultivate the "power of all that is not now" – to honor "the power of the past along with the power of the future." Holistic hope is timeless. It is built on hopes of the past, present, and future. Scioli and Biller suggest that a future orientation toward hope helps to decrease death anxiety by creating symbolic immortality that transcends death. They write:

> "Likely your deepest wishes involve true mastery (of skills and life goals), fulfilling relationships, and a genuine sense of peace. You likely want a hope that is real, not false: one that will extend your creativity, love, and bliss into the future. Presuming this is the case, then your enemy is not death, but instead the total annihilation of hope."

Scioli and Biller suggest six approaches to build your sense of transcendent hope beyond death that include:

- *Doing your "blood work"* – perhaps through attentive parenting or grandparenting (with family members born of blood, adoption, choice, or marriage) and finding ways to deepen and celebrate extended family relationships

- *Being creative* – perhaps through artistic creation, mentoring, gardening, cooking, building, joining neighborhood projects to feed the hungry or house the homeless, creating family or community celebrations, etc.

- *Communing with nature* – whether in your yard or patio, a neighborhood park, the wild untamed countryside, advocating for earth care or animal rights, or experiencing a wilderness adventure like sailing, zip-lining, or bird or whale-watching

- *Strengthening your spiritual beliefs* – whether you are religious or not, exploring and clarifying the experiences, disciplines, practices, traditions, beliefs, rituals, sacred texts, or prayers that are inspiring and uplifting to you that bring you a sense of lasting hope

- *Meditating regularly* – whether you prefer traditional sedentary forms of meditation like mindfulness meditation or centering prayer, or more active forms like tai chi, yoga, walking meditations, fishing, journaling, leisurely biking, using prayer beads, or meditative arts or crafts – meditation can alleviate anxiety and help to foster relaxation, stillness, and clarity of body, psyche, and soul

- *Spreading your love and nurturing relationships with others* in ways suited to you, your circumstances, abilities, and interests – perhaps, being a caring, attentive friend, caregiver, partner, mentor, volunteer, coach, teacher, tutor, donor, pen-pal, or skilled listener who provides hope for others

Among the sources of hope that Scioli and Biller recommend, there is a fundamental source of human hope they return to again and again – the hope that is engendered through relational trust, described as ". . . the assurance of a continued presence . . . someone or something (that) will stay by your side." This "continued presence" can be found with mentors, family, friends, deceased loved ones, nature, God, or some other transcendent or mystical being beyond yourself. At a time when the elder population is growing worldwide, we elders are in a unique position to serve as such a "continued presence" for others (before and after death), deriving a hopeful sense of lasting purpose by doing so.

Consider the good fortune of writer Anthony Breznican, who revealed (in a May 23, 2017 story for *Entertainment Weekly*) how an elder he knew and loved most of his life had a knack for showing up at just the right moment to provide the kind of hope he needed most:

Grieving in the Neighborhood: The Healing Wisdom of a TV Icon

On May 22, 2017, after Anthony Breznican put his four-year-old son to bed, he went online to catch up on that day's news about the Manchester, UK arena bombing. Highlighted within that heart-wrenching story were dozens of examples of people helping people – taxi drivers taking people to safety, families reaching out to find loved ones, people inviting strangers into their homes. Among the posts about the tragedy, there was also the late Fred Rogers, TV host of the PBS children's show, *Mr. Rogers' Neighborhood*, whose friendly face was looking out at Anthony and saying (by way of the attached quote posted and reposted with his photograph):

> "My mother would say to me, 'Look for the helpers. You will always find people who are helping.' To this day, especially in times of disaster, I remember my mother's words, and I am always comforted by realizing that there are still so many helpers — so many caring people in this world."

Rogers, who died in 2003, was known for his ability to help children overcome their fears and anxieties. He served as a slow, deliberate, kindly, and sometimes even silent presence for children who, in recent decades, have been overexposed to a noisy, busy, sometimes disturbing world. Rogers knew how to make his "TV neighborhood" appear smaller and quieter to provide a caring presence like no other children's TV show host before or since. Adults finding solace in his wisdom after the Manchester bombing was a reflection of his widespread influence on generations of viewers.

For Anthony, it wasn't the first time Mr. Rogers showed up for him when he needed him most. Mr. Rogers was from Pittsburgh, Anthony's hometown, so Anthony was one among many who (in his words) "grew up loving this man who taught us to be kind above all and see ourselves as special and good no matter what the world tried to tell us to the contrary."

As Anthony got older, he lost track of Mr. Rogers until he was in college, attending the University of Pittsburgh. It was tough times: Anthony was feeling hopeless and lonely, struggling to put the broken pieces of himself together and pursue his dream of becoming a writer, despite having "only discouragement from home." What's more, he was pained by a grief-striking loss that he couldn't talk about. Even if he could, he didn't know who would listen. One day, when Anthony was at his lowest, he walked out of his dorm room to hear the familiar theme song from Mr. Rogers' Neighborhood: "Won't you be my neighbor. . . " Anthony followed the sound to the empty common room of his dorm floor, where the television was playing to no one. He writes:

> "And there he was – the sweatered one, feeding his fish, checking in with that little trolley that rolled through the wall into the Neighborhood of Make-Believe, and asking me what I do with the mad that I feel . . . I stood mesmerized. His show felt like a cool hand on a hot head. I never sat down, but I watched the whole thing."

That wasn't all. A few weeks later, Anthony planned to take his usual elevator ride from The Pitt News office, where he worked, to the ground floor William Pitt Union lobby. When the doors of the elevator opened, he found Mr. Rogers in the flesh, standing in front of him. Anthony forced himself not to freak out on this living icon of love and tranquility from his childhood. After an initial head nod of acknowledgment, the two rode the elevator down in silence. But just before they parted ways, Anthony turned back to sheepishly thank Mr. Rogers – whose response to Anthony is classic Mr. Rogers. The old man with the "twinkling eyes" asked Anthony if he grew up as one of his television neighbors and when the answer was yes, Mr. Rogers opened his arms and invited Anthony in, saying, "It's good to see you again neighbor."

The two neighbors talked for a bit about the show and just when Mr. Rogers turned to leave, Anthony blurted out his experience a few weeks earlier when he was feeling so low and found Mr. Rogers in the empty-common-room TV with just the right thing to say. Anthony thanked him for that, too. Then, right there in the lobby of the student union, Mr. Rogers invited Anthony to sit beside him on a window ledge and asked, "Do you want to tell me what was upsetting you?" Oh, boy, did he ever. Anthony told him about his grandfather dying – "one of the few good things (he) had." He told him about his broken heart, feeling lost, alone, and overwhelmed with the mad and sad of it. When Anthony finished, Mr. Rogers told him about his own grandfather that he loved and missed. He told him, "You'll never stop missing the people you love."

The conversation took only a few minutes, but it was plenty of time for one lasting gift to become another and yet another. Among them: A vivid reminder that Mr. Rogers not only teaches us to look for the helpers, he also teaches us how to be one.

※ ※ ※

It is rare for a TV personality to be so attuned to the interpersonal needs of their viewing audience. Fred Rogers was a father and grandfather figure to generations of children (and adults) who knew him as an intentional, patient, dependable, and loving elder – the best of the best when it comes to providing hope for others. Traditionally, we think of elders as storytellers, imparting history and wisdom, biography and life lessons that entertain, instruct, and uplift – which Mr. Rogers did and continues to do posthumously. But he also knew how to listen to the stories of others. At a time in our cultural history when intimate personal conversations are oftentimes disrupted by the busyness of our workaday technocentric lives, a hallmark trait of the practicing elder is an ability and willingness to be an attentive listening presence.

One of my honored elders is the writer Brenda Ueland who died at age 93. She was one of the most prolific writers of the 20th century and lived into her final decades with vitality, boldness, and creativity. In addition to writing, Ueland walked several miles a day well into old age, enjoyed swimming (and set an international record for people over 80), spent time improving her handstands, and was an animal rights activist. Moreover, Ueland had a pronounced ability to listen deeply and truthfully as another human being poured out what was on their mind and in their heart. In her final decades, she was passionate about using her listening skills to encourage others in their personal growth, art, creativity, and relationships. Ueland's vast ability to listen was one of her greatest contributions to her writing students and those close to her. In her book, *Strength to Your Sword Arm*, Ueland asserts:

> "Unless you listen, people are wizened in your presence; they become about a third of themselves. Unless you listen, you can't know anybody. Oh, you will know facts and what is in the newspapers and all of history, perhaps, but you will not know one single person. You know, I have come to think listening is love, that's what it really is."

Only a few of us in old age will become TV icons like Mr. Rogers, or celebrated writers and athletes who can rock a handstand like Ueland. But in our own way, every one of us with a mind to, can become an expert listener and hope provider.

⋏ ⋏ ⋏

> Take a moment to ask yourself: *"Is there anyone who regards me as a cherished hope provider – someone who is heartened with comfort, courage, wisdom, love, or laughter because of my caring presence?"* Imagine how you might serve as a hope provider for someone now or in the future.

⋏ ⋏ ⋏

Scioli and Biller write:

> "A good hope provider offers availability, presence, and contact. If given in the right way at the right time, and in the right amount, such gifts can inspire trust and openness. Moreover, availability, presence, and contact can lead to the development of hopeful imprints, or lasting images of positive and supportive relationships . . . To be clear, it is not possible or even appropriate to be completely available, present, and involved with every member of your social network. As the saying goes, 'You can't be all things to all people.' Dispensing hope in an emotionally intelligent manner requires an awareness of your interpersonal skills and limits as well as of the actual hope needs of the other."

As you strive to be an emotionally intelligent hope provider for others, be sure to keep an eye peeled for elders who can serve as hope providers for you, too. For me, my beloved "Pappaw" who died before my fifth birthday was a continual source of hope. He pulled out of his sleeve an endless supply of stories, life lessons, kindnesses, jokes, and adventures, and he invited me to work side-by-side with him in his garden for what seemed like hours. . . no words, just humming softly under his breath. My grandpa's presence in my early years inspired me to adopt elders after his death who served as a nurturing elder presence in his stead – worthy mentors and role models who instill comfort, courage, wisdom, love, and laughter in good times and bad. Some of these elders are personal friends and relatives. Some I never met in person and some reach out to me from beyond as my Pappaw now does. They are writers I admire, like Maya Angelou, Pablo Neruda, Brenda Ueland, and Walt Whitman, or mentors and spiritual leaders like Jane Goodall, Nelson Mandela, Fred Rogers, and Howard Thurman.

Take a moment to ask yourself: *"Who are my cherished elders that (in their own way) impart hope in difficult times?"* These hope providers may be elders who are living, old elders, young elders, or those who precede you in death. They may be close friends or relatives, or elders you never met in the flesh. As you call each one to mind, express gratitude for their presence in your life.

One of the greatest gifts an elder can impart is to steep expertise and experience into a brew of healing wisdom that helps others to believe in themselves, one another, and the goodness of life and relationships even in the worst of times. So, if you don't have an elder in your life who can help you to spin suffering into gold, get yourself one. And if you're an elder with time on your hands who knows how to grieve from a place of abundant hope, find somebody in need of your heartening presence. There are lots of us out there. Opportunities to serve as a hope provider are endless.

Guidepost 52

Provide yourself with evidence of immortality: Count the blessings you receive from your elders that will continue to be blessings after they are long gone.

Escaping Pain for Good
Tempering in Elderhood

When you age into old, you bring a lifetime of losses along. Even so, old age is often generous in adding to grief's storehouse. So, the old myths that tell us "there is no other way but through," harping on the necessity of "doing your grief work," and "facing your pain until it subsides" can be especially damaging to an elder's heart, body, mind, and spirit. When you have a bulging storehouse of grief within you, burying yourself at the bottom of it can be the end of you and your motivation for living fully. It's nigh impossible to face the pain of grief 24/7 and survive, much less thrive. So, be grateful for tempering escape valves that serve to release the ache of your suffering from time to time. Building a repertoire of go-to tempering responses can help you to wear your grief loosely without making light of your pain or allowing it to fester in the dark.

One lifesaving tempering strategy for old people is to put the gifts and limitations of old age in perspective. Despite our cultural tendency to view old age through a lens of negativity, research tells us that the only aspect of being that declines significantly in old age is the physical body. So, a good source of tempering grief among the old can be found by delving into research that offers some surprisingly good news: If you are not suffering from cognitive disease or mental illness (the vast majority among the old are not), you can expand your mental capacities, emotional intelligence, spiritual depth, and social skills exponentially until the day you die. A big part of this expansion depends upon your willingness to keep honing your mental, emotional, spiritual, and social life skills.

What's more, even as you accept the challenges of inhabiting an aging body, you may discover that caring for your physical body as an aging organism and aspiring for age-relative physical fitness provides beneficial side effects such as a clear mind, open heart, enriching spiritual experiences, and social encounters that add valued meaning and enjoyment to elderhood. For me, learning to care for my aging physical body helped me to discover one of the only sure tempering responses I can count on to relieve my grief-related suffering:

Walking Away From Pain: An Athlete's Story of Healing

It was an especially difficult stretch of grieving for me. The burn in my chest was so chronic and intense that I was forced to find a reprieve from my pain. I feared that if I didn't, I might literally die of a broken heart. At the time, I noticed that after exercise (usually biking or hiking), the pain in my chest subsided. So, I began to do much of my editing work and reading on a stationary bike at an easy pace that kept my legs moving for a good part of the day. My spouse Andrew and I lived in Pennsylvania at the time and we made good use of the Rails-to-Trails bike path near our home that went on for miles.

Unexpectedly, my new commitment to exercise reconnected me to a time in my past when I identified myself as an athlete – playing softball and running track from age eight through my mid twenties. Physical exercise not only lifted the pain from my body; it also reminded me of my warrior spirit that inspired me to give my best effort to overcome obstacles. But, paradoxically, re-engaging my inner athlete also stirred up many regrets and losses that I suffered as a youth competing in sports in my home state of Iowa – where girls athletics was well-appreciated (even in the 1960s and '70s).

Although my early sports experiences were a source of fun, camaraderie, and a boost to my self-esteem, in high school my track seasons were plagued with setbacks. In my freshman year, a vengeful coach refused to let me run individual events or participate at the state meet (after anchoring our qualifying relay teams) because I didn't play on his basketball team the sports season before. In my as-yet-undefeated sophomore season, I was unable to compete in my four qualified state meet events due to an untimely move to another school district. Then, as a defending state champion in the 200-meter dash my senior year, a knee injury from the long jump smashed my final hopes in my most promising season yet. The injury played havoc with athletic scholarship offers and college recruitment. But worst of all was the death of my best friend and teammate, Sheri, who died in the fall of my senior year.

In adulthood, whenever I reminisced about high school athletics, it was difficult to recall anything but the losses and defeats. Although my knee eventually healed, and I was able to play softball again, competitive track was over for me... or so I thought. Then, at the age of 55, I was stranded in the Minneapolis/St. Paul airport for several hours. As I walked the airport, I saw a poster for the National Senior Games being held there that year. Since physical activity was a go-to tempering response for me, I looked through the list of National Senior Games sports to find one that might ease my grief-related pain, help me to reclaim my identity as an athlete, and transform the long-standing regrets I carried from the past.

As I searched for my curative sport, I knew track sprints and softball were likely to reinjure my knee. I wanted to enjoy my new sport for the rest of my life – even if I live to be ancient. So, I honed in on sports that are easiest on aging bodies: swimming, archery, bicycling, and what is... racewalking?

Long story short, I am now one of those funny-looking walkers who awkwardly speed by the slowest joggers and recreational walkers I encounter on the many trails and tracks I now inhabit regularly. I'm told by my racewalking mentors that I was born for the sport (an Olympic track and field event since 1904). Who could guess that I would compete again in my beloved sport of track and field as an up-and-coming old woman? What's more, a few years back, I made the acquaintance of a racewalker three decades my senior, who (at 90-plus) is busy setting record times for me to beat when (and if) I get that far.

✣ ✣ ✣

My passion for this wiggly sport that my daughter affectionately describes as "fish running on land" is a godsend. It motivates me to temper grief-related pain in a way that no other approach to tempering does for me. It's a healthy habit that keeps my physical, emotional, mental, and spiritual well-being in balance, largely because exercise raises endorphin levels – the feel-good hormone that makes tempering more possible. To stay healthy and injury-free in a deceptively tough sport, I eased my way into the shorter race distances (that range from 1500 meters to 50 km). I take plenty of recovery days and I use cross-training (biking, hiking, and swimming) to avoid overuse injuries. I also gave my body a good three years to adjust to the unfamiliar form of racewalking before stepping up my training program significantly.

If you decide to take up a new sport or physical activity to temper your grief, be sure to get a physical exam before embarking on any exercise program; then, work your way into it. Even committing to five minutes a day can be motivating and get your engine going. You can add a few minutes every few days from there. It also helps if you choose an activity you enjoy that is low impact to avoid injury – swimming, biking, yoga, tai chi, hiking, or walking are promising choices for older athletes.

But if athletics isn't for you, no worries. There are many ways to temper your suffering, however you're able and willing to do it – perhaps through:

- *Physical activities:* Gardening, building, singing, playing a musical instrument, massage, physical release therapies, therapeutic touch, or physical nurture
- *Distractions:* Watching a funny or enlightening film or reading a good novel, artistic endeavors, knitting, playing music, deep prayer or meditation, guided visualization, research, travel, outdoor adventures, or any type of work or project that helps take your mind off of your pain
- *Deep Sleep:* When you're having trouble sleeping, explore evening activities that invite sleep – listen to soothing music, create white noise with a fan, stay away from the stimulating effect of electronic devices, drink chamomile tea or try a natural supplement, like L-tryptophan, to see what works for you
- *A New Mission:* Consider taking up a social mission that can take your focus off of your suffering and help you to do some good in the world – perhaps through neighborhood or community service projects, volunteer opportunities, mentoring, political activism, or serving as an elder that others can count on

Pay attention to your daily activities that give you a reprieve from your suffering, even if it's a momentary wave of relief that you can revisit whenever you choose.

The Tempering Joys of Grandparenting

One revered role that elders often serve in our culture is the role of grandparent. For some elders, there is no better road to tempering the pain of grief. When I was in graduate school, learning about the traditions in the Black/Afro-American church community, a peer of mine enlightened me that in her tradition a woman is honored as a mother and grandmother of the entire community – whether she gives birth or adopts a child, or not. In U.S. culture, I imagine this tradition might be useful on a broader scale. Rather than regarding the growing numbers of old folks among us as a drain on our economy and healthcare system, what if we began to revere old people as cherished grandparents? What if we regarded grandparenting as a defining metaphor for eldering? It's a natural leap because the true embodiment of these roles of *grandparent* and *elder* is the same: serving as a mentor, consultant, advocate, listener, storyteller, artist, performer, teacher, leader, community-builder, and more.

I'm not advocating that every adult over the age of 60 go out immediately and adopt a whole litter of grandchildren. I almost fell off my chair a few years back when a health care provider imagined aloud that I probably couldn't wait to be a grandmother. (At the time, neither of my adult daughters was pregnant or married, for that matter – if it matters.) I laughed and said, "I don't have time to be a grandmother!" The truth is, I am still thrilled to watch my own children grow and change. Although I will celebrate big if either chooses to become a parent, I won't encourage them to do it for my sake. As a family educator and spiritual director, I am doing plenty of peripheral grandparenting to last a lifetime. Yet, I witness that for many in old age, grandparenting (or something akin to it) is a tempering refuge that serves as a blessed and welcome distraction from grief-striking pain.

In Lesley Stahl's book, *Becoming Grandma: The Joys and Science of the New Grandparenting*, she claims that her success as a journalist and 60 Minutes reporter pales in comparison to the experience of becoming a grandparent. Stahl regards grandparenting as the most vivid and transformative experience of her life. Her metamorphosis into "grandma" inspired her to research the history, influence, and meaning of grandparenting. She found evidence that attentive grandparents have therapeutic effects on their grandchildren and that historically as humans evolved, it was the presence of grandmothers caring for and providing additional nutrition for their grandchildren that improved fitness to survive.

An especially curative aspect of grandparenting is that "grand affection" is generally a two-way street. Loving grandparents stand to gain at least as much as their grandchildren from the relationship. For example, Stahl's previous roommate Carol and her spouse, Ralph, provide care for each of their grandsons (Oliver and Syrus) one day a week. Stahl writes:

> "They call her 'Nanny' and her husband, Ralph, 'Abo,' which is how Oliver first pronounced Opa, 'grandpa' in Dutch... 'You should call your book *The Return of Laughter*,' Carol tells me... 'One of the greatest joys,' she says, 'is seeing how Ralph just erupts in laughter all the time.' As she tells me this, she smiles, her eyes crinkle up and I think she has fallen in love with her husband all over again.

> " 'What is it with a grandchild?' I ask her... 'It's such unconditional love on our part...' She pauses to think. 'And they love us back! They love us unconditionally too.' "

Of course, in today's complex and mobile society, some grandparents and grandchildren live miles away from each other or are alienated from one another due to family conflicts. Even so, an elder can serve as a grand companion to any available and willing young person. If such a relationship isn't readily available in your neighborhood or other circles of community, there are foster grandparenting programs around the country that match a child or youth with a willing elder, and others that match youth and young adults with elders who need reciprocal help and nurturing. Some elders volunteer as cradle cuddlers – who hold, feed, and comfort premature babies or those going through drug withdrawal. Others attend intergenerational daycares where elders and their young companions have opportunities to interact while being provided needed care and supervision from others.

In family circles, attentive grandparenting can be a healing force and motivate parents and grandparents to forgive or forget conflicts of the past. This was certainly the case for my spouse, Andrew, with his father. Our daughters, Morgan and Willa, were nothing less than miracle workers when it came to healing a father-son relationship that was packed with grief from the long-ago and not-so-distant past:

Love Isn't Lame
A Grandparent's Story of Healing That Transcends Death

Days before our daughter Morgan's birth, Andrew resigned from his job as VP and General Manager of his father's corporation. Unsurprisingly, Andrew's dad, Jim, was livid. For five years, father and son had been work partners in a successful and lucrative business. When Andrew turned in his resignation letter, Jim raged at him. Andrew gave him a few days to cool off and then called to try to bury the hatchet. Jim said that he'd "bury it all right" – in Andrew's head. Resentment was monumental on both sides.

Jim's rage was understandable. Since he was a teenager, selling products on the black market during his stint in the Navy, Jim was an incurable entrepreneur who navigated his way through one get-rich-quick ploy after another. He lived, ate, dreamed, and schemed about discovering that one irresistible business idea that could make him millions, and he found it by manufacturing printing parts to undercut the big names in the printing equipment industry. But what was even more difficult than discovering the "one big idea" was finding someone with the skills to run the business and manage the corporation at its central office and main warehouse in Chicago – especially as the business grew with franchise stores and an expanding international clientele.

Finally, it dawned on Jim that Andrew was the one. Andrew started in the business as a youth, sweeping floors in the warehouse and working his way from the bottom up. By his late teens, it became apparent that he had a natural gift for management and a thorough understanding of present and future needs for maintenance and growth of the company. So, when Andrew resigned it felt to Jim as if someone had just cut off his right testicle – at least, concerning his future business success and his family legacy, having planned for Andrew to inherit the business one day.

Andrew's deep resentment was understandable too. Other than their business relationship, Andrew's dad had been fairly absent in his life as a child and youth. Although Jim provided for his family financially, he was mostly unavailable due to workaholism, heavy drinking, and an extra-marital relationship that provided Jim with a home away from home. By the time Andrew was twelve, he and his older siblings deemed Jim the "weekend visitor."

Although there was deep affection between Andrew and his dad, as work partners, old tensions festered and were heightened at times by Jim's excessive drinking, aggressive and argumentative personality, and habit of hiring his drinking buddies to work in the warehouse (leaving the firing responsibilities to Andrew). As Andrew imagined more ideal working conditions for their other tried-and-true 30+ employees that included profit sharing and increasing benefits, Jim was quick to nix Andrew's proposals. What's more, when we became pregnant with our eldest daughter, Morgan, Andrew was discovering a natural gift and interest in early childhood teaching. He found it impossible to justify bearing the lion's share of responsibility for the business and working long hours at a job that made it difficult for him to live out his priorities and values as a boss, spouse, father, and teacher.

After Andrew resigned, his Dad didn't speak to him for five years. Then one day out of the blue, Jim called Andrew and said he had already missed too many birthdays and Christmases with his granddaughters. He asked if he could finally meet them (they were now three and five). A few weeks later, he showed up at our house in Louisville, Kentucky with his new spouse, Dorothy, and two life-size dolls in hand. During his visit, he also took his granddaughters on a shopping spree to buy roller skates, puzzles, games, hula hoops, and more. He thought these toys made up for all the gifts he hadn't given, but the real gift was showing up and displaying his deep affection and interest for his grandchildren who, at the time, he knew only by way of their shared DNA.

That was the beginning of a love affair between Grandpa Jim and two little people who became his biggest fans. By that time in his life, Jim had curbed the heavy drinking of earlier years and further explored his spiritual beliefs, which allowed him to be more attentive to his intimate relationships. Despite his sometimes overactive grumpy-old-man trait (which he was careful not to turn on his granddaughters), he was usually a barrel of fun with his grandchildren around. In our family time with him, he told us stories, performed one-man skits (that sometimes failed miserably, except that by the end we were laughing hysterically), took Morgan and Willa fishing (for five minutes once, because it required far more patience than he could muster even for them), introduced them to the bliss of sugary desserts that they weren't allowed to eat at home, taught them the secrets of winning at blackjack, and was never short of some never-before-experienced adventure that he wanted his granddaughters (and us by association) to experience with him.

Morgan and Willa were reason enough for Jim to let go of his past anger at Andrew and build a stronger, more compassionate relationship with his son. Seeing Jim's face light up when Morgan and Willa walked into a room, or climbed comfortably into his lap, or believed that he really did "own part of the ocean," or laughed at his "dad jokes" or his bawdy tasteless Irish grandpa jokes (as they got older) was more than enough to inspire Andrew to let go of his resentments, too.

Years after his death, Jim remains a loving presence in all our lives. Once in a while, the four of us pull out a memorial album I made for Andrew a few months after his dad died that includes a pocket stuffed with an entire collection of Jim's too-bad-not-to-laugh-at jokes. We found a pile of them in his office after his death – written on three-by-five cards he used so he could learn them by heart. Now, we continue to learn them by heart, just as we continue to learn *him* by heart in our memories and stories, and his ongoing influence in our lives. He is an undeniable presence for us now because he was willing to be an undeniable presence for us then. Foremost, he was willing to place himself in the heart space of his grandchildren, so that we could meet him there and make space for him in our hearts, too.

※ ※ ※

There is nothing like love to temper the pain and suffering of grief. Love can offer a reprieve from grief and it can outlive your pain. So, whoever it is – a grandchild, neighbor, partner, co-worker, student, teacher, relative, or friend – find someone willing to share heart space with you, someone whose presence can help to wash away your pain for a good long minute or more. And maybe, just maybe, each time you bask in their presence, a little bit of your grief will get washed away for good.

Guidepost 53

Love may be an angel in disguise.

In the Crucible of Life & Death
Integrating in Elderhood

Some of the great healers of our time are those who live long, suffer much, and brilliantly integrate grief-striking loss in ways that serve to heighten the beauty, goodness, and meaning of life amid loss. Such healers have an immeasurable impact on others. So, when you come across an elder who is able and willing to live fully in the crucible of life and death, joy and sorrow, pleasure and pain, be sure to sit up and take notice.

Writer, poet, and activist Maya Angelou (1928-2014) is one such elder healer. The documentary film celebrating her life, *And Still I Rise*, reveals that Angelou's traumatic childhood was the catalyst for her to develop a phenomenal ability to lift grief into a holy place. Angelou endured grave racial injustice growing up as a displaced Southern Black girl in the little village of Stamps, Arkansas where she was raised by a kind and attentive grandmother. She was abandoned by her parents at the age of three and suffered rape by her mother's boyfriend at the age of seven. Angelou was mute for three or four years afterward because she felt that speaking the rapist's name was the reason he ended up dead. She learned that her voice was that powerful.

Paradoxically, it was during that time of silence, when she "used to think of (her) whole body as an ear . . . absorbing sound," that her love affair with the spoken and written word was consecrated. Her love of poetry lured her out of that dark time and showed her the good that might yet come from the evil and hardship she encountered. Throughout her adult life, Angelou's childhood losses continued to motivate her to serve boldly as a performing artist, storyteller, and wordsmith, and as a mentor and elder to others. Her autobiographical novel, *I Know Why the Caged Bird Sings*, is now a classic. In a literary fashion, the novel depicts the trauma Angelou experienced as a child. It invites readers to enter the soulful death that her grief-striking losses represent and to celebrate the soulful rebirth that comes to her through a love of literature, family, and community. Countless readers speak of the book's curative effect to help them grieve and heal similar losses.

Angelou was at once a rebel and a peacemaker. She was a champion of Black/Afro-American pride and civil liberties who helped to carve out a more spacious sense of abundance for her Black brothers and sisters – socially, artistically, and politically. In her presence and through her social interactions, she commanded respect for women, the young, and the old. She wore the mantle of elderhood with a fiery certainty and humble generosity that was transformative in its effect. What's more, she extended her healing hand to all of us – no matter our race, economic class, sexual identity, or gender. In her sweepingly inclusive inaugural poem, "On the Pulse of the Morning," commissioned for President Clinton's inauguration on January 20, 1993, Angelou encouraged all of us to "Give birth again/To the dream," to release ourselves from fear, admit past mistakes, look into one another's eyes as sister and brother, and to dare a new beginning.

Angelou used her keen intellect, purposeful artistry, and comfortability with her earthy sensuality to create natural inroads to healing for herself and others. Despite her larger-than-life personality and her regal countenance, she displayed vulnerable humanness that let us know she was not so different from us. She was a warrior queen with a past and she made it her life's calling to show us that if she could transcend the internal and external obstacles that blocked her way, then we could transcend ours, too.

In the opening voiceover of the documentary about her life and loves, we hear Angelou's philosophy of grieving and healing loud and clear:

> "We may encounter many defeats but we must not be defeated. That, in fact, it may be necessary to encounter defeats so we can know who the hell it is that we are. But, can we overcome? What makes us stumble and fall and somehow miraculously rise, and go on?"

In the remainder of the documentary, the filmmakers show some of the great elder's answers to these questions. Through the lens of the film, Angelou's life and words bid us to:

- Revel in the wonder of the world and those we love
- Speak boldly through the beauty of the arts
- Tell our grief stories in such a way that our revelations serve as a healing portal for others
- Wield intelligent anger that paves the way to peaceful and lasting change
- Know who we are and where we came from
- Love ourselves and encourage others to do the same
- Be courageous to impart to the young a loving empathy and acceptance that instills a sense of integrity to offer one's best and show respect to oneself and others
- Walk the talk

Angelou assists her readers, listeners, and companions to clear a path to our true selves by the difficult work of speaking the terrible and beautiful truth to one another. She is like the Mother Theresa of the U.S. When she died, it left a gaping hole in the soul of our nation. Perhaps the actress Alfre Woodard says it best,

> "All of us have different fingerprints, but some of our fingerprints are so indelible on the lives of other people when they touch us. Miss Maya is gone and nobody is gonna talk like she talked or walk like she walked. I mean she left us plenty of things, we can't be greedy but, man, the curtain goin' down on that act. Thank God I got to live in that time."

We can give thanks, too, that Maya Angelou is still present in every story, poem, and wise word she offered to banish our personal and cultural poverty of soul – the far-reaching ill effects of which we as a nation often fail to fully comprehend. Fortunately, in this respect, Angelou left us rich, as elder healers always do. Now it is our task to invest the riches she left behind.

As you reflect on Maya Angelou's far-reaching influence, call to mind an elder who serves you as a role model or guide – one who helps you to integrate grief in ways that foster beauty, goodness, and cherished meaning. What elder do you look to for guidance? It may be someone who is living or deceased, a public figure, or an intimate relative or friend. Write a list of ways that this elder guides you to integrate your grief, making room for both the difficulties and blessings of change that accompany your loss experiences.

⋏ ⋏ ⋏

Surprisingly, to me, my father is one of my role models in this regard. It isn't because my dad knew how to integrate grief vibrantly as Angelou did. No, for most of his life my dad found it excruciatingly difficult to integrate grief and loss. That's why the poem he wrote for me (when I was seventeen) about the death of my best friend Sheri, instantly became a blazing beacon of love and hope for me. The poem itself was a cherished gift, but what was especially awe-inspiring as I searched for a harbor of healing, was the fact that my dad wrestled with this loss deeply enough to put words to its difficulties and blessings in the only poem I ever knew him to write. Until he was in his mid-sixties, the first few weeks immediately following Sheri's death was one of the few times I witnessed him facing grief with clarity and courage, and I know the reason he did it was out of his love for me.

Fortunately, as my dad got older and embraced the inevitable reality of death, he was able to integrate grief more fully. He began to look at loss experiences and regrets of his past. He confessed wrongdoings and apologized for his shortcomings. He retired from his job as an insurance agent (something family members thought he would never do) so he could travel and relocate from Des Moines, Iowa to a retirement community in Sun City West, Arizona. He deepened his spiritual insights and experiences, refocused on his relational priorities, and found new ways to be of service to others.

When Dad was told he had only months to live, he went on a trip around the country by himself, visiting each of his children and their families. In his final months, his greatest priority was spending time with his intimate loved ones. Thankfully, my family and I were able to move close to him to share his final five months on earth. During that time, we soaked in the hundreds of little lessons he taught us about living and dying with cancer. Dad generously shared with us the blessings, deep meaning, and intense difficulties of that time. He showed us how to die with courage, clarity, and love. I regard this gift as my father's greatest legacy.

⋏ ⋏ ⋏

What do you imagine your legacy will be? In life and death, what lasting gifts might you impart? How might you inspire others to integrate the blessings and difficulties of loss-related change?

Making Peace with Death

Elders who integrate the difficulties and blessings of death are in a unique position to lead the way to personal and cultural healing surrounding our human mortality. Planning for a good death (for yourself or another) whenever the time comes, can allay unnecessary fears and troubles. It can serve as motivation for living a good life that is filled with love, cherished meaning, purpose, hope, and freedom.

Stephen Jenkinson, better known by some as Griefwalker (the title of the documentary about him by Tim Wilson), believes that the reality of death serves as "the crucible for making human beings." For five years, Jenkinson led the counseling team of Canada's largest palliative home care program for the dying and their families. He became known as the "angel of death" for his healing presence whenever death hovered near. Jenkinson believes that it is our alienation from death in North American culture that promotes an insistent denial and terror of death when it becomes unavoidable.

Jenkinson's message is simple and life-shifting in its effect: He asserts that it is not death, but our denial and terror of it that keeps us from being fully alive. Jenkinson tells us that genuine love of life doesn't come from not dying, it comes from the fact that we will. In the film, he describes grief as "the great awakening . . . the sign of life stirring towards itself." He believes that a person's death is like a great offering to the living and that when the time comes, the job of the dying is to "die extravagantly." Says Jenkinson,

> "Your life is in the loop. Your life is the loop. You're part of the loop . . . even your death is not for you . . . be grateful for the stuff that doesn't benefit you in the least . . . Now you're getting somewhere. Now you're willing for life to be bigger than your lifespan or your children's lifespan. And now you're getting somewhere.

> " . . . the twin of grief as a skill of life is the skill of being able to praise or love life – which means wherever you find one authentically done, the other is close at hand. Grief and the praise of life side-by-side. To honor this. Room at the head table. And they're toasting you – grief and the ability to love life. They're clinking their glasses and toasting the living."

Grief and death are not your enemies; they are your great awakeners. If they could speak in words, they would open their arms wide and proclaim with one voice: "Come close and do not be afraid. Call me death or call me life. Call me grief or call me love. We are the same. As you die, so will you live, and as you live, so will you die." If ever you doubt it, hollow within your grief a space for love because love always hollows a space for grief. This is the great truth to which healing leads us.

When you make peace with your death as my father did, there may come a time when you realize that preparing for your death is the easy part. Helping to prepare others – particularly those who look to you as a cherished parent, grandparent, mentor, teacher, or guide – can be far more challenging. As a practicing elder, your immortal influence on others lies not in your superhuman resistance to death, but rather in how well you make yourself dispensable, how well you equip others to be fully alive without you. So, tap into your elder wisdom often and learn to integrate death so brilliantly into the landscape of your life and relationships, that death shines as a light on that part of your soul that is eternal. That is the part of you that will be of service to others when you are no longer physically present. As Maya Angelou puts it, "A great soul serves everyone all the time. A great soul never dies. It brings us together again and again." Our ultimate task as elder healers is to impart a greatness of soul that lives beyond our flesh, blood, and bone.

Integrating Death as a Teacher

Death is pervasive in my work as a chaplain and spiritual care provider. I have attended many deaths, communed with the dying, and accompanied terminally ill patients through their contemplations of death and plans for their last days on earth. Even so, my encounters with the dying don't make it any easier when death looms large for me or my loved ones. Each intimate death experience is unique because each life inhabits its own cherished space within me.

When a family member or friend dies, death may demand your undivided attention. But death may also be the music playing in the background when you or a loved one is ill or injured. Death may sweep through you during an accident or near-death experience and then disappear as quickly as it came. Each of these death encounters and more can help you to integrate death and impart lessons on life, mortality, and love. It is up to you to pay attention.

Integrating Pet Death

Since pets generally have shorter life spans than their people, pets give us more frequent opportunities to integrate death – not only when an animal companion dies but also when a pet suffers a severe injury or life-threatening illness. Unfortunately, integrating the deaths of our cherished animals can be problematic for many pet lovers because animals are not generally regarded as family in the same way we regard people in our culture. But the death of a cherished pet can hit as hard as any – especially if a pet is your primary companion.

As I finished writing this chapter, our family dog Barrington (Bear) suddenly died of congestive heart failure. For twelve years, Bear was our "angel dog" – a pure white goldendoodle who got us through some tough times – made us laugh, comforted us when we were sad, made sure everyone felt loved. Although he had arthritis and was showing other signs of age, his physical demise occurred in less than 24 hours. We didn't have time to prepare for it. That night, and for several nights afterward, every time I woke, I burst into tears. For days and months, everywhere I turned was empty of his presence. It isn't a new experience for me. We have been through this before with our dogs, Shadow and Riley, and our cat, Caspian. But these experiences didn't make it any easier to digest the grief that Bear's death evoked for me.

When a cherished pet is ill or injured, acknowledge your grief and anxiety with friends and family members. When death comes, ask others to help you memorialize, remember, and express love and gratitude for the life of an animal companion. If the Griefwalker's claim is true – that death can be given by the dying as a gift to the living, then we honor our animals by receiving the gifts they offer as they depart the earth. In my last hours with Bear, we intentionally thanked one another for the love and companionship we shared for twelve years. These expressions of compassion and connection as death drew near are some of the greatest gifts Bear ever bestowed. He found a way through his pain to bless me with his undying love.

Integrating Brushes with Death

Encounters with death don't need to be fatal to invoke a heightened awareness that life and death are inseparable. Recall the non-fatal encounters with death that are significant for you and your loved ones. In my extended family history, we share brushes with death due to a gunshot wound, severe frostbite, drug overdose, life-threatening illness, suicidal behaviors, and a car accident, to name some. In such cases, relief for the well-being or resurrection of the living may divert you from attending to the residual trauma, sense of loss, or grief you carry within you. It may also keep you from mining healing wisdom that each death encounter offers. When you pause to receive these residual gifts, brushes with death can be positively life-changing.

For example, when my youngest daughter Willa was born, she came so speedily that the midwife who was to attend our planned home birth didn't have time to get there. To our surprise, Willa was born with her umbilical cord wrapped twice around her neck. Fortunately, Andrew and I knew enough to unwrap it, but Willa was not breathing and didn't start for what we experienced as the longest few minutes of our lives. As I held Willa and rubbed her back, my mind raced to find the knowledge of what else I might do for her, at the same time my heart was pierced by the thought that she would never take a breath, that we would have to welcome her to earth and let her go in one fell swoop. Just then, she gurgled her first breath and came to life before our eyes.

Willa's dramatic birth experience heightened our awareness that each of her days on earth is a gift rather than a given. Although this knowledge might have encouraged parental overprotection, for me it did the opposite. It's a good thing. Willa was a daredevil from the beginning and I was more able and willing to trust her sense of adventure because I experienced a maternal "letting go" when she was born.

⋏ ⋏ ⋏

Contemplate your encounters with death that were not fatal or did not result in permanent injury. What do these brushes with death teach you about mortality, life, death, loss, or love?

The Meaning You Discover in Death

As you integrate the reality of death more fully, you may find that death sheds light on every shred of love, wonder, and delight in your vicinity. Death may spur you to consider a new perspective of the afterlife, foster ongoing connections with loved ones who die, or reveal to you how you will be a healing presence for others after you depart the earth.

One perspective of death that helps me resolve some of my ambivalence about my death is to recognize the limited resources of the earth and to think of my death as a parting blessing to make room for another human to inhabit my space here – to eat my portion of food, drink my portion of water, use my share of energy that I now consume. I strive to create useful resources (through my writing and mentoring) to leave behind for those still living and those to come in the future. Now that I am past the middle of middle-aged, I find that the meaning of time becomes a bit more gracious and pliable. I can relax and enjoy each day more fully.

⋏ ⋏ ⋏

> Pause to contemplate a significant death experience. Perhaps you recall the death of a friend, family member, or cherished pet, or remember a near-death experience or a brush with death that made it impossible to ignore death's sting. Perhaps you or a loved one were given a diagnosis that included a projection of death in the near future. Along with your sense of loss or grief, were there any life lessons or gifts you received in this encounter with death?

⋏ ⋏ ⋏

Whatever death experiences you encountered in the past, it can be helpful to contemplate your relationship with death in the present and future. The reality of death provides a boatload of meaningful questions to contemplate. If you're up for it, ask a few to find out what cherished meaning death might hold for you:

- If I died today, what makes me proudest or happiest about how I lived my life?
- If I died today, what is my biggest regret?
- If I were on my death bed, what would I want to say to each of my loved ones before departing?
- If a loved one were dying, what would I celebrate or regret about our time together? What would I want to say or do for my loved one?
- What does my ideal death look and feel like? (Who do I hope will be present? Where do I wish to die? What music, words, touch, silence, solitude, beauty, setting, etc. do I imagine for my ultimate departure?)

- How can I prepare meaningfully for the moment of my death no matter how or where I die – perhaps through meditation, guided visualization, breathing exercises, prayer, reciting a mantra or scripture passage, etc.?
- What last wishes do I desire to communicate with my loved ones? How would I like for others to respond to my medical care, resuscitation, or letting me go?
- How would I like for others to celebrate my life before and after my death?
- What do I want to leave in my will or trust for others? What sentimental tokens would I like to bequest to specific loved ones and why?
- What do I want others to remember about me after my death? What legacy do I desire to leave behind?

Let your sure knowledge of death be a motivator to create more meaningful relationships with yourself and others, daily pleasures, work, the natural world, and with the reality of death itself. For more inspiration, see resources on "Dying a Good Death" on page 325.

When my daughter Morgan was in her mid-twenties and grieving cumulative losses, she struggled to integrate the reality of death in general and my future death in particular (although I was in my fifties and healthy). So, in the tradition of my father, I allowed my massive love for Morgan to inspire me to make peace with my fears surrounding my death. I wrote her a poem (and a series of poems) that became, for her, a lasting reminder that my mortal self is not the only presence I offer her:

> Have Me With You
> for my daughter, Morgan
>
> The more devastating thought
> than leaving you behind:
> That you, dear one,
> might succumb to the grief of my death
> by resisting life for even a heartbeat.
>
> Your grief cannot bring me back –
> At least not in the form you imagine
> You want and can't have
> After I fly this satin cocoon.
>
> Have me with you by remembering
> To watch for the streaming star,
> Touch the sorrow-stained tear,
> Hear each unexpected silence
> and every guffaw of laughter.

Have me with you by remembering
to attend the smallness of life.
Surround yourself with those you love
in that place where time stands still:
Fall into the nuances of one another's faces.

Have me with you
by remembering
to note the tremors of eternity
that rumble just beneath the surface
of all things temporal.
Straddle the multi-million miracles of a moment.

Have me with you
by remembering.
To live.
Now.

    For a while, Morgan read this poem each night before she slept. Eventually, she had the words "have me with you" tattooed on her forearm with an image of the big dipper and little dipper. Thus, she returns the gift to me. Each time I see the words on her skin, I am reminded that it is death that makes life so precious. It is death that provides sustenance and regeneration for this beautiful world and for we humans who inhabit it. Do your best to learn and live this wisdom and generously give it away to others. The healing it inspires may be your greatest legacy.

Guidepost 54

Preparing to die extravagantly, whenever the time comes, is another way to live brilliantly in the present.

Responding Healer-to-Healer
Companionship Needs of The Grieving Elder

Some say that becoming an elder requires you to leave adulthood behind. But elderhood is an expansion of adulthood, not its demise. The healing triage of grief support is the same for the grieving elder as the grieving adult. You're called to prioritize and negotiate among the most pressing needs for support by:

- Being responsible for your own grieving and healing process
- Being responsive to the grieving and healing needs and preferences of others
- Welcoming others to be equally responsive to you

Being responsive grievers and healers requires us to become less attached to ready-made answers, to stop trying so hard to be grief-fixers and people-fixers, to stop making fleeting judgments about grievers crying too much or not enough, working too hard or shirking day-to-day responsibilities, venting 24/7 or withdrawing into a silent cocoon. Whether such judgments are clearly spoken or expressed in subtle or silent innuendos, they can demean a person's grieving and healing process and may send you or a loved one spiraling further into an abyss of pain and suffering. What's more, if you stop trying to figure out how to "fix" grief, you will have more time to listen, observe, ask, care, and learn to trust that a genuine healing process is as unique as the person who embodies it.

One of the greatest challenges among adult grievers is developing relationships in which we provide *mutual support* for one another. Unfortunately, even among practicing elders, those who are especially skilled at being there for other grievers don't always receive reciprocal assistance from others. Moreover, those who are the focus of family loss – for example, an addict, or one who is mentally ill, permanently injured, or dying – may become a family's primary concern at great cost to the grieving and healing needs of other family members. Relationships may suffer.

In some families, there is that one person that everyone leans on hard when grief descends – whether the leaning is positively or negatively focused, whether a family sees a certain individual as the saving grace who helps to bring healing to all or the troublemaker who is to blame for the grief suffered. The same person can play both roles – at times, being the hero and at others, the villain – depending upon which way the winds of suffering blow.

⋏ ⋏ ⋏

> Think about yourself: Do you tend to lean on others or allow others to lean on you when grief descends? Think about your family: Is there someone among you who is usually sought out by others as a comforter, problem-solver, or helper to unravel grief-related trouble? Do others give that person the same level of support and encouragement? Or, perhaps there is someone who is often perceived as the one to blame for your family troubles? Do your family members tend to let off steam by scapegoating or alienating one of your own?

Subtle and obvious differences in the grieving responses of various family members may cause rifts within a family that intensify personal or social suffering. For example:

- An emotionally sensitive family member who is prone to venting about grief may repel other family members who take a quieter, more internal approach
- A griever who is silent and withdrawn may irritate or enrage another griever who equates emotional intensity with caring
- A griever who is devoted to their work to support the family and seek diversion from continual suffering may become resentful that another family member is sleeping 24/7
- A family member who can't seem to get out of bed may resent the other for acting as if life ought to go on as usual, despite the cataclysmic pain

As a grieving companion, it is not your job to heal grief for another. It is your job to heal grief for yourself. Even so, motivation for self-healing is often discovered in your relationships with others – in your efforts to empower others to grieve and heal, and allow others to empower you.

Unfortunately, we elders are often ill-prepared to respond to the grief of another. Indeed, there is a silent mantra that commonly arises among adults of all ages whenever a family member, friend, co-worker, neighbor, or acquaintance is grieving a loss. It goes something like this: "I feel so useless; I don't know what to do or say to help." This experience of discomfort may cause you to spout ready-made answers to fill the void or to fall silent and quietly slip away to allow a griever to figure out their approach to grieving and healing on their own. Sometimes, that may even be what the other person prefers. But, when someone you know is hurting, it's not the time to succumb to your feelings and thoughts of inadequacy.

Newsflash: No one (and I mean *no one*) always knows the perfect response to human suffering. No one (and I mean *no one*) has the magic words that will heal another's grief-related pain. But don't let that stop you. Serving as a grieving companion for another requires a good bit of vulnerability and risk-taking. Sometimes you will feel awkward and unsure of yourself. Sometimes you will even do or say the wrong thing. Mistakes are part of the learning process. Whatever happens, be willing to admit your learning curve and try again until you get it right. It may help to speak your doubts aloud to the one who is hurting: "I feel so useless. I don't know what to say or do to help." If that's all you can think to say, it's a first step to being useful because you are being responsive to someone else's grief in a way that communicates your caring. As the Chinese philosopher Laozi once said, "A journey of a thousand miles begins with a single step." From that starting place, you can continue to hone your skills as a grieving companion. The following section offers plenty of provisions for taking your journey of a thousand miles one step at a time.

Polaris: Serving as a North Star for Grieving Adults of all Ages

In the Northern hemisphere, when you look at the sky on a cloudless night, there is a star called "Polaris," or the "North Star," that can be found at the end of the handle of the Little Dipper constellation. Mistakenly, some believe Polaris is the brightest star in the sky. Although brighter than most, the star's most distinguishing quality is not that it is the brightest but that it is the easiest by which to navigate. Polaris resides by the Northern celestial pole and appears never to move while the other stars in the sky turn around it. For this reason, it was named by the indigenous people of the Great Plains as the "Star That Never Walks." In various myths and legends, it is the star that guides home those who are lost – no matter which direction home is.

As a grieving companion, the symbolism of Polaris reminds you to be someone who stays the journey and doesn't walk away when the going gets rough. It reminds you to be the kind of grieving companion who offers another griever hope of finding "home" again in a world that has shifted. When you serve as another's North Star, you provide any or all of the seven gifts that the word P-O-L-A-R-I-S represents:

P is for Presence:

Sometimes just "being there" for someone is enough. As Thelma Davis puts it, "When someone is going through a storm, your silent presence is worth more than a million empty words." Make yourself available and let another griever know that you recognize their suffering. Whether you sit quietly with the other, engage in meaningful or diversionary activities together, or offer to do yard work, clean house, or cook a meal – your physical presence can speak volumes. If the person or family desires to be alone, respect their wishes and check in with them again periodically – in an hour, day, or week, as is fitting. This is especially important with losses that are not acknowledged socially among friends and family. Some grievers tell me that their loved ones scattered in the weeks and months following a divorce. Even if you don't know what to do or say, be there and keep offering to be there in a respectful way. Sometimes, a griever may send you away, but keep checking for the welcome mat to be set out again as grieving and healing needs and preferences change. Even if a person chooses to be alone in their grief, it's good for a griever to know that there is a choice in the matter. There is a world of difference between suffering loneliness and choosing solitude.

O is for Observe:

Offer loving attention and observe how a griever approaches their loss. Imagine what support and encouragement might be helpful. Check out your hunches with anyone you hope to support, remembering that you can only experience a fraction of another's grieving process. More often than not, a griever knows best what encouragement might be useful to them. However, keen observation skills can help you to choose wisely concerning how, where, and when to offer a helping hand, silent presence, word of empathy, or shoulder to cry on.

L is for Listen:

Some grievers talk about their grief with anyone willing to listen. Others choose only one or two with whom to confide. Grief counseling can be helpful for some grievers, but most grievers process the details and nuances of their loss and the grief that accompanies it with friends and family members. So, when a griever is willing to confide in you, do your best to listen without judging the other's grieving responses or recounting your own similar loss.

Don't try to "fix" the other person or their grief. Allow the other's words to tumble out as prolifically or as haltingly as they may. Don't react immediately if you disagree with something the person says that appears inaccurate or is unfair to another. Allow a griever to let off steam and then clear up discrepancies or present a different perspective when the time is right. Before you do, be sure to put yourself in the other's shoes and strive to understand their experience from their unique vantage point. Loving attention and empathy come first.

If listening to another griever's woes intensifies your suffering or you feel you don't have the knowledge or inner resources to help, be clear with the griever that you may not be the best choice as a listening companion. Help the other to identify who might serve better – perhaps another trusted friend or family member, counselor, therapist, life coach, spiritual director, or clergyperson. If there is no one else available, it may be helpful to establish some rules for talking and listening with your loved one that enhance health and well-being for both of you.

For example, concerning damaging family conflicts (including my parents' divorce), my mom and I agreed to avoid rehashing old wounds and to let each other know when a conversation about past family troubles is doing either of us more harm than good. Paradoxically, because of our willingness to set some limits on lamenting to one another about our family woes, I am more able to listen to my mom's past grievances about my father from time to time and even develop empathy for her perspective – although, posthumously, my father remains one of my best friends. Being clear about your limitations as a listener is another way to listen with compassion – for yourself and others, too.

A is for Ask:

The easiest way to figure out what another adult griever needs from you is to ask. However, some questions are likely to be more helpful than others. For example, asking "Is there anything I can do?" may be too vague for a griever to process quickly and can elicit an immediate negative response. Ask questions that are more specific and relevant to the situation at hand.

Depending on your relationship with a griever, you might ask:

- What can I do for you this afternoon (or this week)? (If the other is hesitant or can't think of anything, you might add, "Think about it and feel free to make me a list.")

- Would it be helpful to talk to someone about your loss? (You might add, "I'm a good listener," or "I can get some references for a grief counselor, spiritual care provider, or support group if you're interested.")
- Would you like me to stay or would you rather have some time to yourself?
- Would you like for me to ask everyone to leave now so you can get some rest? (This may be a tough one for grievers to do for themselves as they don't want to offend those who show up to offer support and caring.)
- Would you like for me to come over and care for your children so you can get some time to yourself?
- Would you like for me to make phone calls? (Write notes? Organize meals from friends and family? Do laundry? Clean house? Go grocery shopping? Help with memorial plans or funeral arrangements?)
- Would it be all right for me to. . . ? (If you see a need that you can fulfill, don't assume that the other desires for you to do it. It may not be the right timing or may be something that the person desires to do for themselves or have someone else do for them.)

Don't pepper a griever with questions, but when a relevant question arises, be sure to ask it and keep asking from time to time. Answers may change as needs and preferences evolve.

R is for Respond:

If a griever confides in you or asks something of you, be sure to respond at the moment and let them know you're listening. You don't need to do or say a lot except to make it clear that you're engaged and interested – even if you say something as simple as "Thank you for trusting me with what you've shared," "I wish I knew what to do or say to help," or "I'm so sorry this happened to you." Be sure not to ignore or belittle a griever's verbal acknowledgment of grief or their request for help, and don't change the subject to avoid your discomfort.

If a griever asks something of you, be clear whether or not it is something you can provide. If not, be willing to help a griever think through other possibilities or identify someone else who might be better able to assist. If you promise to be of assistance and then don't follow through, show up, or call, you only add insult to injury. So, if you can't be readily available to a griever who is hurting, respond thoughtfully in a way that is doable for you: write a letter, card, or email, call to check on the person regularly, offer a handcrafted gift, plan a timely visit, etc. It's better to follow through with a small gesture of care than to let a griever down when grieving support matters most.

I is for Intervene:

There may come a time when a griever you know and love has difficulties adapting to a grief-striking loss. Some people are not as well-equipped as others to grieve severe losses or tolerate grief-related suffering, just as some people have a lower threshold for physical pain. What's more, some losses are more complex to navigate than others and a griever may become overwhelmed. Do not hesitate to intervene or get professional help for a griever you know who engages in self-harming behaviors, becomes reclusive, lashes out violently at others, develops unhealthy addictions to numb the pain, or becomes more vulnerable to emotional disturbances or mental illness to which they are already inclined. Those closest to the griever will need to make tough decisions about when and how to intervene and decide if professional help is needed immediately or in the long run.

Read about the behavior, addiction, emotional disturbance, or mental illness that your loved one displays. Even if they are benefiting from professional help, find out what you can do to support your loved one's grieving and healing process. If possible, identify others who care and round up more wide-reaching support so that you are not the only intimate support person the other counts on. We each need a sense of "family" to undergird our personal and social efforts to grieve and heal – even if the family who gathers is the most ragtag and unexpected collection of well-wishers. Your true family is comprised of those who remind you that your healing matters as much to them as it does to you.

S is for Strategize:

In your circles of community, invite other grievers to reflect on personal and social approaches to healing the grief of shared losses. Consider the skills and abilities each griever might offer and create a network of healing support. Brainstorm possibilities from three different perspectives:

1. What can I do for the sake of my own grieving and healing process?
2. What can others do to support my grieving and healing efforts? (Be specific about who, what, when, and how.)
3. What can I do for others who are grieving and healing? (Again, be specific.)

Clarify with your intimates what might be helpful for you and ask them to do the same. As you do, pay attention to how your willingness to honor the grief of another helps to heal your own grief.

In his book, *Meditations of the Heart,* minister, mystic, and civil rights activist Howard Thurman captures the essence of what it means for practicing adults and elders to serve one another as grieving companions in his meditation, "For a Time of Sorrow:"

> "I share with you the agony of your grief,
> The anguish of your heart finds echo in my own.
> I know I cannot enter all you feel
> Nor bear with you the burden of your pain;
> I can but offer what my love does give:
> The strength of caring,
> The warmth of one who seeks to understand
> The silent storm-swept barrenness of so great a loss,
> This do I in quiet ways
> That on your lonely path
> You may not walk alone."

Thurman's words stream tenderly into the expanses of grief, like the light of Polaris streaming through the skies on a cloudless night in the north. Here is the eternal compass, the mainstay of hope: that we humans may hear the echo of another's grief within our own.

Guidepost 55

It is a darker sky that lends itself to a brighter star.

Do-It-Yourself

Self-Guided Contemplations for the Elder Within You

Here are a few more ideas for self-guided contemplations – this time focusing on the healing wisdom of elderhood. Choose what's helpful to you. Use these ideas as they are, revise them, or create contemplations of your own.

- ⬥ **Mixing Your Memoir Metaphors:** Check out the book, *Where to Go From Here: Discovering Your Own Life's Wisdom in the Second Half of Life* and allow the authors James E. Birren and Linda Feldman to inspire you to take stock of your life as an "autobiographical story with a past, present, and future yet to be plotted." The book prompts you to "appreciate all (you've) been through, survived, and accomplished; figure out what is missing; and decide how (you) want to (approach) the rest of (your life)." As you write about each stage of your life (infancy, childhood, youthhood, adulthood, and elderhood), consider your grief-striking losses and challenges as well as experiences of healing and periods of genuine contentment. Integrate life and death, joy and sorrow, pain and pleasure into your writing, and show how each gives meaning to the other in the context of your life story as a griever and healer.

- ⬥ **Imparting Remembrances to the Young:** While many elders are capable storytellers when it comes to recounting stories of their own lives, a cherished gift to give to your child or grandchild (or any loved one you witnessed grow from early childhood) is for you to impart the other's life stories as a lasting gift. There is a brilliant and touching book written by Bill Martin Jr. and John Archambault, entitled *Knots on a Counting Rope*, in which a grandfather tells the story of his grandson's life – the challenges, passages, and victories that were pivotal in the boy's life to the present moment. With each telling, the boy is coaxed to help his grandfather tell his life story; then, another knot is tied in the counting rope. The grandfather tells his grandson that when the rope is full of knots, the boy will know the story by heart and can tell it himself. Thus, a grandfather imparts an invaluable gift that will last beyond his death. Consider weaving together the life story of a loved one from your perspective as an elder. You may want to write it down or commit it to memory. You might share it at birthdays, significant life passage celebrations, or whenever it can serve as a beacon of encouragement. Add stories as your loved one matures.

- **Befriending Death:** In a culture in which death is often resisted like the plague, we elders do well to befriend death in ways that add to the fullness of life. Gather wisdom about death from your conversations with others, in the themes and insights of films you watch, or in your reading. To integrate death more fully into your consciousness, you may want to read the novel, *The Book Thief* by Markus Zusak – lovingly narrated from the perspective of death itself, or you might keep a journal of your ongoing conversations with death, recording your intimate encounters with death and the cherished meaning you derive from your reflections.

- **Imagining Your Pain Away:** Your imagination can be a powerful tool to transform pain through the use of guided visualization. This meditative practice may strike you as being too "supernatural" for your tastes, but there's nothing especially supernatural about it. It's a common cognitive process that requires imaginative capabilities that may or may not come naturally to you. It's akin to experiencing a spontaneous "waking dream" that you can consciously control. One simple approach to self-led guided visualization is to close your eyes, breathe naturally, relax your mind and body, and imagine a setting or experience that offers a sense of calm, peace, hope, love, joy, or inspiration, perhaps:

  - Your personal healing: imagining your grief-related pain being released and your body being filled with light, love, or a gentle healing presence
  - A peaceful death, meaningful afterlife, or reunion with a loved one in spirit
  - Visiting a place that holds cherished meaning for you
  - Enjoying intimate relationships with others
  - Accomplishing a challenging feat in the future, or
  - Whatever vision helps you to release your pain and encourages calm, peace, hope, love, joy, or inspiration

  More than being a momentary pleasure, your imaginative visions can gently persuade your subconscious that, whatever your present state of suffering, more pleasurable realities exist for you now and in the future. For more on guided visualizations, see "Mindfulness & Meditation" resources on page 332.

- **Miss & Tell:** In the larger context of life, some losses may seem like "no big deal." You get into a car accident but don't get a scratch. A friend or romantic interest stands you up when you were feeling especially lonely already. Your dog was lost for three days and then returned. Losses don't have to be severe to cause you grief. It may be that a brush with death, recurring loneliness, or the possibility of losing an important relationship with a friend or pet is the cause of your pain. Acknowledging the little losses can prevent a series of them from adding up to a looming sense of loss that sticks with you. So, whenever you experience a subtle loss that grieves you, acknowledge it to yourself. It may be helpful to share your experience with a trusted confidante who will listen empathetically without belittling your loss or trying to fix it. If you note your "little losses" in a journal, when grief descends and you aren't sure what the source of your suffering is, you may be able to trace it back to a series of losses that didn't seem all that problematic when they occurred. The trick is not to recite every little loss as a litany of complaints. Alongside the losses, take note of your gratitude, relief, and learning that is interwoven with your grief.

⟡ **Tending Your Bucket List:** It is never too early or too late to make a bucket list. Even when death is imminent or illness is debilitating, imagine what life experiences you might yet enjoy. Make a list and pursue opportunities to accomplish each desire as you're able. For example, my mom sometimes regrets not pursuing a career as a professional musician after high school, but she finds other ways to share her music. In her 80's, she continues to play her grand piano and share her music at the retirement community where she lives, sometimes with her neighbors hovering to listen just outside her door.

Your bucket list might include trips you hope to take, new hobbies to try, or new friendships to build. You may desire to mentor or teach those of younger generations, return to school, or seek training in a new area of interest. You may even decide to launch a new career, like Jim Arruda Henry, who started learning to read at the age of 92 (after cleverly hiding the fact that he was illiterate from almost everyone he knew). Jim lost interest in reading for a while after his wife's death, but at the age of 96, pursued his literacy goal again and eventually published his first book at the age of 98. His inspiration: George Dawson, the son of slaves, who learned to read at 98 and wrote a book at the age of 101 called *Life Is So Good*. Another writer, David Seidler who was nominated for his first Oscar for his screenplay of *The King's Speech* at the age of 73, mused upon winning the award, "My father always said I would be a late bloomer." But, who knows, if Henry and Dawson are any indication, the award-winning playwright may have some more bloom in him yet.

How about you? What do you imagine doing or being as you age into old?

An Elder's Healing Chest
Approaches to Grieving and Healing in Elderhood

Look through the following list of approaches to grieving and healing from Part III, "The Healing Chest: Gathering Your Own Best Medicine." Which approaches might be especially useful for you to grieve and heal solo or alongside others?

- Abuse Awareness & Prevention
- Addiction Prevention & Recovery
- Apologies
- Art & Creativity
- Bibliotherapy
- Breathing & Relaxation
- Caregiving
- Ceremonies & Celebrations
- Cinematherapy
- Cognitive Healing
- Community-Building
- Conscious Eldering
- Crying
- Dance
- Death Care
- Dreaming & Visitations
- Dying a Good Death
- Emotional Healing & Expressing Feelings
- Exercise, Body Awareness & Physical Release
- Forgiveness
- Funeral Planning & Memorial Services
- Grieving & Healing Perspectives
- Habit-Building
- Helping Others
- Hope
- Illness Tending
- Integrative Care & Complementary Therapies
- Laughter & Humor
- Listening
- Massage, Reiki & Comforting Touch
- Meaning-Making
- Memoir & Autobiography
- Memorials & Remembrance
- Metaphors, Objects & Symbols
- Mindfulness & Meditation
- Movement, Yoga & Posture
- Music & Sound Therapy
- Nature
- Natural Remedies for Pain Relief
- Parenting Mindfully
- Pets & Animals
- Pilgrimages, Labyrinths & Hiking Treks
- Play, Fun & Games
- Poetry
- Prayer
- Repairing Broken Relationships
- Sanctuary & Sacred Space
- Self-Injury & Recovery
- Sexual Healing & Recovery
- Sleeping
- Stories & Storytelling
- Suicide Prevention & Survivor Support
- Talking Cures
- Theater & Speech
- Trauma Recovery
- Wonder
- Writing

☙ Part III ☙
The Healing Chest

Gathering Your Own Best Medicine

Truly, the greatest gift you have to give
is that of your own self-transformation.

Lao Tzu

┊Endless Possibilities for Doing Grief in Real Life┊

Wisdom from Everyday Grievers, Professional Healers, Artists & Care Providers

As you gather your best medicine for healing, imagine the possibilities. The examples I offer here are meant to spark your interest for further exploration. Some are cutting-edge discoveries, old classics, or little-known offerings that speak quietly from the margins of our information-loaded lives. Some will pull your heartstrings, require brain power, bring you down to earth, or lift your spirits. Some are rich with research, others are first-person accounts or practical guides. Some conflict with one another in their approach or outlook; not all will appeal to your values, knowledge base, beliefs, or worldview. *Find what is right for you.* Track down authors, films, educators, experts, grievers, and healers whose voice and guidance speak vibrantly to you and whatever your healing requires.

┊Healing Through Nonfiction and (Mostly True) Stories┊

(pb) indicates picture book; (cb) indicates child/youth chapter book

Abuse Awareness & Prevention (also see Trauma Recovery)
"An ounce of prevention is worth a pound of cure." – Benjamin Franklin

Confessions of a Former Bully by Trudy Ludwig (pb; middle grade readers)

Dear Bully: Seventy Authors Tell Their Stories by Megan Kelly Hall (14 and up)

Doing Right by Our Kids: Protecting Child Safety at All Levels by Amy Tiemann and Irene van der Zande

In Love and in Danger: A Teen's Guide to Breaking Free of Abusive Relationships by B. Levy

The Macho Paradox: Why Some Men Hurt Women and How All Men Can Help by Jackson Katz

No Visible Bruises: What We Don't Know About Domestic Violence Can Kill Us by Rachel Louise Snyder

The Safe Child, Happy Parent *picture book series* by Pro Familia, Illustrated by Dagmar Geisler; 15 titles, including *I Can Stand Up to Bullies* and *My Body Belongs to Me* (pb)

Violent No More: Helping Men End Domestic Abuse by Michael Paymar

Addiction Prevention & Recovery (also see Emotional Healing; Habit-Building)
"I'm not telling you it's going to be easy. I'm telling you it's going to be worth it. " – Art Williams

Addict in the House: A No-Nonsense Family Guide Through Addiction & Recovery by R. Barnett

Addiction in the Family: Helping Families Navigate Challenges, Emotions & Recovery by Louise Stanger (substance use disorders)

Chasing the High: A Firsthand Account of One Young Person's Experience with Substance Abuse by Kyle Keegan and Howard Moss

Food: The Good Girl's Drug: How to Stop Using Food to Control Your Feelings by Sunny Sea Gold

High: Everything You Want to Know About Drugs, Alcohol, and Addiction by David Sheff and Nic Sheff (middle grade readers and up)

Irresistible: The Rise of Addictive Technology and the Business of Keeping Us Hooked by Adam Alter

I Want More: How to Know When I've Had Enough from the "Safe Child, Happy Parent Series," Illustrated by Dagmar Geisler (pb)

Love First: A Family's Guide to Intervention by Jeff Jay and Debra Jay

The Mindfulness Workbook for Addiction: A Guide to Coping With Grief, Stress & Anger That Trigger Addictive Behavior by Rebecca E. Williams & Julie S. Kraft

This Naked Mind: Control Alcohol, Find Freedom, Discover Happiness & Change Your Life by Annie Grace

Out of the Shadows: Understanding Sexual Addiction by Patrick Carnes

Recover to Live: Kick Any Habit, Manage Any Addiction: Your Self-Treatment Guide to Alcohol, Drugs, Eating Disorders, Gambling, Hoarding, Smoking, Sex & Porn by Christopher Kennedy Lawford

Sexploitation: Helping Kids Develop Healthy Sexuality in a Porn-Driven World by Cindy Pierce

Unbroken Brain: A Revolutionary New Way of Understanding Addiction by Maia Szalavitz

Understanding Addiction and Recovery Through a Child's Eyes by Jerry Moe

Women, Food, and God: An Unexpected Path to Almost Everything by Geneen Roth

Your Brain on Porn: Internet Pornography and the Emerging Science of Addiction by Gary Wilson

Apologies (also see forgiveness)

"Be willing to apologize. Proper apologies have three parts: 1) What I did was wrong. 2) I'm sorry that I hurt you. 3) What can I do to make it better?"
– Randy Pausch

Effective Apology: Mending Fences, Building Bridges & Restoring Trust by John Kador

This is Just to Say: Poems of Apology & Forgiveness by Joyce Sidman (pb)

Art & Creativity
(also see Dance; Music; Play, Fun & Games; Theater & Speech; Wonder; Writing)

"Art opens the closets, airs out the cellars and attics. It brings healing."
– Julia Cameron

250 Brief, Creative & Practical Art Therapy Techniques by Susan I. Buchalter

Art From Her Heart: Folk Art from Clementine Hunter by Kathy Whitehead, Illustrated by Shane W. Evans (pb)

The Art of Knitting: Stitching Together Our Lives in a Fractured World by Loretta Napoleoni

The Children's Year: Crafts and Clothes for Children and Parents to Make by Stephanie Cooper, Christine Funes-Clinton, and Marye Rowling

Colors of Loss and Healing: An Adult Coloring Book for Getting You Through Tough Times by Deborah Derman, Illustrated by Lisa Powell Braun

Creative Healing: How to Heal Yourself by Tapping Your Hidden Creativity by Michael Samuels

Draw What You See: The Life and Art of Benny Andrews by Kathleen Bensen, Illustrated with paintings by Benny Andrews (pb)

Frederick by Leo Lionni (pb)

Help Me Say Goodbye: Activities for Helping Kids Cope When a Special Person Dies by Janis Silverman

Harold and the Purple Crayon by Crockett Johnson (pb)

Helping People With Developmental Disabilities Mourn: Practical Rituals for Caregivers by Marc A. Markell

I Ain't Gonna Paint No More! by Karen Beaumont, Illustrated by David Catrow (pb)

Looking at Mindfulness: 25 Ways to Live in the Moment Through Art by Christophe Andre

The Noisy Paint Box: The Colors and Sounds of Kandinsky's Abstract Art by Barb Rosenstock (pb)

Snips and Snails and Walnut Whales: Nature Crafts for Children by Phyllis Fiarotta

Toymaking with Children by Freya Jaffke

Wonder: The Art and Practice of Beatrice Blue by Beatrice Blue

Zentangle Art Therapy: Meditative Drawing to Reduce Stress, Increase Wellbeing and Enhance Relaxation by Anya Lothrop

Bibliotherapy (also see Memoir and "Healing Through Novels & Picture Books," p. 341)

"I did what came naturally to me when I was scared, upset or unhappy. I turned to the book in my lap and began to read." — Indu Muralidharan

Connecting Children With Classics by Meagan Lacy and Pauline Dewan

The Enchanted Hour: The Miraculous Power of Reading Aloud in an Age of Distraction by Meghan Cox Gurdon

Healing Stories: Picture Books for the Big and Small Changes in a Child's Life by Jacqueline Golding

Homemade Books to Help Kids Cope: An Easy to Learn Technique for Parents & Professionals by Robert G. Zeigler

Reading to Heal: How to Use Bibliotherapy to Improve Your Life by Jackeline Stanley

Using Literature to Help Troubled Teenagers Cope with Health Issues, edited by C. A. Bowman

Breathing & Relaxation (also see Mindfulness & Meditation)

"Breathing is simple, gracious, soothing and always there for you" — Karenina Ana Murillo

The Art of Breathing: The Secret to Living Mindfully by Danny Penman

Breathe With Me: Using Breath to Feel Strong, Calm, and Happy by Mariam Gates, Illustrated by Sarah Jane Hinder (pb)

Breathe: The Simple, Revolutionary 14-Day Program to Improve Your Mental and Physical Health by Dr. Belisa Vranich

Breathe Like a Bear: 30 Mindful Moments for Kids to Feel Calm and Focused Anytime, Anywhere by Kira Willey, Illustrated by Anni Betts (pb)

The Healing Power of the Breath: Simple Techniques to Reduce Stress and Anxiety, Enhance Concentration, and Balance Your Emotions by Richard P. Brown and Patricia L. Gerberg

How to Relax by Thich Nhat Hanh (series includes *How to Eat*, How to *Walk, How to See*, etc.)

The Mindful Teen: Powerful Skills to Help You Handle Stress One Moment at a Time by Dzung X. Vo

Self-Healing with Breathwork by Jack Angelo

Caregiving (also see Death Care; Helping Others; Parenting Mindfully)

**"It is not the load that breaks you down. It's the way you carry it."
— Lena Horne**

Authentic Healing: A Practical Guide for Caregivers by Kathi J. Kemper

Cruising Through Caregiving: Reducing the Stress of Caring for Your Loved Ones by Jennifer L. Fitzpatrick

The Gift of Caring: Saving Our Parents from the Peril of Modern Healthcare by Marcy Cottrell Houle and Elizabeth Eckstrom

The Gifts of Caregiving: Stories of Hardship, Hope & Healing by Connie Goldman

Learning to Speak Alzheimer's by Joanne Koenig Coste

Top Screwups Doctors Make and How to Avoid Them by Joe Graedon and Teresa Graedon

Trauma Stewardship: An Everyday Guide to Caring for Self While Caring for Others by Laura van Dernoot Lipsky and Connie Burk

Wilfrid Gordon McDonald Partridge by Mem Fox, Illustrated by Julie Vivas (pb)

Ceremonies & Celebrations (also see Funeral Planning & Memorial Services)

" . . . the power of ceremony. It marries the mundane to the sacred. The water turns to wine; the coffee to a prayer." — Robin Wall Kimmerer

The Children's Year: Crafts and Clothes for Children and Parents to Make by Stephanie Cooper, Christine Funes-Clinton, and Marye Rowling

Crossing the Bridge: Creating Ceremonies for Grieving and Healing from Life's Lessons by Sydney Barbara Metrick

Emma's Gift by Deborah Delaronde, Illustrated by Jay Odjick (pb)

Festivals, Family and Food by Diana Carey and Judy Large (Seasonal, Christian, Secular)

Finding Sanctuary in Nature: Simple Ceremonies in the Native American Tradition for Healing Yourself and Others by Jim PathFinder Ewing

Fry Bread: A Native American Family Story by Kevin Noble Maillard, Illustrated by Juana Martinez-Neal (pb)

Healing Ceremonies: Creating Personal Rituals for Spiritual, Emotional, Physical & Mental Health by Carl A. Hammerschlag and Howard D. Silverman

I'm in Charge of Celebrations by Byrd Baylor, Illustrated by Peter Parnall (pb)

Knots on a Counting Rope by Bill Martin, Jr. and John Archambault, Ill. by Ted Rand (pb)

Living Passages for the Whole Family: Celebrating Rites of Passage from Birth to Adulthood by Shea Darian

My Jewish Year: 18 Holidays, One Wondering Jew by Abigail Pogrebin

Night of the Moon: A Muslim Holiday Story by Hena Khan, Illustrated by Julie Paschkis

On The Day You Were Born by Debra Frasier (pb)

On the Night You Were Born by Nancy Tillman (pb)

Oskar and the Eight Blessings by Richard Simon and Tanya Simon, Illustrated by Mark Diegel (pb)

Sacred Ceremony: How to Create Ceremonies for Healing, Transitions, and Celebrations by Steven D. Farmer

Sacred Dying: Creating Rituals for Embracing the End of Life by Megory Anderson

The Way to Start a Day by Byrd Baylor, Illustrated by Peter Parnall (pb)

We Are Grateful: Otsaliheliga by Traci Sorell, Illustrated by Frane Lessac

The Wild Edge of Sorrow: Rituals of Renewal and the Sacred Work of Grief by Francis Weller

Cinematherapy (also see "Healing Through Movies & Documentaries," page 347)

"Movies offer an unusually safe, enjoyable way to peek at all we've denied—our dark sides and our light." – Marsha Sinetar

E-motion Picture Magic: A Movie Lover's Guide to Healing and Transformation by Birgit Wolz

Cognitive Healing (also see Emotional Healing)

"The mind is everything. What you think, you become." – Buddha

The Brain That Changes Itself: Stories of Personal Triumph from the Frontiers of Brain Science by Norman Doidge, M.D.

The Dialectical Behavior Therapy Skills Workbook: Practical DBT Exercises for Learning Mindfulness, Interpersonal Effectiveness, Emotion Regulation & Distress Tolerance by Matthew McCay, Jeffrey C. Wood and Jeffrey Brantley

No Drama Discipline: The Whole Brain Way to Calm the Chaos and Nurture Your Child's Developing Brain by Daniel J. Siegel and Tina Payne Bryson

The Owner's Manual for the Brain: The Ultimate Guide to Peak Mental Performance for All Ages by Pierce J. Howard

Retrain Your Brain: Cognitive Behavioral Therapy in Seven Weeks: A Workbook for Managing Depression and Anxiety by Seth J. Gillihan

The Suicidal Thoughts Workbook: CBT Skills to Reduce Emotional Pain, Increase Hope & Prevent Suicide by Kathyrn Hope Gordon

Whole-Brain Child: 12 Revolutionary Strategies to Nurture Your Child's Developing Brain by Daniel J. Siegel and Tina Payne Bryson

Community-Building

"There is no power for change greater than a community discovering what it cares about." – Margaret J. Wheatley

A Hidden Wholeness: The Journey Toward an Undivided Life by Parker J. Palmer

Be the Bridge: Pursuing God's Heart for Racial Reconciliation by Natasha Morrison

Extra Yarn by Mac Barnett, Illustrated by Jon Klassen (pb)

The Invisible Boy by Trudy Ludwig, Illustrated by Patrice Barton (pb)

It Gets Better: Coming Out, Overcoming Bullying, and Creating a Life Worth Living by Dan Savage and Terry Miller

Modern Loss: Candid Conversations About Grief. Beginners Welcome by Rebecca Soffer and Gabrielle Birkner

The Power of One by Trudy Ludwig, Illustrated by Mike Curato (pb)

The Racial Healing Handbook: Practical Activities to Help You Challenge Privilege, Confront Systemic Racism, and Engage in Collective Healing by Anneliese A. Singh

Rebellious Mourning: The Collective Work of Grief, edited by Sandy Milstein

The Shelter of Each Other: Rebuilding Our Families by Mary Pipher

Start a Community Food Garden: The Essential Handbook by Lamanda Joy

Stone Soup by Heather Forest, Illustrated by Susan Gaber (pb)

Conscious Eldering (also see Parenting Mindfully)

"In a troubled time, the willingness to proceed like you're needed is a radical act." – Stephen Jenkinson

Aging as a Spiritual Practice: A Contemplative Guide to Growing Older and Wiser by Lewis Richmond

Becoming Grandma: The Joy and Science of the New Grandparenting by Leslie Stahl

Conscious Living, Conscious Aging: Embrace and Savor Your Next Chapter by Ron Pevny

Crones Don't Whine: Concentrated Wisdom for Juicy Women *by Jean Shinoda Bolen*

Do Not Go Quietly: A Guide to Living Consciously and Aging Wisely for People Who Weren't Born Yesterday by George & Sedena Cappannelli

Elderhood: Redefining Aging, Transforming Medicine, Reimagining Life by Louise Aronson

Knots on a Counting Rope by Bill Martin, Jr. and John Archambault, Illustrated by Ted Rand (pb)

Second Wind: Navigating the Passage to a Slower, Deeper, and More Connected Life by Dr. Bill Thomas

Women Rowing North: Navigating Life's Currents and Flourishing as We Age by Mary Pipher

Crying

"What soap is for the body, tears are for the soul." – Jewish Proverb

Crying: A Natural and Cultural History of Tears by Tom Lutz

Crying is Like the Rain: A Story of Mindfulness and Feelings by Heather Hawk Feinberg, Illustrated by Chamisa Kellogg (pb)

Tears by Sibylle Delacroix (pb)

Tears Heal: How to Listen to Our Children by Kate Orson

When Tears Sing: The Art of Lament in the Christian Community by William Blaine-Wallace

Why Do We Cry? by Fran Pintadera, Illustrated by Ana Sender (pb)

Why Humans Like to Cry: Tragedy, Evolution, and the Brain by Michael Trimble

Dance (also see Movement, Yoga & Posture)

"Dance, when you're broken open. Dance, if you've torn the bandage off. Dance in the middle of the fighting. Dance in your blood. Dance when you're perfectly free." — Rumi

Boys Dance! (American Ballet Theater) by John Robert Allman, Illustrated by Luciano Lazono

The Creative Habit: Learn It and Use It for Life by Twyla Tharp

Dancing Mindfulness: A Creative Path to Healing and Transformation by Jamie Marich

How Do You Dance? by Thyra Heder (pb)

I Will Dance by Nancy Bo Flood (pb)

Mao's Last Dancer by Li Cunxin (memoir; adult & young reader versions)

Returning to Health: With Dance, Movement & Imagery by Anna Halprin

Sweat Your Prayers: Movement as Spiritual Practice by Gabrielle Roth

Death Care (also see Dying a Good Death; Funeral Planning & Memorial Services)

"Tell your friend that in his death, a part of you dies and goes with him. Wherever he goes, you also go. He will not be alone." — Jiddu Krishnamurti

A Beginner's Guide to the End: Practical Advice for Living Life and Facing Death by B.J. Miller and Shoshanna Berger

The American Book of Living & Dying by Richard Groves and Henriette Anne Klauser

Dear Life: A Doctor's Story of Life and Love by Rachel Clarke

Final Gifts: Understanding the Special Awareness, Needs, and Communication of the Dying by Maggie Callanan and Patricia Kelley

Finding Peace at the End of Life: A Death Doula's Guide for Families and Caregivers by Henry Fersko-Weiss

Living into Dying: A Journal of Spiritual and Practical Deathcare for Family and Community by Nancy Jewel Poer

The Needs of the Dying by David Kessler

Present Through the End: A Caring Companion's Guide for Accompanying the Dying by Kirsten DeLeo

Sacred Dying: Creating Rituals for Embracing the End of Life by Megory Anderson

Sacred Passage: How to Provide Fearless, Compassionate Care for the Dying by Margaret Coberly

Using the Power of Hope to Cope With Dying: The Four Stages of Hope by Cathleen Fanslow

Dreaming & Visitations

"When we are asleep in this world, we are awake in another." — Salvador Dali

Dreams at the Threshold: Guidance, Comfort, and Healing at the End of Life by Jeanne Van Bronkhorst

Grief Dreams: How They Help Heal Us After the Death of a Loved One by T.J. Ray

Healing Dreams: Exploring the Dreams That Can Transform Your Life by Marc Ian Barasch

Why We Dream: The Transformative Power of Our Nightly Journey by Alice Robb

Dying a Good Death (also see Death Care; Funeral Planning & Memorial Services)

"To die proudly when it is no longer possible to live proudly . . . in the midst of children and witnesses: so that an actual leave-taking is possible while (the one) who is leaving is still there." – Friedrich Nietzsche

Advice for Future Corpses: A Practical Perspective on Death and Dying by Sallie Tisdale

The Art of Dying Well: A Practical Guide to a Good End of Life by Katy Butler

Being Mortal by Atul Gawande

Comforting Thoughts About Death That Have Nothing to Do With God by Greta Christina

Deathing: An Intelligent Alternative for the Final Moments of Life by Anya Foos-Graber

Dying Well: Peace and Possibilities at the End of Life by Ira Byock

Extreme Measures: Finding a Better Path to the End of Life by Jessica Nutik Zitter

Facing the Final Mystery: A Guide to Discussing End-of-Life Issues by Laura Larsen

The Five Invitations: Discovering What Death Can Teach Us About Living Fully by Frank Ostaseseki

The Four Things That Matter Most: A Book About Living by Ira Byock

I'm Dead, Now What?: Important Information About My Belongings, Business Affairs, and Wishes (a "peace of mind" planner) by Peter Pauper Press

Life Lessons by Elizabeth Kübler-Ross and David Kessler

Hope for the Flowers by Trina Paulus (pb)

Living Our Dying: A Way to the Sacred in Everyday Life by Joseph Sharp

Living Fully Dying Well: Reflecting on Death to Find Your Life's Meaning by Edward W. Bastian and Tina L. Staley

Sadako and the Thousand Paper Cranes by Eleanor Coerr (cb)

Emotional Healing & Expressing Feelings (also see Cognitive Healing)

"But feelings can't be ignored, no matter how unjust or ungrateful they seem." — Anne Frank

50 Ways (and *50 More Ways*) *to Soothe Yourself Without Food* by Susan Albers

50 Ways to Feel Happy: Fun Activities and Ideas to Build Your Happiness Skills by Vanessa King, Val Payne & Peter Harper, Illustrated by Celeste Aires (pb)

The Depression Cure: The Six-Step Program to Beat Depression Without Drugs by Stephen S. Ilardi

EMDR: The Breakthrough "Eye Movement" Therapy for Overcoming Anxiety, Stress, and Trauma by Francine Shapiro

Healing Through the Dark Emotions: The wisdom of grief, fear, and despair by Miriam Greenspan

In My Heart: A Book of Feelings by Jo Witek, Illustrated by Christine Roussey (pb)

My Heart by Corinna Luyken (pb)

Retrain Your Brain: Cognitive Behavioral Therapy in Seven Weeks: A Workbook for Managing Depression and Anxiety by Seth J. Gillihan

Wonder: From Emotion to Spirituality by Robert C. Fuller

Exercise, Body Awareness & Physical Release (also see Movement)

" . . . regular exercise is about as close to a magic potion as you can get."
— Thich Nhat Hanh

The Body Awareness Workbook for Trauma by Julie Brown Yau and Lisa Genova

Healing Your Grieving Body: 100 Physical Practices for Mourners by Alan D. Wolfelt and Kirby J. Duvall

Healthy Healing: A Guide to Working Out Grief by Michelle Steinke-Baugard

Running Home: A Memoir by Katie Arnold

Trauma Releasing Exercises (TRE): A revolutionary new method for stress/trauma recovery by David Berceli

Ultra-Marathon Man: Confessions of an All-Night Runner by Dean Karnazes

Yoga for Grief Relief: Simple Practices for Transforming Your Grieving Mind and Body by Antonio Sausys

Forgiveness (also see Apologies)

"Not forgiving is like drinking rat poison and then waiting for the rat to die."
— Anne Lamott

The Apology by Eve Ensler

Forgive for Good: A Proven Prescription for Health and Happiness by Fred Luskin

How Can I Forgive You: The Courage to Forgive, the Freedom Not To by Janis Abrams Spring

Why Won't You Apologize: Healing Big Betrayals and Everyday Hurts by Harriet Lerner

Funeral Planning & Memorial Services (also see Death Care)

"The connections we make in the course of life—maybe that's what heaven is."
— Fred Rogers

The Art of Dying: Honoring & Celebrating Life's Passages by Salli Rasberry and Carole Rae Watanabe

Celebrating a Life: Planning Memorial Services and Other Creative Remembrances by Faith Moore

Dealing Creatively With Death: A Manual of Death Education and Simple Burial by Ernest Morgan

The End of Something Wonderful: A Practical Guide to a Backyard Funeral by Stephanie V. W. Lucianovic, Illustrated by George Ermos (pb)

The Funeral by Matt James (pb)

A Good Goodbye: Funeral Planning for Those Who Don't Plan to Die by Gail Rubin

The Goodbye Book by Todd Parr (pb)

The Green Burial Guidebook: Everything You Need to Plan an Affordable, Environmentally Friendly Burial by Elizabeth Fournier

The Party of Your Life: Get the Funeral You Want by Planning It Yourself by Erika Dillman

The Tenth Good Thing About Barney by Judith Viorst and Erik Blegvad (pb)

Grieving & Healing Perspectives

"Grief does not change you, Hazel. It reveals you." — John Green

The 100 Practical Ideas Series by Alan D. Wolfelt (including *Healing Your Grieving Heart After a Cancer Diagnosis, Healing the Adult Sibling's Grieving Heart, Healing Your Traumatized Heart, Healing Your Holiday Grief*, etc.)

The American Book of Living & Dying by Richard Groves and Henriette Anne Klauser

Bearing the Unbearable: Love, Loss & the Heartbreaking Path of Grief by Joanne Cacciatore

Bereaved Children and Teens: A Support Guide for Parents & Professionals, edited by Earl A. Grollman

Cry Heart, But Never Break by Glenn Ringtved, Illustrated by Charlotte Pardi (pb)

Doing Grief in Real Life: A Soulful Guide to Navigate Loss, Death & Change by Shea Darian

Empty Arms: Coping With Miscarriage, Stillbirth and Infant Death by Sherokee Ilse

The End is Just the Beginning: Lessons in Grieving for African Americans by Arlene Churn

The Fall of Freddie the Leaf: A Story for All Ages by Leo Buscalia (pb)

Getting Grief Right: Finding Your Story of Love in the Sorrow of Loss by Patrick O'Malley

Grief is a Journey: Finding Your Path Through Loss by Dr. Kenneth Doka

Grieving Beyond Gender: Understanding the Ways Men and Women Mourn by Kenneth J. Doka and Terry L. Martin

The Grieving Teen: A Guide for Teenagers and Their Friends by Helen Fitzgerald

Grieving While Black: An Anti-Racist Take on Oppression and Sorrow by Breeshia Wade

Healthy Healing: A Guide to Working Out Grief by Michelle Steinke-Baugard

Helping People With Developmental Disabilities Mourn: Practical Rituals for Caregivers by Marc A. Markell

It's Ok That You're Not Ok: Meeting Grief and Loss in a Culture That Doesn't Understand by Megan Devine

Legacy: Trauma, Story, and Indigenous Healing by Suzanne Methot

Lifetimes: The Beautiful Way to Explain Death to Children by Bryan Mellonie and Robert Ingpen (pb)

Mourning & Mitzvah: A Guided Journal for Walking the Mourner's Path Through Grief to Healing by Anne Brener

"A New Mourning: Synthesizing an interactive model of adaptive grieving dynamics" by C. D. Bagbey Darian; *Illness, Crisis & Loss* Vol. 22(3), pages 195-235. (https://doi.org/10.2190/IL.22.3.c)

Opening to Grief: finding your way from loss to peace by Claire B. Willis and Marnie Crawford Samuelson

Option B: Facing Adversity, Building Resilience, and Finding Joy by Cheryl Sandburg and Adam Grant

Rebuilding: When Your Relationship Ends by Bruce Fisher (divorce or breakup)

Unattended Sorrow: Recovering from Loss and Reviving the Heart by Stephen Levine

The Wild Edge of Sorrow: Rituals of Renewal and the Sacred Work of Grief by Francis Weller

Habit-Building (also see Addiction Prevention & Recovery)
"We create our future self by default or design." — Nicole Cody

Atomic Habits by James Clear

One Small Step Can Change Your Life: The Kaizen Way by Robert Maurer

The Power of Habit by Charles Duhigg

The Way to Start a Day by Byrd Baylor (pb)

Helping Others (also see Caregiving)
"They say to serve is to love. I think to serve is to heal, too." — Viola Davis

The Art of Being a Healing Presence: A Guide for Those in Caring Relationships by James E. Miller

Be Kind by Pat Zietlow Miller (pb)

Crossing Bok Chitto: A Choctaw Tale of Friendship & Freedom by Tim Tingle, Illustrated by Jeanne Borek Bridges (pb)

Each Kindness by Jacqueline Woodson, Illustrated by E.B. Lewis (pb)

How to Be a Friend to a Friend Who's Sick by Letty Cottin Pogrebin

How to Heal a Broken Wing by Bob Graham (pb)

Peace is an Offering by Annette LeBox, Illustrated by Stephanie Graegin (pb)

Please Be Patient: I'm Grieving by Gary Roe

Hope
"But I know, somehow, that only when it is dark enough can you see the stars." — Martin Luther King, Jr.

Hope in the Age of Anxiety by Anthony Scioli and Henry B. Biller

Hope Rising: How the Science of Hope Can Change Your Life by C. Gwinn and C. Hellman

Scared by Struggle, Transformed by Hope by Joan Chittister

The Suicidal Thoughts Workbook: CBT Skills to Reduce Emotional Pain, Increase Hope & Prevent Suicide by Kathryn Hope Gordon

Using the Power of Hope to Cope With Dying: The Four Stages of Hope by Cathleen Fanslow

Illness Tending (also see Memoir & Autobiography)
"When peoples care for you and cry for you, they can straighten out your soul." — Langston Hughes

A Perfect Shelter by Clare Helen Welsh, illustrated by Asa Gilland (pb)

Dancing With Elephants: Mindfulness Training for Those Living With Dementia, Chronic Illness or an Aging Brain Disease by Jarem Sawatsky

Good Night Hospital Room by M. L. and C. Robertson, Illustrated by Melissa Gerhold (pb)

How to Be a Friend to a Friend Who's Sick by Letty Cottin Pogrebin

How to Help Children Through a Parent's Serious Illness by Kathleen McCue

Identity Theft: Rediscovering Ourselves After Stroke by D. E. Meyerson and D. Zuckerman

My Parent Has Cancer and It Really Sucks: Real Life Advice From Real Life Teens by Marc Silver and Maya Silver

My Stroke of Insight: A Brain Scientist's Personal Journey by Jill Bolte Taylor

The Tide by Clare Helen Welsh, Illustrated by Ashling Lindsay (pb)

The Wet Engine: Exploring the Mad Wild Miracle of the Heart by Brian Doyle

Integrative Care & Complementary Therapies
(also see Massage, Reiki & Comforting Touch; Natural Remedies & Pain Relief)

"The natural healing force within each one of us is the greatest force in getting well." – Hippocrates

The Art of Healing: Uncovering Your Inner Wisdom and Potential for Self-Healing by Bernie Siegel and Cynthia J. Hurn

The Body Keeps the Score: Brain, Mind, and Body in the Healing of Trauma by Bessel van der Kolk

The Brain That Changes Itself: Stories of Personal Triumph from the Frontiers of Brain Science by Norman Doidge

The Magic Feather Effect: The Science of Alternative Medicine and the Surprising Power of Belief by Melanie Warner

Laughter & Humor (also see Play, Fun & Games)

"Laugh till you weep. Weep till there's nothing left but to laugh at your weeping. In the end it's all one. – Frederick Buechner

Amelia Bedelia series by Peggy Parish (young readers – pb)

The Best Christmas Pageant Ever by Barbara Robinson (cb)

Can't We Talk About Something More Pleasant?: A Memoir by Roz Chast

Click, Clack, Moo: Cows That Type by Doreen Cronin, Illustrated by Betsy Lewin (pb)

The Complete Nonsense of Edward Lear by Edward Lear

Gesundheit!: Bringing Good Health to You, the Medical System, and Society through Physician Service, Complementary Therapies, Humor, and Joy by Patch Adams

Laughter Therapy: How to Laugh About Everything in Your Life That Isn't Really Funny by Annette Goodheart

Pippi Longstocking series by Astrid Lindgren (cb)

The Wonky Donkey by Craig Smith (pb)

Listening (also see Talking Cures)

"When I have been listened to and when I have been heard, I am able to re-perceive my world in a new way and to go on." – Carl R. Rogers

The Art of Listening in a Healing Way by James E. Miller

Communication Skills for Teens: How to Listen, Express & Connect for Success by Michelle Skeen, Ph.D., Matthew McKay, Ph.D., Patrick Fanning and Kelly Skeen

How to Talk So Kids Will Listen and Listen So Kids Will Talk by Adele Faber & Elaine Mazlish

Listen by Holly M. McGhee, Illustrated by Pascal Lemaitre (pb)

The Listening Path: The Creative Art of Attention by Julia Cameron

The Rabbit Listened by Cori Doerrfeld (pb)

"Tell Me More" essay in *Strength to Your Sword Arm: Selected Writings* by Brenda Ueland

Massage, Reiki & Comforting Touch

"Touch comes before sight, before speech. It is the first language, and the last, and it always tells the truth." – Margaret Atwood

Comfort Touch: Massage for the Elderly and the Ill by Mary Kathleen Rose

A Healer's Journey to Intuitive Knowing: The Heart of Therapeutic Touch by Delores Krieger

The Healing Power of Reiki by Raven Keyes

The Little Book of Baby Massage by Jo Kellett

The Massage Book by George Downing

The Modern Book of Massage: Five Minute Vacations and Sensuous Escapes by Anne Kent Rush (focuses on self-massage)

Reiki Healing for Beginners: The Practical Guide with Remedies for 100+ Ailments by Karen Frazier

Meaning-Making

"The question, O me! so sad, recurring—What good amid these, O me, O life?/ Answer./That you are here—that life exists, and identity;/That the powerful play goes on, and you will contribute a verse." – Walt Whitman

The Beauty of What Remains by Steve Leder

Giving Grief Meaning by Lily Dulan

More Beautiful Than Before: How Suffering Transforms Us by Steve Leder

When Bad Things Happen to Good People by Howard S. Kushner

Memoir & Autobiography

"I think many people need, even require, a narrative version of their life. I seem to be one of them. Writing memoir is, in some ways, a work of wholeness." – Sue Monk Kidd

Alone: A Love Story by Michelle Parise

Beautiful Boy: A Father's Journey Through His Son's Addiction by David Sheff

Being Heumann: An Unrepentant Memoir of a Disability Rights Activist by Judith Heumann

Black Indian by Shonda Buchanan

The Boy in the Moon: A Father's Journey to Understand His Extraordinary Son by Ian Brown

Comfort by Ann Hood

Dear Life: A Doctor's Story of Love and Loss by Rachel Clarke

The Diary of a Young Girl by Anne Frank

The Diving Bell and the Butterfly: A Memoir of Life in Death by Jean-Dominique Bauby

The End of Your Life Book Club by Will Schwalbe

Grief Diaries: Surviving Loss by Overdose by Lynda Cheldelin Fell, et. al.

Disability Visibility: First Person Stories from the Twenty-First Century, edited by Alice Wong

Don't Call Me Crazy: 33 Voices Start the Conversation About Mental Health, edited by Kelly Jensen

Expecting Sunshine: A Journey of Grief, Healing, and Pregnancy After Loss by A. M. Chute

H is for Hawk by Helen Macdonald

How to Lose Everything by Christa Couture

I Know Why the Caged Bird Sings by Maya Angelou

If I am Missing or Dead: A Sister's Story of Love, Murder, and Liberation by Jeanine Latus

Invisible Sister by Jessica Handler

Little Matches: A Memoir of Grief and Light by Maryanne O'Hara

Living With No Excuses: The Remarkable Rebirth of an American Soldier by Noah Galloway

The Long Goodbye by Meghan O'Rourke

Look Me in the Eye: My Life with Asperger's by John Elder Robison

May Cause Love: An Unexpected Journey of Enlightenment After Abortion by K. Underwood

Morrie: In His Own Words by Morrie Schwartz

No Time Like the Future: An Optimist Considers Mortality by Michael J. Fox

Notes on Grief by Chimamanda Ngozi Adichie

On My Own Two Feet: From Losing My Legs to Learning the Dance of Life by Amy Purdy

Once More We Saw Stars: A Memoir by Jason Greene

One Child: The True Story of a Tormented Six-Year-Old and the Tormented Teacher Who Reached Out by Torey Hayden

The Other Wes Moore: One Name, Two Fates and *Discovering Wes Moore* by Wes Moore

The Reason I Jump: The Inner Voice of a Thirteen-Year-Old Boy with Autism by Naoki Higashida

The Sad Book by Michael Rosen

Smoke Gets in Your Eyes: And Other Lessons from the Crematory by Caitlin Doughty

Ten Thousand Joys, Ten Thousand Sorrows: A Couple's Journey Through Alzheimer's by Olivia Ames Hoblitzelle

Tuesdays With Morrie: An Old Man, a Young Man, and Life's Greatest Lesson by Mitch Albom

The Wheel of Life: A Memoir of Living and Dying by Elizabeth Kübler-Ross

When Breath Becomes Air by Paul Kalanithi

White Hot Grief Parade by Alexandra Silber

Memorials & Remembrance (also see Metaphors, Objects & Symbols)

"Silently, one by one, in the infinite meadows of heaven,/Blossomed the lovely stars, the forget-me-nots of the angels." — Henry Wadsworth Longfellow

A Day for Rememberin' by Leah Henderson, Illustrated by Floyd Cooper

"Forever After: Helping Children Reconnect with Loved Ones Who Die" by Shea Darian, *Lilipoh Magazine* (online PDF of article available at DoingGrief.com)

The Last Lecture by Randy Pausch

Nadia, The Willful by Sue Alexander, Illustrated by Lloyd Bloom (pb)

The Tenth Good Thing About Barney by Judith Viorst and Erik Blegvad (pb)

The Wall by Eve Bunting, Illustrated by Ronald Himler (pb)

Metaphors, Objects & Symbols (also see Memorials & Remembrance)

"Metaphors have a way of holding the most truth in the least space."
— Orson Scott Card

America's White Table by Margot Theis Raven, Illustrated by Mike Benny

The Hundred Penny Box by Sharon Bell Mathis, Illustrated by Leo and Diane Dillon (pb)

Hope for the Flowers by Trina Paulus (pb)

The Memory Box: A Book About Grief by Joanna Rowland, Illustrated by Thea Baker (pb)

The Memory String by Eve Bunting, Illustrated by Ted Rand (pb)

Spirits of the Earth: A Guide to Native American Nature Symbols, Stories, and Ceremonies by Bobbie Lake-Thom

Wilfrid Gordon McDonald Partridge by Mem Fox, Illustrated by Julie Vivas (pb)

Mindfulness & Meditation (also see Breathing & Relaxation)

"I have lived with several Zen masters – all of them cats."– Eckhart Tolle

10% Happier: How I Tamed the Voice in My Head, Reduced Stress Without Losing My Edge, and Found Self-Help That Actually Works–A True Story by Dan Harris

50 (and 50 More) Ways to Soothe Yourself Without Food: Mindfulness Strategies to Cope With Stress and End Emotional Eating by Susan Albers

A Handful of Quiet: Happiness in Four Pebbles by Thich Nhat Hahn (pb)

Bearing the Unbearable: Love, Loss & the Heartbreaking Path of Grief by Joanne Cacciatore

Buddha's Brain: The Practical Neuroscience of Happiness, Love and Wisdom by Rick Hanson and Richard Mendius

Dancing With Elephants: Mindfulness Training for Those Living With Dementia, Chronic Illness or an Aging Brain Disease by Jarem Sawatsky

Daydreamers by Tom Feelings, Illustrated by Eloise Greenfield (pb)

Guided Meditations, Explorations and Healings by Stephen Levine

I Am Peace: A Book of Mindfulness by Susan Verde (pb)

I Am Yoga by Susan Verde (pb)

The Language of Letting Go: Daily Meditations for Codependents by Melodie Beattie

Lovingkindness: The Revolutionary Art of Happiness by Sharon Salzberg

Mindfulness and Grief: With Guided Meditations to Calm Your Mind and Restore Your Spirit by Heather Stang

"My Stroke of Insight" (Ted Talk – Ted.com) *by Jill Bolte Taylor*

The Tao of Daily Life by Derek Lin

Movement, Yoga & Posture (also see Dance)

"I move, therefore I am." – Haruki Murakami

Body Learning: An Introduction to the Alexander Technique by Michael J. Gelb

I Am Yoga by Susan Verde (pb)

Tai Chi for Beginners and the 24 Forms by Paul Lam

True to Form: How to Use Foundation Training for Sustained Pain Relief and Everyday Fitness by Eric Goodman

The Way of Qi Gong: The Art & Science of Chinese Energy Healing by Kenneth S. Cohen

Yoga for Grief Relief by Antonio Sausys

Yoga for Warriors: Basic Training in Strength, Resilience, and Peace of Mind by B. B. Birch

Music & Sound Therapy

"Without music, life would be a mistake." — Friedrich Nietzsche

Finding Your Voice: A Practical and Spiritual Approach to Singing and Living by Carolyn Sloan

I Got the Rhythm by Connie Schofield Morrison, Illustrated by Frank Morrison (pb)

Music Medicine: The Science and Spirit of Healing Yourself with Sound by Christine Stevens

Rise Up Singing: A Group Singing Songbook: Words, Chords & Sources to 1200 Songs, edited by Peter Blood and Annie Patterson

The Tao of Music: Sound Psychology: Using Music to Change Your Life by John M. Ortiz

Natural Remedies for Pain Relief

(also see Integrative Medicine and Massage, Reiki & Comforting Touch)

"Healing severe or chronic pain, I believe, includes transforming our relationship to the pain, and, ultimately, it is about transforming our relationship to who we are and to life."— **Sarah Anne Shockley**

Life After Pain: 6 Keys to Break Free of Chronic Pain and Get Your Life Back by Jonathan Kuttner and Naomi Kuttner

The Pain Companion: Everyday Wisdom for Living With and Moving Beyond Chronic Pain by Sarah Anne Shockley

Reversing Chronic Pain: A 10-Point All-Natural Plan for Lasting Relief by Maggie Phillips

Trauma Releasing Exercises (TRE): A revolutionary new method for stress/trauma recovery by David Berceli

True to Form: How to Use Foundation Training for Sustained Pain Relief and Everyday Fitness by Eric Goodman

Yoga Therapy as a Creative Response to Pain by Matthew J. Taylor

Nature

"And into the forest I go to lose my mind and find my soul." — John Muir

Bird Therapy by Joe Harkness

Born to Be Wild: Hundreds of Free Nature Activities for Families by Hattie Garlick

Earthways: Simple Environmental Activities for Young Children by Carol Petrash

Finding Sanctuary in Nature: Simple Ceremonies in the Native American Tradition for Healing Yourself and Others by Jim PathFinder Ewing

Healing with Nature: Mindfulness and Somatic Practices to Heal from Trauma by Rochelle Calvert

I Am Phoenix: Poems for Two Voices by Paul Fleischman, Illustrated by Ken Nut

Into the Woods: Families Making Art in Nature by Sue Fiersten

Joyful Noise: Poems for Two Voices by Paul Fleischman, Illustrated by Eric Beddows

Last Child in the Woods: Saving Our Children From Nature-Deficit Disorder by Richard Louv

Sharing Nature with Children by Joseph Cornell

The Nature of Nature: Why We Need the Wild by Enric Sala

To Speak for the Trees: My Life's Journey from Ancient Celtic Wisdom to a Healing Vision of the Forest by Diana Beresford-Kroeger

Wild Comfort: The Solace of Nature by Kathleen Dean Moore

Parenting Mindfully (also see Abuse Awareness; Trauma Recovery)

**"Being a parent is one of the greatest mindfulness practices of all."
– Jon Kabat-Zinn**

The 100 Practical Ideas Series by Alan D. Wolfelt (including *Healing Your Grieving Heart for Teens, Healing Your Grieving Heart for Kids, Healing a Parent's Grieving Heart, Healing a Grandparent's Grieving Heart, Healing Your Grieving Heart After Stillbirth,* etc.)

Adolescent Mental Health Initiative "A Firsthand Account" series, see "Memoir" listing

Bereaved Children and Teens: A Support Guide for Parents & Professionals, edited by Earl A. Grollman

Between Form and Freedom: Being a Teenager by Betty Staley

A Better Man: A (Mostly Serious) Letter to My Son by Michael Ian Black

The Connected Child: Bring Hope and Healing to Your Adoptive Family by Karyn B. Purvis

Grandparents as Parents: A Survival Guide for Raising a Second Family (2nd Edition) by Sylvie de Toledo and Deborah Edler Brown

Grandparents Raising Grandchildren: Expanding Your View: A Guidebook for the Kinship Caregiver by Linda L. Dannison and Andrea B. Smith (booklet/workbook)

How to Help Children Through a Parent's Serious Illness by Kathleen McCue

Living Passages for the Whole Family: Celebrating Rites of Passage from Birth to Adulthood by Shea Darian

Natural Family Living by Peggy O'Mara

Raising Good Humans: A Mindful Guide to Breaking the Cycle of Reactive Parenting and Raising Kind, Compassionate Kids by Hunter Clarke Fields and Carla Naumburg

Sanctuaries of Childhood: Nurturing a Child's Spiritual Life by Shea Darian

Seven Times the Sun: Guiding Your Child Through the Rhythms of the Day by Shea Darian

Simplicity Parenting: Using the Extraordinary Power of Less to Raise Calmer, Happier, and More Secure Kids by Kim John Payne

Raising Cane: Protecting the Emotional Life of Boys by Dan Kindlon and Michael Thompson

Reviving Ophelia: Saving the Selves of Adolescent Girls by Mary Pipher

The Shelter of Each Other: Rebuilding Our Families by Mary Pipher

Trauma-Proofing Your Kids: A Parent's Guide for Instilling Confidence, Joy & Resilience by Peter Levine and Maggie Kline

Pets & Animals

**"Until one has loved an animal, a part of one's soul remains unawakened."
— Anatole France**

Bird Therapy by Joe Harkness

Faraway Horses: The Adventures and Wisdom of America's Most Renowned Horseman by Buck Brannaman and Bill Reynolds

How Animals Grieve by Barbara J. King

I Am Phoenix: Poems for Two Voices by Paul Fleischman, Illustrated by Ken Nut

Losing My Best Friend: Thoughtful support for those affected by dog bereavement or pet loss by Jeannie Wycherley

Lucky Dog: How Being a Veterinarian Saved My Life by Sarah Boston

Making Rounds With Oscar: The Extraordinary Gift of an Ordinary Cat by David Dosa

My Gentle Barn: Creating a Sanctuary Where Animals Heal and Children Learn to Hope by Ellie Laks

The Tenth Good Thing About Barney by Judith Viorst, Illustrated by Erik Blegved

Oh, Theodore! Guinea Pig Poems by Susan Katz, Illustrated by Stacey Schuett

Walking with Petey: The Dog Who Saved My Life by Eric O'Grey

When a Pet Dies by Fred Rogers (pb)

Whole-Pet Healing: A Heart-to-Heart Guide to Connecting and Caring for Your Animal by Dennis W. Thomas

Pilgrimages, Labyrinths & Hiking Treks

**"Faith is not the clinging to a shrine but an endless pilgrimage of the heart."
— Abraham Joshua Heschel**

The Alchemist (autobiographical fiction) by Paulo Coelho

Eat, Pray, Love: One Woman's Search for Everything Across Italy, India and Indonesia by Elizabeth Gilber

Exploring the Labyrinth: A Guide for Healing and Spiritual Growth by Melissa Gayle West

Hiking Through: One Man's Journey to Peace and Freedom on the Appalachian Trail by Paul Stutzman

The Sacred Path Companion: A Guide to Walking the Labyrinth to Heal and Transform by Lauren Artress

Tracks: A Woman's Solo Hike Across 1700 Miles of Australian Outback by Robyn Davidson

Wild: A Journey from Lost to Found by Cheryl Strayed

Play, Fun & Games

**"Play keeps us vital and alive. Without it, life just doesn't taste good."
— Lucia Capocchione**

Best New Games by Dale LeFevre (cooperative and trust-building games)

Cat's Cradle, Owl's Eyes: A Book of String Games by Camilla Griske

Free to Learn: Why Unleashing the Instinct to Play Will Make Our Children Happier,

More Self-Reliant, and Better Students for Life by Peter Gray

Games of Survival: Traditional Inuit Games for Elementary School Children by Johnny Issaluk

Hopscotch, Hangman, Hot Potato & Ha Ha Ha: A Rulebook of Children's Games by Jack McGuire

Play: How it Shapes the Brain, Opens the Imagination, and Invigorates the Soul by Steward Brown and Christopher Vaughan

Step it Down: Games, Plays, Songs, and Stories from the Afro-American Heritage by Bess Lomax Hawes and Bessie Jones

Toymaking with Children by Freya Jaffke

Poetry

"We love the things we love for what they are." — Robert Frost

The Art of Longing: Selected Poems by Robert Neimeyer

The Art of Losing: Poems of Grief & Healing, edited by Kevin Young

Book of a Thousand Poems: A Family Treasury (children's poetry anthology)

The Complete Nonsense of Edward Lear by Edward Lear (pb)

The Dreamkeeper and Other Poems by Langston Hughes (pb)

for colored girls who have considered suicide/ when the rainbow was enuf (a choreopoem) by Ntozake Shange

The Hill We Climb: An Inaugural Poem for the Country by Amanda Gorman

Hip-Hop Speaks to Children: A Celebration of Poetry with a Beat by Nikki Giovanni (pb)

Joyful Noise: Poems for Two Voices by Paul Fleischman, Illustrated by Eric Beddows

Laughing Tomatoes: And Other Spring Poems / Jitomates Risuenos: Y Otros Poemas de Primavera by Francisco X. Alarcon, illustrated by Maya Christina Gonzalez (pb)

A Maze Me: Poems for Girls by Naomi Shihab Nye

Mourning Songs: Poems of Sorrow and Beauty, edited by Grace Schulman

Out of the Dust by Karen Hesse

Poetic Medicine: The Healing Art of Poem-Making by John Fox

Poetry Speaks: Hear Great Poets Read Their Work from Tennyson to Plath, edited by Elise Paschen and Rebekah Presson Mosby

Poetry Speaks to Children, edited by Elise Paschen and Dominique Raccah

Poetry Speaks Who I Am: poems of discovery, inspiration, independence, and everything else . . . , edited by Elise Paschen and Dominique Raccah

This is Just to Say: Poems of Apology & Forgiveness by Joyce Sidman (pb)

Under the Influence: A Journey of Abuse, Trauma, and Grief Through Poetry by Jacqueline Lee

Where the Sidewalk Ends and *A Light in the Attic* by Shel Silverstein (pb)

Prayer

> "I think it pisses God off if you walk by the color purple in a field somewhere and don't notice it. People think pleasing God is all God cares about. But any fool living in the world can see it always trying to please us back."
> — Alice Walker (Shug from *The Color Purple*)

50 Ways to Pray: Practices from Many Traditions and Times by Theresa Blythe

Earth Prayers From Around the World and *Life Prayers from Around the World* by Elizabeth Toberts and Elias Amidon

The Interfaith Prayer Book: New Expanded Edition by Ted Brownstein

Learn to Pray: A Practical Guide to Faith & Inspiration by Marcus Braybrooke

A Praying Congregation: The Art of Teaching Spiritual Practice by Jane E. Vennard

Sleeping With Bread: Holding What Gives You Life by D. Linn, S. F. Linn and M. Linn (pb)

Repairing Broken Relationships (also see Listening)

"The bravest journeys are never taken alone." – unknown

A Baptist Preacher's Buddhist Teacher: How My Interfaith Journey with Daisaku Ikeda Made Me a Better Christian by Lawrence Edward Carter, Sr.

Conscious Uncoupling: Five Steps to Living Happily Even After – How to Break Up in a Whole New Way by Katherine Woodward Thomas

Discovering Your Personality Type: The Essential Introduction to the Enneagram, Revised and Expanded by Don Richard Riso and Russ Hudson

Done With the Crying: Help and Healing for Mothers of Estranged Adult Children by Sheri McGregor, MA

The Four Things That Matter Most: A Book About Living by Ira Byock, MD

Healing the Empty-Nesters Grieving Heart: 100 Practical Ideas for Parents After the Kids Move Out, Go Off to College, or Start Taking Flight by Alan D. Wolfelt

The Racial Healing Handbook: Practical Activities to Help You Challenge Privilege, Confront Systemic Racism, and Engage in Collective Healing by Anneliese A. Singh

The Rest of the Way: Healing Barriers Between Gays, Lesbians, and Their Parents by Enid Duchin Jackowitz

Sanctuary & Sacred Space (also see Nature)

**" There are many ways to hold sanctuary. May I be one of them."
– Sheniz Janmohamed**

Creating Sanctuary: Daily Practices to Achieve Happiness and Well-Being by Jessi Bloom

The Keeping Quilt by Patricia Polacco (pb)

My Gentle Barn: Creating a Sanctuary Where Animals Heal and Children Learn to Hope by Ellie Laks

Finding Sanctuary in Nature: Simple Ceremonies in the Native American Tradition for Healing Yourself and Others by Jim PathFinder Ewing

Sanctuaries of Childhood: Nurturing a Child's Spiritual Life by Shea Darian

Spark Joy: An Illustrated Master Class on the Art of Organizing & Tidying Up by Marie Kondo

Self-Injury Recovery

"The scars you can't see are the ones that hurt the most." – Michelle Hodkin

A Bright Red Scream: Self-Mutilation and the Language of Pain by Marilee Strong

The Dialectical Behavior Therapy Skills Workbook: Practical DBT Exercises for Learning Mindfulness, Interpersonal Effectiveness, Emotion Regulation & Distress Tolerance by Matthew McCay, Jeffrey C. Wood and Jeffrey Brantley

Freedom from Self-Harm: Overcoming Self-Injury With Skills from DBT (Dialectical Behavioral Therapy) *and Other Treatments* by Kim Gratz & Alexander Chapman

The Mindfulness Workbook for Teen Self-Harm by Gina M. Biegel and Stacie Cooper

Self-harm Recovery Journal (by Self-Love Recovery Designs)

Stopping the Pain: A Workbook for Teens Who Cut & Self-Injure by Lawrence E. Shapiro

Sexual Healing & Intimacy

"Sexuality is one of the ways that we become enlightened, actually, because it leads us to self-knowledge." – Alice Walker

Beyond Betrayal: Taking Charge of Your Life after Boyhood Sexual Abuse by Phil Waldrep

Boys & Sex: Young Men on Hookups, Love, Porn, Consent, and Navigating the New Masculinity by Peggy Orenstein

Come As You Are: Revised and Updated: The Surprising New Science That Will Transform Your Sex Life by Emily Nagoski

Girls & Sex: Navigating the Complicated New Landscape by Peggy Orenstein

Life, Reinvented: A Guide to Healing from Sexual Trauma for Survivors and Loved Ones by Erin Carpenter

Out of the Shadows: Understanding Sexual Addiction by Patrick Carnes

The Pleasure Plan: One Woman's Search for Sexual Healing by Laura Zam

Sex Without Stress: A couple's guide to overcoming disappointment, avoidance & pressure by Jessa Zimmerman

Sexual Intimacy for Women: A Guide for Same-Sex Couples by Glenda Corwin

The Sexually Healing Journey: A Guide for Survivors of Sexual Abuse by Wendy Maltz

Your Brain on Porn: Internet Pornography and the Emerging Science of Addiction by Gary Wilson

Sleeping (also see Dreaming & Visitations)

"The best bridge between despair and hope is a good night's sleep. – E. Joseph Cossman

Definitive Guide to Sleep Disorders: 7 Smart Ways to Help You Get a Good Night's Rest by Herbert Ross

Dr. Seuss' Sleep Book by Dr. Seuss (pb)

Goodnight Moon by Margaret Wise Brown, Illustrated by Clement Hurd

Grandfather Twilight by Barbara Helen Berger (pb)

Sleep Rituals: 100 Rituals for a Deep and Peaceful Sleep by Jennifer Williamson

Sleeping With Bread: Holding What Gives You Life by D. Linn, S. F. Linn and M. Linn (pb)

Sweetest Kulu: A Bedtime Poem by Celina Kalluk, Illustrated by Alexandria Neonakis (pb)

Why We Sleep: Unlocking the Power of Sleep and Dreams by Matthew Walker

Stories & Storytelling (also see Memoir, Poetry, Writing)

"Stories have to be told or they die, and when they die, we can't remember who we are or why we're here." – Sue Monk Kidd

How to Tell Stories to Children by Joseph Sarosy and Silke Rose West

Kitchen Table Wisdom: Stories That Heal by Rachel Naomi Remen

Stricken: The 5000 Stages of Grief (essay anthology), edited by Spike Gillespie and Katherine Tanney

Storytelling with Children by Nancy Mellon

Therapeutic Storytelling: 101 Healing Stories for Children by Susan Perrow

Suicide Prevention & Survivor Support

"Rough week, right? Listen, every book in your home is one of us saying to you, please hold on until the end. We want you to stay with us so we can all see, together, how it all turns out. You're not alone. One of us is with you all the time. Hold on tight. See you next week." — Warren Ellis

Depression and Your Child: A Guide for Parents and Caregivers by Deborah Serani

The Dialectical Behavior Therapy Skills Workbook: Practical DBT Exercises for Learning Mindfulness, Interpersonal Effectiveness, Emotion Regulation & Distress Tolerance by Matthew McCay, Jeffrey C. Wood and Jeffrey Brantley

Dying to Be Free: A Healing Guide for Families After a Suicide by Beverly Cobain and Jean Larch

How I Stayed Alive When My Brain Was Trying to Kill Me: One Person's Guide to Suicide Prevention by Susan Rose Blauner

Life After Suicide: Finding Comfort & Community After Unthinkable Loss by Jennifer Ashton

No Time to Say Goodbye: Surviving the Suicide of a Loved One by Carla Fine

The Suicidal Thoughts Workbook: CBT Skills to Reduce Emotional Pain, Increase Hope & Prevent Suicide by Kathyrn Hope Gordon

The Suicide Index: Putting My Father's Death in Order by Joan Wickersham

Talking Cures (also see Listening)

"There is no greater agony than bearing an untold story within you." – Maya Angelou

Communication Skills for Teens: How to Listen, Express & Connect for Success by Michelle Skeen, Matthew McKay, Patrick Fanning and Kelly Skeen

The Dance of Connection: How to Talk to Someone When You're Mad, Hurt, Scared, Frustrated, Insulted, Betrayed, or Desperate by Harriet Lerner

How Your Story Sets You Free by Heather Box and Julian Mocine-McQueen

Therapy 101: A Brief Look at Modern Psychotherapy Techniques & How They Can Help by Jeffrey C. Wood and Minnie Wood

We Need to Talk About Grief: How to Be A Friend to the One Who's Left Behind by Annie Broadbent

Theater & Speech

"We all come to the theatre with baggage. The baggage of our daily lives, the baggage of our problems, the baggage of our tragedies, the baggage of being tired . . . But if our hearts get opened and released – well that is what theatre can do."
– Vanessa Redgrave

101 Drama Games & Activities: Theater Games for Children and Adults by David Farmer

Amazing Grace by Mary Hoffman, Illustrated by Caroline Binch (pb)

How Your Story Sets You Free by Heather Box and Julian Mocine-McQueen

Theater Games for the Classroom: A Teacher's Handbook by Viola Spolin

Trauma Recovery

"There is no timestamp on trauma. There isn't a formula that you can insert yourself into to get from horror to healed. Be patient. Take up space. Let your journey be the balm." — Dawn Serra

The Body Keeps the Score: Brain, Mind, and Body in the Healing of Trauma by Bessel van der Kolk

Childhood Disrupted: How Your Biography Becomes Your Biology and What You Can Do About It by Donna Jackson Nakazawa

Healing Trauma: A Pioneering Program for Restoring the Wisdom of the Body by Peter Levine

Healing with Nature: Mindfulness and Somatic Practices to Heal from Trauma by Rochelle Calvert

The Journey from Abandonment to Healing by Susan Anderson

The PTSD Breakthrough: The Revolutionary Science-Based Compass RESET Program by Frank Lawlis

The Sexually Healing Journey: A Guide for Survivor's of Sexual Abuse by Wendy Maltz

Strong at the Broken Places: Overcoming the Trauma of Child Abuse by Linda Sanford

Surviving Domestic Violence: A Guide to Healing Your Soul and Building Your Future (for women) by Danielle F. Wozniak and Karen Allen

Trauma Stewardship: An Everyday Guide to Caring for Self While Caring for Others by Laura van Dernoot Lipsky and Connie Burk

Trauma Through a Child's Eyes: Awakening the Ordinary Miracle of Healing by Peter Levine

Waking the Tiger: Healing Trauma by Peter Levine

What Happened to You? Conversations on Trauma, Resilience, and Healing by Bruce D. Perry and Oprah Winfrey

Wonder

"(They) who can no longer pause to wonder and stand rapt in awe, is as good as dead; (their) eyes are closed." – Albert Einstein

Wonder: The Art and Practice of Beatrice Blue by Beatrice Blue

Wonder: From Emotion to Spirituality by Robert C. Fuller

Writing

"I can shake off everything as I write: My sorrows disappear, courage is reborn." – **Anne Frank**

The Artist's Way and The Artist's Way Workbook by Julia Cameron

Braving the Fire: A Guide to Writing About Grief & Loss by Jessica Handler

Grief's Courageous Journey: A Workbook by Sandi Caplan and Gordon Lang

Guiding Autobiography Groups for Older Adults: Exploring the Fabric of Life by James E. Birren and Donna E. Deutchman

Homemade Books to Help Kids Cope by Robert G. Ziegler

The Memory Book: A Grief Journal for Children and Families by Joanna Rowland, Illustrated by Thea Baker

Mourning & Mitzvah: A Guided Journal for Walking the Mourner's Path Through Grief to Healing by Anne Brener

The Rewarding Practice of Journal Writing by James E. Miller (willowgreen.com)

The Thorn Necklace: Healing Through Writing and the Creative Process by Francesca Lia Block

Tiny Buddha's Gratitude Journal: Questions, Prompts, and Coloring Pages for a Brighter, Happier Life by Lori Deschene

Writing Down the Bones: Freeing the Writer Within by Natalie Goldberg

Writing as a Way of Healing: How Telling Our Stories Transforms Our Lives by Louise Desalvo

Writing to Heal the Soul: Transforming Grief & Loss Through Writing by Susan Zimmerman

Healing Through Novels & Picture Books

Here are a few possibilities for exploring the healing properties of fiction. Themes and minimum age suggestions for read-alouds or independent reading are included in parentheses.

Abiyoyo by Pete Seeger, Illustrations by Michael Hays (4 and up; overcoming rejection and fear; healing through storytelling, dance, and song)

The Adventures of Pinocchio by Carlo Collodi, Illustrated by Greg Hildebrandt (6 and up; growth through pain, karmic consequences, peer pressure vs. respect for elder advice, laziness vs. work ethic, unconditional love, family, loyalty, honesty)

Are You My Mother? by P.D. Eastman (3 and up; parent-child separation and reunion)

The Art of Racing in the Rain by Garth Stein (14 and up; love, family, illness, death, destiny, spiritual growth)

The Beginner's Goodbye by Anne Tyler (adult; death, grief, healing, growth, hope)

Belle Prater's Boy by Ruth White (12 and up; abandonment, poverty, suicide, friendship, family, belonging)

Big Cat, Little Cat by Elisha Cooper (3 and up; cycle of life; death, loss)

The Book Thief by Markus Zusak (13 and up; literacy and power, death, anti-Semitism, love and hate, courage, hope)

Bridge to Terabithia by Katherine Paterson (10 and up; friendship, death, individuality and conformity, fantasy and escapism, gender roles, appearances vs. reality)

The Butter Battle Book by Dr. Seuss (5 and up; power and competition, futility of war, respecting differences)

Caleb and Kit by Beth Varbel (8 and up; friendship, coping with disability/cystic fibrosis, coming of age, making hard choices, pains of growing up and growing apart)

The Cellist of Sarajevo by Steven Galloway (adult; denigration of the arts, healing power of music, division of ethnic groups, impact of civil war, hope)

Charlotte's Web by E.B. White (6 and up; friendship, sacrifice, death, love)

The Country Bunny and the Little Gold Shoes by Du Bose Heyward, Illustrated by Marjorie Hack (4 and up; bullying, gender expectations, value of "mother" role, overcoming sexism and racism, kindness, value of hard work)

The Day My Daddy Lost His Temper by Carol Santana McCleary (5 and up; witnessing domestic violence, validating experiences and feelings related to domestic violence)

Daydreamers by Tom Feelings, Illustrated by Eloise Greenfield (3 and up; solace of daydreaming; poetry and portrayals of Black children wishing, yearning, and remembering)

The Dogs of Babel by Carolyn Parkhurst (adult; love, depression, mysterious death, suicidal ideation, grief)

Each Kindness by Jacqueline Woodson, Illustrated by E.B. Lewis (5 and up; ostracism, virtue, friendship, determination, missed opportunities, kindness)

Every Time You Go Away: A Novel by Beth Harbison (adult; spouse's death, visitation of the deceased, grief, friendship, reconciliation, healing)

The Fault in Our Stars by John Green (14 and up; living and dying with cancer, family, isolation, young love, religious beliefs and death, courage, identity, existential questioning, mortality, coming of age)

Follow the Drinking Gourd by Jeanette Winter (5 and up; compassion, courage, faith, breaking the bonds of slavery, solidarity, determination)

Frederick by Leo Lionni (3 and up; mindfulness, kindness, individuality, seeking nourishment through art, valuing the artist)

The Funeral by Matt James (3 and up; death, funerals, family, celebration, remembrance)

Genesis Begins Again by Alicia D. Williams (9 and up; colorism, bullying, verbal abuse, consequences of addiction, self-discovery, self-compassion)

Grandpa's Garden by Shea Darian, Illustrated by Karlyn Holman (4 and up; illness, hospitalization of a grandparent, gardening, grandparent-grandchild bond)

Grandpa's Stories by Joseph Coelho, Illustrated by Allison Colpoys (4 and up; grandparent-grandchild bond, grandparent's death, transcendent relationship with deceased, longing, remembrance)

Gwinna by Barbara Helen Berger (6 and up; coming of age, self-discovery, quest, independence, freedom, perseverance, destiny)

Harry Potter series (varies, 8-14 and up; coming of age, friendship, being orphaned, death, confronting fears, love, good overcoming evil, magic, prejudice, fate, acceptance/tolerance)

Holding up the Universe by Jennifer Niven (13 and up; bullying, obesity, face blindness/prosopagnosia, parent's illness, parent's death, grief, love, being seen for who you are)

Holes by Louis Sachar (10 and up; ancestry, multi-generational conflict, fate, friendship, cruelty, survival, integrity, prevailing justice, new beginnings)

Hope for the Flowers by Trina Paulus (life, death, love, revolution, rebirth, hope)

The Hundred Penny Box by Sharon Bell Mathis, Illustrated by Leo and Diane Dillon (6 and up; old age, richness of life, death, music, remembrance, memory loss, personal and family history, love, joy)

I Know Why the Caged Bird Sings by Maya Angelou (14 and up; race, gender influence, prejudice, inequality, segregation, identity, abandonment, rape, murder, grief, healing, family ties, healing refuge of literature, church as a place of sanctuary and punishment)

The Invisible String by Patrice Karst (4 and up; separation anxiety, loss, grief, love, connectedness, kinship, support, reassurance)

Julie of the Wolves by Jean Craighead George (12 and up; abandonment, fear, isolation, survival, self-reliance, traditional wisdom, human-animal connections, quest for family)

The Kindness of Strangers by Katrina Kittle (adult; widowhood, single parenting, child sexual abuse, fear, fury, family loyalty, appearances, compassion, advocacy)

The Knitting Circle by Ann Hood (adult; death of a child, grief, kindness, the healing power of knitting and female companionship)

The Knee-Baby by Mary Jarrell, Illustrated by Symeon Shimin (4 and up; the displacement of an elder sibling when a new baby arrives in the family, love, belonging, acceptance)

Knots on a Counting Rope by Bill Martin, Jr. and John Archambault, Illustrated by Ted Rand (5 and up; blindness, fear, courage, belonging, grandparent-grandchild bond that transcends death, love, family, community, healing through storytelling and ritual)

Last Stop on Market Street by Matt de la Pena, Illustrated by Christian Robinson (3 and up; intergenerational friendship, community, beauty, helping others)

The Lottery Rose by Irene Hunt (12 and up; child abuse, gardening, growth, giving and receiving love)

The Little Engine That Could, retold by Watty Piper, Illustrated by George and Doris Hauman (3 and up; self-belief when times are tough, persistence, overcoming challenges)

The Legend of the Bluebonnet, Illustrated and retold by Tomie DePaola (4 and up; hunger, famine, drought, courage, hope, loyalty, sacrifice, community, helping others)

A Lesson Before Dying by Ernest Gaines (14 and up; education and racism, religious cynicism, hope and strength to overcome suffering, heroism and sacrifice, abandonment, roots, family, community, service, morality, injustice, facing responsibility, redemption in death)

The Light Jar by Lisa Thompson (9 and up; abandonment, domestic abuse, fear, hope, loneliness, friendship, finding the light within)

The Lion, the Witch and the Wardrobe (Narnia series) by C. S. Lewis (7 and up; betrayal, forgiveness, good vs. evil, courage, transformation, the natural world, magic, hope)

The Little Lame* Prince and His Traveling Cloak by Dinah Mulock Craik, Illustrated by Hope Dunlap (age 4 and up; accidental injury, paralysis, imagination, empathy, morality, helplessness, isolation, loneliness, courage, adventure, freedom, independence, coming of age, wise and just leadership – **note: "lame" is not considered to be a respectful word choice by those who are physically disabled; however, this 1875 story is an inspiring tale of a prince who would not be defined by his disability; as a read-aloud, consider deleting or changing this word as you read*)

The Little Match Girl by Hans Christian Anderson, Illustrated by Rachel Isadora (6 and up; poverty, struggle, loneliness, hope, resilience, longing, death)

The Lorax by Dr. Seuss (4 and up; environmental responsibility, ambition, compassion, the beauty of nature)

Love You Forever by Robert Munsch (3 and up; parent-child bond, life cycle, death, nurturing a child and nurturing an aging parent, eternal love, gender roles)

Louisiana's Way Home by Kate DiCamillo (10 and up; abandonment, poverty, home and family, friendship, forgiveness, hope, redemption)

Looking for Alaska by John Greene (14 and up; coming of age, peer pressure, independence, identity, suicide, grief, guilt, meaning of life, mystery of the unknown, loyalty, forgiveness)

The Lucky Stone by Lucille Clifton (6 and up; storytelling, ritual, family history, slavery, freedom, longing, survival, good fortune, wishful thinking)

Maniac McGee by Jerry Spinelli (8 and up; homelessness, family, racism, friendship, the importance of literacy and education, community, courage, heroism, human dignity)

The Memory String by Eve Bunting, Illustrated by Ted Rand (4 and up; ritual, loss, death, grief, transitions, adapting to change, stepparent-child relationship, remembrance)

Miss Rumphius by Barbara Cooney (5 and up; travel, good deeds, leaving the world a better place, generosity, philanthropy, life cycle)

A Monster Calls by Patrick Ness, from an original idea by Siobhan Dowd, Illustrated by Jim Kay (9 and up; parent's terminal illness, fear, courage, grandparent-grandchild relationship, aloneness, reconciling the suffering and relief of death, acceptance, healing)

Mossflower and the *Redwall* fantasy saga by Brian Jacques (8 and up; oppression, good vs. evil, cruelty, courage, compassion, war and peace)

The Moves Make the Man by Bruce Brooks (13 and up; racism, school integration, domestic violence, basketball, parent's mental illness, friendship, loss, grief)

The Music of Dolphins by Karen Hesse (ages 9 and up; what it means to be human, listening, communication, animal-human connection, capture, language acquisition, call of the wild)

Nadia, the Willful by Sue Alexander, Illustrated by Lloyd Bloom (6 and up; death of a sibling/child, suppression of grief, therapeutic talking, remembrance, healing)

The Ocean at the End of the Lane by Neil Gaiman (14 and up; self-identity, child vs. adult perspective, memory, perception, fear, bravery, friendship, death, suicide, healing power of stories)

Old Turtle by Douglas Wood, Illustrated by Cheng-Khee Chee (3 and up; differing perceptions of God, conflict, peace, reconciliation, interconnectedness of all beings)

On the Day You Were Born by Debra Frasier (all ages; birth, welcoming, celebration, family, unity of creation, belonging)

On the Night You Were Born by Nancy Tillman (all ages; unconditional love, wonder, welcoming, celebration, family, unity of creation, belonging)

One Crazy Summer by Rita Williams-Garcia (9 and up; civil rights, injustice, Black pride, racial prejudice, the power of names)

One Wave at a Time by Holly Thompson (5 and up; parent's death, waves of grief, sadness, anger, fear, guilt, numbness, healing, friendship)

The Other Side by Jacqueline Woodson, Illustrations by E.B. Lewis (5 and up; tolerance, race relations communication, friendship, open-mindedness)

Our Only May Amelia by Jennifer L. Hohm (12 and up; coming of age, death, grief, independence, strained father-daughter relationship, gender expectations, identity, abusive grandmother, illness and recovery, family belonging)

Out of the Dust by Karen Hesse (11 and up; the great depression, poverty, loss, death, injury, blame, guilt, forgiveness, love of family, the environment, power of the human spirit to overcome adversity, persistence, return of joy)

Peter Pan by J.M. Barrie (8 and up; courage, love, family, belonging, remembrance, imagination, adventure, belief, difficulties of growing up and leaving childhood behind, good triumphing over evil, coming of age, adult responsibility)

Plainsong by Kent Haruf (adult; loss of innocence, endurance of hardship and cruelty, kindness, small town life – the good and the bad, loneliness, isolation, family, belonging, redemption)

The Rabbit Listened by Cori Doerrfeld (3 and up; listening and its affect on others, sadness, talking about feelings, what helps you feel better when you're sad)

The Rainbabies by Laura Kraus Melmed, Illustrated by Jim LaMarche (4 and up; loss, parent-child bond, love, protection, infertility, adoption, overcoming trials, magic and the supernatural)

Rapunzel, retold by Barbara Rogasky, Illustrated by Trina Schart Hyman (child loss, cruelty, imprisonment, abandonment, jealousy, love, courage, freedom, facing evil and finding beauty in the world, taking responsibility for our actions, the healing power of tears)

Roxaboxen by Alice McLerran, Illustrated by Barbara Cooney (5 and up; childhood, community, peace, imagination, self-expression, creativity, working together)

Saint George and the Dragon, retold by Margaret Hodges, Illustrated by Trina Schart Hyman (5 and up; fear, bravery, perseverance, good triumphing over evil, peace)

The Secret Life of Bees by Sue Monk Kidd (14 and up; guilt, death, abandonment, forgiveness, coming of age, racism, female power, mother-child relationship, appearance vs. reality)

Squirm by Carl Hiaasen (10 and up; power of family, trusting yourself, protecting the environment, divorce, abandonment, adventure, stepfamily relationships, geographic mobility, coming of age, growth)

Stargirl by Jerry Spinelli (12 and up; conformity, individuality, rejection, shunning, self-confidence, belonging, kindness, friendship, love, social pressure, thinking for oneself)

Stone Soup, retold by John Warren Stewig, Illustrated by Marot Tomes (4 and up; hunger, stinginess, giving and receiving, creativity, collaboration, cooperation, community, sharing)

The Story of Jumping Mouse: A Native American Legend by John Steptoe (5 and up; overcoming hardship, compassion, courage, dreams, determination, hope)

Tatterhood and the Hobgoblins by Lauren Mills (5 and up; fear, overcoming adversity, love, equality, gender expectations, individuality, independence, protection, bravery, leadership)

The Things They Carried by Tim O'Brien (adult; Vietnam war, adversity, grief, fear, loss, longing, identity, vulnerability, cruelty, futility of war, guilt, shame, love, self-forgiveness, subjective truth vs. storytelling, power of friendship, integrity, killing, death, remembrance)

The Tenth Good Thing About Barney by Judith Viorst, Illustrated by Erik Blegvad (5 and up; pet loss, grief, funeral, memorializing, remembrance)

The Velveteen Rabbit by Margery Williams (4 and up; becoming your real self, love is hard work and worth the effort, change, illness, loss, grief, inner strength, ongoing connections)

The Underneath by Kathi Appelt (10 and up; love, loss, grief, death, betrayal, animal cruelty, wonder of nature, mystery, magic, friendship, danger, protection, regret, loneliness, listening to wisdom in nature, reunion, redemption)

Walk Two Moons by Sharon Creech (10 and up; grief, loss, disappearance of a loved one, abandonment, death, self-identity, guilt, hope, denial, acceptance, forgiveness, love, family, new beginnings, independence, coming of age, emotional freedom, empathy)

Water for Elephants by Sarah Gruen (15 and up; death, grief, poverty, mental illness, violence, animal cruelty, animal-human connection, belonging, love, compassion, courage, freedom and confinement, suffering, gender roles, old age, fortitude, redemption, fulfillment)

We Were Liars by E. Lockhart (14 and up; grief, death, family, romantic love, wealth, greed, bigotry, lies, memory, family secrets, guilt, consequences)

The Wheel on the School by Meindert DeJong (8 and up; loss, longing, wonder, animal care, purpose, persistence, overcoming obstacles, community, cooperation, friendship, kinship with the natural world and its creatures)

When Sadness Is at Your Door by Eva Eland (3 and up; exploring sadness, being and doing with your sadness, mindfulness, emotional literacy)

Wilfrid Gordon McDonald Partridge by Mem Fox, Illustrated by Julie Vivas (3 and up; intergenerational friendship, helping others, memory loss, sharing memories, compassion, service, difficulties and joys of old age)

Winnie the Pooh by E.H. Shepard (5 and up; lasting friendships, individual differences, overcoming obstacles, loss, empathy, compassion, honesty, learning life lessons, supporting and being supported by others, mindful conversation)

Wonder by R.J. Palacio (8 and up; appearances, living with a facial deformity, kindness, friendship, identity, bullying, rejection, acceptance, being a sibling of someone with a physical deformity, family, belonging)

Healing Through Movies & Documentaries

As you choose films to enjoy, take note of the grieving and healing responses and outcomes of the film's characters or subjects to glean healing wisdom for yourself. The films suggested here include genre, age guide/rating, and major themes. Some children may be uncomfortable or frightened by animation, loud noises, or even mild violence. Films marketed to children often contain adult content that is difficult for a child to comprehend. Choose wisely.

127 Hours: 2010 drama; R – survival, loss, grief, love, overcoming adversity, injury

500 Days of Summer: 2009 romantic comedy-drama; PG-13 – belief in love, loss of a breakup

And Still I Rise: 2016 documentary/biography; NR – the life & influence of Maya Angelou

Anne of Green Gables: 1985 family drama; 6 and up – aloneness, loss, love, belonging

Asperger's R Us: 2016 documentary & 2019 *On Tour With Asperger's R Us* TV series; 12 and up – living with Asperger Syndrome, friendship, family, theater, creativity, coming of age

The Assistant: 2019 drama; R – workplace harassment, sexism, abuse of power

Babe: 1995 family comedy-drama fantasy; 6 and up; purpose in life, family, loss, love

Bambi: 1942 animated drama; 5 and up – birth, death, rebirth, love, friendship, coming of age

Beautiful Boy: 2018 drama; R – addiction, responsibility, blame, relapse, recovery, hope

Being Mortal: 2014 PBS Frontline documentary; NR – mortality, talking with the dying about death

Blindsight: 2006 documentary; NR – six teenagers who are blind climb to a 23,000 foot summit

Boy Erased: 2018 drama; R – sexuality, masculinity, patriarchy, conversion therapy, suicide

Buck: 2011 documentary; 8 and up – biography of the life and work of horse whisperer, Buck Brannaman, animal-human connection, emotional wounds, child abuse, healing

Cast Away: 2000 survival drama; PG-13 – adversity, perseverance, isolation, new beginnings

Cinderella Man: 2000 drama; PG-13 – poverty, love, loss, family, adversity, perseverance

Coco: 2017 animated fantasy drama; 8 and up – death, land of the dead, family, music, legacy

Departures: 2008 Japanese drama; PG-13 – adversity, death, funerals, caring for the dead

Extremely Loud and Incredibly Close: 2011 drama; PG-13 – 9-11 attacks on U.S., death of a parent, grief of a person with Asperger syndrome and autism, parent-child bond

Extremis: 2016 documentary; PG – doctors, patients, and families make difficult end-of-life decisions in a hospital ICU

Fed Up: 2014 documentary; 10 and up – childhood obesity, nutrition, public health policy

Field of Dreams: 1989 comedy-drama; 12 and up – adversity, remembrance, belief, baseball

Finding Nemo: 2003 animated adventure; 4-6 and up – loss, memory, courage, perseverance

Flash of Genius: 2008 drama; PG-13 – invention, corporate greed, perseverance, family neglect

Flight from Death: 2003 documentary; NR – explores relationship of human violence and death anxiety as a possible root cause

Freedom Writers: 2007 drama; PG-13 – prejudice, tolerance, self-worth, overcoming hardship

Fried Green Tomatoes: 1991 comedy-drama; PG-13 – domestic abuse, death, adversity, love

Ghost: 1990 romantic fantasy thriller; PG-13 – death, love, eternal connections, revenge

The Great Debaters: 2007 drama; PG-13 – racism, injustice, self-respect, dignity, courage

Green Book: 2018 comedy-drama; PG-13 – racism, friendship, class, masculinity, music

The Green Mile: 1999 drama fantasy; R – death, murder, compassion, sacrifice, healing

Griefwalker: 2008 documentary; NR – palliative care/hospice work of Stephen Jenkinson

Harriet: 2019 action/drama; PG-13 – slavery, brutality, gendered work of abolition, heroic courage, tensions between Blacks born slave vs. free, spirituality, love, family

The Help: 2011 drama; PG-13 – racial injustice, servitude, loss, grief, gender, class, hypocrisy, caregiver-child bond

The Horse Whisperer: 1998 drama; PG-13 – injury, death, healing, animal-human connection

How to Make an American Quilt: 1995 romance/drama – love, marriage, gender roles, infidelity

The Hurt Locker: 2008 war/action; R – war addiction, rage, recklessness, fear, death, honor

I Am Not Your Negro: 2016 documentary; PG-13 – life and influence of writer James Baldwin

In and Out: 1999 comedy/romance; PG-13 – masculinity, coming out, belonging, acceptance

Inside Out: 2015 animated comedy; 7 and up; mindful emotions, loss, grief, true happiness

Infinitely Polar Bear: 2014 drama; R – manic depression, parent with mental illness, family

The Intouchables: 2011 French comedy/drama; R – paraplegia, class, friendship, respect

Is Anybody There?: 2008 drama; PG-13 – loneliness, old age, coming of age, death, friendship

Joy Luck Club: 1993 drama; R – Asian-American immigration/assimilation, sexism, racism

The King's Speech: 2010 drama; R – overcoming speech impediment/adversity, duty, class, family, warfare, friendship, social/political responsibilities and expectations serving as royalty

Kramer vs. Kramer: 1979 drama; 10 and up – abandonment, divorce, grief, gender roles

Lars and the Real Girl: 2007 romantic drama; PG-13 – love, death, loneliness, belonging

Little Miss Sunshine: 2006 drama/comedy; R – death, family, defining beauty and success

Lorenzo's Oil: 1992 drama; PG-13 – child illness, death, researching cure, perseverance

Marley & Me: 2008 romantic comedy; 7 and up – unconditional love, marriage, pet death

Marriage Story: 2019 drama ; R – dissolving a marriage, love, pain, honoring, remembrance

Mask: 1985 drama; PG-13 – facial deformity, family, friendship, courage, hope, judging others

Men of Honor: 2000 drama; R – military service, racial injustice, courage, determination

Meet Joe Black: 1998 romance/fantasy; PG-13 – accidental death, meaning of life, mortality

Milk: 2008 drama; R – the life and influence of Harvey Milk, a gay activist and politician

Minari: 2020 drama; PG-13 – adversity, illness, faith, work, displacement, survival, resilience

The Miracle Worker: 1962 drama; 9 and up – early life of Helen Keller, blindness, deafness, language acquisition, courage, perception/prejudice of those with physical disabilities

Mrs. Doubtfire: 1993 comedy; PG-13 – divorce hardships on family, loneliness, grief, healing

My Dog Skip: 2000 drama; 9 and up – friendship, loyalty, bravery, bullying, belonging, death

My Flesh & Blood: 2003 documentary; NR – Susan Tom and her 11 special needs children

My Girl: 1991 drama; 12 and up – life, death, funerals, love, family, grief, acceptance

The New World: 2005 drama; PG-13 – retelling of Pocohantas' story, duty, betrayal, love

Old Yeller: 1957 western drama; 12 and up – dog-child bond, masculinity and emotion, fear, courage, loyalty, protection, provision, coming of age, responsibility, death, killing

Open Heart: 2013 documentary; NR – eight Rwandan children seek high-risk heart surgery

Paradise Road: 1997 drama; R – barbarity of war, healing power of music, unity, courage

Peanut Butter Falcon: 2019 adventure/comedy; PG-13 – adversity, family, living with Down syndrome, prejudice, friendship, dreams, coming of age, institutionalization, freedom

The Pieces I Am: 2019 documentary; PG-13 – life and influence of author/editor Toni Morrison

Proof: 2005 drama/mystery; PG-13 – mathematics, genius, mental illness, gender bias, sibling rivalry, caregiving for parent, love, life, death, loss, trust

Precious: 2009 drama; R – childhood sexual abuse and neglect, obesity, race, self-acceptance

The Pursuit of Happiness: 2006 drama; PG-13 – homelessness, survival, determination

Quartet: 2012 comedy-drama; PG-13 – old age, mending broken relationships, music, belonging

Rainman: 1988 drama; R – Savant syndrome, money, guilt/blame, family conflict, meaning

Reason for Hope: 1999 documentary; NR – work and influence of conservationist Jane Goodall

Rent: 2005 musical; PG-13 – value of life, addiction, AIDS, homophobia, poverty, friendship

The Sandlot: 1993 comedy-drama; 8 and up – loss, coming of age, belonging, baseball

Saving Private Ryan: 1998 war/action; R – sacrifice, patriotism, self-doubt, morality, suffering

Seabiscuit: 2003 drama; PG-13 – poverty/wealth, adversity, child death, horseracing, injury

The Sessions: 2012 drama – sex, love, living with severe physical disabilities, God, meaning

Simon Birch: 1998 comedy-drama; 10 and up – belonging, death, destiny, hypocrisy, faith

The Sixth Sense: 1999 Thriller; PG-13 – life, death, supernatural, fear, trauma, empathy

Sound & Fury & *Sound & Fury Six Years Later:* 2000/2011 documentaries; NR – deaf identity, deaf parents conflicted over provided deaf child with a cochlear implant

Smoke Signals: 1998 drama; PG-13; death, grief, stereotypes, forgiveness, community

Stand and Deliver: 1988 drama; 12 and up – inequality, peer pressure, determination, hope

Stand by Me: 1986 drama; R – coming of age, death, abuse, family dysfunction, friendship

Steel Magnolias: 1989 comedy-drama; 12 and up –illness, death, resilience, love, friendship

Stepmom: 1998 drama; PG-13 – stepparent relationship, terminal illness, grief, love, family

Temple Grandin: 2010 drama; 12 and up – autism, rejection, savant skills, courage, empathy

Terms of Endearment: 1983 comedy-drama; 13 and up – broken relationships, death, love

Three Burials of Melquiades Estrada: 2005 western drama; R – death, justice, friendship

Tumbleweed: 1999 drama; PG-13 – mother-daughter bond, domestic abuse, coming of age

Under Our Skin & *Under Our Skin 2:* 2008 /2014; NR – Lyme disease as an emerging epidemic

Up: 2009 animated adventure; 7 and up – old age, grief, life after loss, friendship, love, journey

Whale Rider: 2002 Drama; PG-13 – death, abandonment, tradition, sexism, nature, destiny, environmental degradation, community, coming of age, identity, overcoming adversity

What's Cooking?: 2000 comedy-drama; PG-13 – love, resolving family conflicts and expectations, Thanksgiving, ethnic traditions, unity in diversity, intergenerational relationships

What's Eating Gilbert Grape: 1993, drama: PG-13 – family responsibility, search for freedom, Down syndrome, obesity, love, courage, breaking from tradition

Wizard of Oz: 1939 musical adventure; 8 and up – home, belonging, journey, love, dreams, power, self-belief, good vs. evil, fear, courage, friendship, contentment, gratitude

Healing Through Community Connections

Here are a few ideas for making healing connections in your local community and beyond. Beyond these suggestions, explore what in-person and online resources are available to you and your loved ones, given your unique needs for healing. *These listings are provided for convenience and do not constitute an endorsement of any products, services, or opinions.*

Healing Through Sports & Exercise

Challenged Athletes: Provides programs and equipment to athletes with physical challenges who don't have access to adaptive sports. ChallengedAthletes.org

National Senior Games Association: Individual/team sports for those 50 & up. NSGA.com

Special Olympics: Global movement to provide inclusive sports programs and events for those of all differences and abilities. SpecialOlympics.org

Surfing Programs for Vets: JimmyMillerFoundation.org (at-risk youth) • OperationSurf.org • SurfAction.co.uk (families) • WarriorSurf.org; • WavesofImpact.com

Healing Through the Arts

Threshold Choir: Singing for those at the thresholds of death & birth. ThresholdChoir.org

The Healing Power of Arts & Artists: Community of artists and advocates raising awareness about art as a catalyst for healing. Healing-Power-of-Art.org

Healing Through Nature

Wilderness Programs for Children & Youth: BigCityMountaineers.org (mountaineering) • GenerationWild.com (education and parent support) • OutdoorOutreach.org (hiking, biking, kayaking, climbing) • OutwardBound.org • TheWahineProject.org (surfing)

Wilderness Programs for Vets: • NoBarriers.USA.org (backcountry expeditions) • ProjectHealingWaters.org (fly fishing) • Veterans.Expeditions.com (backpacking, mountaineering, rock climbing, whitewater rafting, mountain biking, golfing)

Healing Through Education & Support Groups

Trauma Survivors Network: traumasurvivorsnetwork.org (peer support groups/resources)

Death Loss: Dougy.org (Dougy Center – excellent online directory to locate grief support groups in your area) • MISSFoundation.org (traumatic loss/child death/care provider education) • HealGrief.com (for young adults) • CompassionateFriends.org (child/sibling death) • FirstCandle.org (miscarriage/infant death) • SoaringSpirits.org (spouse death) • SurvivorsAfterSuicide.org • Anticruelty.org (pet death)

Illness, Special Needs & Caregiving: CancerCare.org • DifferentDream.com (parents of children with special needs & disabilities) • Nancys-House.org (caregivers of children with special needs) • SacredArtofLiving.org (caregivers for the dying) • Willowgreen.com (all caregivers) • CaregiversAction.org (all caregivers)

Healing Through Therapeutic Counseling & Spiritual Direction

Good Therapy: Directory of individual, group, and family counselors listed by specialties. Helpful blog posts and explanations of various types/modes of therapy. GoodTherapy.org

Spiritual Directors International: Directory of spiritual directors by location and specialties. sdiCompanions.org

Index

Artistic Activities
  collaging 88, 89
  creating a grieving map 44–45
  creating a healing map 111
  creating a personal book of meaning 240–242
  creating your grieving hotspot symbols 46–47
  drawing 44, 89
    creating a mural 88
  resources
    art and creativity 319
    community connections
      healing through the arts 350
Cinematherapy 48–49
  A Cinematic Exploration 48–49
  resources 322
    healing through movies and documentaries 347
Companionship Needs
  of the grieving adult 246–248
  of the grieving child 134-141
  of the grieving elder 305–311
  of the grieving infant 108–109
  of the grieving youth 173–185
Crying 99–100, 119, 136
  control patterns 100
  resources 323
Death and Dying
  and relatedness pain 201-204
  and spiritual pain, 196
  child's view of death 127–130
  dying a good death 62–63
    resources 325
  embracing the reality of death 298–304, 313
  pet death 300–301
    resources for pets and animals 335
  resources for death and dying
    community connections
      healing through education and support groups 350
    death care 324
    funeral planning and memorial services 326
    suicide prevention and survivor support 339
Emotional Safe Havens 174–185, 187
  caring relationships 177–178
  clear rules 180–182
  curative spaces & activities 178–179
  healthy daily habits 182–185
  the arts 179–180
Emotions and Healing 166–167, 261–282
  anger 265–268

fear, worry, and pessimism 277–282
happiness 261
in youthhood 166–167
loneliness 268–271
remorse, guilt, and shame 271-277
  remorse 221
resources for emotional healing and expressing feelings 325
sadness and melancholy 262-265
Family Contemplations and Activities 48-49, 87–89
  Creating the Big Picture of Your Family Grieving Dynamics 88
  Grieving Alone and In the Company of Others 89
  "The Language of Grieving: A Cinematic Exploration 48–49
Folktales, Myths, and Fables
  "A hundred grievers walk into a room" 52
  A Mother, the Buddha & Some Mustard Seed 23–24
  Farmer and His Donkey 94
  Harvesting Elder Wisdom 254
  Little Bird 33
  Narcissus and Echo 150–151
  Scylla and Charybdis 12
  Why Angry People Shout 266
Forgiveness 142, 208–222, 267-268
  resources 326
Grandparenting 291–295
  resources
    for parenting mindfully 334
Grief
  and self-awareness 22, 92
  body, heart, mind, and spirit 9, 28–30
    emotional life 29
    physical body 28-29
      benefits of exercise 289–291
    spiritual relationships 29-30
    thinking habits or patterns 29
  defining grief 19–21
  denial of 68-69
  empathic grief 57–58
  intergenerational trauma 57
  physicality of childhood grief 116–123
  physicalizing grief 143
  relationship with grieving 32–33
  sources of 14–16, 24–26
    in childhood 120
  unidentified 27
Grieving
  authentic grieving 38–39
  checklist of grieving responses 77–83
    heartening 79–80
    integrating 80–81
    lamenting 78–79
    tempering 82

four types of grieving responses 42
   balance among four dynamics 54
grieving hotspots 46-47
nonverbal expressions of grief in childhood 120–122
relationship with grief 32–33
resources for grieving
   grieving and healing perspectives 327
   with loved ones 50, 73–76, 87–89
   infant-caregiver bond 108–109
Guided Visualizations
   imagining your pain away 313
   of hope and healing 84–86
Habit-Building 182-185, 258
   Kaizen way 247-248, 258
   resources 328
Healer Within, The 94–95
Heartening 42, 60–63
   defined 42
   in childhood 124–126
   in elderhood 283–288
   in infancy 101–103
   in youthhood 157–160
   modes of 60–61, 79–80, 103, 125–126
Hope 84–86, 223–232, 283–288
   resources 328
Integrating 42, 64–67
   defined 42
   in childhood 131–133
   in elderhood 296–304
   in infancy 106–107
   in youthhood 166–172
   modes of 80–81, 171
Lamenting 42, 55–59
   defined 42
   in childhood 119–123
   in elderhood 261–282
   in infancy 99–100
   in youthhood 150–156
   modes of 58, 78–79
Loss and Losses
   hidden losses during youthhood 169
   impact of grief-related change 64-67
   of childhood 114–115
   of innocence 115–116
   perceptions of loss in childhood 120, 128-133
   types of loss 15–16, 24–26
Meaning-Making 233–245
   and the reality of death 302–304
   resources 330
Memorials and Remembrance 201–207
   altar-building in memory of a loved one 133, 264
   resources 331, 326
      funeral planning and memorial services 326
      memorials and remembrance 331

Model of Adaptive Grieving Dynamics 40–43
Parent-Child Interaction Therapy 102
Play 125–126, 141–142
   resources
      play, fun, and games 335-336
Poems, Meditations, and Blessings
   "All shall be well.." (Julian of Norwich) 84
   Going In (Shea Darian) 237–238
   Have Me With You (Shea Darian) 303–304
   "I share with you the agony of your grief . . . " (Howard Thurman) 311
   "Let us never/Grow too comfortable . . . " (Shea Darian) 16
   resources
      poetry 336
Post-traumatic Growth 158
Quarterlife Crisis 192
Reactive Attachment Disorder 102
Self-injury 170
   resources
      self-injury recovery 338
Sleep 138, 291
   resources 338-339
Smiling 187
Spiritual Pain 22, 196–199
   and spiritual strengths 197–199
   types of 196
      forgiveness pain 196, 208–222
      hopelessness pain 196, 223–232
      meaning pain 196, 233–245
      relatedness pain 196, 200–207
        and death 201–204
Stories and Storytelling
   adoption story 111
   elders imparting remembrances to the young 312
   resources 339
   separation anxiety in childhood 124–125
Talking Cures 140
   resources 339
      community connections
         healing through therapeutic counseling and spiritual direction 350
Tempering 42, 68–72, 82
   defined 42
   in childhood 69, 127–130
   in elderhood 289–295
   in infancy 104–105
   in youthhood 161–165
   modes of 69–70, 82, 130
   selective 70–72
Writing
   free-form writing activity 27
   memoir writing 312
   resources 341

Works Cited

(alphabetized by author or title of film)

Alexander, Sue. *Nadia the Willful*. Illustrated by Lloyd Bloom, Pantheon Books, 1983.

Allen, Thomas B. *Offerings at the Wall*. Turner Publishing, 1995.

And Still I Rise. Directed by Rita Coburn Whack and Bob Hercules, Netflix, 2016.

Angelou, Maya. *On the Pulse of Morning*: The Inaugural Poem. Random House, 1993.

Aristotle. *Art of Rhetoric*. Translated by John Henry Freese. Harvard University Press, 1967.

Austen, Jane. *Emma*. Penguin Classics, 2003.

Becker, Ernest. *The Denial of Death*. The Free Press, 1973.

Birren, James E., and Linda Feldman. *Where to Go from Here: Discovering Your Own Life's Wisdom in the Second Half of Your Life*. Simon & Schuster, 1997.

Blake, William. *William Blake's Songs of Innocence and of Experience*. Tate Publishing, 2007.

Bond, Ruskin. *Scenes from A Writer's Life*. Penguin Random House, 2000.

Braque, George. *Illustrated Notebooks 1917-1955*. Dover Publications, 1971.

Breznican, Anthony. "Remembering Mister Rogers, a true-life 'helper' when the world still needs one." www.ew.com/tv/2017/05/23/remembering-mr-rogers/

Brown, Kelly Williams. *Adulting: How to Become a Grown-up in 468 Easy(ish) Steps*. Grand Central Publishing, 2018.

Buck, Directed by Cindy Meehl. IFC Films, 2011.

Buechner, Frederick. *Wishful Thinking: A Theological ABC*. Harper & Row, 1973.

Campbell, Joseph. *The Power of Myth*. Anchor, 1991.

Card, Orson Scott. *Speaker for the Dead*. Tor: 1994.

Cather, Willa. *O Pioneers*. Virago, 1999.

Chabon, Michael. *Manhood for Amateurs: The Pleasures and Regrets a Husband, Father and Son*. Harper Collins Publishing, 2009.

Chodron, Pema. *The Pocket Pema Chodron*. Shambhala, 2008.

Clear, James. *Atomic Habits: Tiny Changes, Remarkable Results: An Easy & Proven Way to Build Good Habits & Break Bad Ones*. Avery, 2018.

Cohen, David. "Temple Grandin: 'I'm An Anthropologist from Mars." The Guardian, www.theguardian.com/education/2005/oct/25/highereducationprofile.academicexperts.

Darian, Shea. "Forever After: Helping Children Reconnect with Loved Ones Who Die." Lilipoh, Spring 2012, pp. 49-52.

Darian, Shea. Seven Times the Sun. Gilead Press, 1999.

Darian, Shea. Sanctuaries of Childhood. Gilead Press, 2011.

David, Hal. "What the World Needs Now is Love," performed by Jackie DeShannon, Imperial Records, 1965.

Dawson, George, and Richard Glaubman. *Life Is so Good*, 2013.

Demolition. Directed by Jean-Marc Vallée, Fox Searchlight Pictures, 2016.

Duhigg, Charles. *The Power of Habit*. Random House, 2014.

Edgeworth, Maria. *Popular Tales*. C. Mercier and Co., 1804.

Eisenberg, N., R. A. Fabes, and I. K. Guthrie, "Coping with stress: The roles of regulation and development." *Handbook of Children's Coping: Linking Theory and Intervention*, edited by S. A. Wolchik and I. N. Sandler, Plenum Press, 1997, pp. 41–70.

Elders Leading Resilience. Directed by Mathan Ratinam, A short documentary film supported by Global Facility for Disaster Reduction and Recovery. https://ibasho.org/blog/20150510-1461

Elkind, David. *The Hurried Child*. Perseus Publishing, 2001.

Emerson, Ralph. W. *Journals of Ralph Waldo Emerson, 1820-1872*, (1911) Volume 5. Kessinger Publishing, 2010.

Fed Up. Directed by Stephanie Soechtig, Atlas Films, 2014.

Fowler, Therese Anne. *Souvenir*. Ballantine Books, 2008.

Frankl, Viktor E. *Man's Search for Meaning*, Beacon Press, 2006.

Freedom Writers. Directed by Richard LaGravenese, Paramount Pictures, 2007.

Fried Green Tomatoes. Directed by Jon Avnet, Universal Pictures, 1991.

Frost, Robert. "Choose Something Like a Star." *Collected Poems, Prose & Plays*. The Library of America, 1995.

Gandhi. Directed by Richard Attenborough, Columbia Pictures, 1982.

Gillespie, Spike and Katherine Tanney. *Stricken: The 5,000 Stages of Grief*. Dalton Publishing, 2009.

Goldman, Connie. *The Ageless Spirit*. Fairview Press, 2004.

Goodwin, Doris Kearns. *Team of Rivals: The Political Genius of Abraham Lincoln*. Simon & Schuster, 2006.

Grandin, Temple and Margaret M. Scariano. *Emergence: Labeled Autistic*. Warner Books, 1996.

Green, John. *Looking for Alaska*. Penguin, 2006.

The Green Mile. Directed by Frank Darabont, Warner Bros., 1999.

Griefwalker. Directed by Tim Wilson, National Film Board of Canada, 2008.

Groves, Richard F. and Henriette Anne Klauser. *The American Book of Living and Dying*. Celestial Arts, 2005.

Gruwell, Erin and The Freedom Writers. *The Freedom Writers Diary: How a Teacher and 150 Teens Used Writing to Change Themselves and the World Around Them*. Broadway Books, 2009.

Gwyn, Nell. *The Quotable Woman, from Eve to 1799*. Edited by Elaine Partnow, Facts on File Publications, 1985.

Heschel, Abraham Joshua. *Moral Grandeur and Spiritual Audacity: Essays*. Introduction by Susannah Herschel, Farrar, Straus & Giroux, 1996.

Hesse, Eva. *Eva Hesse: Diaries*. Edited by Tamara Bloomberg and Barry Rosen. Hauser & Wirth Publishers, 2020.

Hirsch, Edward. "Coming out into the Light: W. B. Yeats's 'The Celtic Twilight' (1893, 1902)." *Journal of the Folklore Institute*, vol. 18, no. 1, 1981, pp. 1-22. www.jstor.org/stable/3814184

Holloway, Karla FC. "A Name for a Parent Whose Child has Died." *Duke Today*, 26 May 2019 in Opinion.

Honig, A.S. "What Are the Needs of Infants?" *Young Children*, vol. 37, no. 1, November 1981, pp. 3-10.

Hood, Ann. *Comfort: A Journey Though Grief*. W.W. Norton & Co., 2008.

Horney, K. *The Neurotic Personality of Our Time*. W. W. Norton & Co., 1937.

Howard, Pierce J. *The Owner's Manual for the Brain: Everyday Applications from Mind-Brain Research*. Bard Press, 2006.

Hugo, Victor. *William Shakespeare*. HardPress Publishing, 2011.

Indridason, A. *Voices*. Translated by B. Scudder, Harvill Secker, 2006.

Jacoby, Susan. *Never Say Die: The Myth and Marketing of the New Old Age*. Pantheon Books, 2011.

Jane Goodall: Reason for Hope. Directed by Emily Goldberg, PBS special produced by KTCA, 1999.

Julian of Norwich. 'All Shall Be Well:' *Revelations of Divine Love*. 1670 AD.

Karen, R. *Becoming Attached: First Relationships and How They Shape Our Capacity to Love*. Oxford University Press, 1998.

Kettlewell, Caroline. *Skin Game: A Memoir*. St. Martin's Griffin, 2000.

Kiyota, Emi, et.al. "Elders Leading the Way to Resilience." Global Facility for Disaster Reduction and Recovery, 2015. www.ssrn.com/abstract=2575382 or http://dx.doi.org/10.2139/ssrn.2575382

Kramer vs. Kramer. Directed by Robert Benton, Columbia Pictures, 1979.

Kübler-Ross, Elizabeth and David Kessler. *On Grief and Grieving*. Scribner, 2005.

Kübler-Ross, Elizabeth. *On Death and Dying*. The Macmillan Company, 1969.

Lewis, C. S. *A Grief Observed*. Faber & Faber, 1968.

Lewis, C. S. *Mere Christianity*. Macmillan, 1960.

Life is Beautiful. Directed by Robert Benigni, Miramax Films, 1997.

Liston, D., and Garrison J. "Grief as a Gateway to Love in Teaching." *Teaching, Learning, and Loving*, Routledge, 2003.

Martin, Bill and John Archambault. *Knots on a Counting Rope*. Illustrated by Ted Rand. Square Fish / Henry Holt & Co., 2012.

Maurer, Robert. *One Small Step Can Change Your Life: The Kaizen Way*. Workman Publishing, 2004.

Miller, A. and Ward, R. N. *The Drama of the Gifted Child: The Search for the True Self*. Basic Books, 1997.

Morrison, Keith. "Coming Home." https://www.nbcnews.com/id/wbna24818399. May 25, 2008, 2:51 PM MST.

Ness, P. *A Monster Calls*. Walker Books, 2015.

Niebuhr, Reinhold. "Serenity Prayer." Diary entry, 1932.

Nin, Anaïs. *The Diary of Anaïs Nin, 1944-47*. Harcourt, Brace, Jovanovich, 1971.

Norem, J. K. "The Right Tool for the Right Job." *The Positive Power of Negative Thinking*, Basic Books, 2001.

Ogan, Eddie. Mikey's Funnies (limited archive): "The Rich Family In Church." www.mikeysfunnies.com/archive/richFamily/index.html

Oliver, Mary. "To Begin With, the Sweet Grass." *Devotions: The Selected Poems of Mary Oliver*. Penguin Press, 2017.

Oliver, Mary. "Wild Geese." *Wild Geese: Selected Poems*. Bloodaxe World Poets, 2004.

Parrott, W. G. *The Positive Side of Negative Emotions*. The Guilford Press. 2014.

Pausch, Randy. *The Last Lecture*. Hyperion, 2008.

Perry, B.D, and Szalavitz.M. *The Boy Who Was Raised As a Dog: And Other Stories from a Child Psychiatrist's Notebook: What Traumatized Children Can Teach Us About Loss, Love, and Healing*. Basic Books, 2008.

The Phone of the Wind: Whispers to Lost Families. Directed by Ryo Urabe and Tomohiko Yokoyama, NHK, 2017.

Pogrebin, Letty Cottin. *Stories for Free Children*. McGraw-Hill, 1982.

The Power to Live and Forgive: Interview with Eva Mozes Kor. Buzz Feed Video, 2017.

Ritchie, G. C. & Sherrill, E. *Return from Tomorrow*. Fleming H. Revell, 1978.

Robbins, Alexandra & Wilner, Abby, *Quarterlife Crisis: The Unique Challenges of Life in Your Twenties*. Tarcher-Perigee, 2001.

Robert Brault, *Short Thoughts for The Long Haul*. CreateSpace, 2017.

Ross, H. *Steel Magnolias*. Dramatists Play Service, 1987.

Sarton, M. *Mrs. Stevens Hears the Mermaids Singing*. W.W. Norton & Co., 1975.

Schopenhauer, A. *The Essays of Arthur Schopenhauer: Counsels and Maxims*. Translated by T. Bailey Saunders, Book Jungle, 2009.

Scioli, Anthony, and Henry B. Biller. *Hope in the Age of Anxiety*. Oxford University Press, 2009.

Sendak, M. *Where the Wild Things Are*. HarperCollins, 2013.

Shange, Ntozake. *for colored girls who have considered suicide when the rainbow is enuf*. Scribner, 1975.

Silverstein, S. *The Missing Piece*. Harper & Row, 2006.

Silverstein, S. *The Missing Piece Meets the Big O*. HarperCollins, 1981.

Smith, Tiffany Watt. *The Book of Human Emotions: An Encyclopedia of Feeling to Anger to Wanderlust*. Profile Books, 2015.

Solter, A. J. *Helping Young Children Flourish*. Shining Star Press, 1989.

Spitz, R.A. and K.M. Wolf. *Grief: A Peril in Infancy: a film*. The Research Project, 1947. resource.nlm.nih.gov/9505470

Stahl, Lesley. *Becoming Grandma: The Joys and Science of the New Grandparenting*. Blue Rider Press, 2017.

Styron, William. *Darkness Visible: A Memoir of Madness*. Random House, 1990.

Swannell S.V., et.al. "Prevalence of nonsuicidal self-injury in nonclinical samples: systematic review, meta-analysis and meta-regression." *Suicide Life Threat Behav*. 2014 Jun;44(3):273-303. doi: 10.1111/sltb.12070.

Tapscott, Stephen. *100 Love Sonnets. Cien sonetos de amor*. University of Texas Press, 1986.

Tedeschi, R. G., and L. G. Calhoun. (2004). Target Article: "Posttraumatic Growth: Conceptual Foundations and Empirical Evidence". *Psychological Inquiry*, 15(1), 1–18. doi.org/10.1207/s15327965pli1501_01.

Thompson, Hunter S. *The Proud Highway: Saga of a Desperate Southern Gentleman, 1955-1967*. Ballantine Books, 1998.

Thurman, Howard. *Meditations of the Heart*. Beacon Press, 1953, 1981. " A Time for Sorrow" (pp.211-212). Used by permission of The Thurman Estate.

Tolkien, J.R.R. *The Fellowship of the Ring*. Houghton Mifflin Company, 1994.

Tolle, Eckhart. *The Power of Now*. Hodder Paperback, 2001.

Tolstoy, Leo. *Anna Karenina*. Translated by David Magarshack, New American Library, 1961.

Trevarthen, Colwyn. "The Self (of the infant) is looking for the vital will and imagination..." See more on Colwyn Trevarthen at www.pmarc.ed.ac.uk/people/colwyntrevarthen.html

Twain, Mark. *Which Was the Dream? and Other Symbolic Writings of the Later Years*. Edited by John S. Tuckey, University of California Press, 1967.

Ueland, Brenda. *Strength to Your Sword Arm: Selected Writings*. Holy Cow! Press, 1993.

Valente, Catherynne M. *The Girl Who Fell Beneath Fairyland and Led the Revels There*. Square Fish, 2013.

van Gelder, Tom. *The Six Basic Exercises by Rudolf Steiner*. Online PDF: tomvangelder.antrovista.com/pdf/basic.pdf.

Westerhoff, Nikolas. "Set in Our Ways." *Scientific American Mind*, vol. 19, no. 6, 2008, pp. 44–49., www.jstor.org/stable/24940018

Whitman, Walt. *Leaves of Grass*. Penguin Classics, 2017.

Williamson, Marianne. *A Return to Love*. HarperCollins, 1996.

Wood, Tara. *That Time My Daughter Talked to a Stranger*. https://community.today.com/parentingteam/post/untitled_1476901511. Posted on October 19, 2016.

Zusak, Markus. *The Book Thief*. Knopf Books for Young Readers, 2007.

❧ Gratitude ❧

Nothing mends the heart
like gratitude.

S. D.

Those Who Helped & Inspired

Doing Grief in Real Life is more than a book to me – it is a mission. I've been living, eating, breathing, and dreaming this book into being for over a decade. Along the way, I grew rich with support from those who offered their wisdom and inspiration to make the dream real. Without you, I might still be wandering in a forest of ideas. Thank you for helping me find my way into the clearing where ideas were transformed into healing substance – for me as much as anyone.

Eternal thanks to. . .

- The eighty-plus readers who pored over early manuscript drafts: you were willing to dive into the muck and mystery of grief, come up breathing, and ask for more – especially Brian Berumen, Vanessa Chamberlain, Andrew Darian, Willa Darian, Barb Doerrer-Peacock, Kay Klinkenborg, Brent Tillotson, Demetra Anne Woodyard, and Morgan Darian, whose endless supply of encouragement and editing skills were invaluable

- My friend, David Boninger – without you, it's likely that this book would sit on a shelf and gather dust for another decade; you believed in me and my work when I barely believed in myself

- The students in Dr. Boninger's Understanding Death & Dying course at Glendale Community College (AZ) who were some of my early readers – you let me know that this book can heal and change lives

- Those who allowed me to enter into the inner sanctum of your grief in my work as a healer – you are some of my greatest teachers

- My family and friends who live the dream with me: We heal one another best by healing ourselves

- The many grievers and healers who allowed me to tell your stories in these pages – your healing is our healing

- And finally, Andrew, Morgan, and Willa, my loves – you inspired every word; you are with me at every ending and each new beginning

Those Who Led the Way

In their life and through their death, my dear departed have been my guides to help me heal and transform the grief of a lifetime. Their eternal love and influence resonate in these pages and in my work as a healer.

In Loving Memory

- William Hubert Woodyard (1887 - 1964)
- Sheri Lynn Carey (1961-1977)
- Dana Lynn Waddell (1985-2002)
- James Edward Hughes (1934-2004)
- Charles ("Chuck") Strother Bagbey (1929-2005)
- Mary Thienes Schunemann (1960-2007)
- Pauline ("Polly") Hamann (1923-2010)
- Effie (Cobbs) Bagbey (1931-2012)
- William Kyle Bagbey (1987-2014)
- William Hardwick Bagbey (1922-2016)
- And my furry companions who are family to me: Francie, Sham, Shadow, Caspian, Riley, and my darling, Barrington

About the Author

Shea Darian is a grief educator, spiritual care provider, and award-winning author of three parenting books on family spirituality and healing, including *Sanctuaries of Childhood* (Foreword Book Awards), *Living Passages for the Whole Family* (Nautilus Book Awards), and *Seven Times the Sun*. She is the creator of the Model of Adaptive Grieving Dynamics, published in the journal *Illness, Crisis & Loss*, Vol. 22 (3), 2014. Shea lives with her spouse, Andrew, in Sun City, Arizona. Connect@DoingGrief.com.

Praise for *Doing Grief in Real Life*

Shea Darian has transformed her own grief and loss into a tour de force. *Doing Grief in Real Life* is chocked full of resources, ideas and prompts for navigating grief and has something for everyone. The personal stories, her own and others, that show how people survive grief and loss . . . gave me hope.

> **Peggy O'Mara**, former editor and publisher, *Mothering* magazine
> and author of *Natural Family Living*

Shea has written a book that speaks to the heart and soul of who we are as humans. The compass she offers us for navigating the change and loss that we will all experience is nothing short of life-changing. And Shea does it with a voice that embraces readers and makes them feel like they are sitting in their living room with her as she shares her wisdom. *Doing Grief in Real Life* will be a gift to all readers who have the good fortune to open up its pages.

> **David Boninger, Ph.D.**
> Professor of Psychology, Glendale Community College

Shea Darian's book *Doing Grief in Real Life: A Soulful Guide to Navigate Loss, Death and Change* is a treasure trove . . . giving grief—in whatever form it shows up—the space and honor it needs. As a spiritual director who encounters individuals' grief and processing of loss on a daily basis, this book is an incredible resource.

> **Rev. Teresa Blythe**, founder of the Phoenix Center for Spiritual Direction
> and author of *Spiritual Direction 101* and *50 Ways to Pray*

Books come to us at special moments in our lives...before I knew it, I was enmeshed...taking notes and doing the Contemplations. Soon, I was in dialogue with Shea Darian, and I was in dialogue with myself. Shea delivers her main points with a punch to help us become more ourselves. She trusts we can do it, and she is there to guide us...she prods us to confront our fears as we find small ways to awaken tender memories and celebrate them. Through stories, poetry, personal contemplations, helpful quotations, and research she shows that each person's grief is unique. Her subtitle is "A Soulful Guide to Navigate Loss, Death & Change." She promises this, and she delivers it with grace and love.

> **Betty Staley, M.A.**, Waldorf Educator and author of *Tending the Spark*
> and *Between Form and Freedom*